Copyright © 2002 A.D.A. EDITA Tokyo Co., Ltd.
3-12-14 Sendagaya, Shibuya-ku, Tokyo 151-0051, Japan
All rights reserved. No part of this publication may be reproduced,
stored in a retrieval system, or transmitted, in any form or by any means,
electronic, mechanical, photocopying, recording, or otherwise,
without permission in writing from the publisher.

The drawings of Frank Lloyd Wright are
Copyright © The Frank Lloyd Wright Foundation 2002
Text Copyright © The Frank Lloyd Wright Foundation 2002
Copyright of photographs © 2002 GA photographers: Yukio Futagawa &
Associated Photographers

The red square with FRANK LLOYD WRIGHT in block letters is a
registered trademark belonging to The Frank Lloyd Wright Foundation.
The Frank Lloyd Wright Foundation grants permission for
A.D.A. EDITA Tokyo to use the mark in its block.

"GA" logotype design: Gan Hosoya

ISBN4-87140-616-4 C1352

Printed and bound in Japan

Frank Lloyd Wright
Elegant Houses

Edited and Photographed by Yukio Futagawa
Text by Bruce Brooks Pfeiffer

006

Frank Lloyd Wright
Elegant

28	**"Wingspread", Herbert F. Johnson House**	
	Wind Point, Wisconsin, 1937	
70	**Leigh Stevens House, "Auldbrass Plantation"**	
	Yemassee, South Carolina, 1939	
104	**Lowell Walter House, "Cedar Rock"**	
	Quasqueton, Iowa, 1945	
132	**Herman T. Mossberg House**	
	South Bend, Indiana, 1946	
162	**Kenneth Laurent House**	
	Rockford, Illinois, 1949	
176	**David Wright House**	
	Phoenix, Arizona, 1950	
188	**William Palmer House**	
	Ann Arbor, Michigan, 1950	
208	**Isadore J. Zimmerman House**	
	Manchester, New Hampshire, 1950	
228	**Harold Price House, "Grandma House"**	
	Paradise Valley, Arizona, 1954	
248	**Gerald Tonkens House**	
	Cincinnati, Ohio, 1955	

Cover: Herman T. Mossberg House

Houses

Elegant Houses *by Bruce Brooks Pfeiffer*

The elegant Frank Lloyd Wright house is not matter of size or cost, but of completeness. How well it is furnished is just as important as the architectural excellence of the building itself. How well it has been maintained is just as important as how well it was built in the first place. Wright frequently described organic architecture as an architecture in which the parts are related to the whole as the whole is related to its parts: "In organic architecture then, it is quite impossible to consider the building as one thing, its furnishings another and its setting and environment still another. The spirit in which these buildings are conceived sees all these together at work *as one thing*."[1] The result is a sense of harmonious proportion. Elegance in a Wright house is common and invariably evokes a sense of quiet repose, stimulating to the eye and restful to the soul.

Interior space is central to any Wright building or, as the architect described it, is "the reality of building". Believing that "a house is more a home by being a work of Art",[2] he carefully worked out interior details, the placement of furnishings, and the landscaping plan. His clients often wrote to him that the house changed their way of life by changing the way their saw, moved through and interacted with the world around them. They note with wonder that every day is different, the placement of the house capturing changes in the sunlight within and without, enhancing their enjoyment of the interior space and the surrounding natural environment of which the house is a part.

The selection of homes for this volume is not meant in any way to suggest these are the only "elegant" Wright houses. The prairie houses have purposefully been omitted, since a volume in this series is devoted to them, but this volume could easily include Wright's own Home and Studio in Oak Park, the Susan Lawrence Dana house (Springfield, Illinois) (GA TRAVELER 004 Prairie Houses), the Ward Willits house (Highland Park, Illinois) (ibid.), the Arthur Heurtley house (Oak Park, Illinois) (ibid.), the F. F. Tomek house (Riverside, Illinois) (ibid.), the Meyer May house (Grand Rapids, Michigan) (ibid.), the Darwin D. Martin house (Buffalo, New York) (ibid.) and Frederick Robie house (Chicago, Illinois) (ibid.). Other examples would be the Frederick Bogk house (Milwaukee, Wisconsin), Hollyhock House and the John Storer house (Los Angeles, California), and the Jean and Paul Hanna

フランク・ロイド・ライトのエレガント・ハウスは，大きさやコストによらない。その完全性を問うものである。家具調度がそこにふさわしく配されていることは，建物そのものが建築的に素晴らしいことと同様に大切である。ライトはよく，有機的建築について，部分が全体に結びつき，全体が部分と結ばれている建築と説明していた。「それゆえに，有機的建築に於いては，建物を一つのものとして，次にその家具調度を別なものとして，さらにまた，その敷地の状況や周辺環境を別のものとして考えることはまったく不可能なのである。これらの建物のうちに表現されている精神は，そうしたすべてが〈一つのものとして〉共に働き合うものと考えるのである。」[1] そこに生まれるのは調和に満ちた均整の感覚である。ライトの住宅が持つ優雅さは，共通して，常に変わらず，目を刺激し，心に安らぎを与え，静かな平安を呼び覚ましてくれる。

　内部空間は，ライトのどの建物に於いても，中心となるもの，あるいは建築家自身が説明しているように「建物の本質(リアリティ)」なのである。「住宅は，芸術作品であることによって，より深く我が家といえるものになる」[2] ことを信じながら，彼は細心の注意を込めてインテリアの細部，家具の配置，ランドスケープのプランを決めていった。彼のクライアントは，家の中をすみずみまで歩き回り，周囲の世界と交流することで，物の見方が変わり，家が私たちの生活の在り方を変えました，とよく書き送ってきた。毎日が違ったものとなり，家の配置は，内や外の陽射しの変化を捕らえ，内部空間と，家もその一部である周囲の自然がもたらす喜びを高めてくれます，と彼らは感嘆をこめて記している。

　この巻のために選ばれた住宅のみが，ライトの"エレガント"な住宅作品であることを意味するわけではまったくない。プレイリー・ハウスはこのシリーズの別の巻にまとめられているために，ここでは意図的に外しているが，オーク・パークのライト自邸とスタジオ，スーザン・ローレンス・ダナ邸（スプリングフィールド，イリノイ）(GA TRAVELER 004 Prairie Houses)，ウォード・ウィリッツ邸（ハイランド・パーク，イリノイ）(前掲書)，アーサー・ハートレイ邸（オーク・パーク，イリノイ）(前掲書)，F・F・トメック邸（リヴァーサイド，イリノイ）(前掲書)，メイヤー・メイ邸（グランドラピッズ，ミシガン）(前掲書)，ダーウィン・D・マーティン邸（バッファロー，ニューヨーク）(前掲書)，フレデリック・ロビー邸（シカゴ，イリノイ）(前掲書)がここに含まれるものであることは疑いない。その他の例には，フレデリック・ボック邸（ミルウォーキー，ウィスコンシン），ホリホックの家とジョン・ストーラー邸（ロサンジェルス，カリフォルニア），ジャン＆ポール・ハンナ邸（スタンフォード，カリフォルニア）(GA TRAVELER 005 Usonian Houses)がある。エドガー・J・カウフマンの"落水荘"は恐らく，エレガント・ハウスの心髄が表れている作品であるが，この住宅は，ライトの自邸であるタリアセン（スプリンググリーン，ウィスコンシン）とタリアセン・ウェスト（スコッツデール，アリゾナ）同様に一冊の巻にまとめられる。この巻に選ばれた住宅はすべて，一つのカテゴリーには収まりにくい，ライトの後期に属する作品である。

house (Stanford, California) (GA TRAVELER 005 Usonian Houses). Edgar J. Kaufmann's "Fallingwater", perhaps the quintessential example, is covered in its own volume, as are Wright's own homes, Taliesin (Spring Green, Wisconsin) and Talicsin West (Scottsdale, Arizona). The houses selected here are all examples of Wright's later work which do not easily fit into a single category.

"Wingspread", Herbert F. Johnson House, Wind Point, Wisconsin, 1937

Wright named this house "Wingspread" for the four wings that extend out from the spacious "Great Hall":

"Wingspread, the Herbert Johnson prairie house is another experiment in the articulation which began with the Coonley House at Riverside, built 1909, wherein Living Room, Dining Room, Kitchen, Family sleeping rooms, Guest Rooms were each separate units grouped together and connected by corridor.

The plan is oriented so that sunlight falls in all of the rooms and shows a logical expression of the zoned house.

At the center of the four zones the spacious Living Room stands. A tall central chimney-stack with five fireplaces divides this vertical space into spaces for the various domestic functions: Entrance Hall, Family Living Room, Library Living Room, and Dining Room. Extending from this lofty central room are four wings—three lows and one with mezzanine. The one with mezzanine floor and galleries is for the master, mistress, and young daughter. Another wing extends from the central space for their several boys; a playroom at the end, a graduated deep-pool in conjunction—another wing for service and utilities—another for guests and five motor cars. Each wing has independent views on two sides, each has perfect privacy—the whole being united by a complete house telephone system. Lighting is integral. Heating is integral, in the floor slab as in the S. C. Johnson Co. Administration Building and the Jacobs House at Madison.

This extended wing plan lies, very much at home, integral with the prairie landscape, which is made more significant and beautiful through it. In this case, especially, growth will claim its own; wild grape vines pendant from trellises; extensive collateral gardens in bloom; a great mass of evergreens in the entrance court; single tall associate of the building. Lake Michigan lies off to the middle distance seen over a wild-fowl-pool stretching away in that direction from just below the main terrace of the house.

This structure is of the common type, proving it a good one for a home in the climate around the Great Lakes. It is popularly known as brick veneer. Outside members are cypress planks, roofs tiled, floors of concrete, 4'-0" square concrete-slab-tiles.

This house, while resembling the Coonley House at Riverside,

ウィングスプレッド，ハーバート・F・ジョンソン邸，1937年

ライトはこの家を，広々とした"グレート・ホール"から4つのウィングが広がっているために"ウィングスプレッド"と名付けた。

「ウィングスプレッド，すなわちハーバート・ジョンソンのプレイリー・ハウスは，1909年リヴァーサイドに建ったクーンレイ邸に始まる空間分節に関わる実験的試みのまた別の例証である。クーンレイ邸ではリビングルーム，ダイニングルーム，台所，家族の寝室，ゲストルームがそれぞれまとまりを持つ別のユニットを構成し，廊下で結ばれている。
　プランは，陽光がすべての部屋に射し込み，ゾーン分けされた住宅の論理的表現を示すように配置されている。
　4つのゾーンの中心に広々としたリビングルームが立ち上がる。5つの暖炉を束ねた背の高い組み合わせ煙突が，この垂直の空間を様々な住宅機能に分割する。エントランスホール，ファミリー・リビングルーム，ライブラリー・リビングルーム，そしてダイニングルーム。このロフト風の中央空間から4つのウィングが広がる──3つは低層で，一つには中2階がついている。中2階とギャラリーのあるウィングには主人と夫人，そして若い3人の娘の部屋がある。中央空間から伸びる別なウィングには息子である少年たちの部屋があり，末端に遊び場，それに続いて段々に深くなるプールがある──もう一つのウィングはサービスとユーティリティ──もう一つにはゲストルームと5台分のガレージがある。どのウィングも両側に個別の眺望が開け，それぞれ完璧なプライバシーを持ち，完備したホームテレフォン・システムが全体を結んでいる。照明は一体化されている。暖房も，S・C・ジョンソン社管理棟や，マディソンのジェイコブズ邸のように床下に統合されている。
　この，手を四方に差し伸ばしたウィング・プランは，周囲の環境に非常によく調和し，プレイリーの風景と一体化し，その風景を通してさらに魅力と美しさを深めながら広がっている。この家の場合は特に，成長した草木がその独自性を主張するようになるだろう。蔓棚から垂れ下がる野葡萄，両側に広がる花盛りの庭，エントランスコートの常緑樹の大きな茂み──これは建物に寄り添う唯一背の高い存在である。少し離れた中景には，メイン・テラスの真下から湖の方向に広がる，野生のカモやガンが生息する池の先にミシガン湖が見える。
　この建物は，五大湖周辺の気候に相応しい住宅であることが証明されている一般的なタイプのものである。それは，化粧張り煉瓦造としてよく知られている。外部の部材にはサイプレスの厚板が使われ，屋根はタイル葺き，床は4フィート角のコンクリート板タイル敷きである。
　この住宅は，イリノイ州リヴァーサイドのクーンレイ邸に似ているが，より恒久的な材料を使ったその形態と扱いはさらに大胆で，力強く，直截である。カソタ砂岩の重厚な水平の層が基部を構成し，それは私が今まで見たなかで最も優れた煉瓦積み工事である──そして建設に使われている材料はどこをとってもすべてが頑丈なものである。内部には，建

Illinois, is much more bold, masculine, and direct in form and treatment—executed in more permanent materials. The house has a heavy footing course of Kasota sandstone, the best brickwork I have seen in my life—and the materials of construction throughout are everywhere substantial. The house is architecturally furnished in keeping with the character established by the building."[3]

A technique called "blind nailing" was used on the interior woodwork at Wingspread. With a very sharp knife, the craftsman pulls up a sliver of wood about the size of a small fingernail. Holding the sliver carefully so that it will not detach or splinter off, he then inserts the nail, puts a small amount of glue under the sliver and the result is flawless cabinetwork done in natural wood with no evidence of nails or nailing.

Johnson flew his own plane, taking off and landing on a small strip not far from the house site. This gave Wright the idea to add a small observation tower for the Johnson children (an adult cannot stand up in it), rising with the main chimney mass above the tile roof with a 360-degree view. A spiral metal stairway connects the tower to the mezzanine of the main Living Room.

Leigh Stevens House, "Auldbrass Plantation", Yemassee, South Carolina, 1939

"Auldbrass is the historical name," Wright wrote, "given this southern plantation scheme by Leigh Stevens because Auldbrass was the name of the old place ruined there by Sherman's march to the sea"[4]:

"The ranch type scheme spreads out beside a typical Southern swamp. The grade level of the fields is about 7 feet above the water level, with large moss-hung trees round about the whole area on which the rambling cypress buildings are placed. The place is designed for country life involving farmers, stables, cattlesheds, dog kennels, birdhouses as well as machine sheds and barn. Guesthouse and caretaker's cottage are adjacent to the commodious residence of Mr. and Mrs. Leigh Stevens themselves. The materials of construction were natural cypress plank walls standing on gravity-heated concrete floors (see GA TRAVELER 005 Usonian Houses p.12). The copper roofs are treated blue by way of a simple process. The sloping walls are natural to the kind of framing used (or vice versa) and the general plan-form is of a type yielding greatest intimacy with the beauty of the surrounding forest-glade. If there is anything needed to complete this domicile for Southern plantation life it is because neither Mr. Stevens nor his architect could imagine it."[5]

For a plantation in the South, Wright has evoked the feeling of the antebellum plantations without using the Neo-Classic vocabulary of

物が確立している性格に調和した建築的な家具調度が配されている。」[3]

　ウィングスプレッド内部の木工品には"隠し釘打ち"と呼ばれる技術が使われた。非常に鋭いナイフで，職人は指の爪ほどの小さな木の細片を引き上げる。剥離したり，裂けたりしないように細片を慎重に持ちながら，その跡に釘を差し込み，細片の下側に少量の糊をつけてかぶせる。その結果，自然木でつくられた，釘や釘打ちの跡の見えない，完璧な高級木工家具が生まれる。
　ジョンソンは自家用飛行機を飛ばしており，家の敷地からほど遠くない場所にある小さな滑走路で離着陸していた。これが，ライトに，ジョンソンの子供たちのために，屋根の上，中央の大きな煙突に沿って立ち上がり，四方を見晴らせる小さな展望塔（大人はその中で立つことはできない）を加えようというアイディアを思いつかせた。金属製の螺旋階段が展望塔を中央のリビングルームの中2階と結んでいる。

リー・スティーヴンス邸，"オールドブラス・プランテーション"，1939年

「オールドブラスとは，シャーマン将軍の海へ向かう進軍によって廃墟となったこの場所の昔の名前であるために，リー・スティーヴンスによるこの南部のプランテーション計画に与えられた歴史的な由来を持つ名前である」[4]とライトは書いている。

　「この大農場タイプの計画案は，典型的な南部の湿地の傍らに広がっている。農場の土地は水面より7フィートほど高く，サイプレス材でつくられた建物が不規則に建ち並ぶ土地全体を，コケ類の垂れ下がる大木が囲んでいる。この場所は，農夫たちの家，厩，牛舎，犬小屋，鳥小屋，機械置場，納屋などのある田舎での生活に合わせて設計されている。ゲストハウスと管理人のコテージはリー・スティーヴンス夫妻自身のゆったりして使い易い住宅の隣にある。建設材料は，重力暖房（グラヴィティ・ヒート）（GA TRAVELER 005 Usonian Houses p.13参照）で暖められたコンクリート床に，自然な仕上げのサイプレスの厚板を使った壁を立てている。銅葺き屋根は単純なプロセスを用いて青い色に加工処理されている。傾きを持つ壁は，使われている枠組みの一種にとって自然であり（またはその逆も言える），そして全体プランは周囲の森の湿地の美しさと非常に密接な関わりをもたらすものである。この，南部のプランテーションでの生活を完成させるのに，もし他に何か必要なものがあるとすれば，それは，スティーヴンス氏も建築家もプランテーションでの生活を想像することが出来なかったがゆえに他ならない。」[5]

　この南部のプランテーションに対して，ライトは，かつての新古典的ヴォキャブラリーを使わずに，南北戦争前のプランテーションの情景を呼び起こすことに成功している。当時の邸宅は，際立った形式性と壮大さを備えていたが，ライトはそうしたものを注意深く避けたのである。

that time. There was a marked formality and grandeur in those earlier establishments, which Wright has carefully avoided. Although this plantation has certain elements associated with the gracious living and entertaining of the South, the major feature of the work is its relaxed informality. The traditional separation of the main kitchen from the house itself was maintained here, however, with Wright locating the kitchen away from the main living area, but still linked to the living room by a covered passageway. Recent renovation has enclosed the pergola and converted it into a dining area.

The overall perspective shows how the main house is connected to the guesthouse, while the farm buildings, machine sheds, stables, and kennels form their own grouping separated from the owner's quarters. The main house and guesthouse (which was not built) are laid out on a hexagonal unit system—a device, which by its very nature creates a more flexible plan. The sloping cypress plank walls echo the sloping trunk of the oak trees of the region. The walls not only slope in as they rise, but also from left to right, a type of construction seen here for the first time in Wright's work. Copper downspouts at the corners of the roof emulate the Spanish moss hanging from the trees around the plantation.

Lowell Walter House, "Cedar Rock", Quasqueton, Iowa, 1945

In 1945, *Ladies' Home Journal* published Wright's design for "The Glass House—Opus 497". It was a plan concept that he would employ in other works, the Lowell Walter house being the first constructed. The house is situated on a bluff overlooking the Wapsipinicon River and expansive plate glass windows (hence, Glass House) afford views on three sides, two toward the river and one onto a terrace with flower gardens and lawn beyond. Low planting areas bordered in brick contain flowers, shrubs, and vines running the periphery of the aptly named Garden Room on two sides. The fourth side provides processional entry into the room as well as the fireplace with built-in seating. The central section of the room has a raised ceiling with nine square skylights as well as clerestory windows that provide natural light for extensive indoor plantings. The long bedroom wing rotates 120-degrees from the square living room plan. The workspace is placed at the point where the rotation occurs. A distinctive feature of the house is the upturned, reinforced concrete roof. The house is brick with interior partitions, shelving, cabinets, and all furniture constructed in fine walnut. The rounded edges of much of the shelving repeat the curves of the roof.

At the river's edge Wright built a "River Pavilion", the upper story flush with the embankment and providing a screened, roofed area for cool summer breezes and tranquil evenings by the water. The lower area is for boat storage, with a ramp down into the river and a wharf nearby.

このプランテーションには，南部の優美な生活やもてなしに通じるいくつかの要素がありはするが，その主要な特徴は，寛いで，形式張っていないところにある。主厨房を住宅そのものから切り離す伝統はここでも守られている。しかしライトは，厨房を中心となる生活空間から離して位置させる一方で，屋根付きの通路でリビングルームと依然として結んでいるのである。最近の改装ではこのパーゴラに囲みを付けてダイニング・エリアに変えている。

　全体透視図は，農場の建物，機械置場，厩，犬小屋がオーナーの領域と分けてグループをつくる一方で，主屋がゲストハウスとどのようにつなげられているかを示している。主屋とゲストハウス（建設されなかった）は六角形のユニット・システムに基づいて展開されている——これはまさにその六角形ユニットの性質を利用してより柔軟性のあるプランをつくりだす工夫である。サイプレスの厚板の壁に付けられている傾斜は，この地域に生えるカシの木の傾いた幹に呼応する。壁は上に行くに従って傾斜するばかりでなく，左から右に向かっても傾斜しているが，これはライトの作品のなかで，ここで初めて登場する方式である。屋根の角につけられた銅製の縦樋は，プランテーションを囲む木々から垂れ下がるサルオガセモドキを模したものである。

ローウェル・ウォルター邸，"シーダー・ロック"，1945年

1945年，『レディース・ホーム・ジャーナル』誌は，ライトの"ガラスの家：作品497"のデザインを掲載した。これは，彼が他の作品にも採用することになる計画案で，それに基づいて最初に建てられたのがローウェル・ウォルター邸である。この家はワプシピニコン川を見晴らす崖上にあり，大きな板ガラスの窓が三方に開き（このためにガラスの家という），二面からは川の眺めが，残る一面からは花壇のあるテラスとその先の芝生が見える。煉瓦で縁取られた，花や灌木や蔓草など背の低い植物を植え込んだプランターが，ガーデン・ルームと相応しい名前を与えられた部屋の二面に沿って巡らされている。4番目の側面は造付けの座のある暖炉と，この部屋へ進んでくるエントリーを構成する。部屋の中央部は天井が高く，高窓と9個の方形の天窓が付いて，室内に広く置かれている植物に自然光を注ぐ。寝室のある細長い翼がリビングルームの方形平面から120度角度を振って伸び出している。この分岐点にワークプレイスが配置されている。この家の際立った特徴は縁が上に反った鉄筋コンクリートの屋根である。建物は煉瓦造で，間仕切り，棚，戸棚，家具のすべては良質のウォールナット製である。ほとんどの棚の角につけられている丸みは，屋根の曲線を繰り返したものである。

　川の縁に，ライトは"リヴァー・パヴィリオン"を建てた。上の階はちょうど土手と同じ高さで，スクリーンで囲まれ，屋根で覆われたこのエリアは，水辺での，夏の涼しいそよ風と静かな夕べを与えてくれる。下の階はボートの収納庫で，川と近くの埠頭に降りて行くランプが付いている。

Wright's apprentice, John DeKoven Hill, worked on the drawings and supervised the construction of the Walter house. Hill and Wright personally selected all of the decorative elements: glass figures, ceramics, flower vases, lamps, tabletop ware, and delicate works of art, many of which came from the Wright-designed V. C. Morris Shop in San Francisco. Thus, everything about the house including the meticulous and lavish landscaping was orchestrated through Wright's direction.

Herman T. Mossberg House, South Bend, Indiana, 1946

Wright's original sketches for the Mossberg house were for a single story structure with an elongated plan, the living room extending out 90-degrees at the far end. The building regulations for residences in this neighborhood, however, mandated that all homes be two stories. Wright accordingly placed the daughter's bedroom on an upper level, which he labeled "Mezzanine". This level was given three balconies, one overlooking the two-story living room, an outdoor one balcony on the street side and a third on the opposite side, overlooking the lawn and gardens. The stairs to the upper level are thin concrete slabs hung on steel rods from the roof rafters above. The slabs are carpeted on both sides, and the polished steel rods take the place of a railing.

On the main floor, the street entrance separates the master bedroom from the long wing that includes dining room, workspace, two bedrooms, bathroom, and the carport. It was rare for Wright to place the master bedroom so close to the main entrance, and possibly this was done at the request of the clients. The carport is reached via the driveway through a gate at the end of the building. Steps from the carport lead up to the gallery for the main floor bedrooms and the workspace and down to a small basement for utilities. The slope of the property accounts for these various levels. The living room extends out from the master bedroom area and features a splendid ceiling-high, full wall-width window facing the garden. Composed of hexagonal units, the central section is framed on either side by brick piers and narrower glass panels.

The location of the house is on a city lot, an uncommon choice for Wright, who usually urged his clients to go as far away from the city as possible. To compensate for this, he has made the street side somewhat fortress-like with few window openings. The brickwork throughout the house is of the highest quality. One particular detail that deserves special mention is the brick paving that starts at the entry hall and continues though the dining room and into the workspace beyond. The result is a harmonious melding of floor and wall. The dining room, although not entirely separated from the entry hall, loggia, and living room, is more defined than is usual. This independent treatment of the dining room and the placement of the master bedroom right at the front door make this a more conventional plan than that seen in most of Wright's contemporary residential designs.

ライトの見習い生，ジョン・デコーヴェン・ヒルがウォルター邸の図面と工事監理を担当した。ヒルとライトは装飾品のすべてを自ら選択した。ガラスの彫像，陶器，花瓶，ランプ，卓上用の飾り，そして繊細な芸術作品で，これらの多くは，ライトが設計したサンフランシスコのＶ・Ｃ・モリス商店から入手したものであった。こうして，この家のあらゆるものは，細部まで行き届き，豊かなランドスケーピングを含め，ライトの指揮によって編成されている。

ハーマン・Ｔ・モスバーグ邸，1946年

　モスバーグ邸のためのライトの最初の案は，平屋の，長く伸びたプランで，リビングルームは終端部で直角に差し出されている。しかし，この地区の建築規制は，建物はすべて2階建てとすることを命じている。従ってライトは娘の寝室を，彼が"メザニン"と名付けた上階に置いた。この階には3つのバルコニーが配され，一つは2層吹き抜けたリビングルームを見下ろし，道路側には屋外バルコニー，3つ目はその反対側にあり，芝生と庭園を見晴らしている。上階への階段は，頭上を覆う屋根の垂木からスティール・ロッドで吊られた薄いコンクリート・スラブである。スラブは両面ともカーペットで覆われ，磨き仕上げのスティール・ロッドが手すりの代わりをしている。

　主階では，道路からのエントランスが主寝室をダイニングルーム，ワークスペース，2寝室，浴室，カーポートを含む細長いウィングから分けている。ライトが主寝室をメイン・エントランスの近くに配することは希で，これはたぶんクライアントの要請によりなされたのかもしれない。カーポートへは，建物の終端にある門を入りドライヴウェイを経て行く。カーポートから階段を上がると主階寝室とワークスペースのギャラリーに導かれ，階段を降りればユーティリティーのある小さな地下室に出る。敷地の傾斜がこうした様々なレベル差が生まれた理由を説明している。リビングルームは主寝室エリアから広がり，際立った天井の高さと庭園に面した壁全面の幅を持つ窓に特徴がある。六角形ユニットで構成されたその中央部分は，両側が，煉瓦の窓間壁と他より幅の狭いガラス面で枠取られている。

　この家の場所は市街地にあるが，普通，クライアントに対し，できるだけ市内から離れるように強く勧めるライトにしては珍しい選択である。これを埋め合わせるために，彼は道路側を，窓の開口の少ない，どこか要塞に似た構成としている。煉瓦工事の質は全体に非常に高い。特筆に価する素晴らしいディテールは，エントリー・ホールに始まり，ダイニングルームに続きその先のワークスペースに至る，煉瓦敷きである。これによって，床と壁が調和しながら溶け合っている。ダイニングルームは，エントリー・ホール，ロッジア，リビングルームと完全には分離されていないながら，通常よりはっきりと区分されている。このダイニングルームの独立した扱いと，主寝室を正面扉のすぐ右手に配置するやり方は，この家のプランを，ライトの現代住宅デザインの大半よりむし

However, so masterfully has he executed the plan that the Mossberg house ranks among his finest.

Wright designed, or was instrumental in the selection of, all of the furnishings including furniture, carpets, textiles, and lighting fixtures. He also took great care in the landscape planning: brick flower boxes and flower gardens surround the outdoor terrace and the kitchen gardens are directly adjacent to the workspace. Large trees native to the site and flowering shrubs complete the plan.

Kenneth Laurent House, Rockford, Illinois, 1949

Two gentle curves facing each other form a football-shaped lozenge that is the general plan of the Kenneth Laurent house. It is a simple form punctuated by two large, square forms: one that houses the workspace, dining area, and seating cove with fireplace; the other for the master bedroom and its fireplace. Between the master bedroom and the workspace, there is a bathroom and another bedroom. The reverse curve is outdoors, providing a terrace with a garden set close to the glass doors, along with a small fountain pool. The great ease of circulation throughout the house, the wide doorways and double doors at the entry were designed to accommodate the client's wheelchair to which he was confined following an accident at the end of the Second World War. The house is built of brick and cypress, with the architect's furnishings throughout. The careful attention to all the details, from the building itself to interiors and landscaping makes this one of the finest examples of Wright's moderately priced residential work.

David Wright House, Phoenix, Arizona, 1950

David Wright, the architect's son, was in the concrete block business in Phoenix. It was only logical, therefore, for Wright to design his son's house with standard concrete block. On the conceptual sketch seen here, he called the design "How to Live in the SW" [Southwest]. This sketch clearly shows an already well-developed scheme, ready to be fleshed out by his apprentices. On this one large sheet of paper, there is a freehand sketch of the house, a compass-drawn plan of the circular structure, central patio and garden area, two elevations and section with dimensions. The information on this one sheet of paper is so complete that from this drawing alone his apprentices were able to develop the presentation drawings.

The building site was a field surrounded by citrus trees with a dramatic view of Camelback Mountain. To take advantage of these elements, Wright raised the main living quarters of the house up off the ground to the height of the trees, the general plan resembling a rising spiral. The house rests on substantial concrete block piers, the open area below the house offering a shady retreat. A narrow garden bor-

ゲーム・パズル

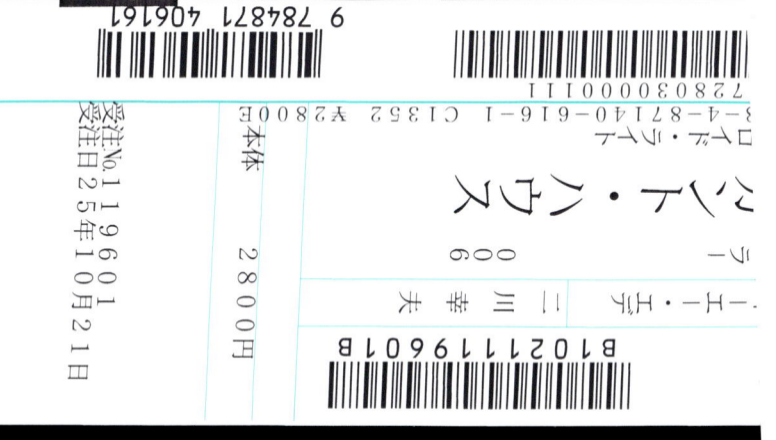

ナンシー・ペンス

二川　幸夫　訳

978-4-87140-616-1　C1352　¥2800E

本体　2800円

受注No.119601
受注日 25年10月21日

2001134 *

ろ伝統的なものにしている。しかし彼はこのプランを実に巧みに扱い，モスバーグ邸は彼の最も優れた作品の一つに位置づけられるものとなった。

　ライトは，家具，カーペット，テキスタイル，照明器具を含む内部装飾のすべてをデザインするか，またはその選択に力を貸している。彼はまた，ランドスケープ構成にも細心の注意を払った。屋外テラスを囲む煉瓦のプランターや花壇，そしてワークスペースと隣り合うキッチン・ガーデン。敷地に原生する大木や花の咲く灌木がこうした構成を完結させている。

ケネス・ローレント邸，1949年

　互いに向き合う2つの緩やかな曲線がフットボールの形をした菱形を形成する，それがケネス・ローレント邸の全体プランである。それは，一方の弧を2つの大きな方形が穿つシンプルな形をしている。方形の一つにはワークスペース，ダイニング・エリア，暖炉の付いた座を構成する窪みがあり，もう一方には，主寝室とその暖炉がある。主寝室とワークスペースの間に浴室ともう一つの寝室がある。もう一方の逆転する弧は，ガラス扉近くに置かれた庭と噴水付きの小さなプールのある戸外テラスを構成する。幅の広い戸口，エントリーの観音開きの扉など家全体が非常に動きやすくできているのは，第二次大戦の終わりに起きた事故の後，引きこもらざるを得なくなったクライアントの車椅子に合わせてデザインされたためである。建物には煉瓦とサイプレス材が使われ，家全体の家具調度もライトの手になるものである。建物そのものからインテリア，ランドスケーピングに至るまで，あらゆるディテールに細心の注意が払われた結果，ライトの，手頃な価格の住宅作品として最も優れたものの一つに数えられる。

デイヴィッド・ライト邸，1950年

　ライトの息子であるデイヴィッド・ライトは，フェニックスでコンクリート・ブロック関係の仕事をしていた。従って，ライトが自分の息子の家を標準的なコンクリート・ブロックを用いてデザインすることは，ごく自然なことであった。この家のコンセプチュアル・スケッチについて，ライトはそのデザインを"SW（南西部）に住む方法"と名付けた。このスケッチは既に十分に展開済みで，ライトの見習い生の手で肉付けする準備ができていることが明らかに解る。この1枚の大判の紙の上に，フリーハンドの家のスケッチ，コンパスで描いた円形の建物，パティオと庭園のプラン，2つの立面図と寸法の入った断面図が収まっている。1枚の紙の上にこめられた情報は，ここから彼の見習い生がプレゼンテーション用の図面を展開するに十分なものである。

　建物の敷地はキャメルバック山の印象的な眺めを望む，レモンの木で囲まれた野原である。これらの要素を生かすために，ライトはこの家の

ders the ramp that ascends to the living level. The entrance, like so many others, is understated, quiet, and contained. A turn to the left brings one into the main living-dining area, a space that opens onto an outdoor balcony overlooking the circular court below. On the opposite side, the living room opens onto another outdoor balcony that runs the full perimeter of the house. Three bedrooms and two bathrooms complete the plan, with the bedrooms also opening onto the balcony. A second circular mass on the ground level for utilities houses a stairway to the workspace above, which is separated from the living room by a circular fireplace. From the outside another, steeper ramp circles around the workspace mass and ascends to a roof terrace over the living room, with spectacular views in all directions. The woodwork, carpentry, and cabinetwork in this house are superb. The striking geometric pattern of the ceiling with its lapped mahogany boards is the perfect complement to the cool gray of the concrete blocks. The living room carpet, of Wright's design, adds refreshing colors and pattern to the interior.

William Palmer House, Ann Arbor, Michigan, 1950

The William Palmer house is laid out on a unit system based on the equilateral triangle and features the triangle itself: in the center of the opus as the living room and its roofed terrace, as two bedrooms and the study, and as the storage room. Wright has sited the house on sloping terrain, with the carport at one end slightly above grade and contained within a low brick retaining wall while the study, at the opposite end, is built into the hill. The living room, in the center of the plan, is level with the finished grade, and its terrace opens out onto a grassy knoll. Due to the change of levels, the carport is well below the level of the living room, and broad steps ascend from the carport to the entry hall and living room. The workspace is accessed by an interior stairway directly up from the covered carport. The bedroom wing, several steps above the entry, contains three bedrooms, two bathrooms, and a study. The main building material is brick, with specially designed concrete blocks that are perforated for daylight in the gallery of the bedrooms, and in the workspace as well. The blocks are at counter level and above the cabinets, providing delicate filigree light from two sources. There is also a skylight above. Combined with the fine brickwork is the equally fine woodwork, evident in the wall partitions, shelving, and ceiling. The living room was specially designed for concerts and musical entertainment, a grand piano fitting perfectly into the triangular space. The landscaping is especially well designed, and includes a Japanese stroll garden.

When asked about living in the house, the Palmers replied: "The impact of a Wright home upon the owner and those who visit it is one of excitement and tranquility. The multi-dimensional qualities of the design, the infinite care in the handling of every detail, the in-

中心的な住空間を地面から木の高さまで持ち上げ，上昇する螺旋に似た全体プランをつくった。家は頑丈なコンクリート・ブロックの支柱に載り，家の下に空いたスペースは日影になった隠れ場所を提供する。リビング階に上って行くランプを植え込みが細く縁取っている。エントランスは，他の多くと同じように，控えめで，静かで，落ち着いている。左手に曲がるとメインのリビング／ダイニング・エリアに導かれ，そこは下に広がる円形コートを見下ろす戸外のバルコニーに開かれた空間である。その反対側では，リビングルームが，建物の周縁全長に回されたもう一つの戸外バルコニーに開いている。3寝室と2浴室がプランを完結し，寝室もまたバルコニーに面している。2つ目の円形部分の1階はユーティリティで，その上の階にあるワークスペースに至る階段が付いている。ワークスペースは円形の暖炉でリビングルームと分けられている。もう1本の勾配の急なランプがワークスペースの外壁に沿って巻き上がり，リビングルームの上の屋上テラスへ続き，そこからは広大な眺めを四方に見晴らせる。この家の木工細工，大工仕事，木工家具の仕事はとびきりに素晴らしい。マホガニーの板を重ねた，人目を引く天井の幾何学パターンは，コンクリート・ブロックの冷たいグレイを完璧に補っている。ライトのデザインしたリビングルームの絨毯が，インテリアに新鮮な色彩とパターンを添えている。

ウィリアム・パーマー邸，1950年

ウィリアム・パーマー邸は，正三角形に基づいたユニット・システムで展開され，三角形そのものが特徴となっている――それは建物中央ではリビングルームとその屋根付きのテラスを，また2つの寝室と書斎を，そして収納部を構成する。ライトはこの家を斜面地に配置し，カーポートをその一端に，わずかに地盤面から上げて，低い煉瓦の擁壁内に納める一方で，反対側の端部を丘のなかに組み入れている。プラン中央のリビングルームは整地面と高さをそろえ，テラスが草深い小丘の上に向かって広がる。レベル差のために，カーポートはリビングの高さからはかなり下になり，幅の広い階段がそこからエントリー・ホールとリビングルームに上っている。ワークスペースへは，屋根の付いたカーポートから内部階段を経て直接入ることができる。エントリーから数段上がった寝室翼には，3寝室，2浴室，書斎がある。主要な建築材料は煉瓦で，寝室のギャラリー，またワークスペースにも，昼光を差し入れる孔を穿った特別なデザインのコンクリート・ブロックが一緒に使われている。カウンターの高さとキャビネットの上の有孔コンクリート・ブロックは，上下2つの光源となって繊細優美な模様を描く光を差し入れる。頭上にはスカイライトも付いている。精緻な煉瓦工事と組み合わされているのは，間仕切り壁や，棚，天井にはっきりとうかがえる，同じように繊細な木工細工である。リビングルームはコンサートや音楽を楽しむためにデザインされ，グランドピアノが三角形の空間に完璧に収まっている。ランドスケープは際立って見事に構成され，回遊式の日本庭園もある。

tegrity in the use of materials, and above all the precious evidence of the creative genius at work make each day a delight in the fresh realization of harmonious relationships of part to part to the whole. Mr. Wright's architecture is like a Beethoven quartet. It is vibrant. It is exciting. It is harmonious."[6]

Dr. Isadore J. Zimmerman House, Manchester, New Hampshire, 1950

The Isadore Zimmerman plan is straightforward and relatively simple—an elongated plan with the master bedroom jutting out beside the living room terrace. The single entry on the street side serves both the living room on the right and the workspace and guestroom on the left. With this particular configuration, a guest is guaranteed more freedom and privacy with the opportunity to come and go without disturbing the owners. High windows on the street side of the living room and entry provide light through specially cast concrete blocks with glass inserts. In contrast to the red bricks of the house these blocks are white, and present a striking pattern of geometric shapes running the full length of the brick wall under the overhanging roof. The garden side of the plan has glass doors in the dining area, opening onto an outdoor terrace, while the living room fenestration is treated in a unique and novel way: four window bays are set between brick piers. Each bay has mullions that create a central square window with the fixed glass around the edges set into reglets in the brick walls on the sides, the ceiling above, and a ledge at the bottom. The effect is a suspended "picture frame" that looks out over a low planting box outside and onto the landscape beyond.

The Zimmermans completely furnished their home with furniture of Wright's design or specifications. There is a Wright-designed quartet stand in the living room similar to the ones in the architect's homes in Wisconsin and Arizona. Some oriental works of art, especially a fine Japanese screen at the end of the living room, add graceful elements to the interior. Over the years the Zimermans opened their house to anyone who came by wishing to see it; many visitors were served lunch or dinner, several were put up overnight in the guestroom. Dr. and Mrs. Zimmerman realized that they possessed more than just a home; they possessed a fine work of art and generously shared it. Eventually they bequeathed their house to the Currier Gallery of Art in Manchester, and following a complete program of conservation, the house is once again open to the public with all its original furnishings and art works intact.

Harold Price House, "Grandma House", Paradise Valley, Arizona, 1954

In 1954, Harold and Mary Lou Price (clients for the Price Tower in Bartlesville, Oklahoma) commissioned Wright to design a home for

この家での生活について聞かれた時，パーマー一家はこう答えた。「ライトの住宅から，私たち，そしてここを訪ねてきた人たちが受けた衝撃は，興奮であり静けさというものでした。デザインが備えている多彩な尺度，一つ一つのディテールの扱い方に対する測り知れないほど大きな配慮，材料の使い方に見られる一体性，そして何よりも，そこに働いている創造的な天分のかけがえのない刻印が，毎日を，その部分と部分，そして全体が見事に調和し結びついていることを新たに気づかせてくれる喜びに浸してくれます。ライトさんの建築は，ベートーヴェンの協奏曲のようなものです。生き生きとしていて，心を高揚させ，音楽的な調和に満ちているのです。」[6]

イサドア・J・ジマーマン博士邸，1950年

　イサドア・ジマーマン邸のプランは率直で，比較的単純なものである——長く伸びたプランで，リビングルームのテラスの脇から主寝室が張り出している。エントリーは一ヶ所で，道路側に面し，右手のリビングルームと，左手のワークスペースとゲストルームの両方に通じている。この通常とは異なる配置によって，客は，オーナーを煩わすことなく出入りでき，より多くの自由やプライバシーを保証される。リビングルームとエントリーの道路側にとられた高窓が，ガラスをはめ込んだ特別に成型したコンクリート・ブロックを通して光を差し入れる。住宅に使われている赤煉瓦とは対照的に，これらのブロックは白で，張り出した屋根の下の煉瓦壁の全長に伸び，印象的な幾何学パターンを見せている。プランの庭側では，ダイニング・エリア内にガラス扉があり，戸外のテラスに開く一方，リビングルームの窓割りはユニークでそれまでにない方法で扱われている。煉瓦の窓間壁の間に4つの窓区画がとられているのである。各区画にはマリオンがあり，両サイド，上の天井，下の横桟，そして煉瓦壁の溝にはめこまれた周囲のはめ殺しガラスと共に，中央に方形の窓をつくりだしている。この結果，宙に浮いたような"ピクチャー・フレーム"が生まれ，外にある低いプランターを越えて，その先に広がる風景が見える。

　ジマーマン一家は，彼らの家を，ライトのデザインした，あるいは指定した家具調度ですべてを整えた。リビングルームには，自邸であるウィスコンシンやアリゾナの家にあるものに似た，ライトがデザインした，本などを立てかける四つ組のスタンドが置かれている。いくつかの東洋の美術品，特に，リビングルームの終端に置かれている繊細な日本の屏風が室内に気品のある，優雅な雰囲気を添えている。何年にもわたって，ジマーマン家は，彼らの住宅を，見たいと訪れる人には誰にでも開放し，多くの来訪者がランチやディナーをふるまわれ，幾人かはゲストルームで一夜を過ごしてもいる。ジマーマン博士夫妻は単なる住宅以上のものを手にしていることに気づいていた。彼らは一つの芸術作品を所有したのであり，それを寛大に分かち合ったのである。最後には，彼らはその家をマンチェスターのカリアー美術館に遺言によって寄贈し，完全な補

them in Phoenix where they always spent the winter. Of primary concern was Mrs. Price's desire to have a place where her grandchildren could visit her during their vacations from school. This prompted Wright to name the design "The Grandma House".

The plan extends along one long plane from the court at the west end to a play yard at the far east end. Due to the slope of the site, a series of level changes mark the procession from the car court along the walkway on the south wall to where the entrance gains a square atrium. Past the atrium, steps rise still higher to the bedroom wing where there are four bedrooms, three bathrooms, and an enclosed play yard for the children. On the other side of the atrium is the living-dining room, and finally the workspace here treated more as a kitchen, with service stairs down to the car court. Rotated 120-degrees, another wing contains two guestrooms, bathroom, and carport. The central atrium is the dominant feature of the plan, and it is taller than the other wings, with mahogany doors set between the concrete block piers, the panels of the doors decorated in abstract murals by Wright's secretary and business manager, Eugene Masselink. The atrium is covered over, but the clerestory space above the doors has been left open. The doors, however, provide protection against the typical windstorms of the region. There is a fireplace at one corner of the atrium, and in the center there is a fountain, but with a grate set at water level so that children cannot fall in.

The Price house is an excellent example of Wright's frequent use of standard building materials: concrete block and steel. The ceiling is "Tectum Boards" which are pre-formed by compressing a mixture of wood shavings and Portland cement into panels. Steel frames then support the panels, left their natural tan color. All the steel throughout the house is painted turquoise blue. The gray blocks and blue steel suggest coolness both inside and out, welcome relief on the desert. The block courses in some of the walls rise vertically, slightly battered inwards, while others are battered outwards. This gives a strong sculptural character to the house. The concrete block columns, in particular, are handled in a unique manner and become a strong element in the overall design. They step out on all four sides as they rise, growing more massive as each course extends beyond the one below it. Surprisingly, Wright stopped them two feet short of the ceiling and devised a thin pipe column of turquoise-colored steel to rise out of the center of the massive block column up to the ceiling. The effect is a roof that virtually floats over the entire opus. Lights placed inside the block columns and aimed at the ceiling above further intensify, at night, this sense of a roof hovering over the house.

Gerald Tonkens House, Cincinnati, Ohio, 1955

Following the Depression in the early 1930s, Wright set to creating a *building system* that would greatly reduce the cost of home construc-

修計画がなされた後，オリジナルの家具調度や元通り完全な状態の芸術作品と共に一般に公開された。

ハロルド・プライス邸，"おばあちゃんの家"，1954年

1954年，ハロルドとメリー・ルー・プライス（オクラホマ州バートルズヴィルに建つプライス・タワーのクライアント）は，いつも冬を過ごしているフェニックスで住宅の設計をライトに依頼した。最重要事項は，孫たちが学校の休暇中に彼女を訪ねてくることが出来る場所が欲しいというプライス夫人の願望であった。このことが，ライトにこのデザインを"おばあちゃんの家"と名付ける気持ちにさせたのである。

　プランは，西端にあるコートからはるか先の東端にある遊び場まで，一つの長い面に沿って広がっている。敷地に傾斜があるため，南壁に面した通路に沿ったカーポートから，エントランスが方形のアトリウムを構成している所まで続く道筋を高低の変化が特徴づけている。アトリウムを過ぎると，依然として高い位置にある寝室翼へ向かって階段が上っている。寝室翼には4寝室，3浴室，子供たちの囲まれた遊び場がある。アトリウムのもう一方の側は，リビング／ダイニングルームがあり，最後にワークスペースがくるが，サービス階段がカーポートに降りていて，ここではワークスペースは台所としての性格がより強いものとして扱われている。120度角度を振って張り出しているもう一つの翼には，ゲストルーム2つ，浴室，カーポートがある。中央のアトリウムはこのプランを支配する特徴的存在で，他の翼よりも高い位置にあり，コンクリート・ブロックの柱の間にマホガニー材の扉が収まり，その扉板は，ライトの秘書でありビジネス・マネージャーのユージース・マセリンクによる抽象的な壁画で飾られている。アトリウムは頭上を覆われているが，扉上の高窓のスペースは開け放たれたままである。しかし，扉が，この地方の典型的な暴風に対する守りとなっている。アトリウムの一角には暖炉があり，中央には噴水がある。水面の高さには格子が被されているので，子供が水に落ちることはない。

　プライス邸は，標準的な建築材料であるコンクリート・ブロックと鉄をライトがふんだんに使用したものとして素晴らしい例である。天井は"テクタム・ボード"で，これは木屑とポートランドセメントを混ぜ，パネルとしてあらかじめ圧縮成型したものである。次にスティール・フレームがこのパネルを支え，その自然な黄褐色はそのまま残される。家中のスティールはすべてターコイズブルーに塗装されている。グレイのコンクリート・ブロックと青いスティールは，家の内外とも，涼しさを感じさせ，砂漠にある，人を歓待する憩いの場所の存在を暗示する。壁のいくつかの部分で，ブロックの層は垂直に立ち上がり，上方に行くに従って少し内側に傾く一方，他の部分は外側に傾いている。これは，この住宅に強い彫刻的性格を与えている。特にコンクリート・ブロックの柱は，独特な扱いがなされ，デザイン全体のなかの力強い要素になっている。これらの柱は上に行くにつれて四方に張り出し，各層ごとに下の

tion for families of moderate incomes. This system, which he called the Usonian house, required the labor of carpenters and masons at a time when their wages were relatively inexpensive. How this was achieved is explained in a separate volume in this series (GA TRAVELER 005 Usonian Houses). By the end of the Second World War, however, labor costs had escalated considerably and the era of the Usonian House as a cost effective product was ended. In 1949, Wright again addressed system-built construction methods and came up with a solution he called the Usonian Automatic. His aim was once again to give the building industry a design that would be affordable, beautiful, and practical at the same time. "Usonian" was a word Wright preferred to identify the United States of America, and the word "Automatic" refers to a system of such basic simplicity and uniformity that the client himself could, if he so desired, participate in the construction of his home. The primary building material is the concrete block, but a specially designed block 1' x 2', coffered on one side, smooth on the other. The coffered block was lighter in weight, thereby making it possible for a one person to lift and place the block. Wright reckoned that if it required two persons to hoist the block into place, the system defeated itself. Unlike the richly varied geometric patterns of the California textile block houses, this new scheme derived its ornamental character through the use of perforated blocks, sometimes open as in terrace walls, others in the house set with glass. This is a far more sophisticated solution achieving rhythm, charm, and beauty by the simplest means possible. Even the ceilings are coffered blocks connected with reinforcing rods to a concrete slab above, matching the pattern of the walls. In some cases, the interior blocks are covered with mahogany plywood, as are the interior partitions.

The plan for the Gerald Tonkens house is common to Wright's residential designs: at one end is the large living-dining room, with workspace and utilities nearby. The bedrooms extend in a long line from the workspace to the study. At right angles to this wing, near the study, is the carport. The ceiling height in the bedroom wing and carport is eight feet, in the living room twelve feet, and in the workspace and utility area fourteen feet. In the living room, glass doors open onto an enclosed outdoor terrace. At the far end, the study also enjoys doors opening onto a smaller terrace. Two-foot square glass panes, set in metal frames, appear throughout for ventilation, and are combined with perforated blocks with fixed glass inserts. The placement of these operable windows presents a quiet repetitive pattern running the full length of the house that faces the south lawn. The combination of perforated blocks and square windows provides for a well-lit interior as well as a well-ventilated one. The entrance is near the utility and workspace with access directly to the workspace and the living room beyond. The entrance into the living room is another example of Wright's magical use of space: a low deck of coffered

層より先に広がりながら量を増して行く。驚いたことに，ライトは天井より2フィート下で柱の高さをとめ，ターコイズブルーに塗ったスティール・パイプの細い柱を考案し，ブロックのマッシヴな柱の中央から天井まで立ち上げた。これによって，屋根が建物全体を覆って浮かんでいるように見えるのである。ブロックの柱の内側に，天井に向けて設置された照明が，夜には，この，家の上に浮かんでいるような屋根の感じをさらに強める。

ジェラルド・トンケンズ邸，1955年

1930年代初頭の大不況に引き続いて，ライトは，中間所得者層の家族のために，住宅建設のコストを大幅に引き下げることになる〈ビルディング・システム〉の創造に心を向けた。彼がユーソニアン・ハウスと呼んだこのシステムは，当時はその賃金が比較的安価であった大工や組積工の労働力を必要とした。これがどのように実現されたかは，このシリーズの別の巻（GA TRAVELER 005 Usonian Houses）で説明されている。しかし，第二次大戦直後，労働賃金は大幅に上昇し，費用効率のよいプロダクトとしてのユーソニアン・ハウスの時代は終わった。1949年，ライトは再び，システムに基づいた建設方式をつくることを表明し，ユーソニアン・オートマティックと彼が呼ぶ方法が生まれた。彼の目的は，建設産業界に再び手頃な値段の，美しく実際的なデザインを供与することだった。"ユーソニアン"は，ライトがアメリカ合衆国を言及するのに好んで用いた言葉であり，"オートマティック"という言葉は，望めばクライアント自身が，自分の家の建設に参加できるような，基本的に単純で一貫性を備えたシステムを指すものである。主要な建築材料はコンクリート・ブロックであるが，特別にデザインされた1フィート×2フィートのブロックで，片側に格間が施され，片側は滑らかになっている。格間を施したブロックは通常のブロックより軽いので，一人で持ち上げ，据えることができる。ライトは，ブロックを扱うのに2人の手を必要としたら，システムそのものが破綻することを認めていた。カリフォルニア・テキスタイル・ブロックの住宅が持つ豊かで多彩な幾何学パターンとは違い，この新しい方式は，その装飾性を，時にはテラスの壁としてオープンなままに，他方では家の内部でガラスをはめて設置される有孔ブロックを使用することから生まれている。これは，リズム，魅力，美しさを，可能な限り単純な方法でつくりだす，遥かに洗練された方法である。天井でさえ，壁のパターンに合わせて格間のついたブロックを使い，上のコンクリート・スラブと補強用の鉄筋で連結している。いくつかの場合，屋内のブロックは内部の間仕切りとしてマホガニーの合板で覆われた。

　ジェラルド・トンケンズ邸のプランは，ライトの住宅デザインに共通するものである。一端に広いリビング／ダイニング・ルームがあり，ワークスペースとユーティリティがそのそばにある。寝室はワークスペースから書斎まで長い線を描いて伸びている。この翼に直角に，書斎の近

blocks offers quiet passage between the high ceilings of the entry and living room, focusing one's attention on the spatial experience. The gallery along the bedroom wing has an eight-foot coffered ceiling gilded in gold leaf. High perforated blocks with fixed glass run along the wall above a series of storage cabinets to provide light.

Although the Usonian Automatic was conceived as a system of construction for more moderate income clients, this was not the case with the Gerald Tonkens house. Wright's grandson, Eric Lloyd Wright, supervised its construction and the architect himself made several trips to the site. Each detail speaks of elegance: furniture, fabrics, carpets, and the several objects of Oriental art that are placed in the various rooms. In 1967 the Frank Lloyd Wright Foundation sent out a questionnaire to clients and current owners of Wright's works to inquire the state and condition of each building. To the question "Condition of your building" several blank lines were provided for the response. Gerald Tonkens simply wrote "Impeccable".

Bruce Brooks Pfeiffer

Taliesin West August 2002

1: *An American Architecture*, Edgar Kaufmann, ed. (New York: Barnes & Noble Books, 1998) pp.55-56
2: Frank Lloyd Wright, *The Natural House*, (New York: Horizon Press, 1954) back endpapers
3: Frank Lloyd Wright, *Architectural Forum*, January 1938, p.56
4: William Tecumseh Sherman (1820-1891), Union Civil War general who drove the Confederate Army from Atlanta, and then began his march to the sea through Georgia and South Carolina, leaving ruin and devastation of the South behind him in 1864-65.
5: Frank Lloyd Wright, *Architectural Forum*, January 1948, p.95
6: Frank Lloyd Wright Archives, mss. AV#2401.566

くにあるのはカーポートである。天井の高さは，寝室翼とカーポートが8フィート，リビングルームが12フィート，ワークスペースとユーティリティが14フィートである。リビングルームでは，ガラスの扉が囲まれた戸外テラスに開いている。一番端にある書斎にもガラス扉が付き，小さなテラスを楽しめる。金属枠にはめ込まれた2フィート角のガラス板が通気のために家全体に使われ，はめ殺しガラスを入れた有孔ブロックと組み合わされている。これらの開閉できる窓の配置は，南の芝生に面した家の全長にわたって伸びる反復する静かなパターンを見せている。有孔ブロックと方形の窓の組み合わせは，通風もよく，日射しもよく入るインテリアをつくりあげる。エントランスは，ユーティリティやワークスペースの近くにあり，ワークスペースとその先にあるリビングルームに直接通じている。このリビングルームへ至る部分は，ライトの魔法のような空間の使い方のまた別の例である。格間を施したブロックで構成された低いデッキが，エントリーとリビングルームの高い天井の間に静かな通路を提供し，そこを行く人の注意をその空間体験に集中させる。寝室翼に沿ったギャラリーには，金色の葉を飾った8フィートの高さの格間天井がついている。外の光を採り入れるために，はめ殺しガラスの入った有孔ブロックが，一連の収納戸棚の上の壁に沿って高い位置に並んでいる。

　ユーソニアン・オートマティックは中間所得階層のための建設システムとして考えられたものではあるが，ジェラルド・トンケンズ邸はこのケースにはあてはまらない。ライトの孫，エリック・ロイド・ライトがその工事を監理し，ライト自身も現場を何回か訪れている。それぞれのディテールは優雅さを語りかけてくる。様々な部屋に置かれている，家具，ファブリック，カーペット，いくつかの東洋の美術品。1967年，フランク・ロイド・ライト・ファウンデーションは，ライトの建物のクライアントと現在のオーナーに対して，各建物の現状についての質問表を送った。"あなたの建物の状態" という質問には答えを書き込むための数行の空欄が添えられていた。ジェラルド・トンケンズは，簡潔に "非のうちどころなし" と記入してきた。

ブルース・ブルックス・ファイファー
　　　　　　　　　　　　タリアセン・ウェストにて　2002年8月

註：
1："An American Architecture", Edgar Kaufmann, ed. (New York: Barnes Books, 1998) pp.55-56
2：Frank Lloyd Wright "The Natural House" (New York. Horizon Press. 1954) 裏面見返し。
3：Frank Lloyd wright, "Architectural Forum", January 1938, p.56
4：William Tecumseh Sherman (1820-1891)　南北戦争当時の将軍で，アトランタから南軍を追い払い，1864年から1865年にかけて，ジョージアとサウスカロライナを通って海まで進軍し，南部に廃墟と破壊の跡を残した。
5：Frank Lloyd Wright, "Architectural Forum", January 1948, p.95
6：Frank Lloyd Wright Archives. mss. AV#2401.566

"Wingspread", Herbert F. Johnson House
Wind Point, Wisconsin, 1937

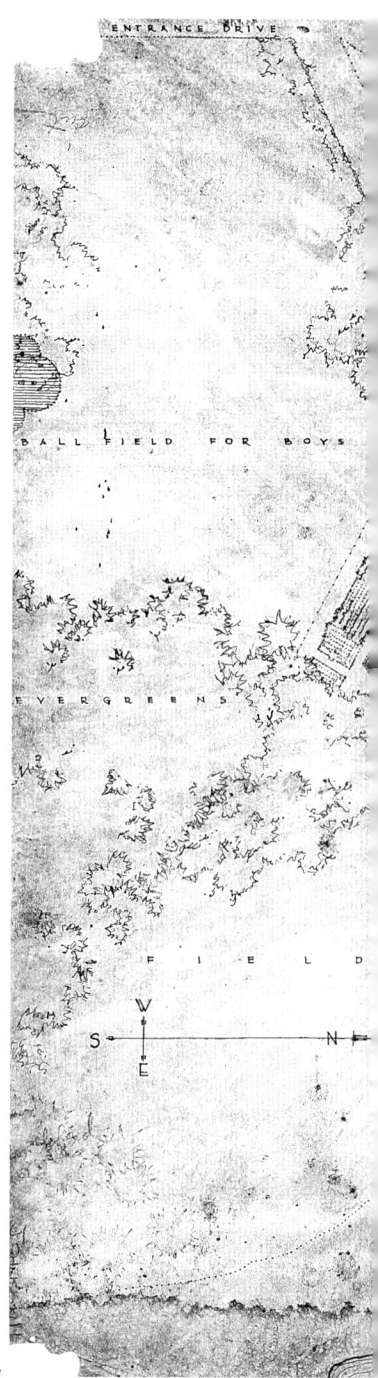

Site plan

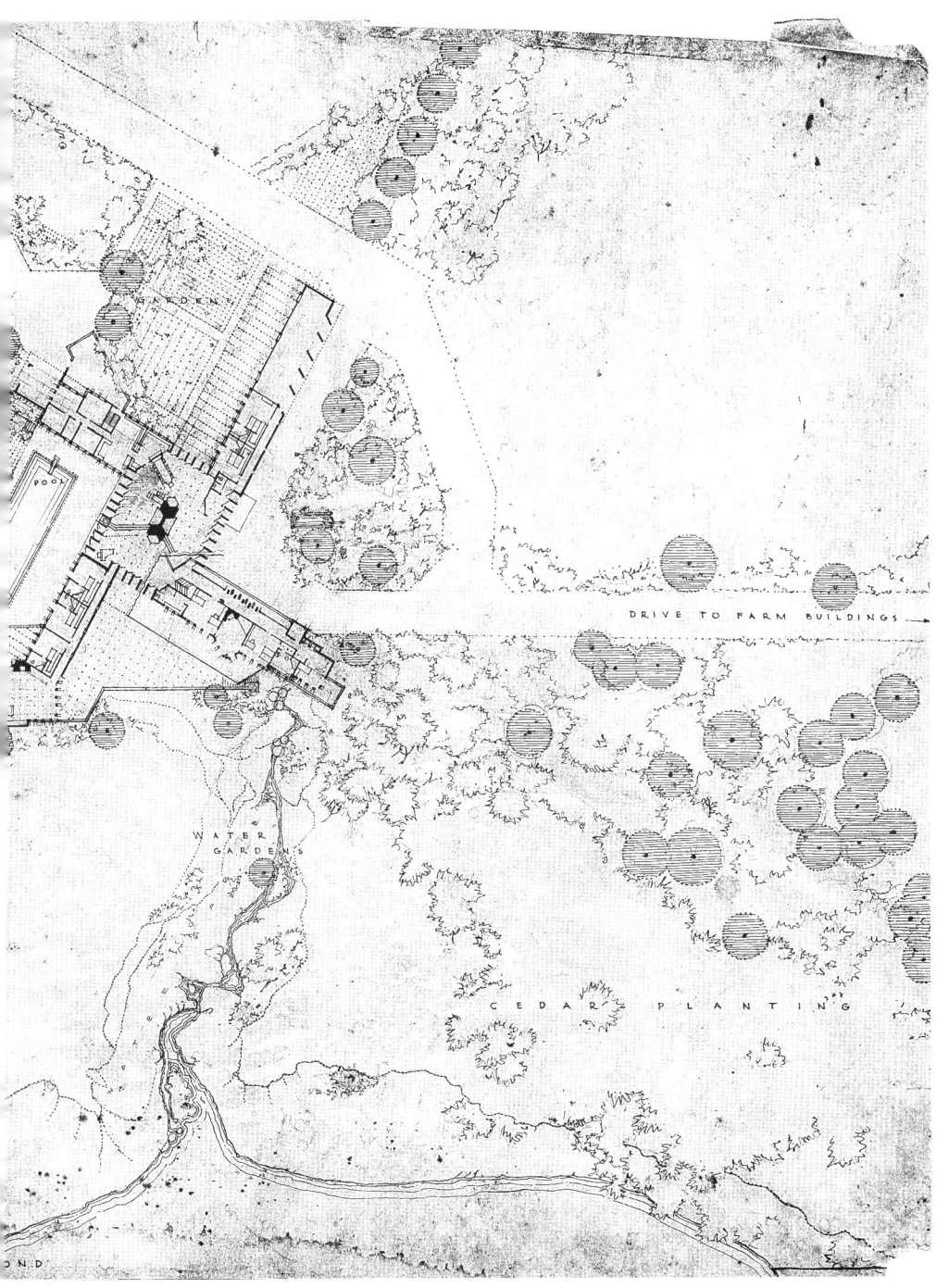

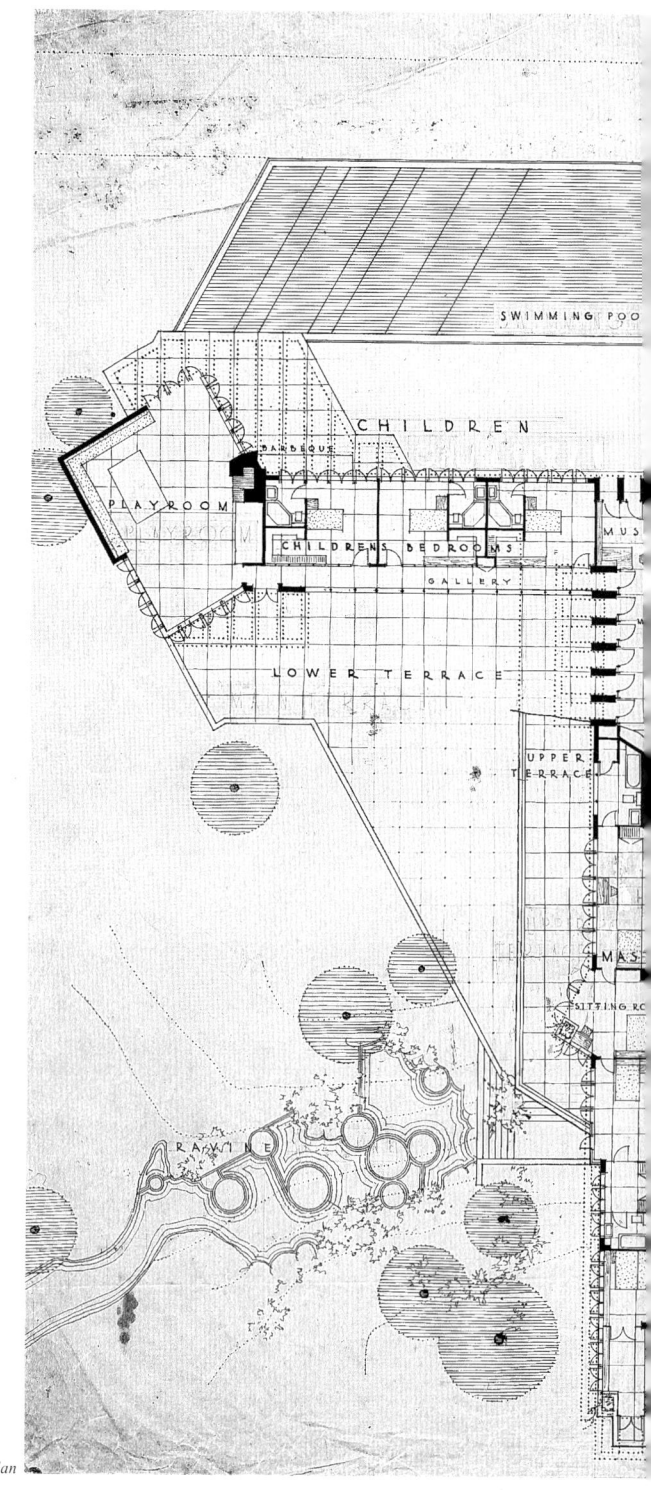

Plan

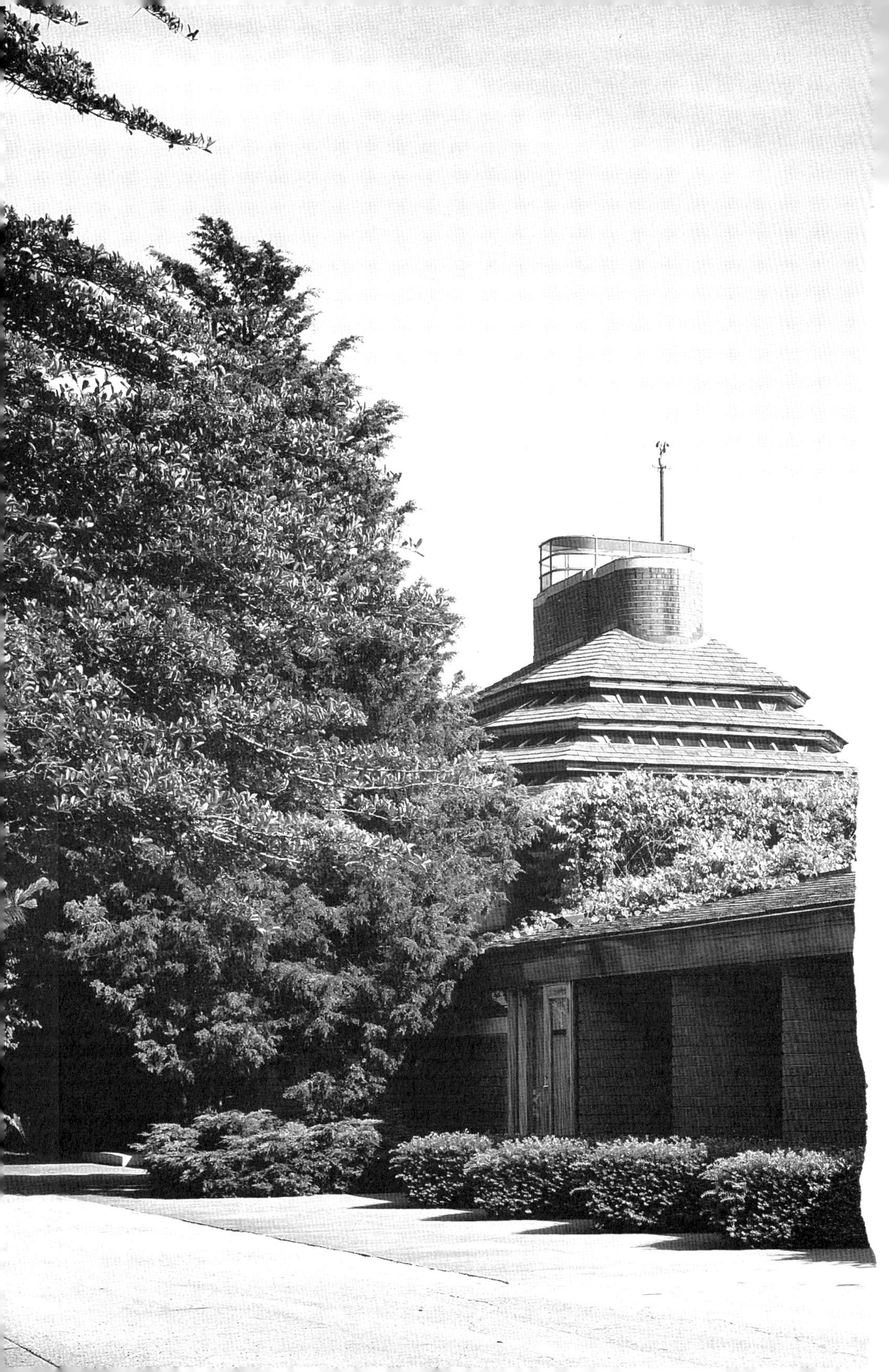

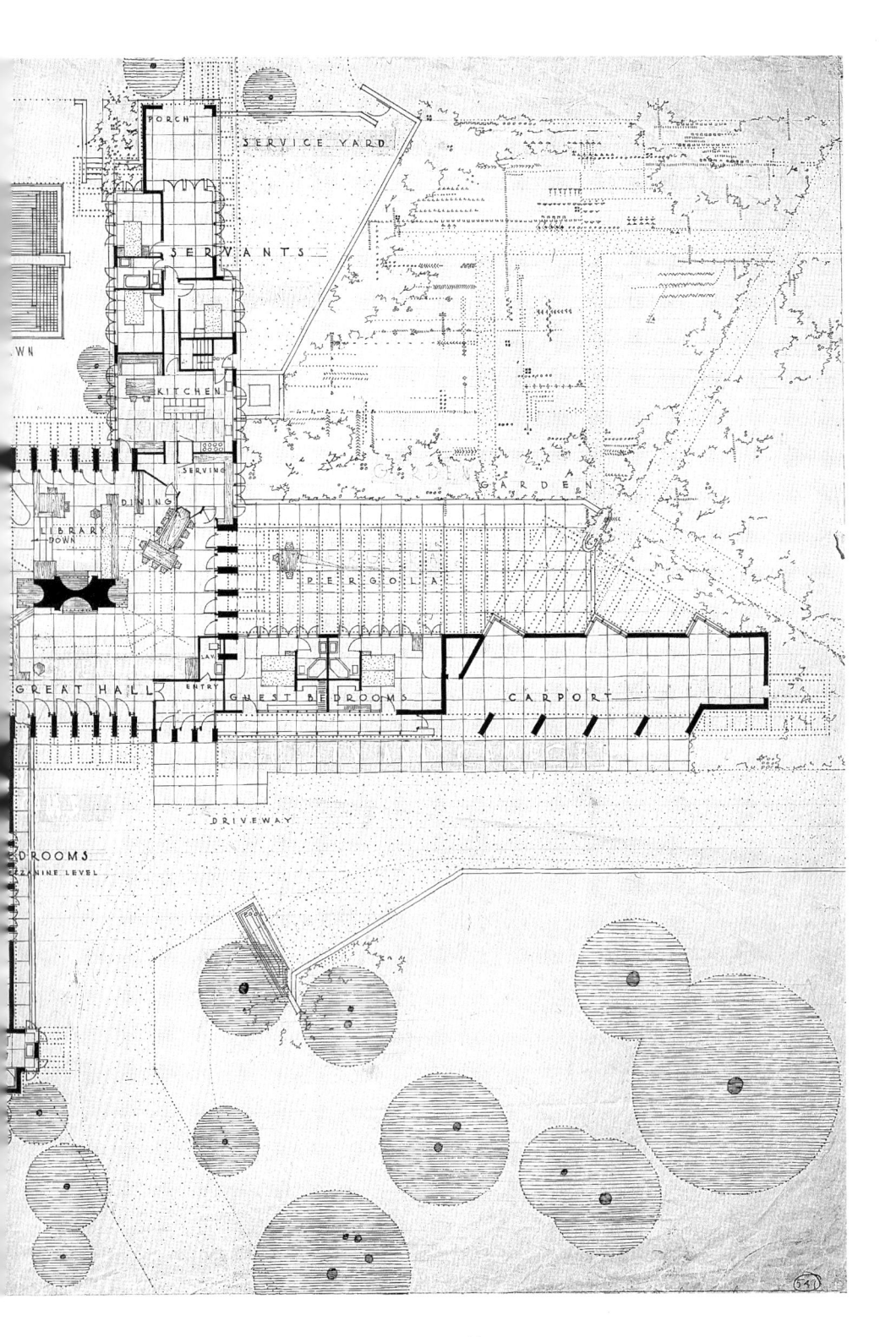

PORCH
SERVICE YARD
SERVANTS
KITCHEN
SERVING
DINING
LIBRARY
DOWN
GARDEN
PERGOLA
GREAT HALL
ENTRY
GUEST BEDROOMS
CARPORT
DRIVEWAY
DROOMS
ZZANINE LEVEL

31

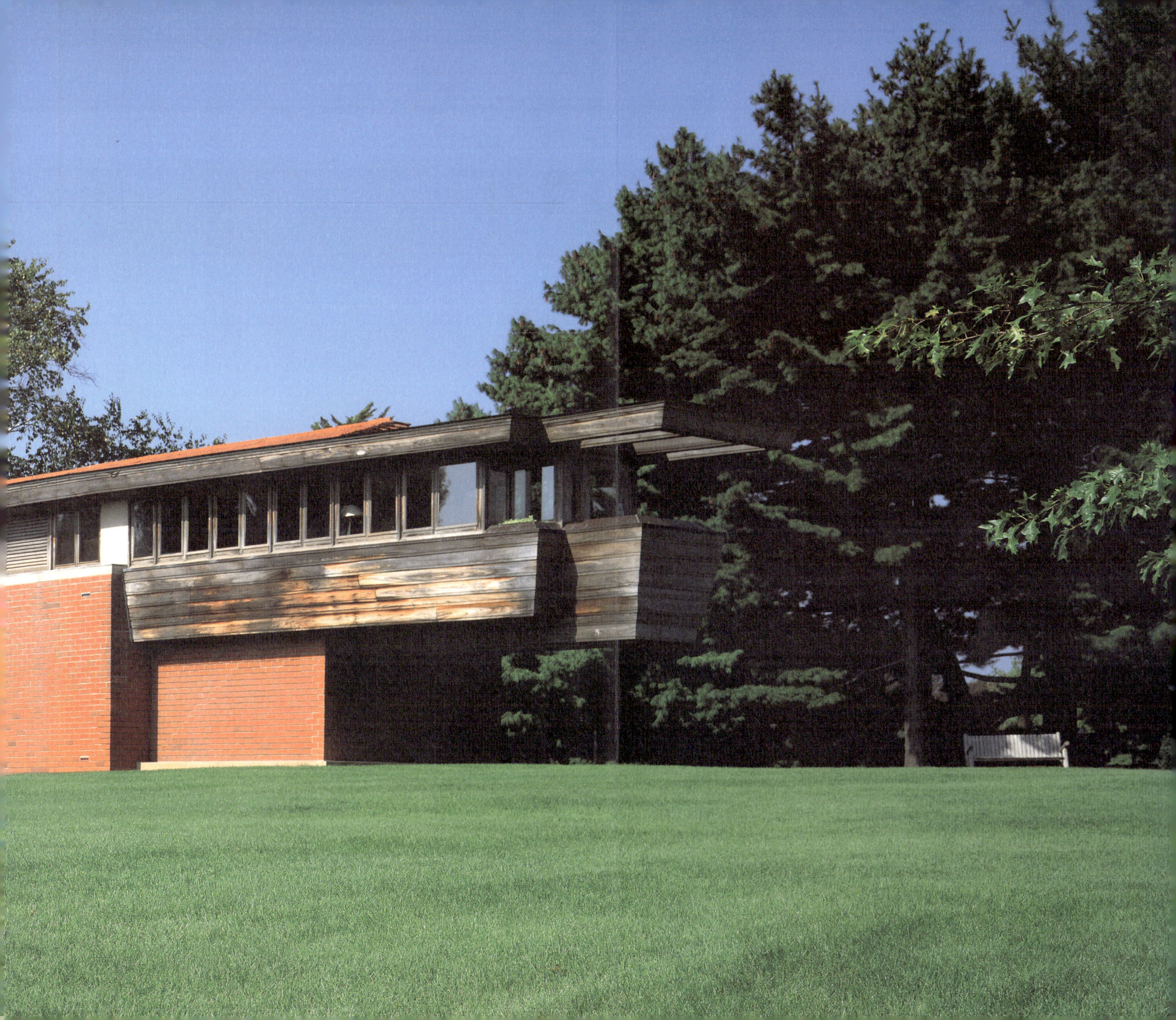

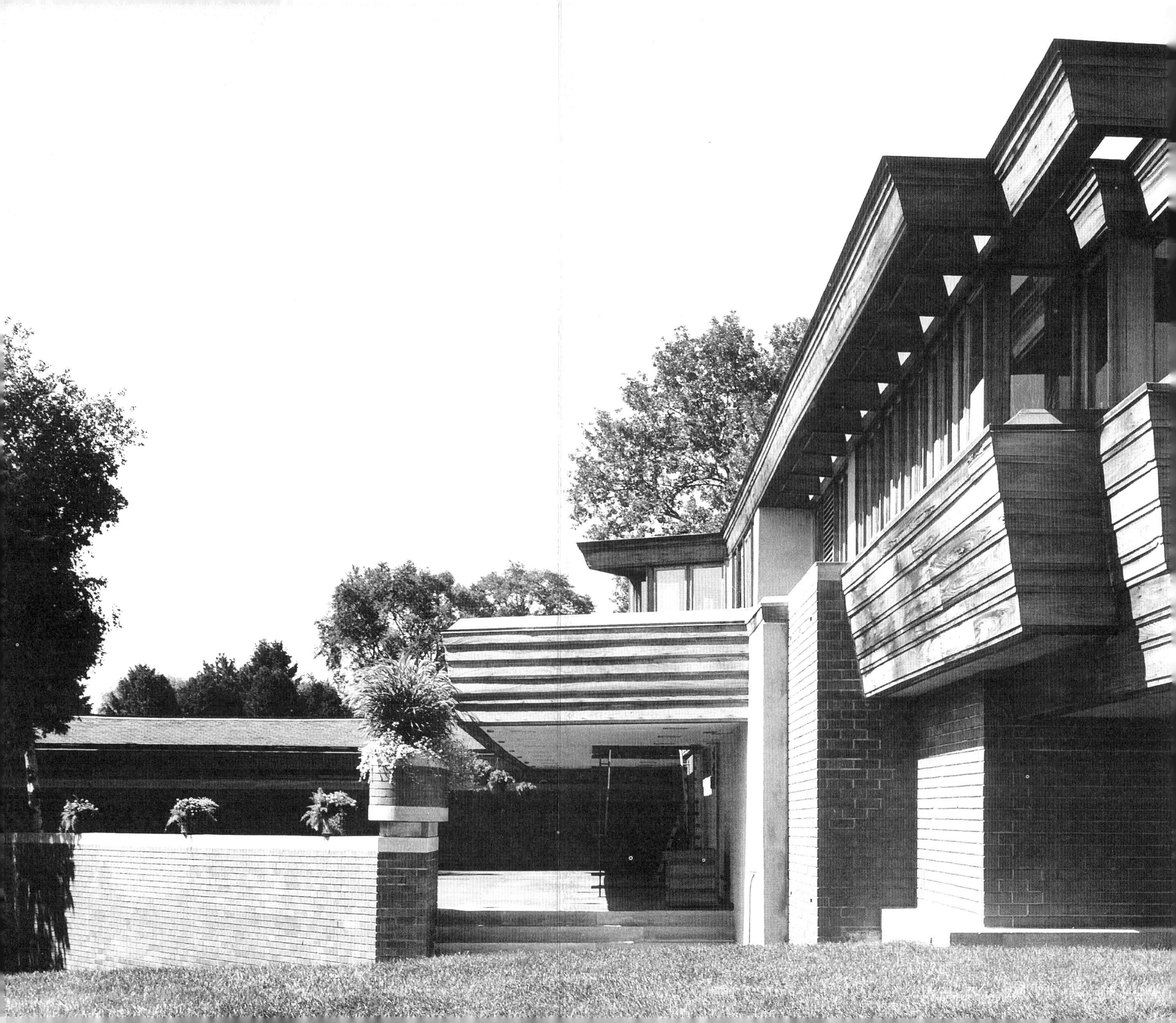

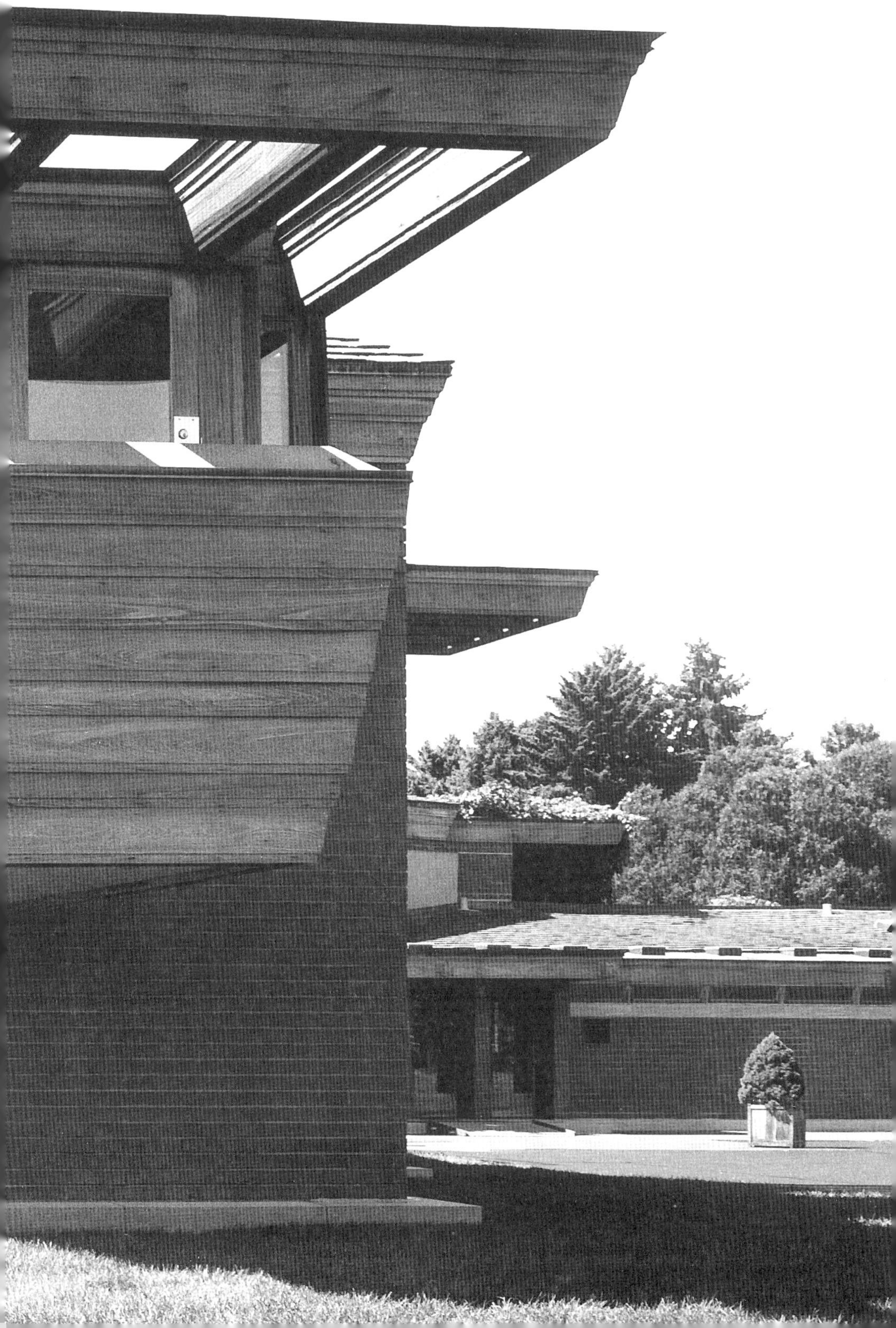

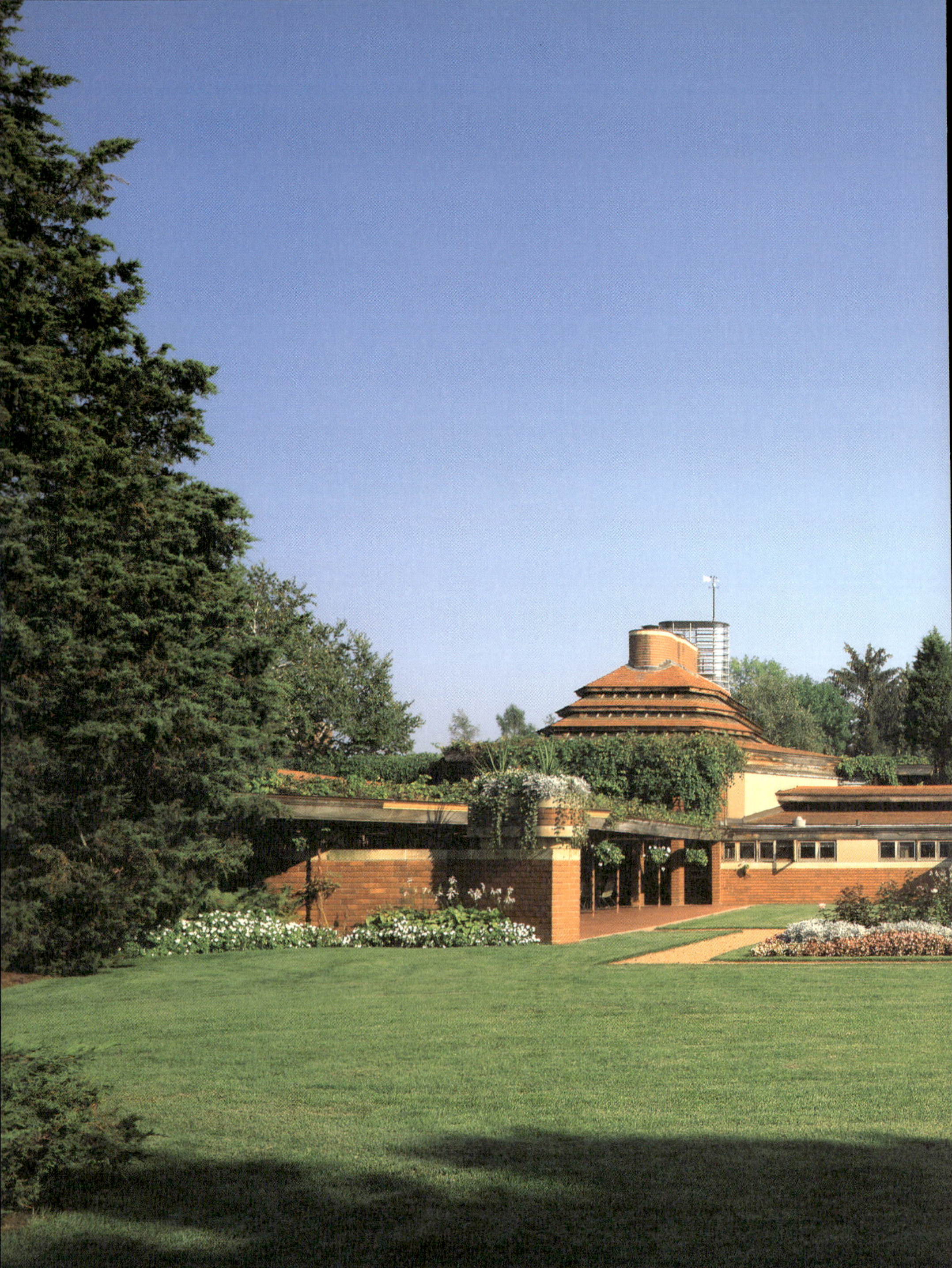

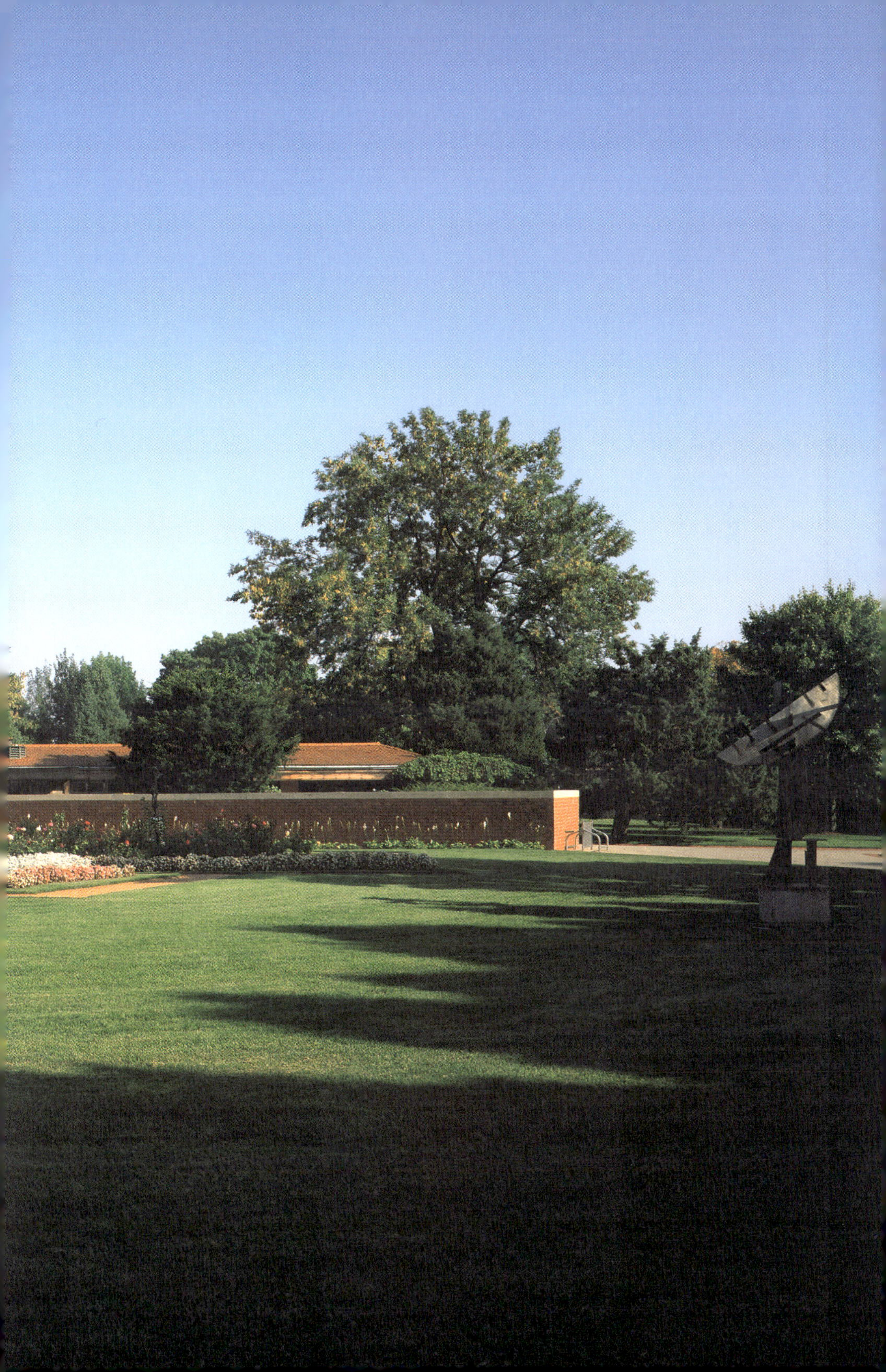

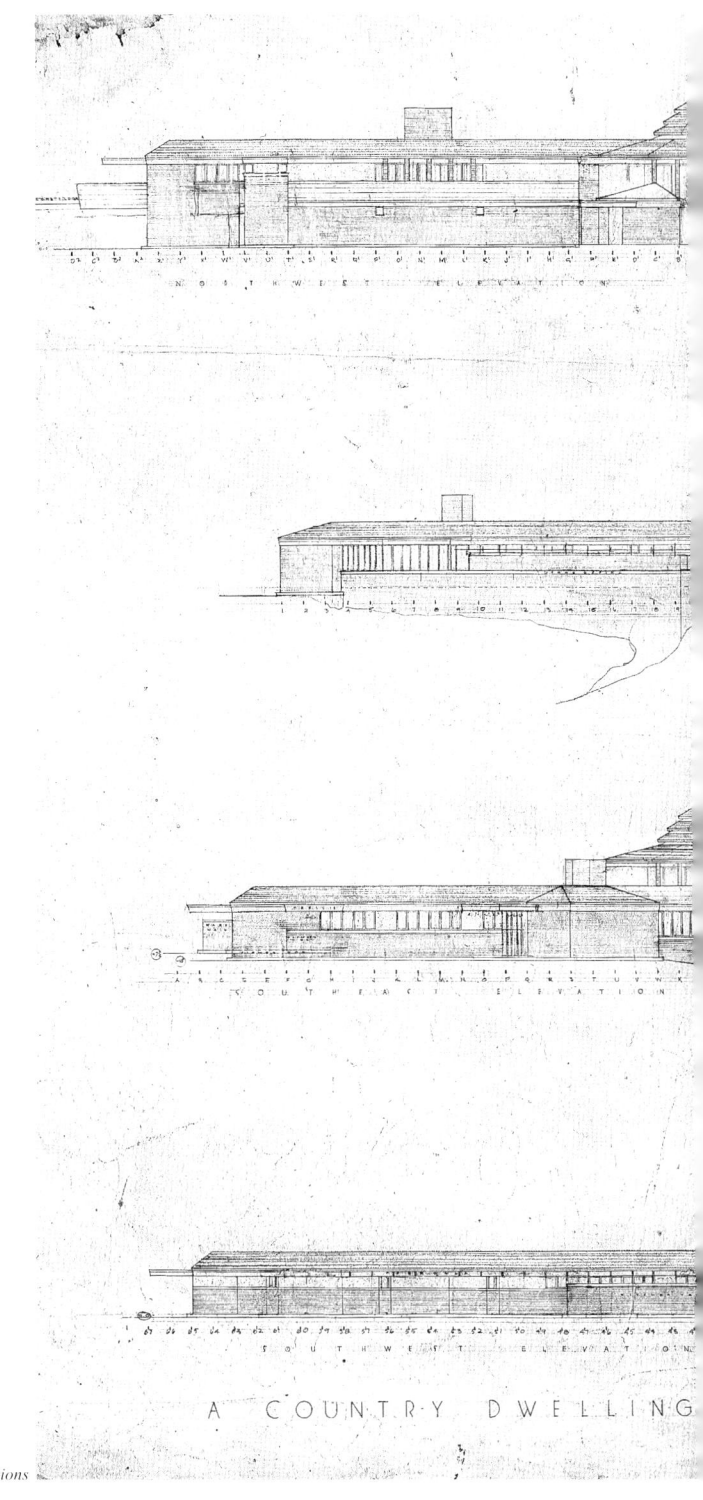

A COUNTRY DWELLING

Elevations

FOR MR AND MRS HERBERT F JOHNSON JR
WINDY POINT RACINE WISCONSIN
FRANK LLOYD WRIGHT ARCHITECT

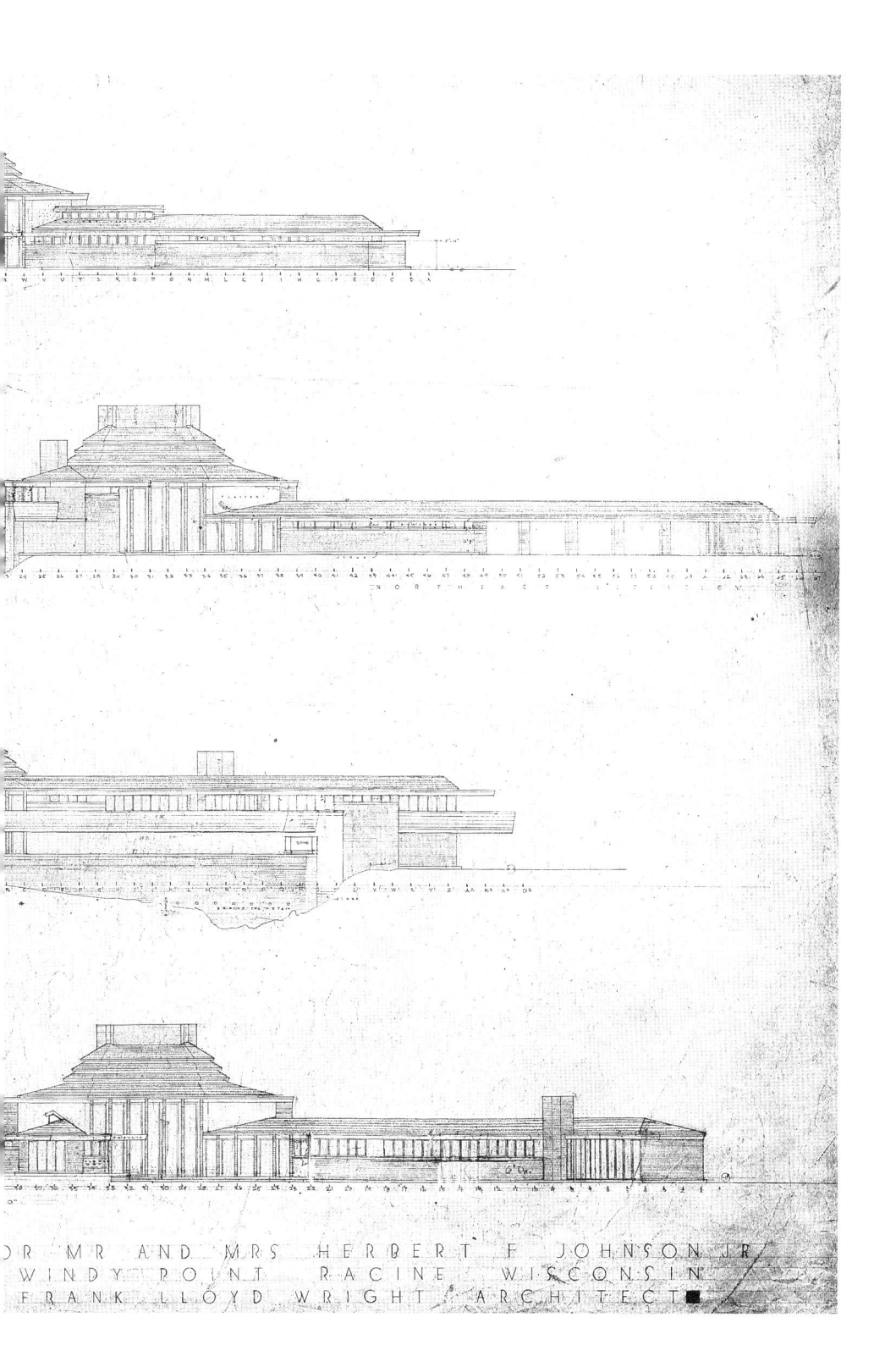

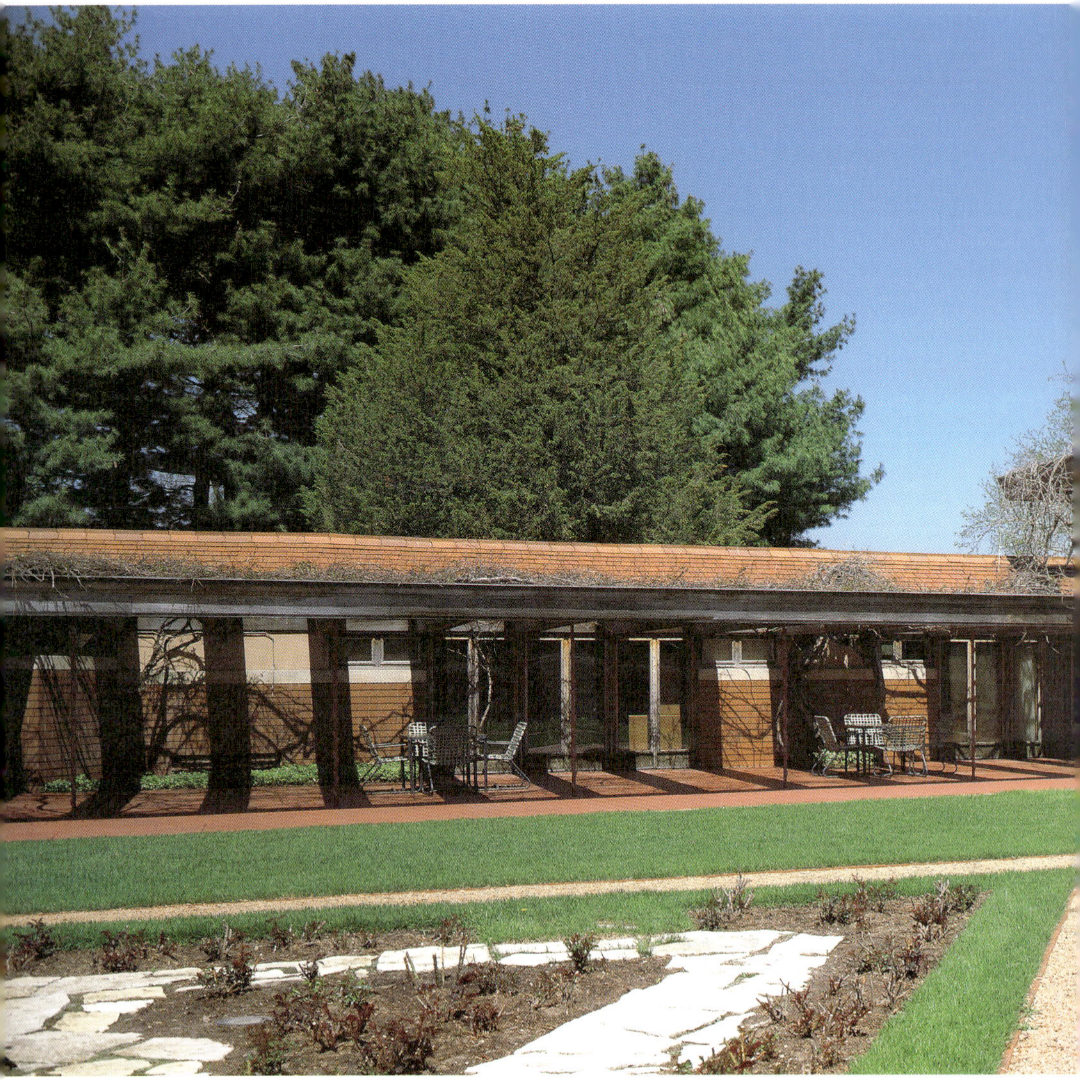

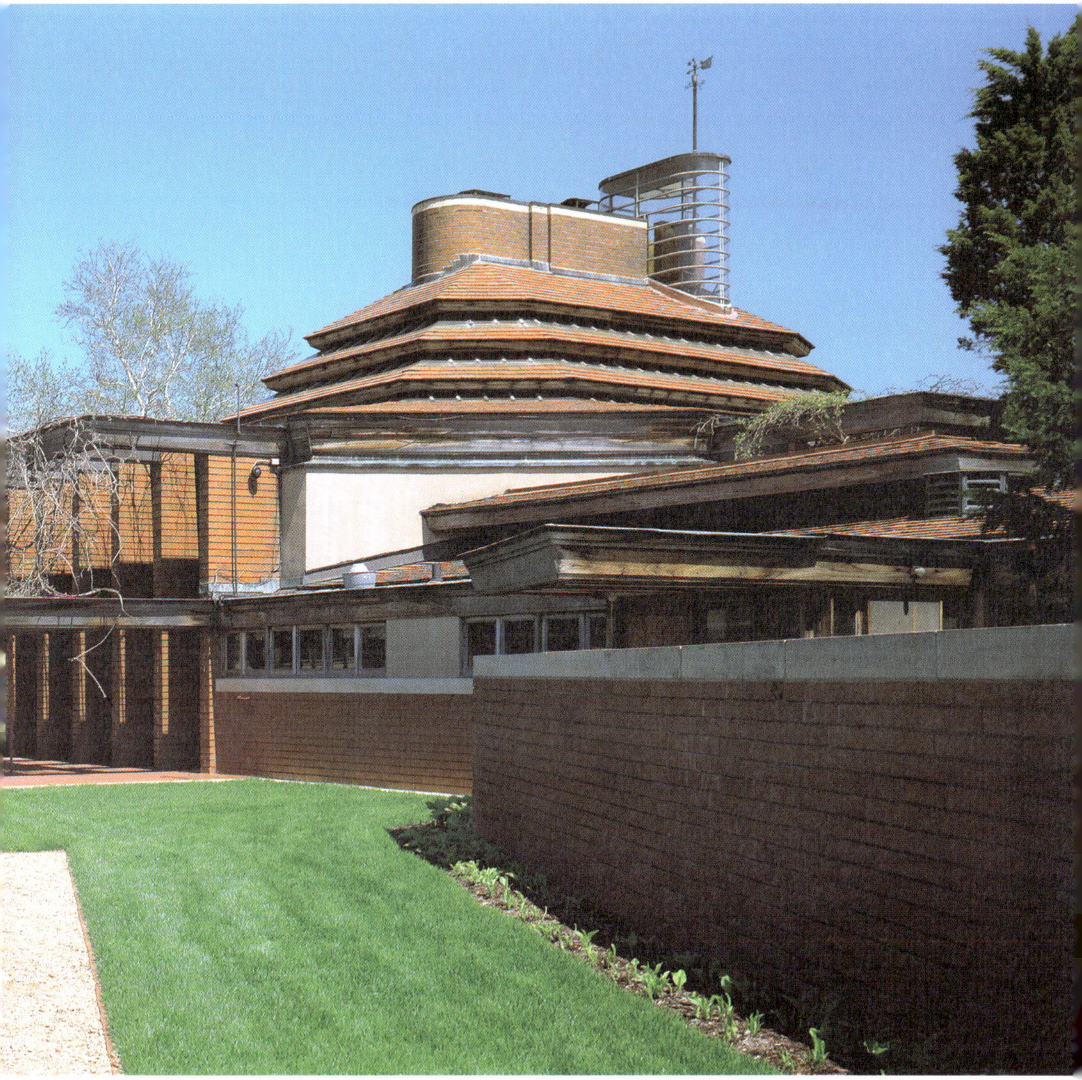

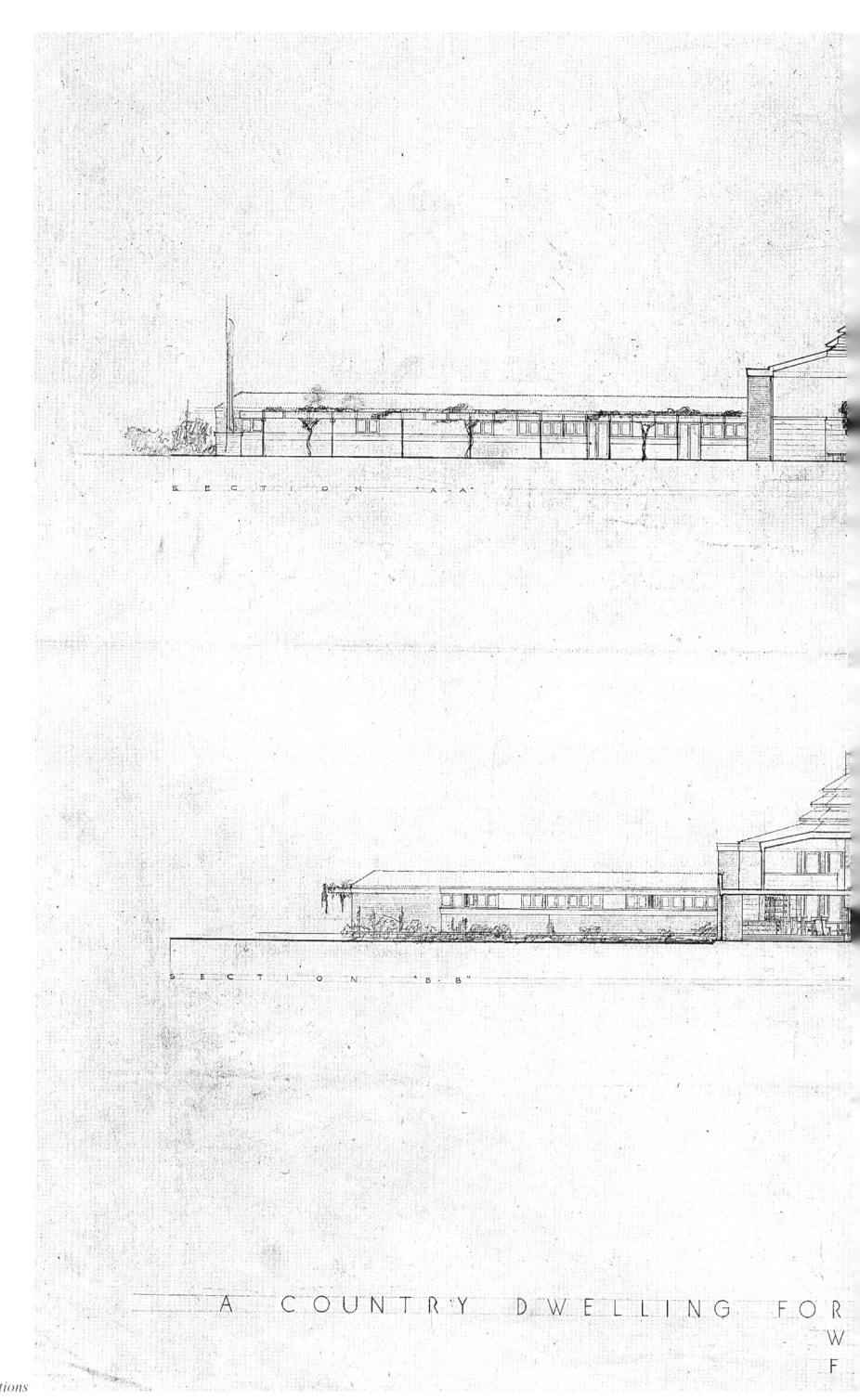

SECTION A-A

SECTION B-B

A COUNTRY DWELLING FOR
W
F

Sections

MR AND MRS HERBERT F JOHNSON JR ·
DY POINT   RACINE   WISCONSIN
NK LLOYD WRIGHT   ARCHITECT

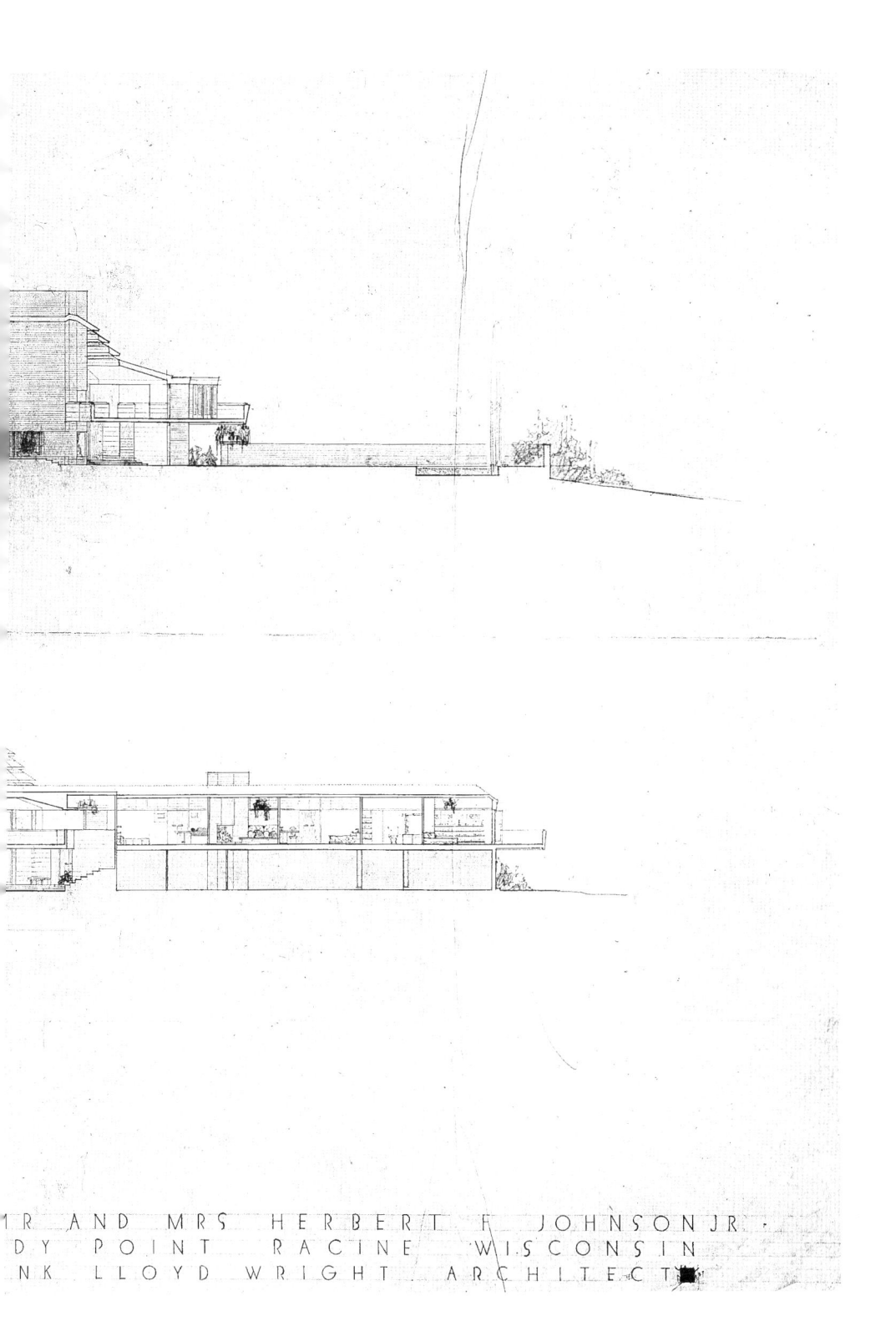

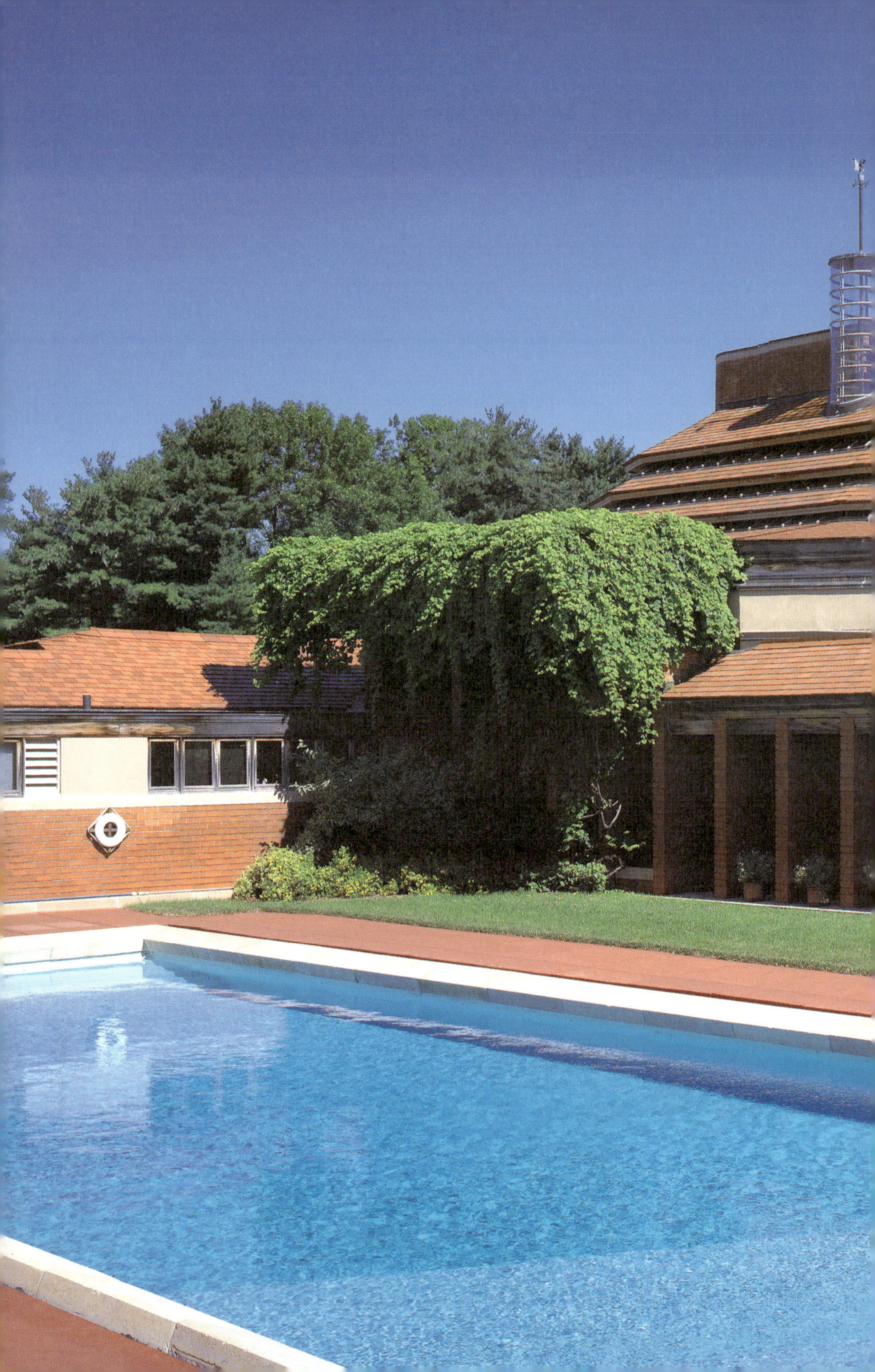

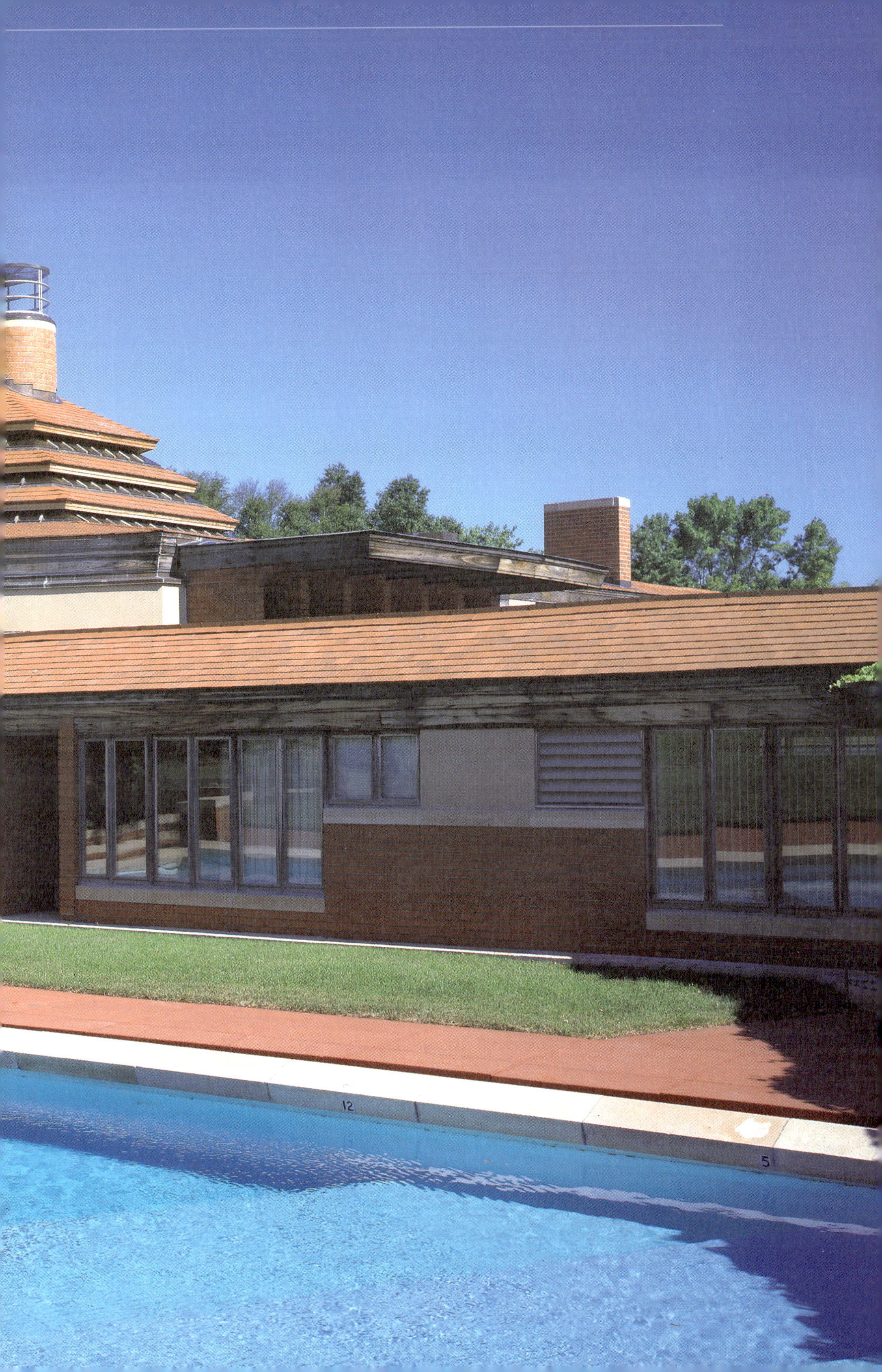
12
5

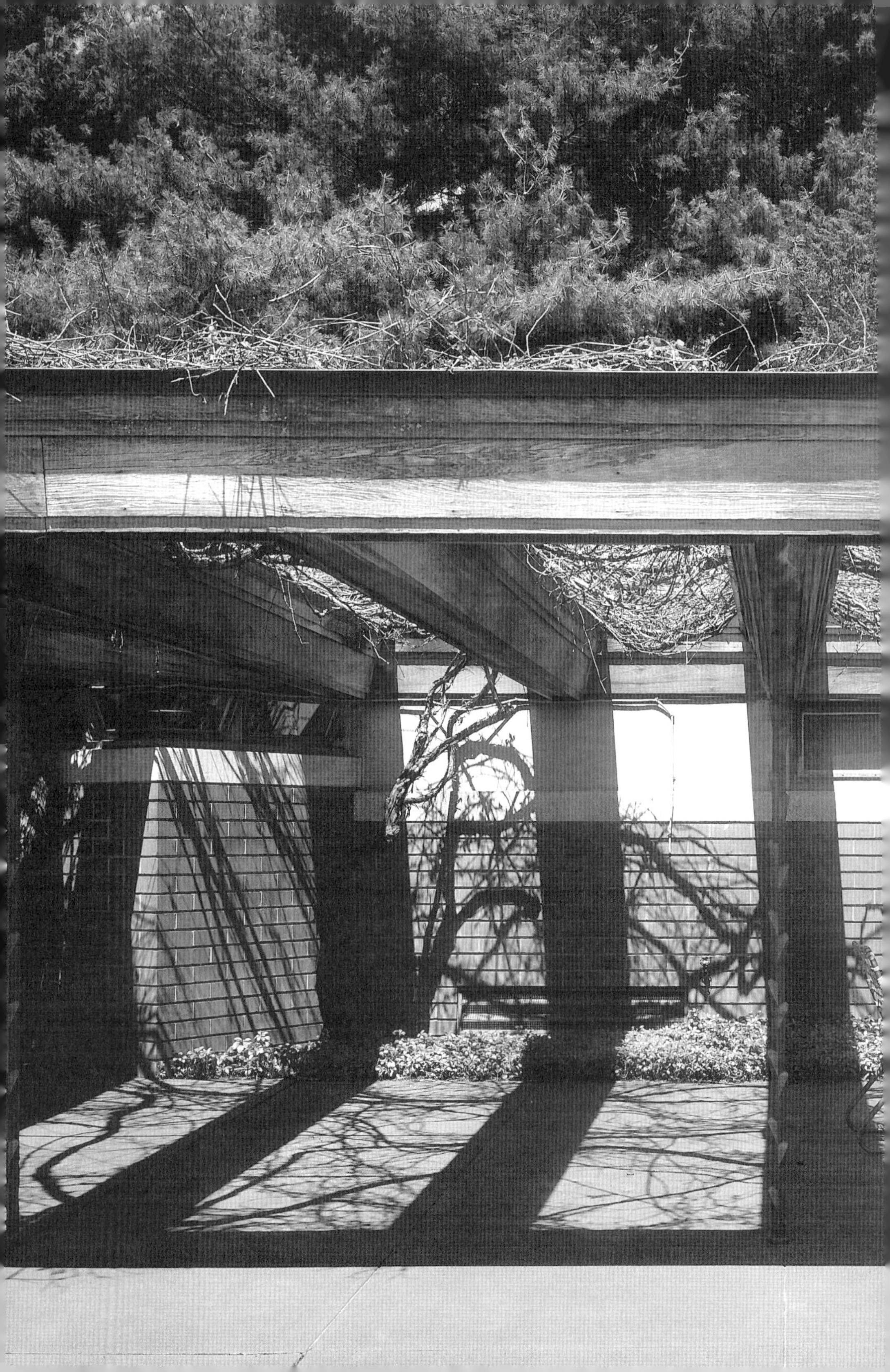

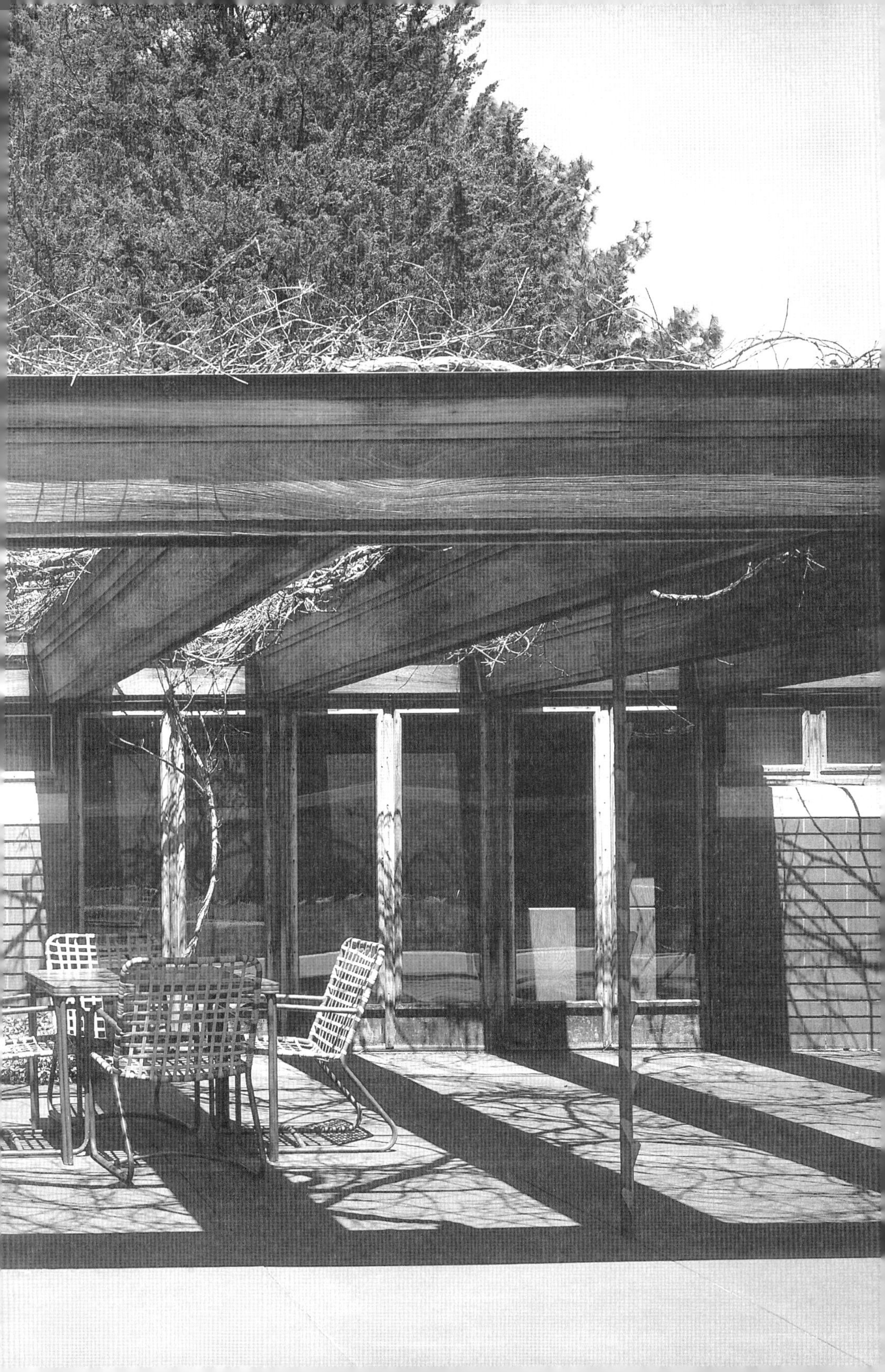

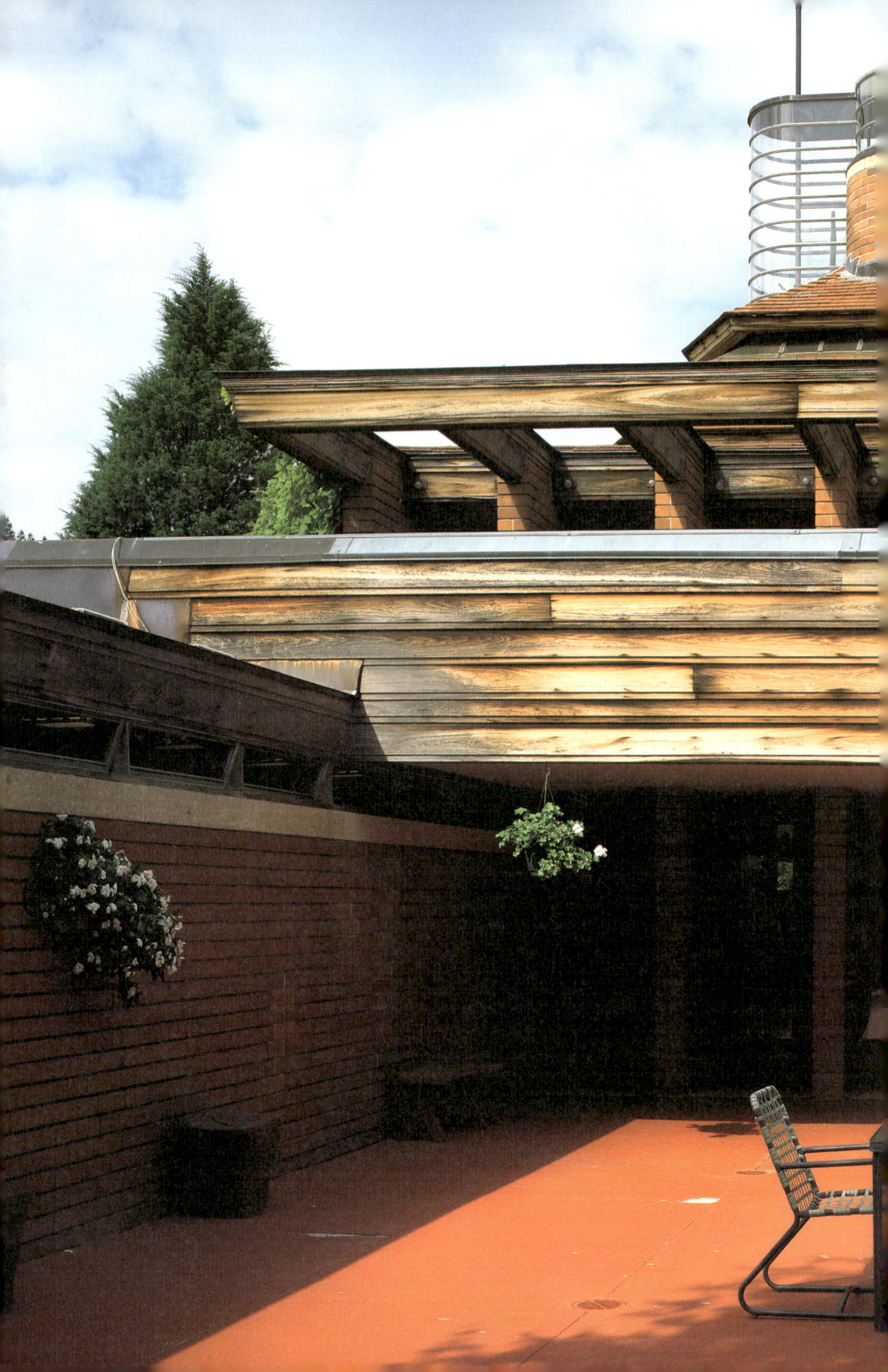

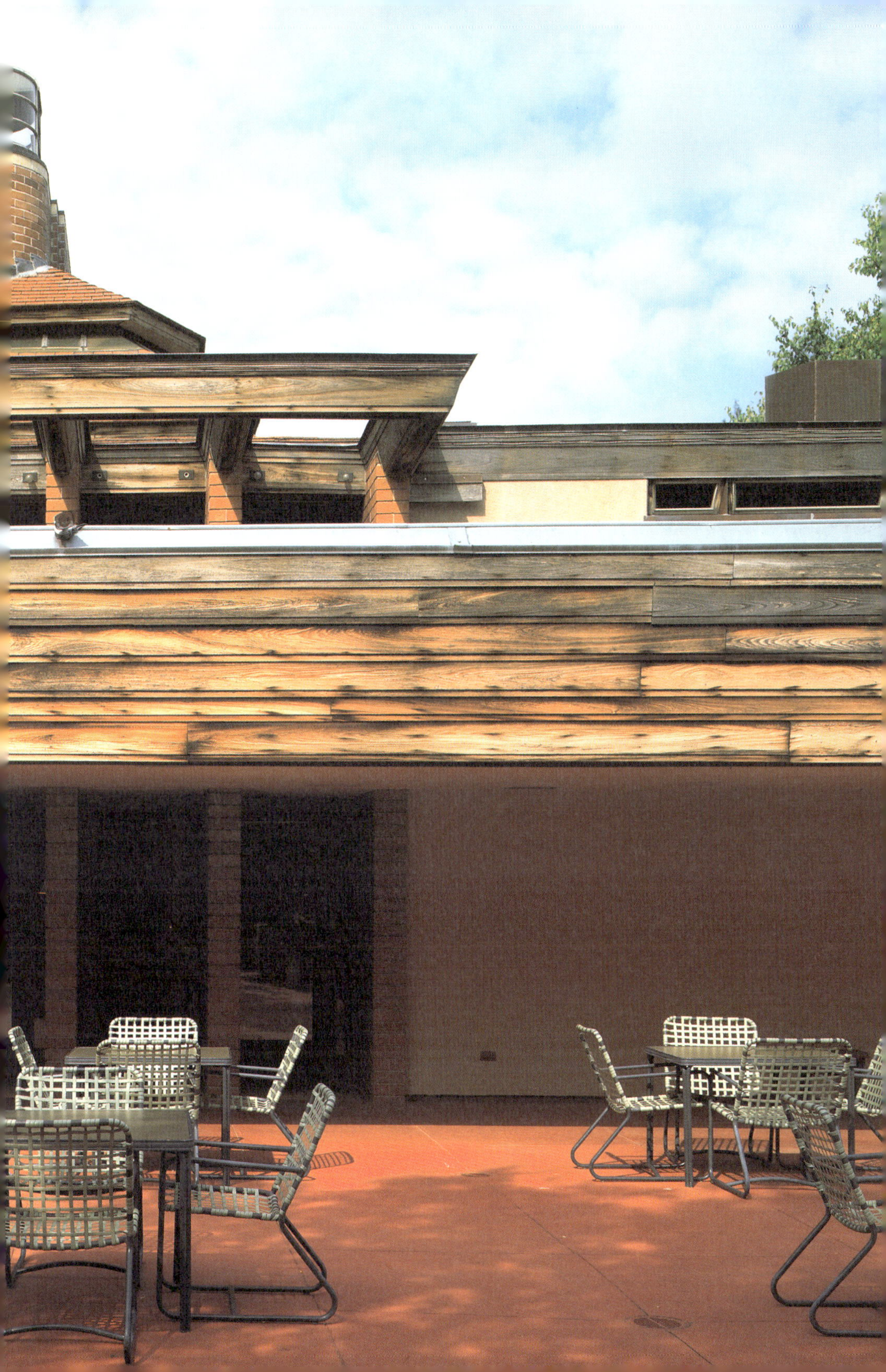

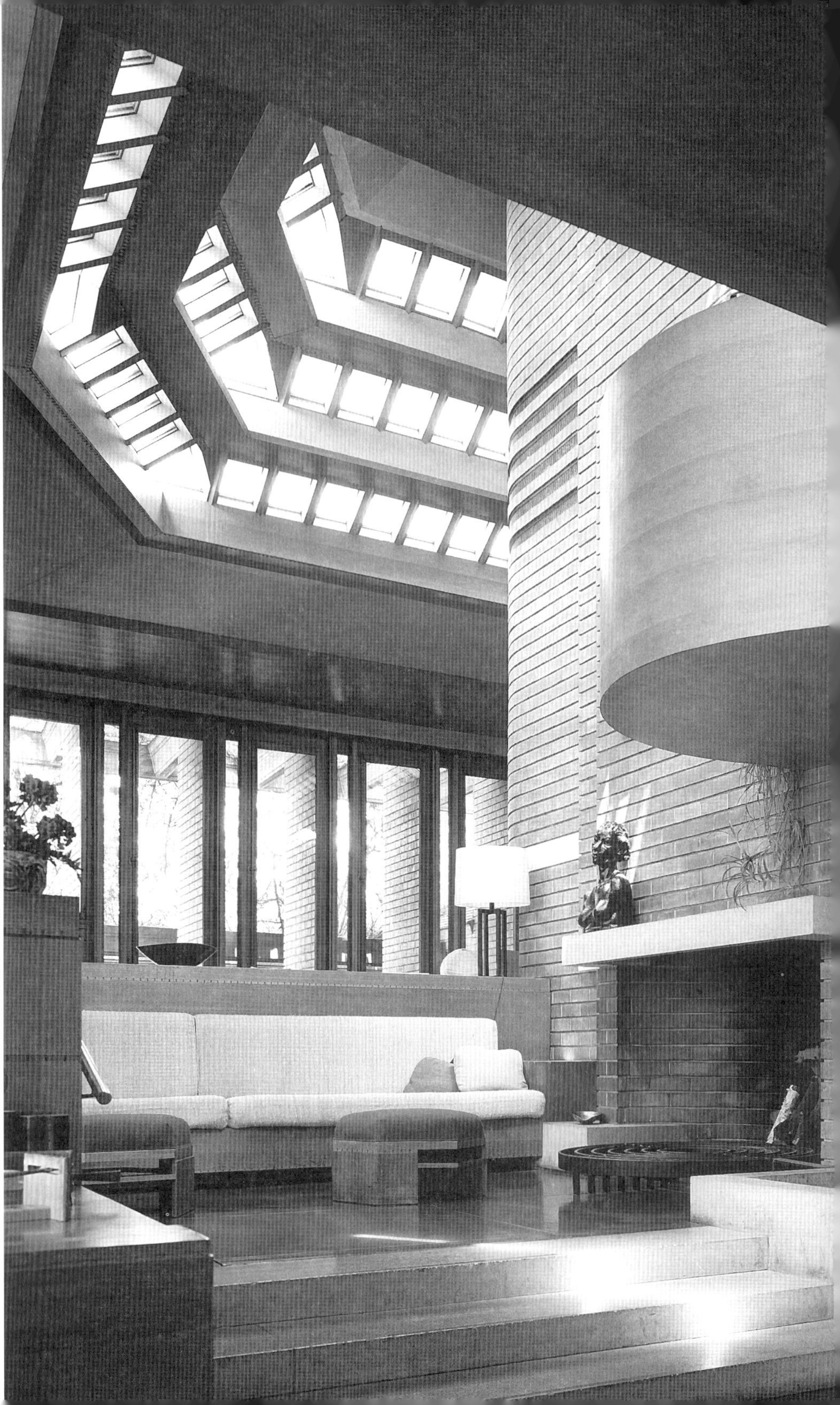

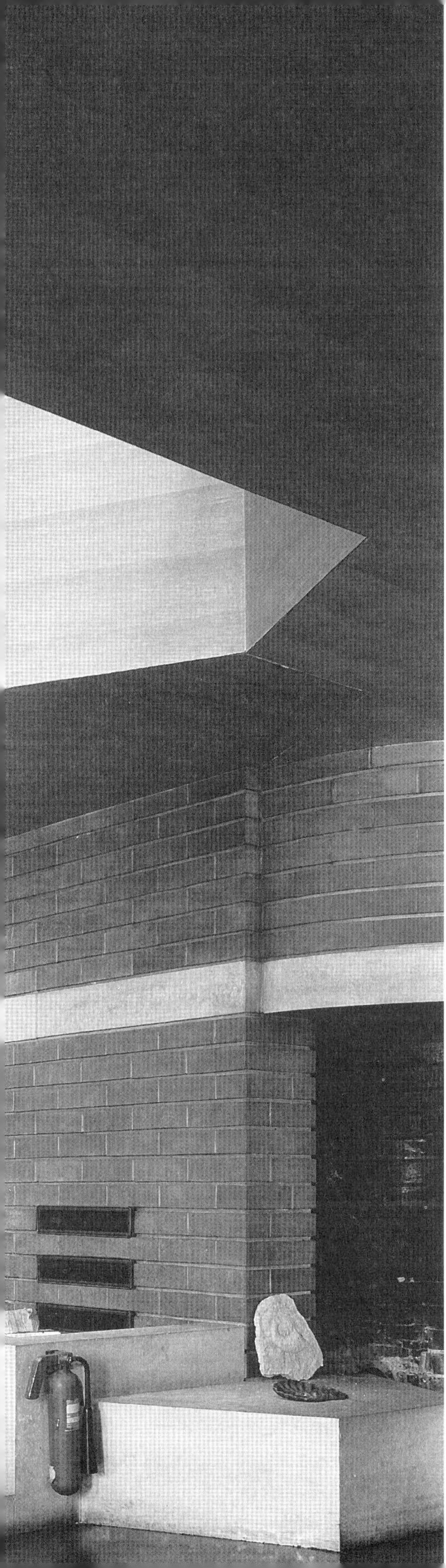

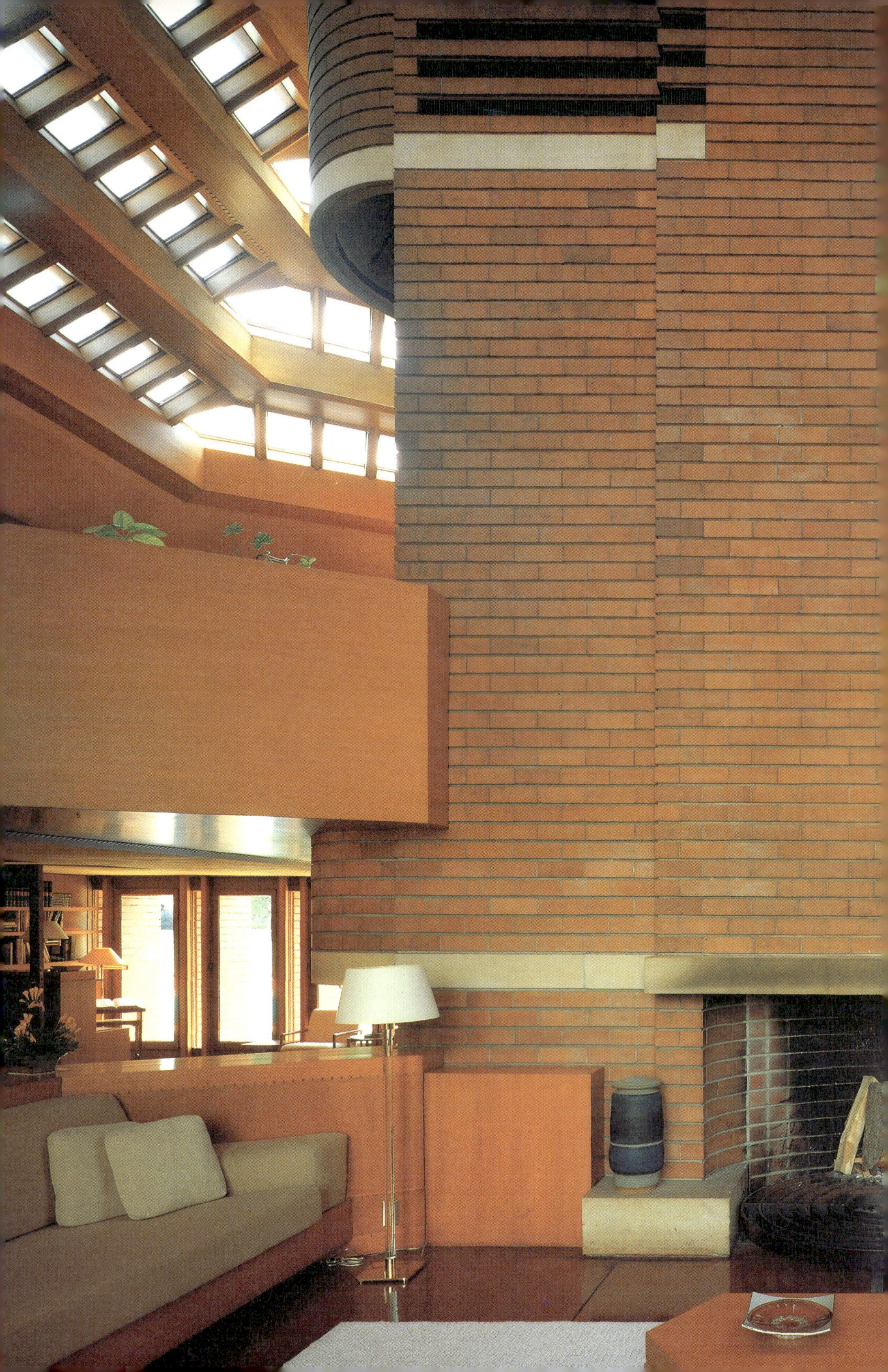

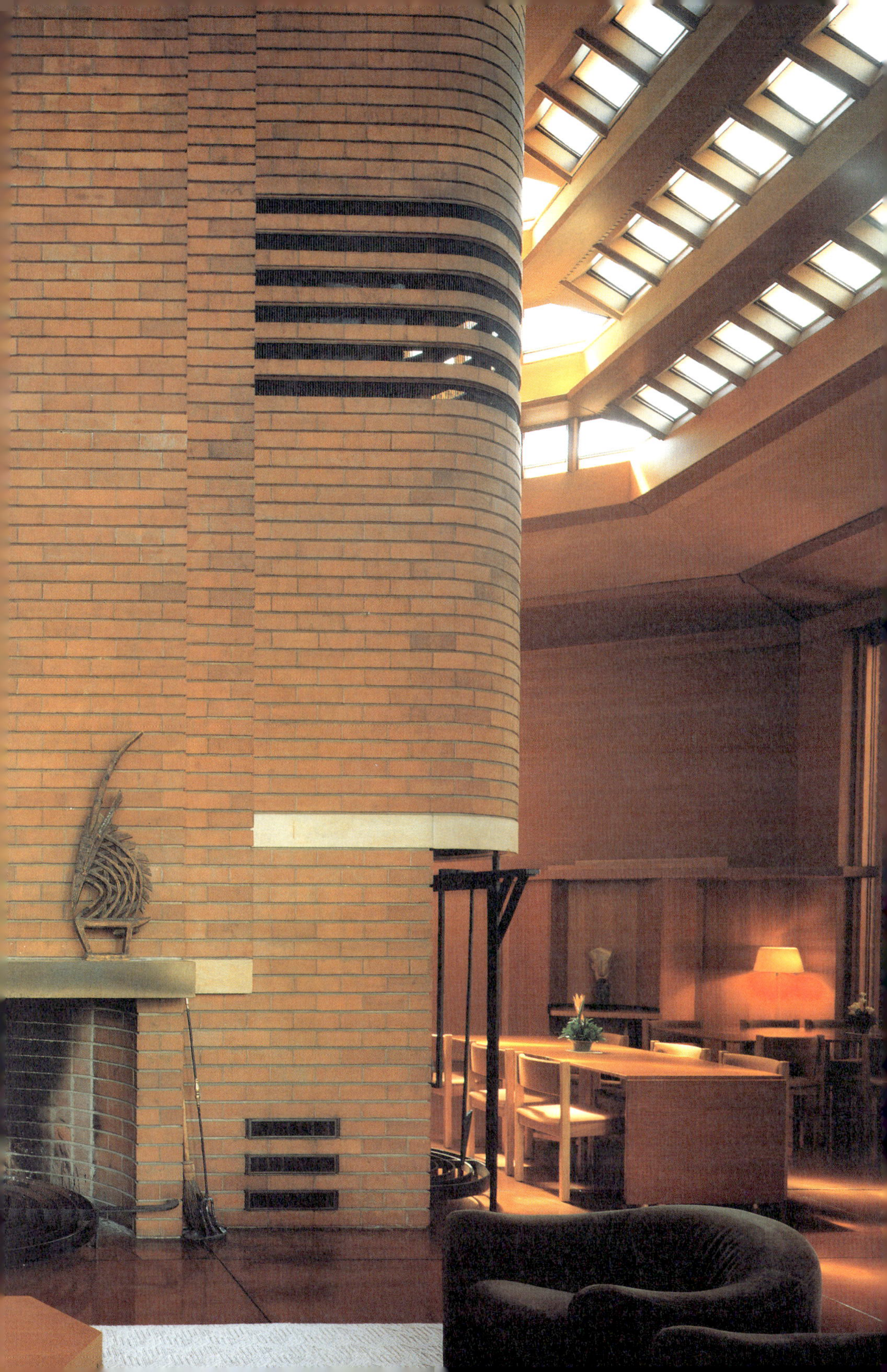

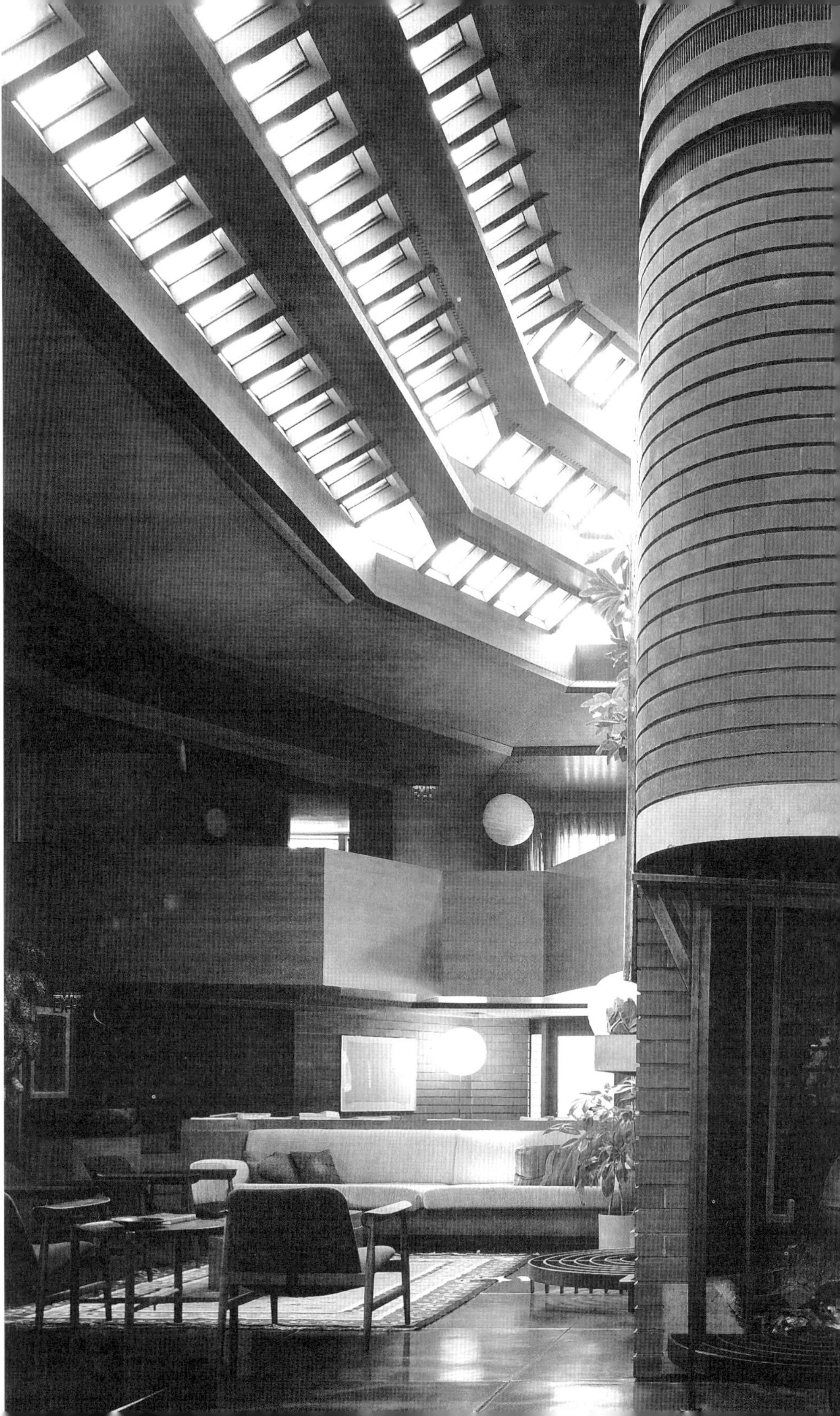

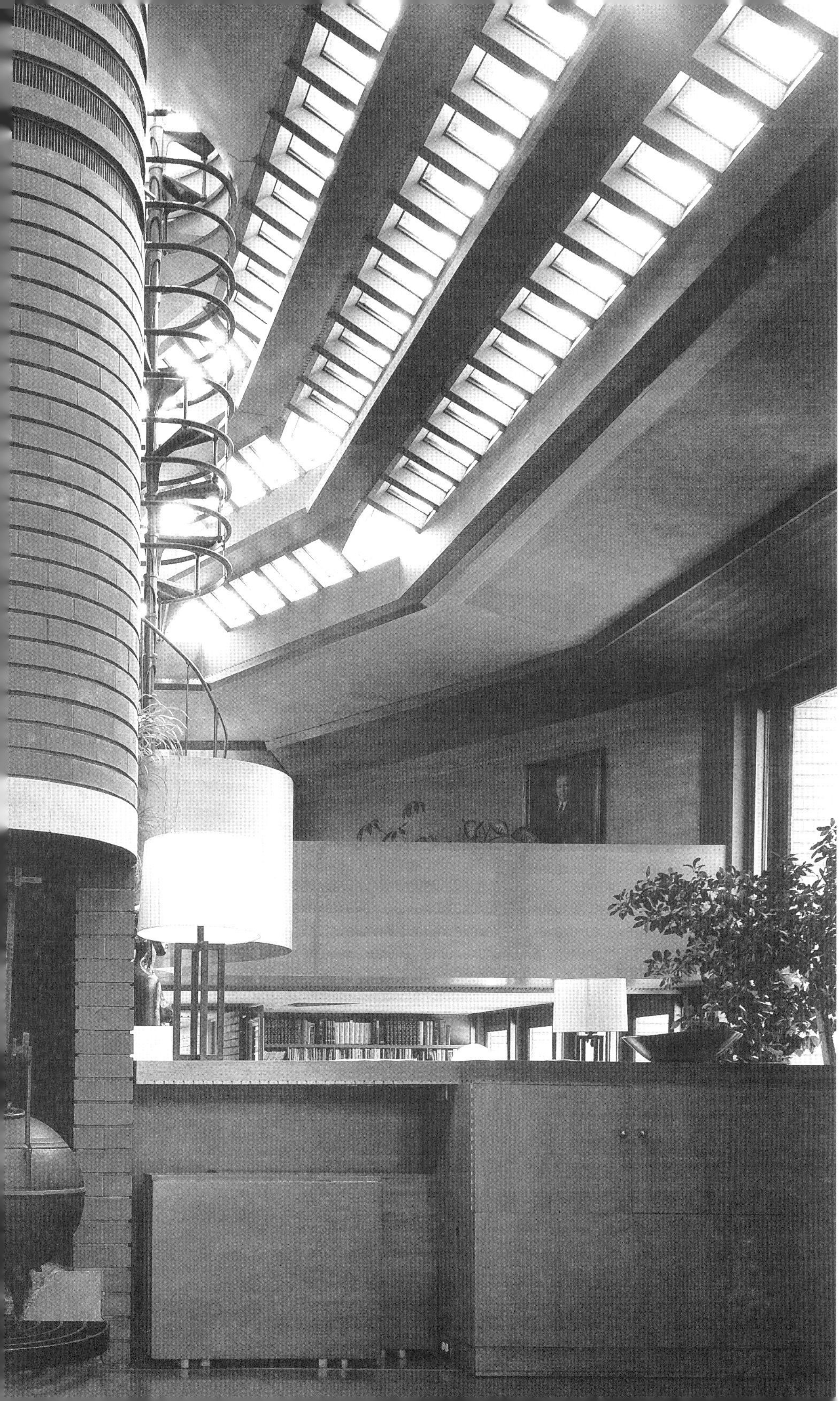

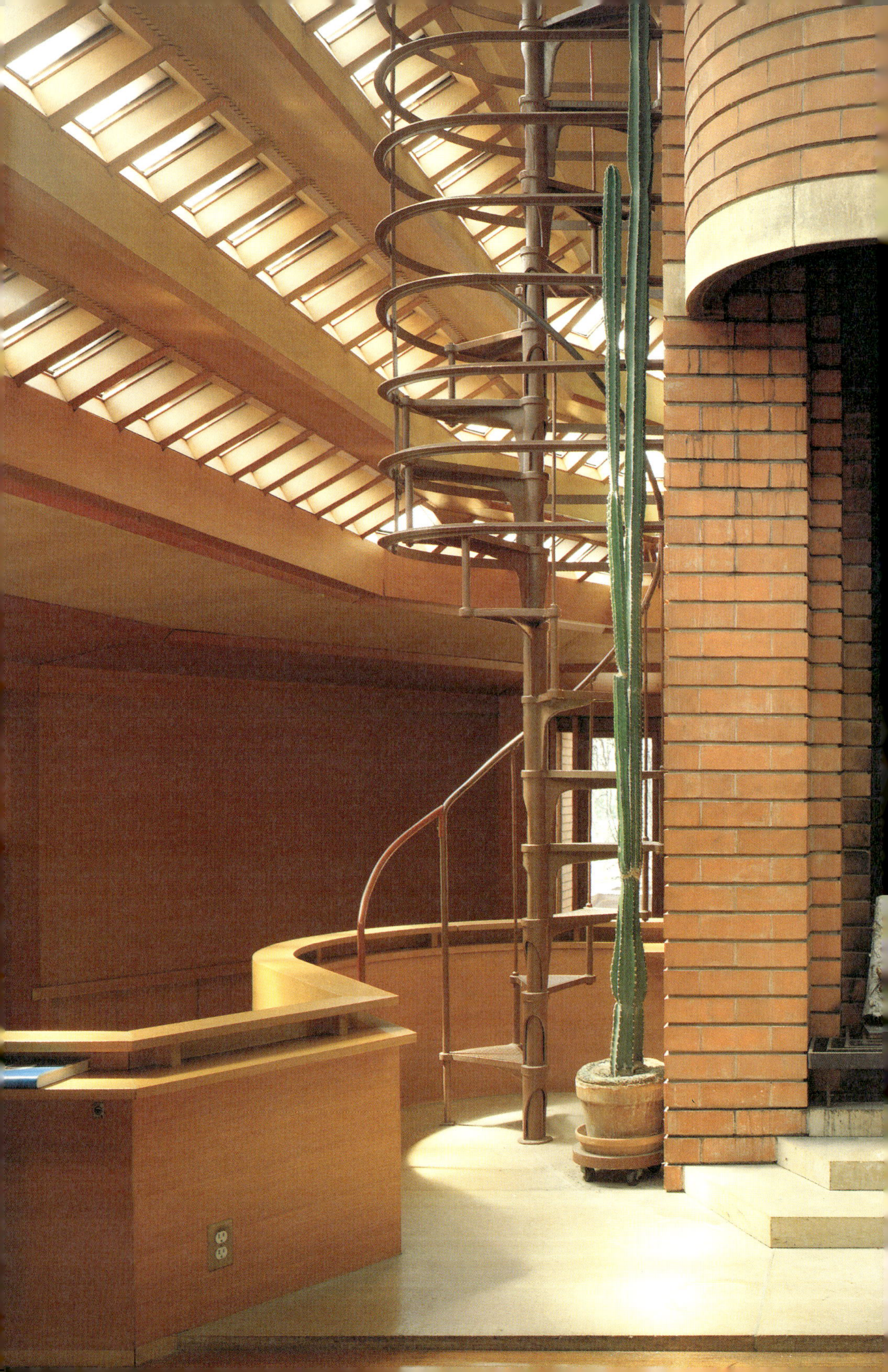

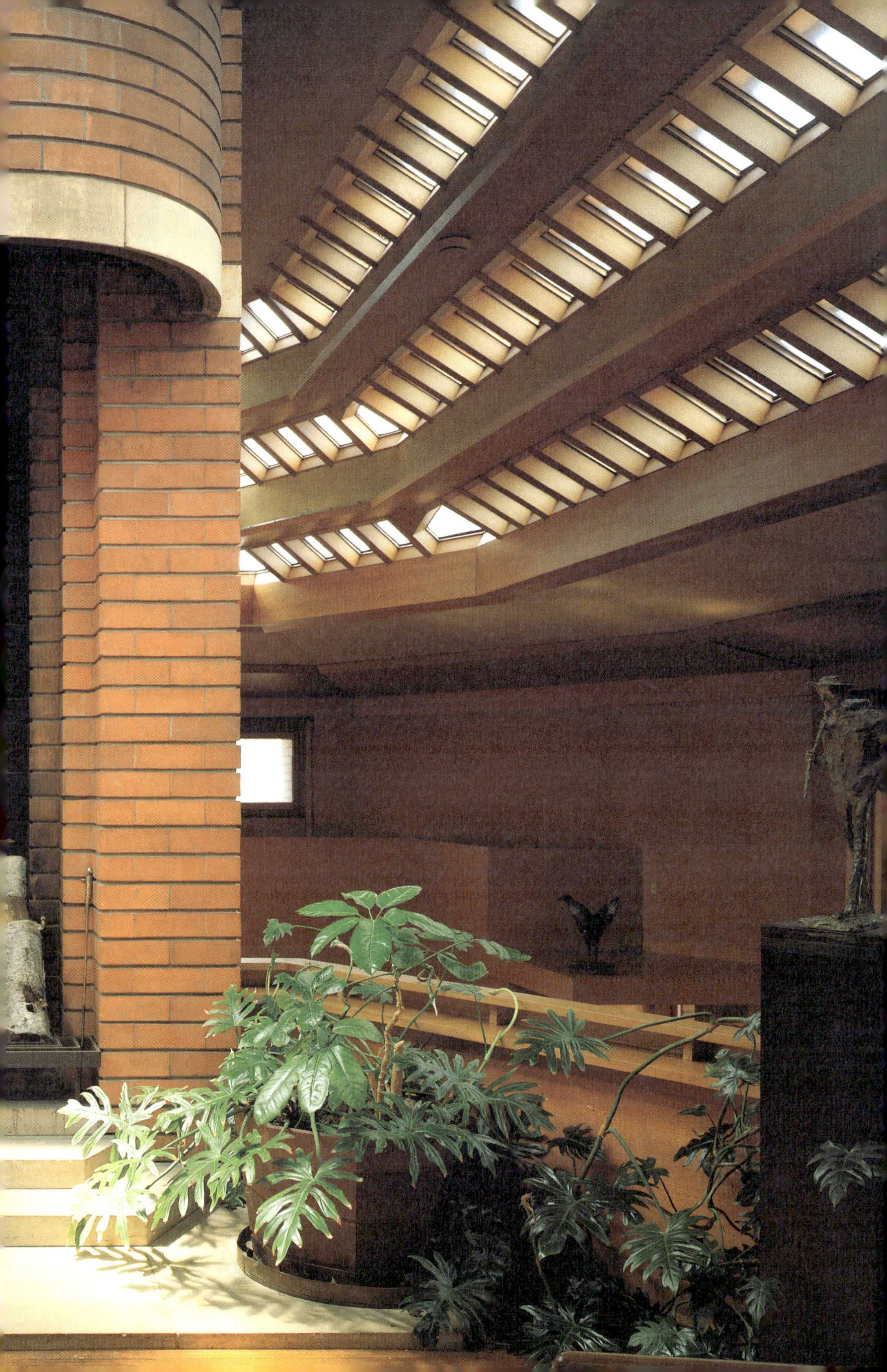

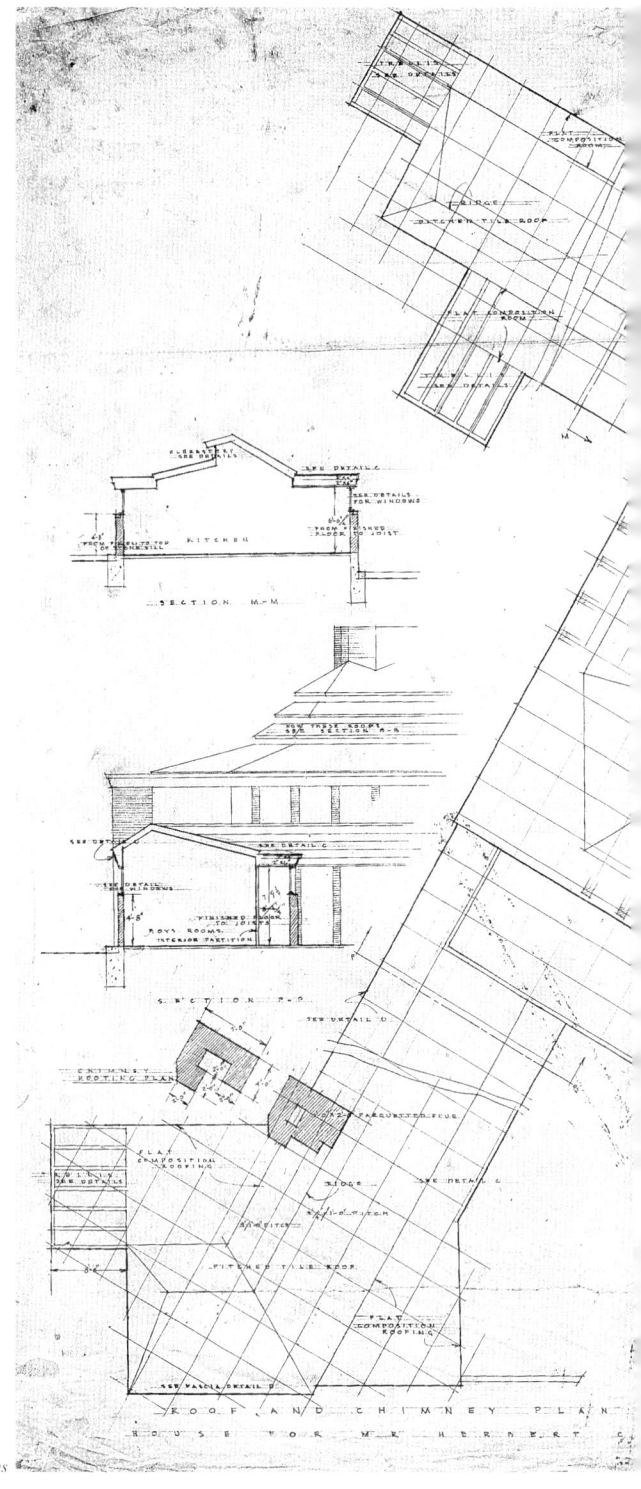

Roof and chimney plan with typical sections

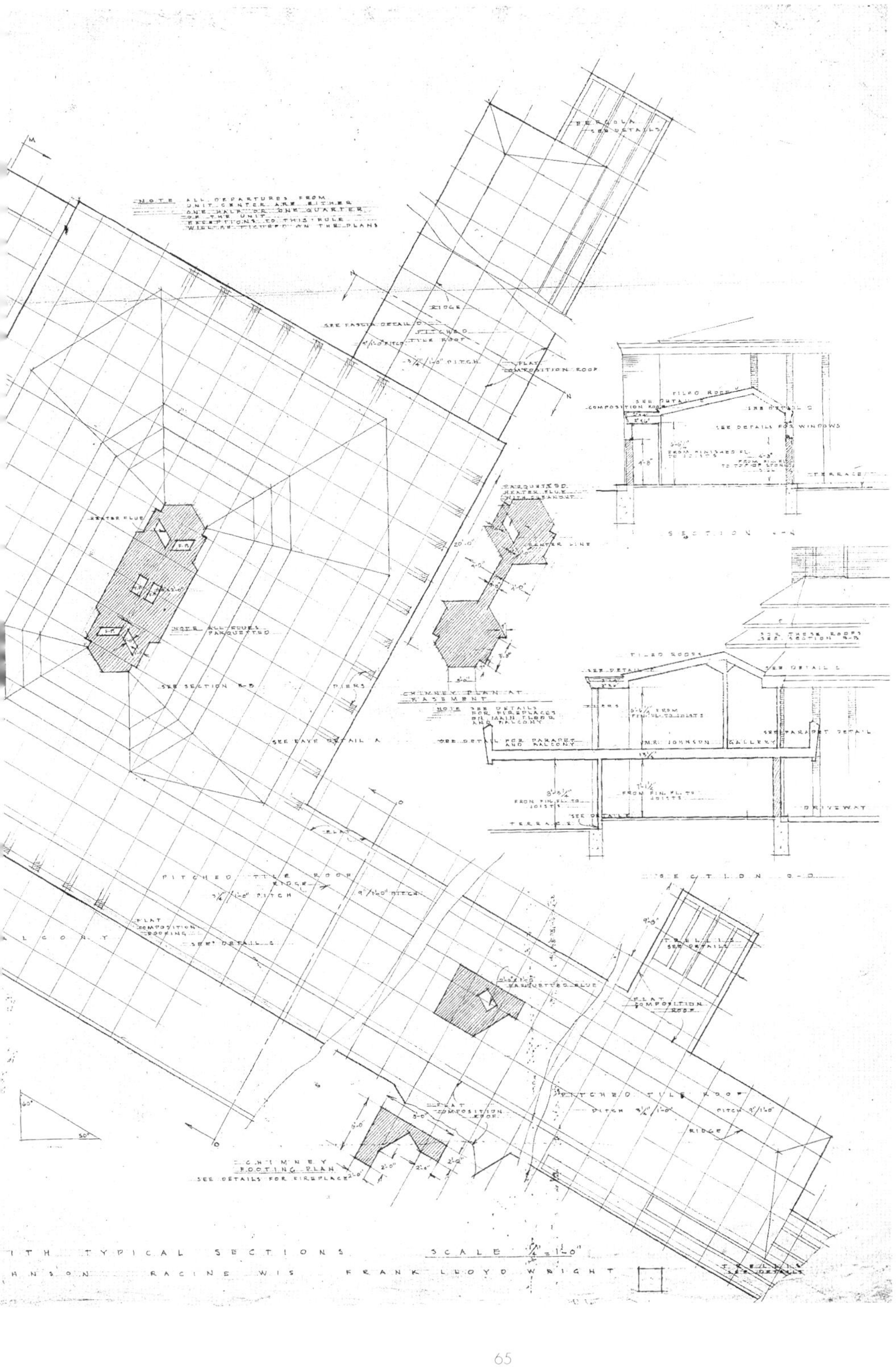
NOTE ALL DEPARTURES FROM UNIT CENTER ARE EITHER ONE HALF OR ONE QUARTER OF THE UNIT. EXCEPTIONS TO THIS RULE WILL BE FIGURED ON THE PLANS
PERGOLA SEE DETAILS
RIDGE
SEE FASCIA DETAIL D
PITCHED TILE ROOF
FLAT COMPOSITION ROOF
NOTE ALL FLUES PARQUETTED
SEE SECTION B-B
PIERS
SEE EAVE DETAIL A
CHIMNEY PLAN AT BASEMENT
NOTE SEE DETAILS FOR FIREPLACES ON MAIN FLOOR AND BALCONY
SECTION A-A
SEE DETAILS FOR WINDOWS
TERRACE
TILED ROOFS
SEE DETAIL FOR PARAPET AND BALCONY
MR. JOHNSON GALLERY
DRIVEWAY
SECTION C-C
PITCHED TILE ROOF
TRELLIS SEE DETAILS
PARQUETTED FLUE
CHIMNEY FOOTING PLAN
SEE DETAILS FOR FIREPLACE
ITH TYPICAL SECTIONS SCALE 1/4" = 1'-0"
HNSON RACINE WIS FRANK LLOYD WRIGHT

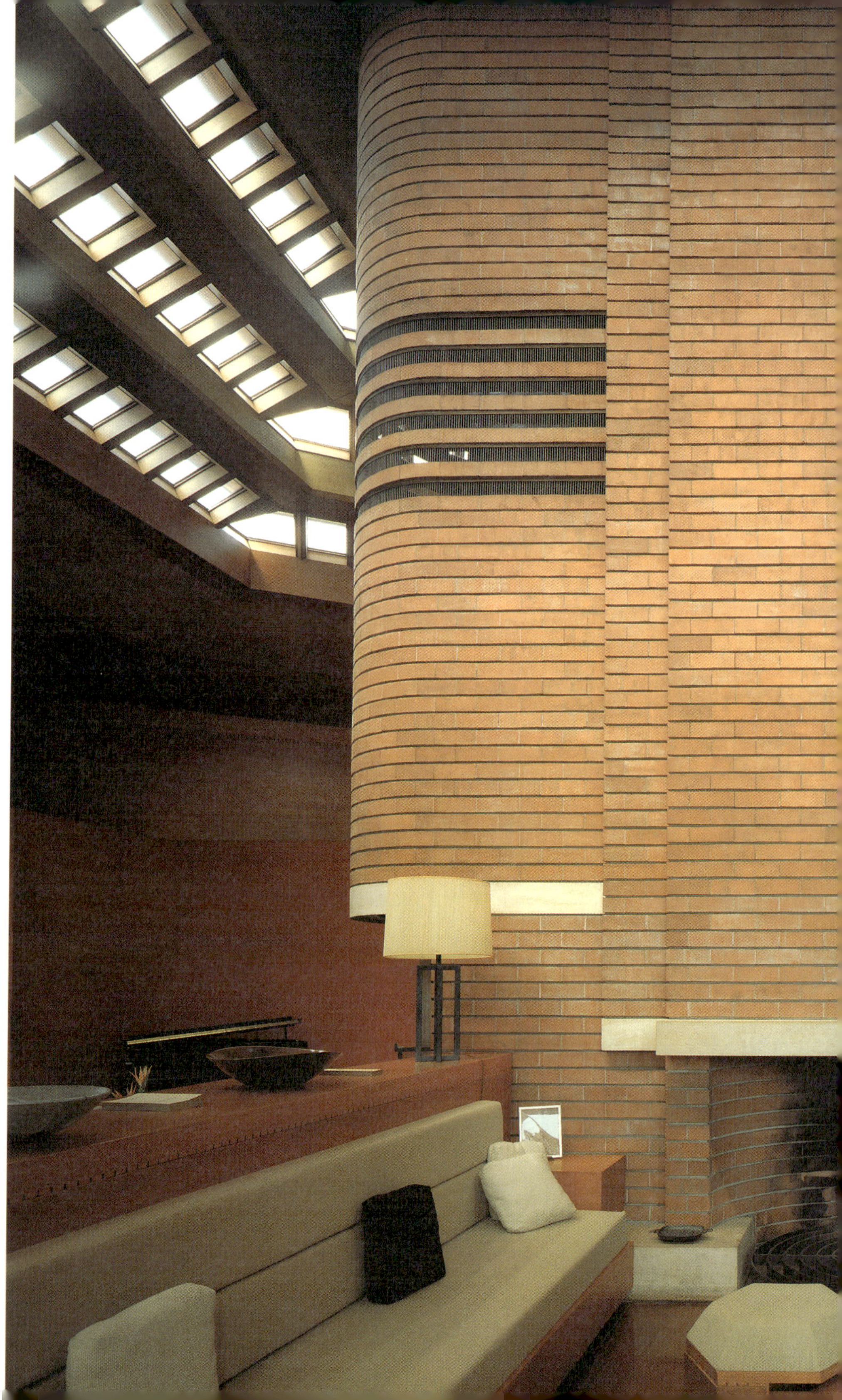

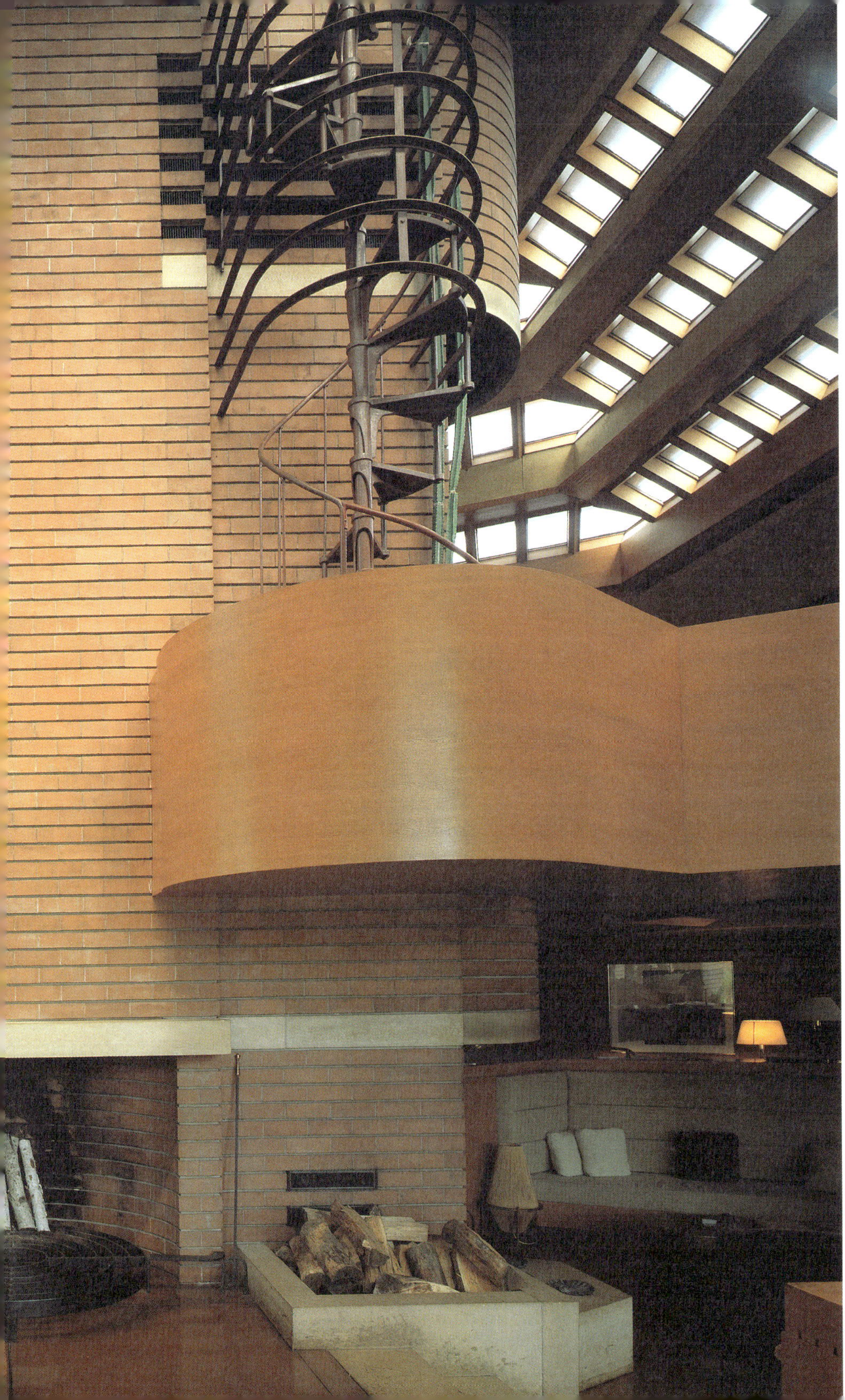

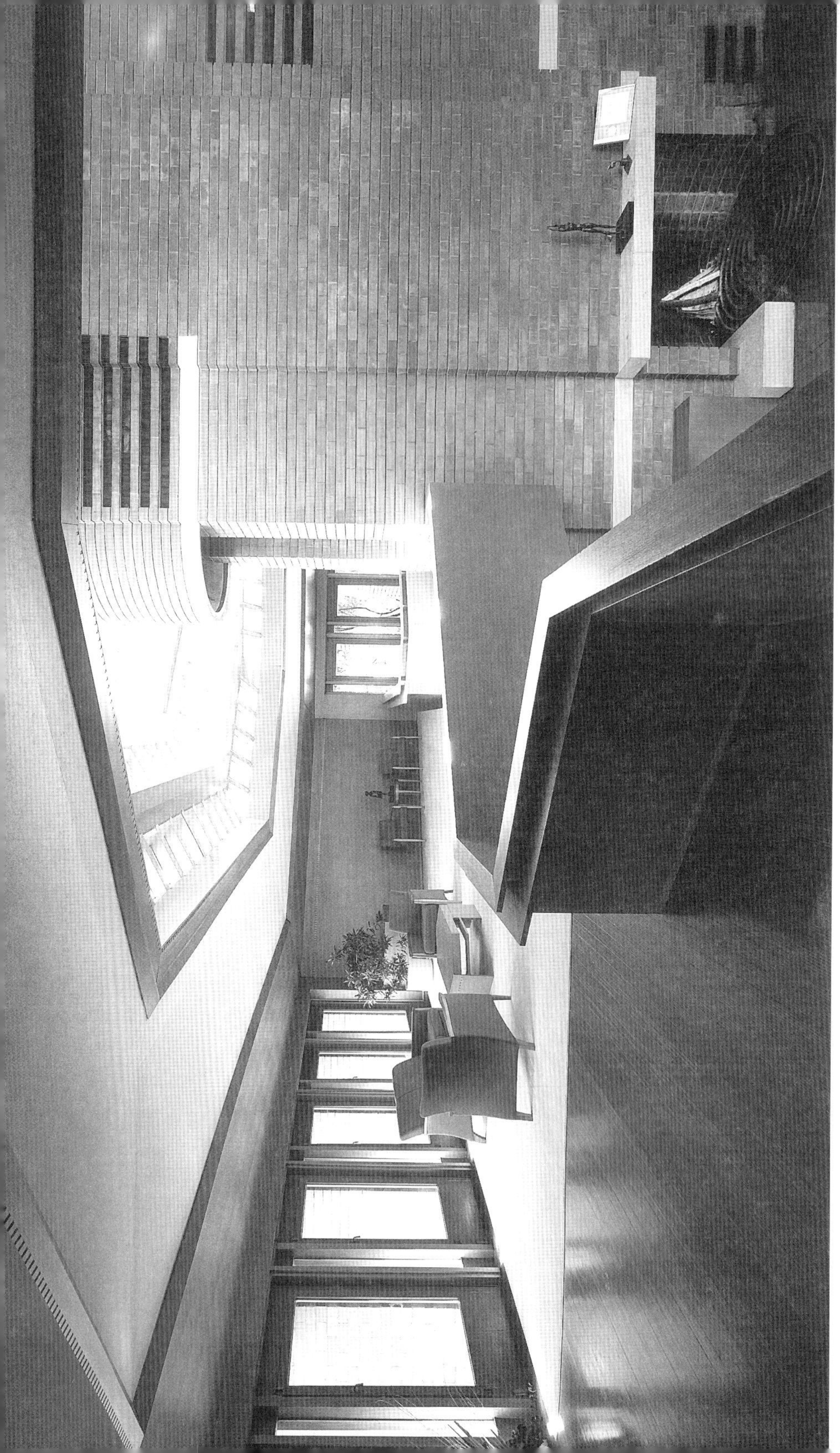

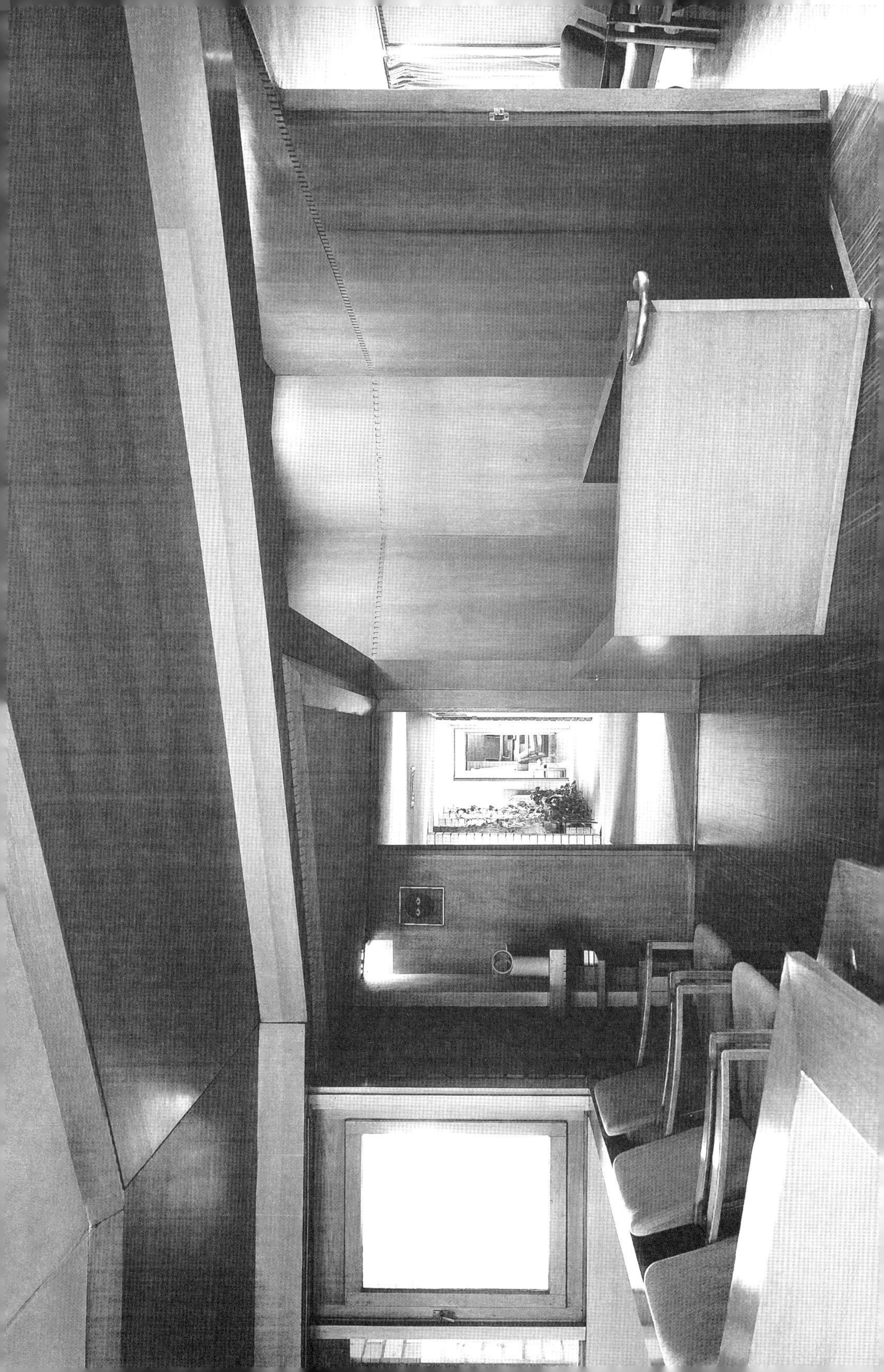

Leigh Stevens House, "Auldbrass Plantation"
Yemassee, South Carolina, 1939

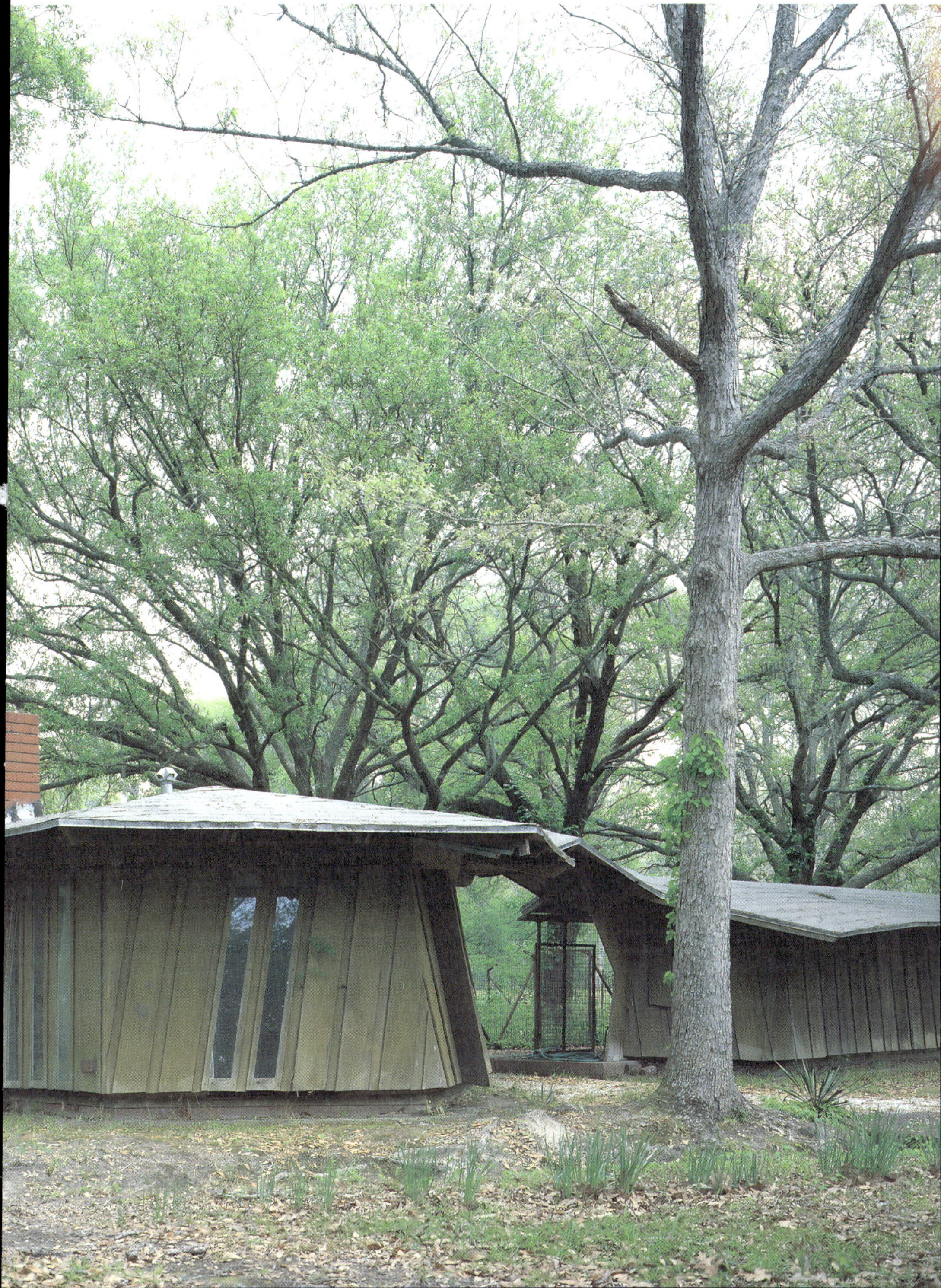

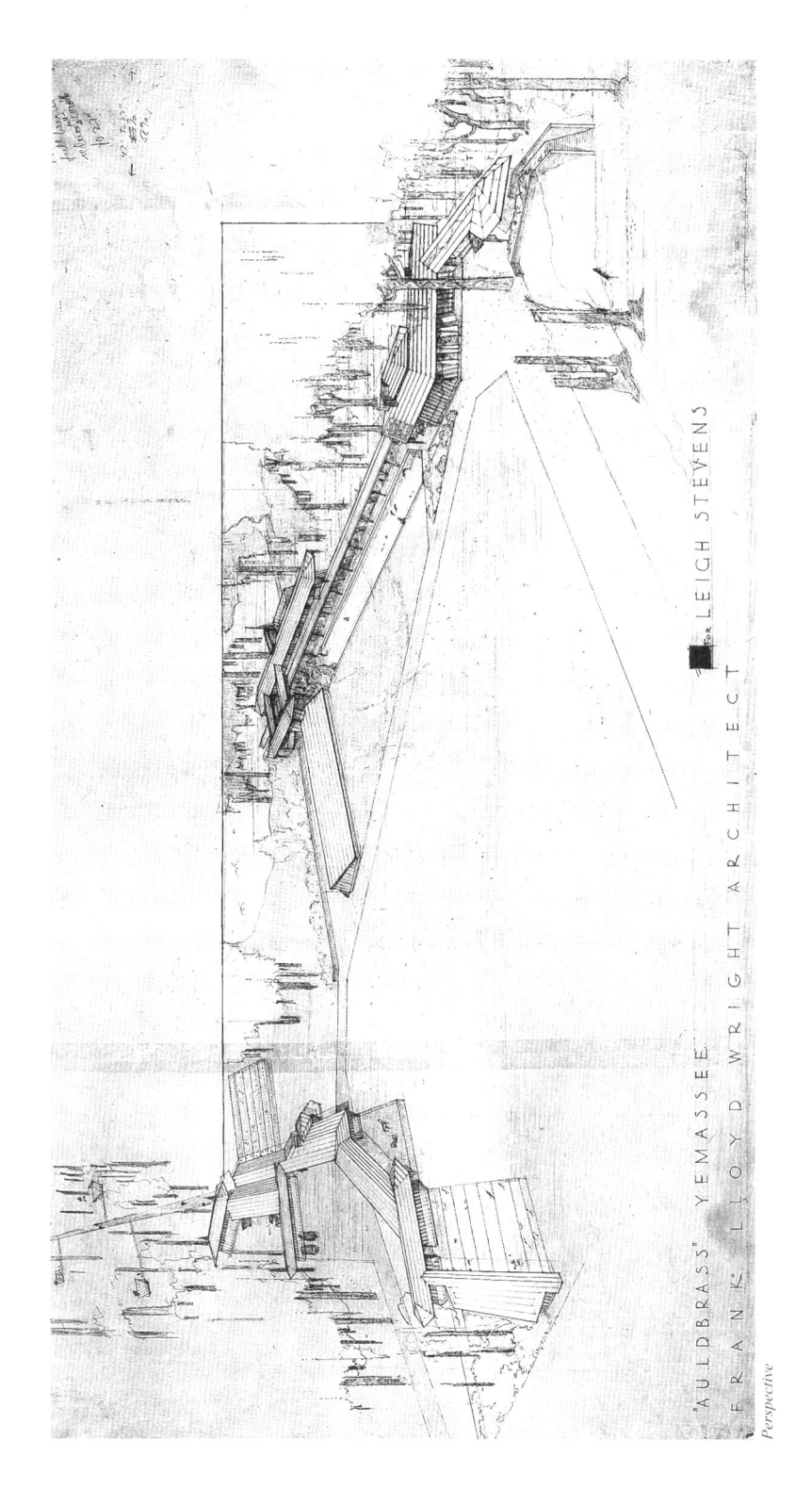

"AULDBRASS" YEMASSEE
FRANK LLOYD WRIGHT ARCHITECT for LEIGH STEVENS

Perspective

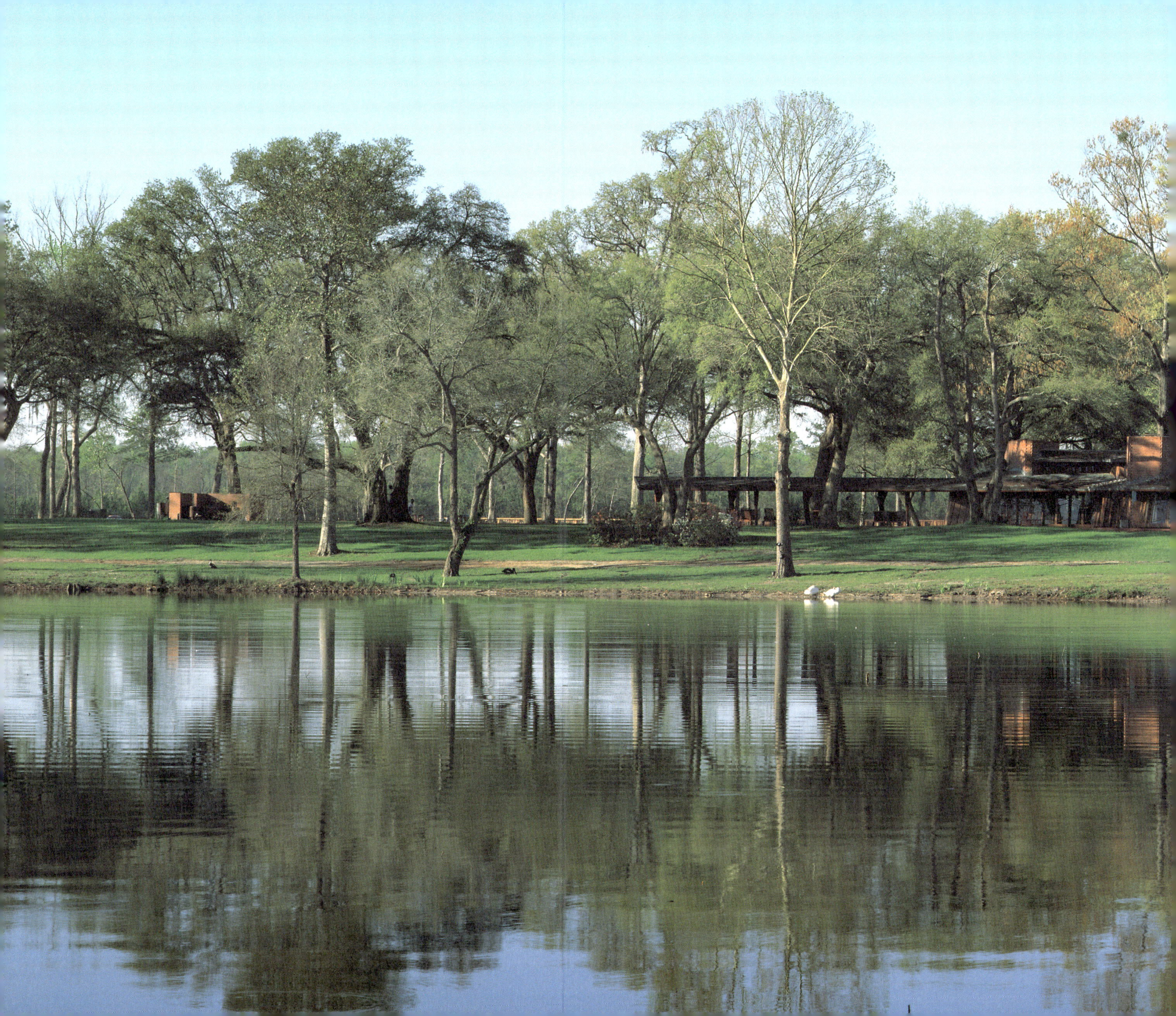

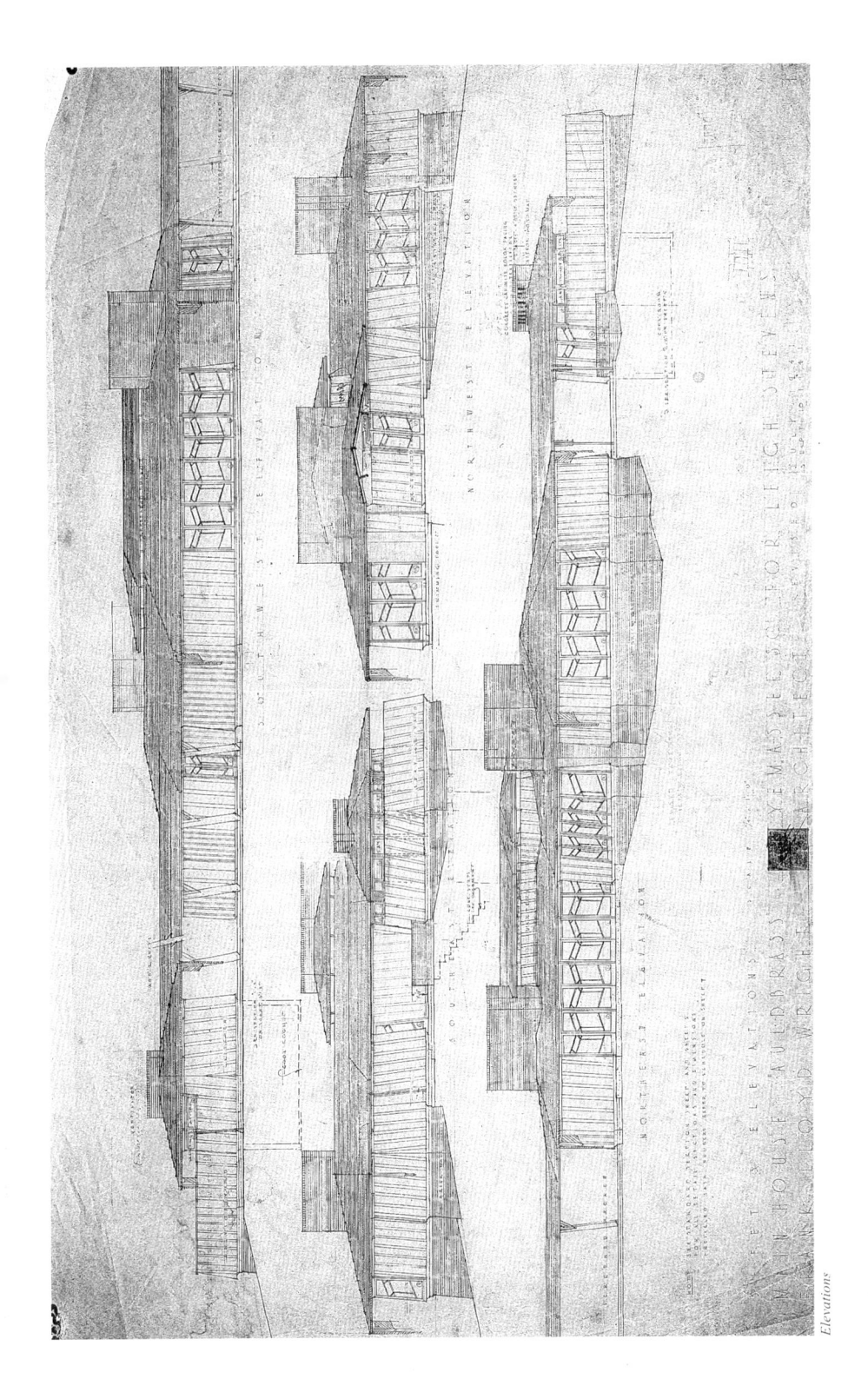

Elevations

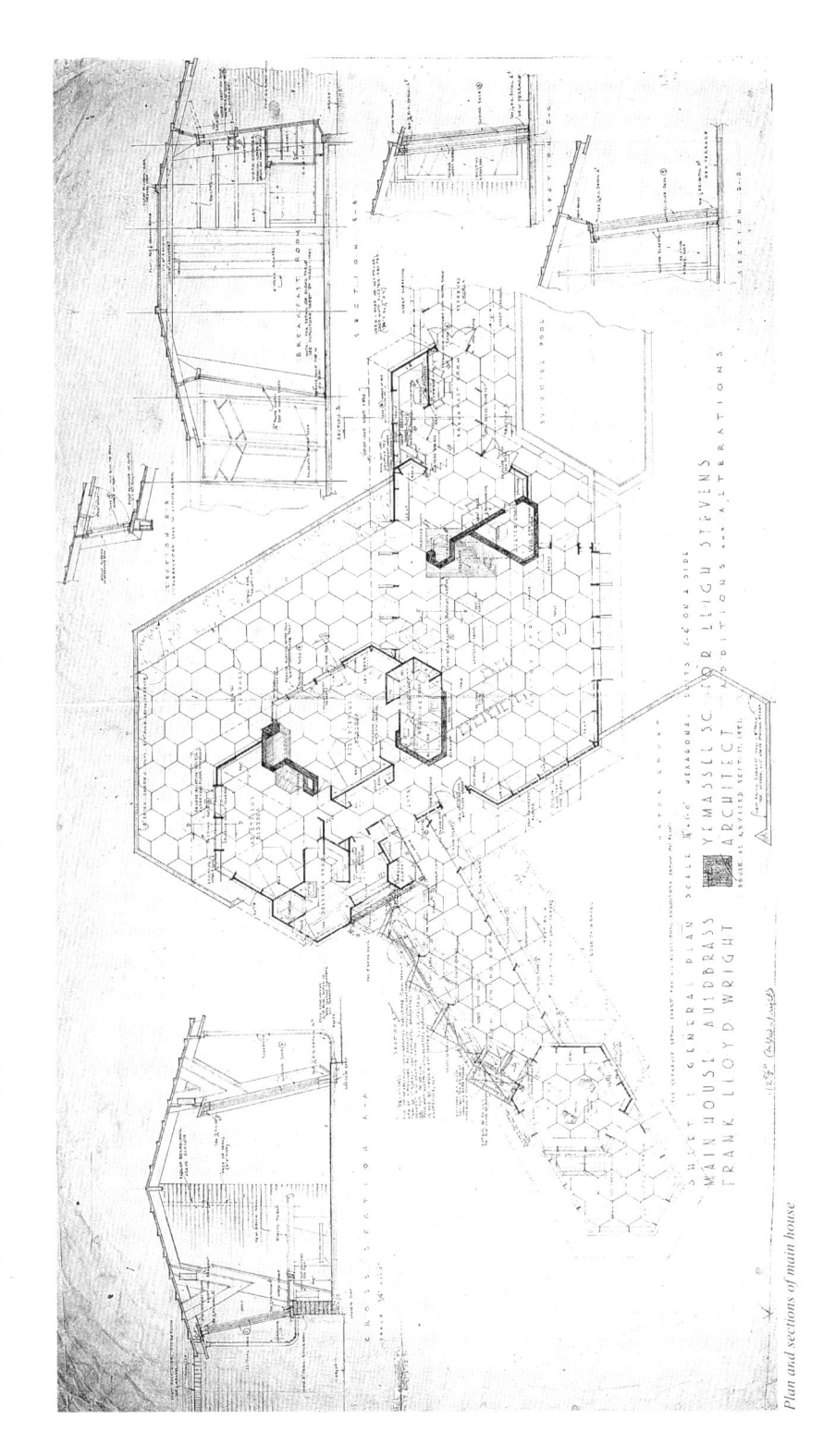

Plan and sections of main house

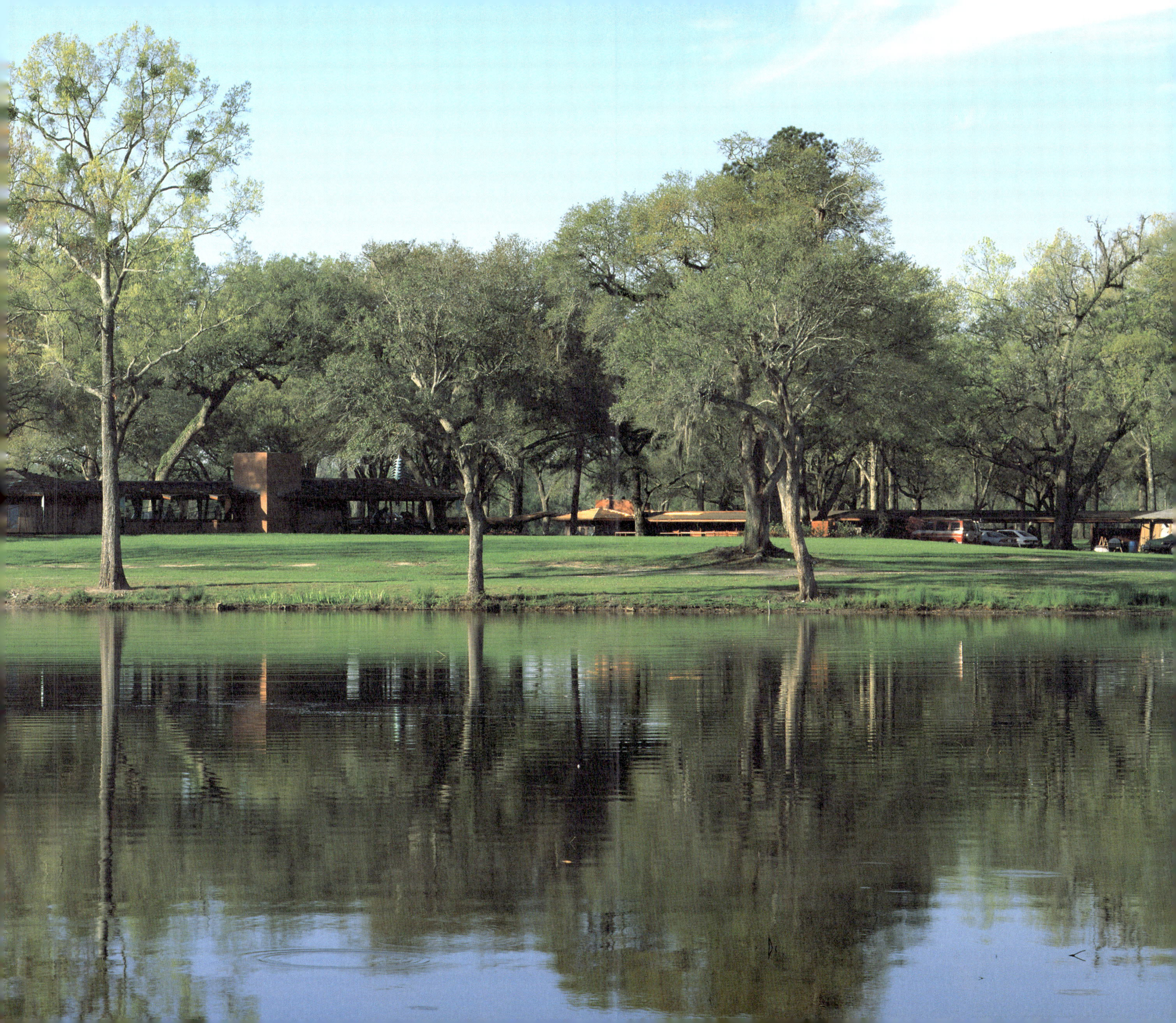

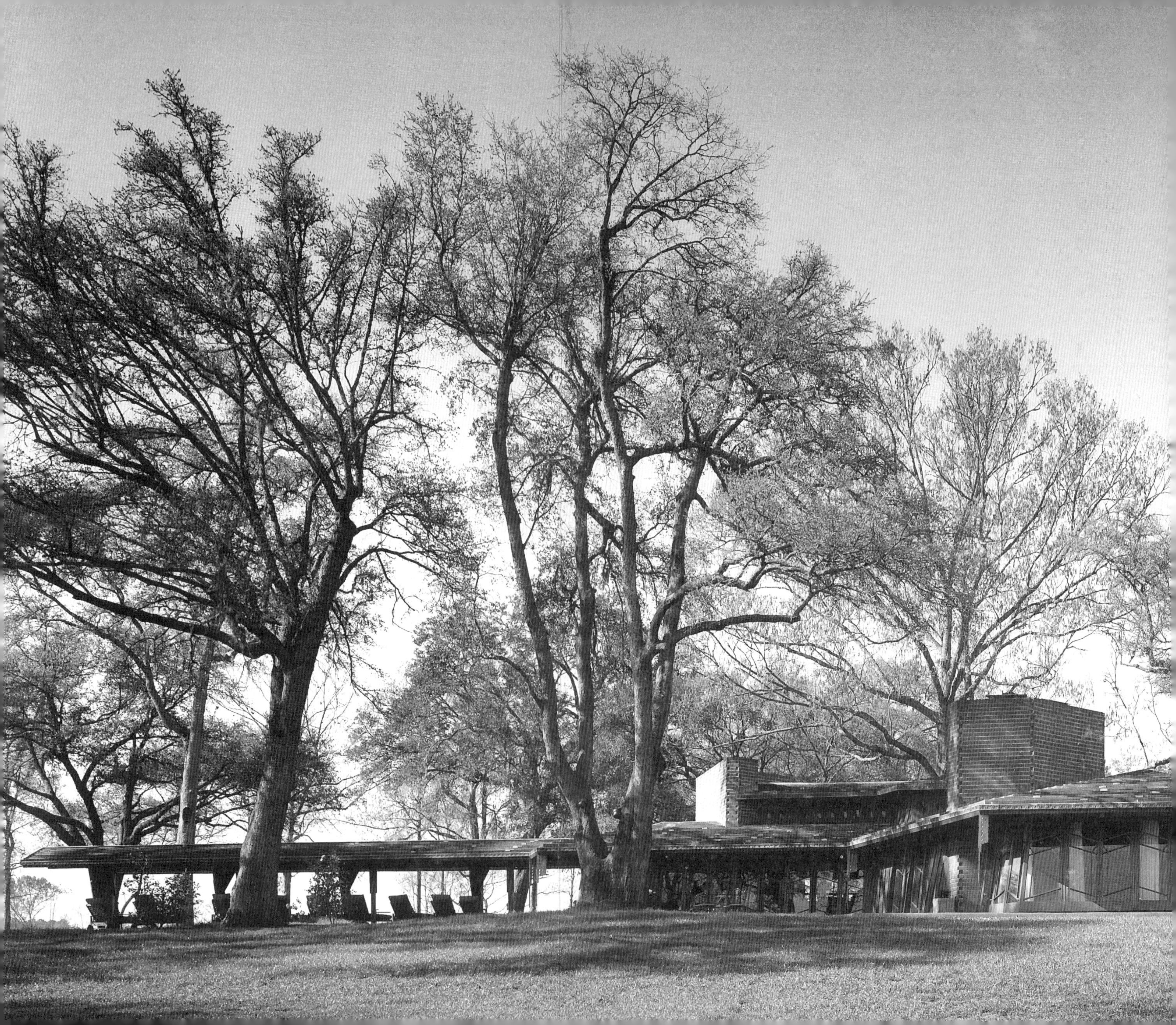

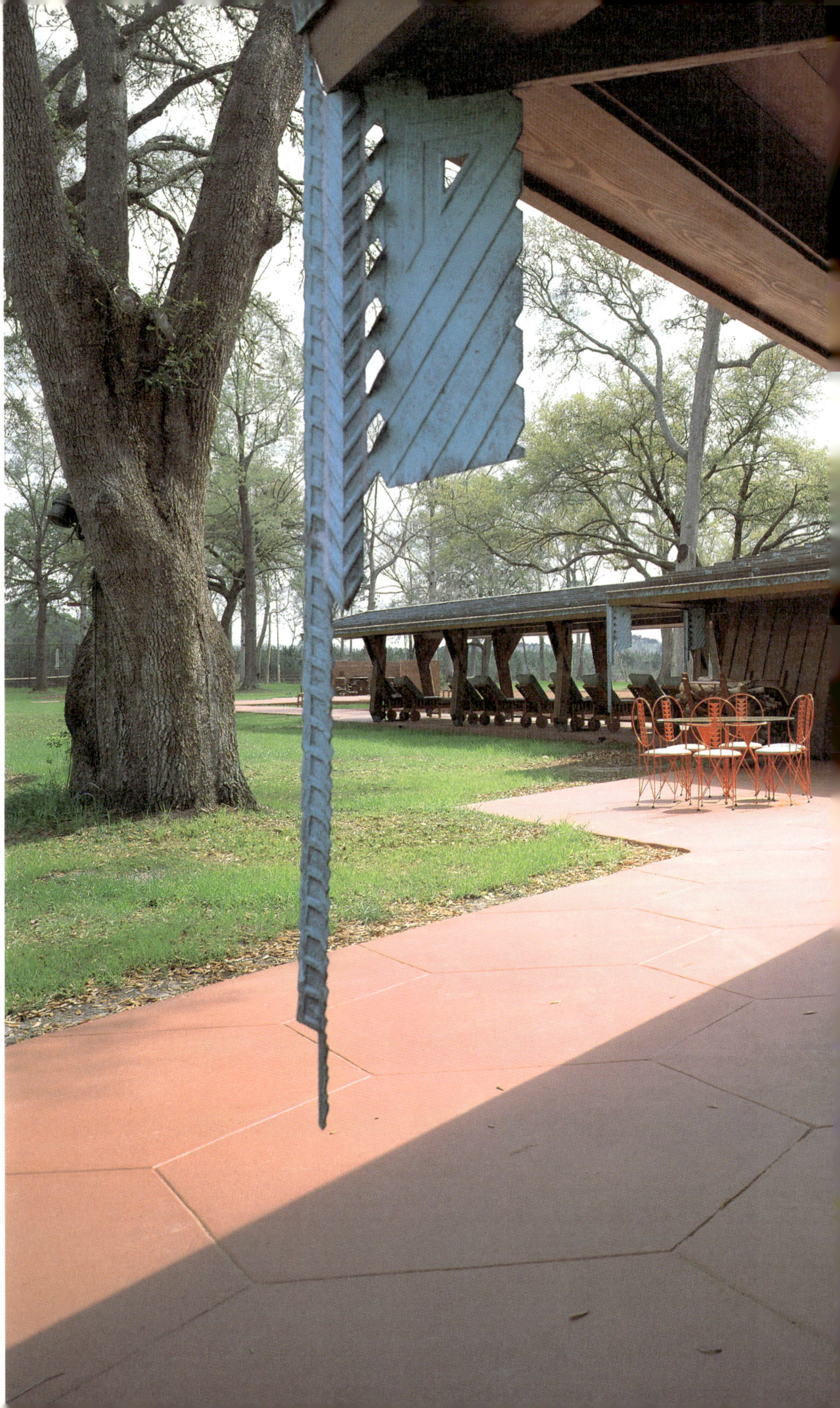

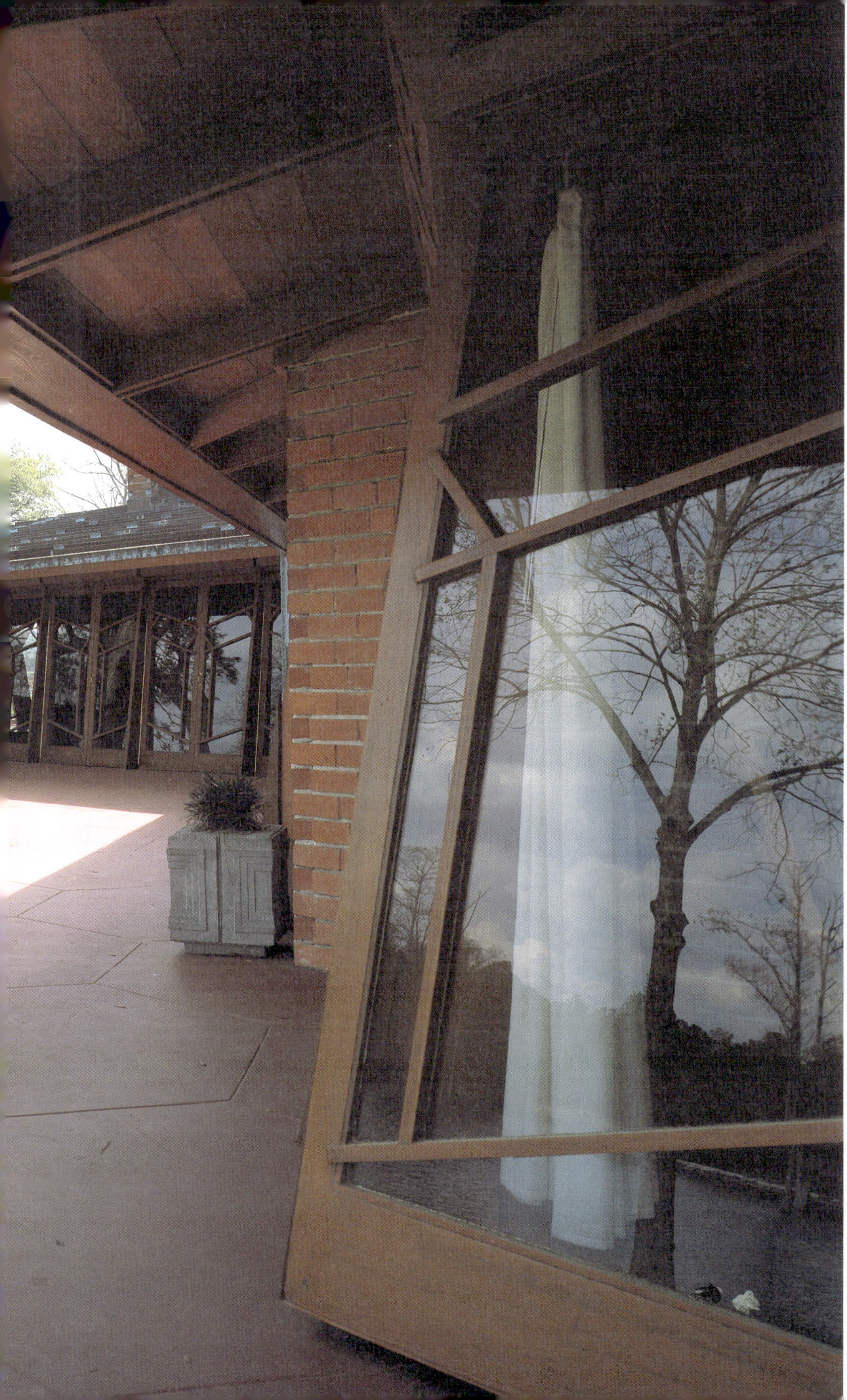

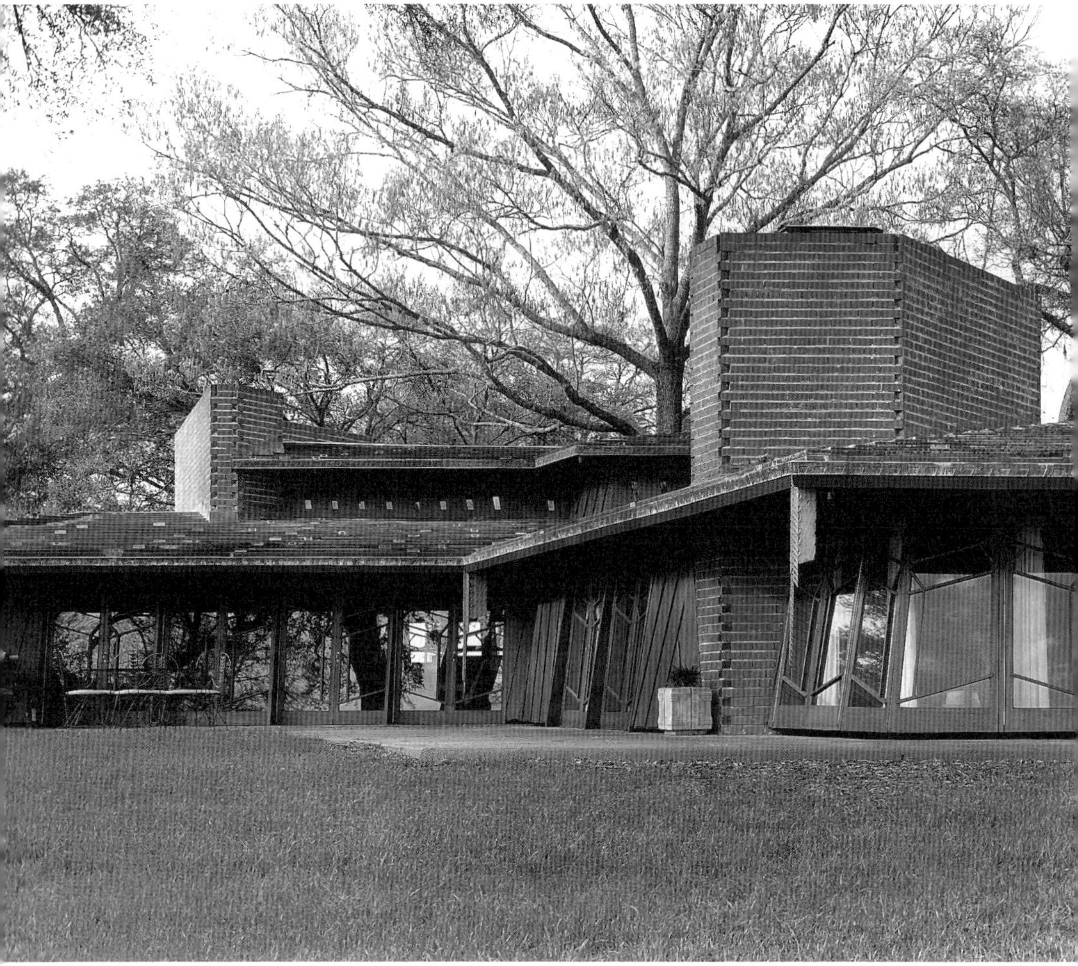

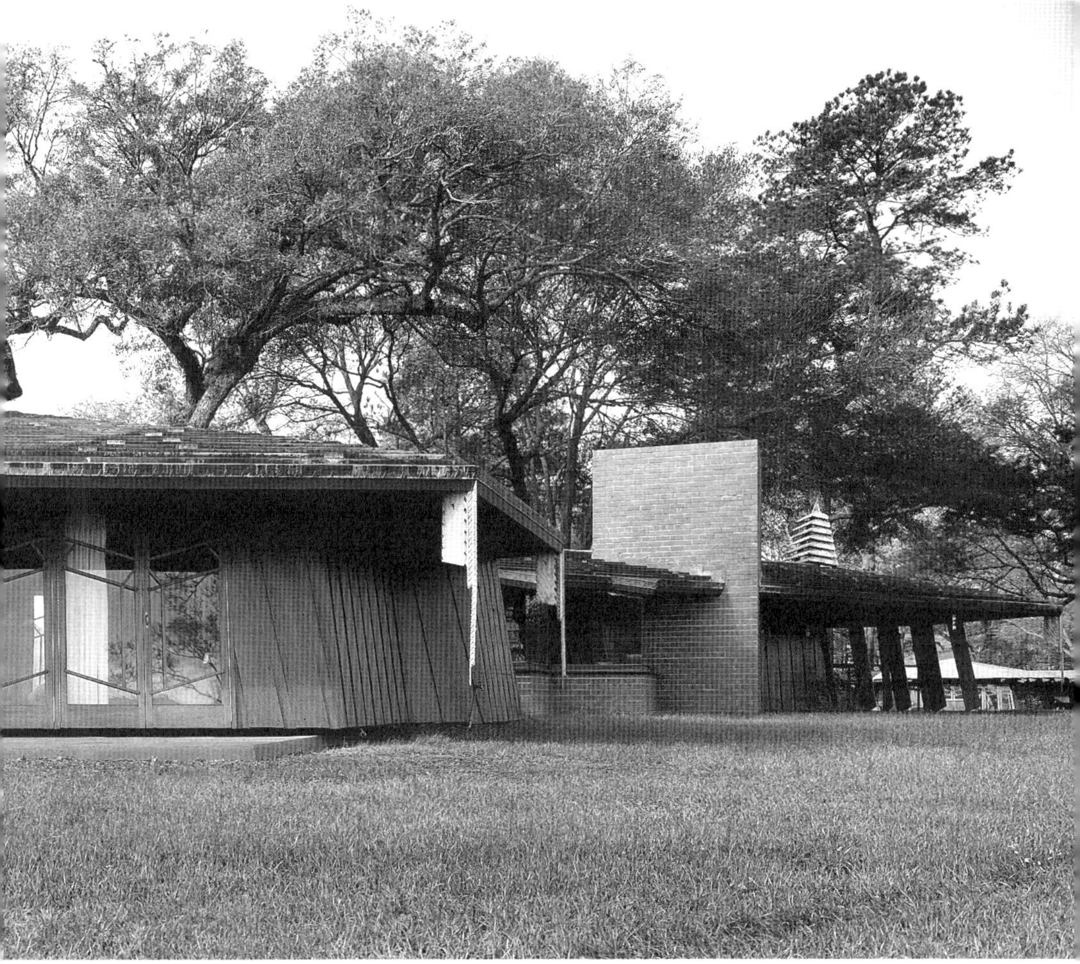

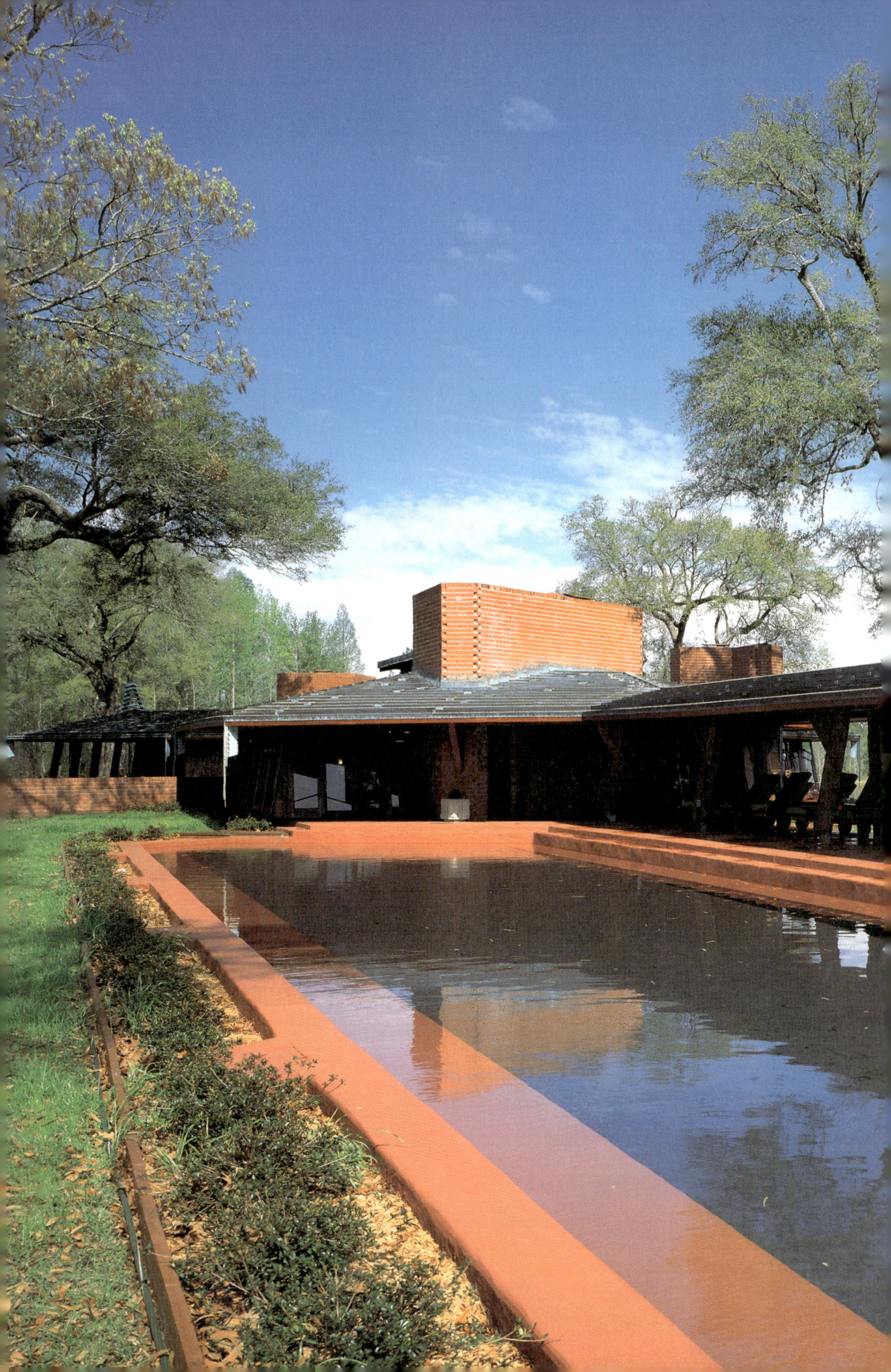

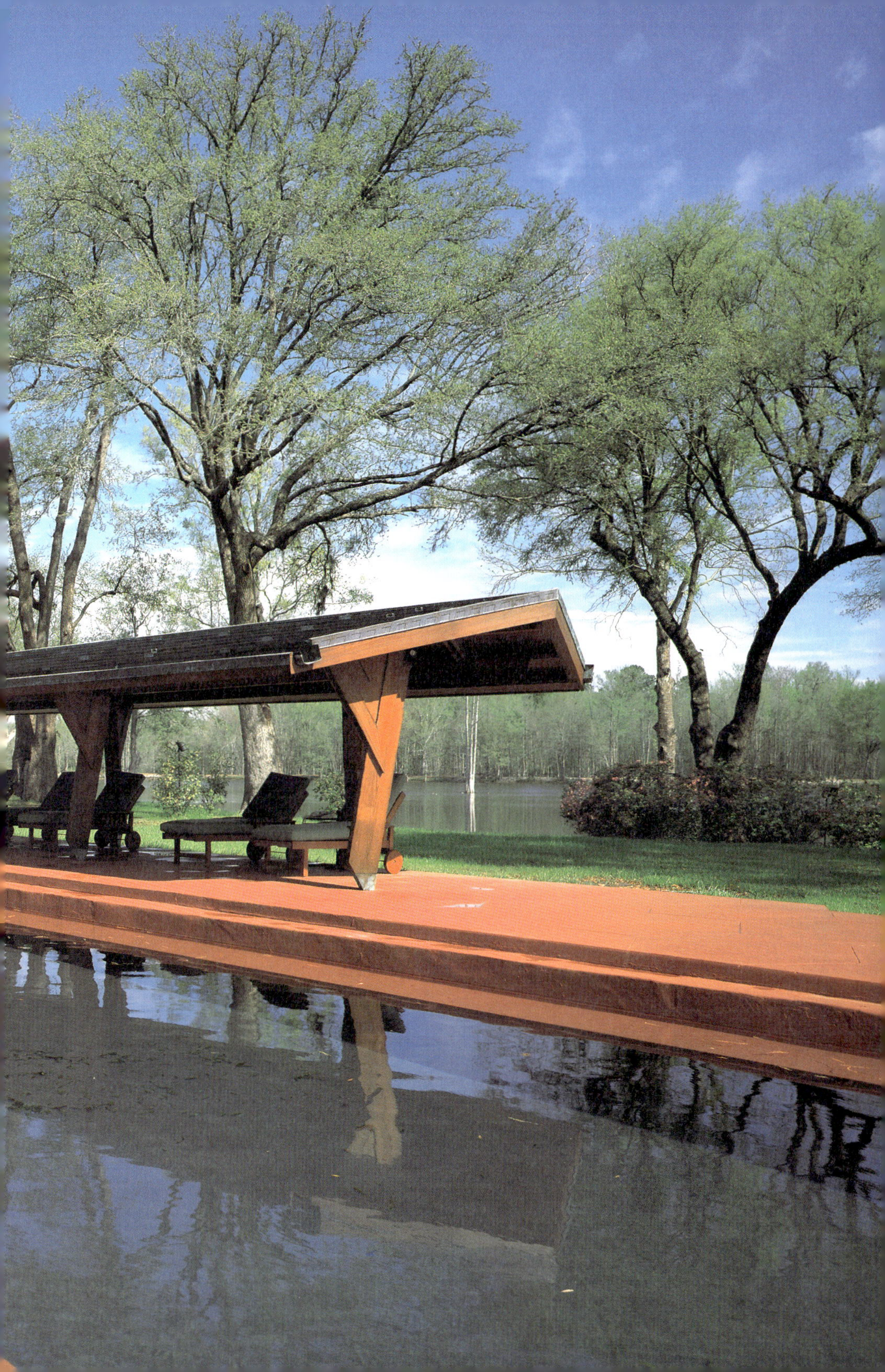

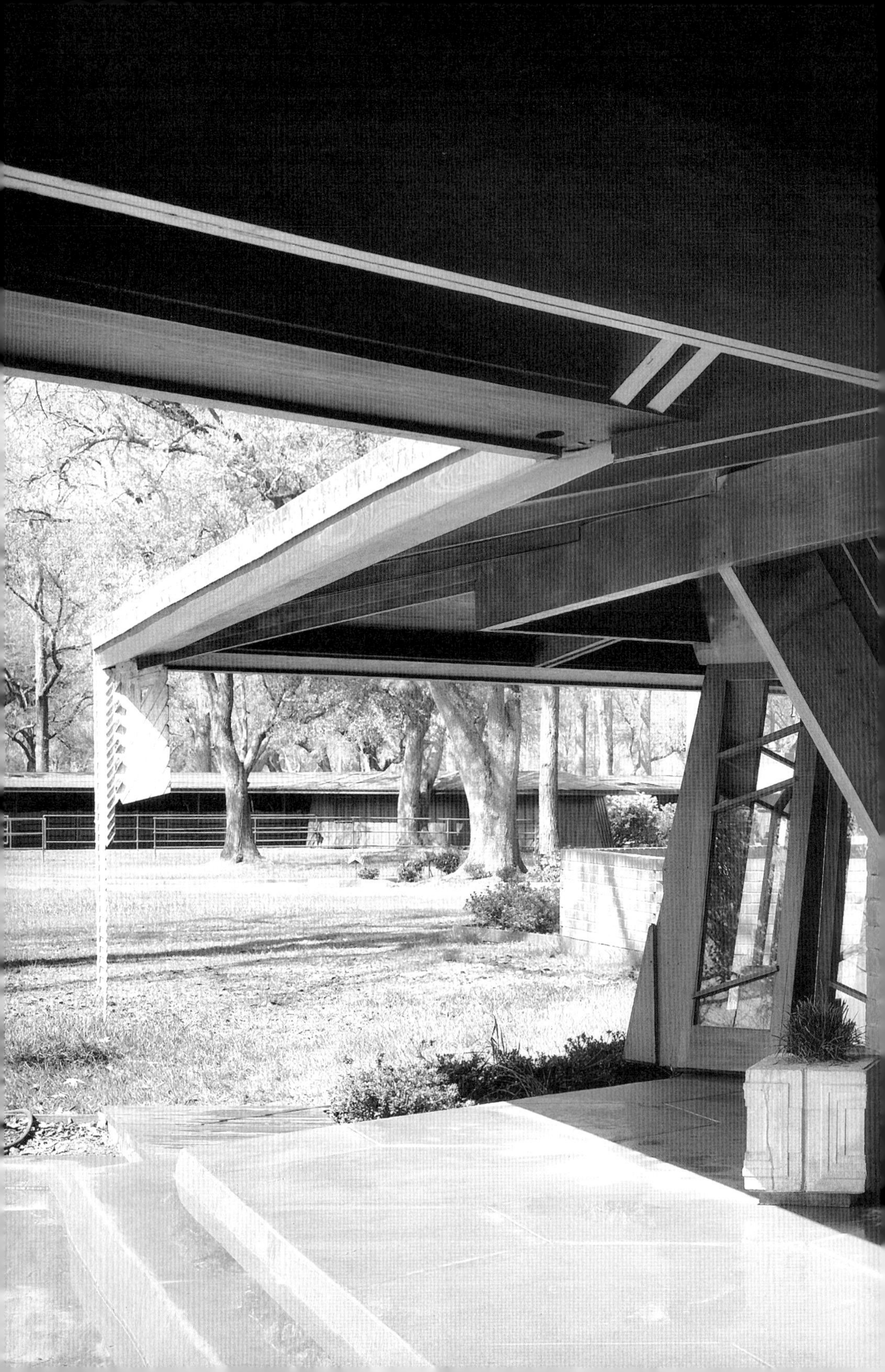

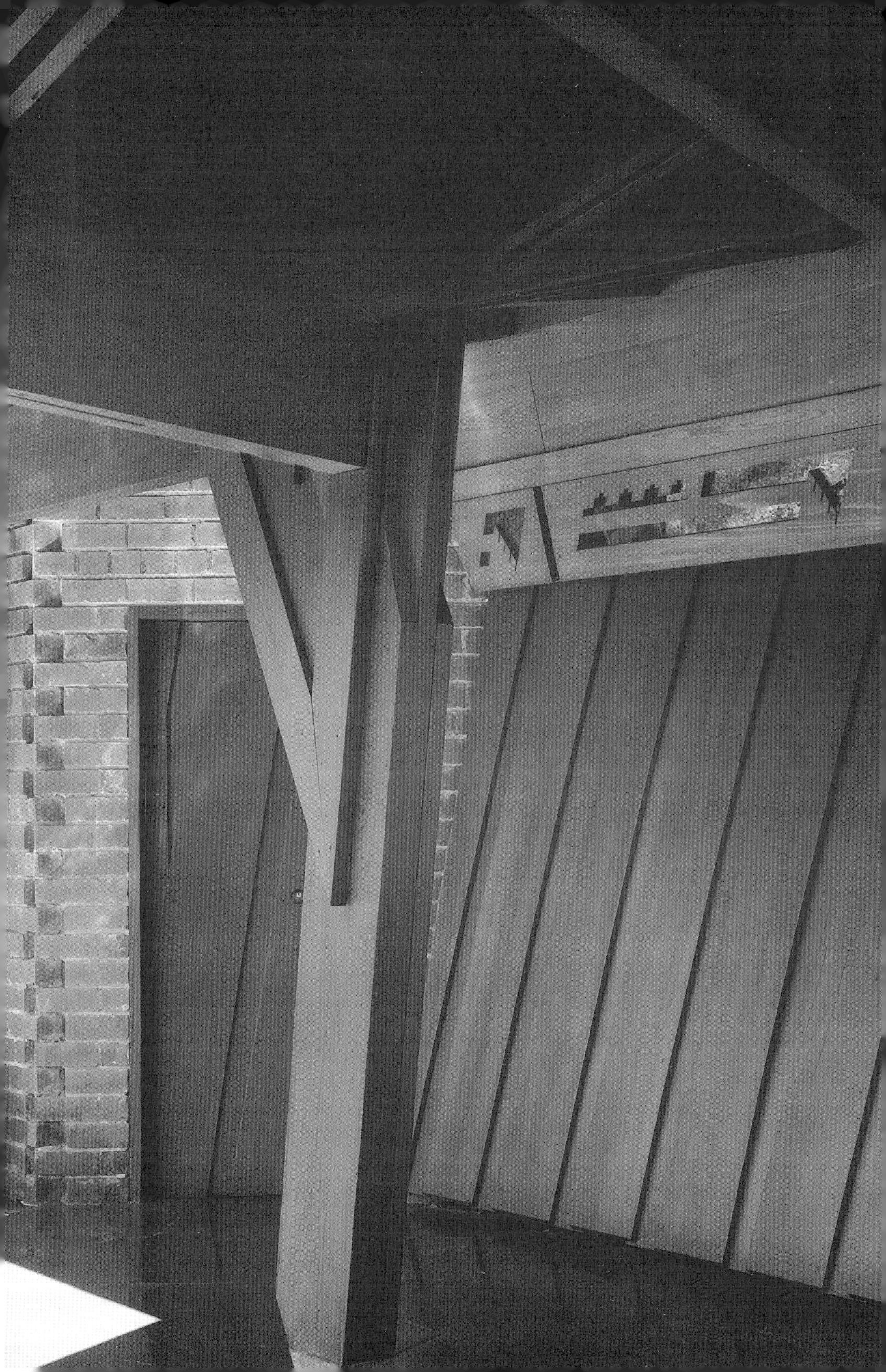

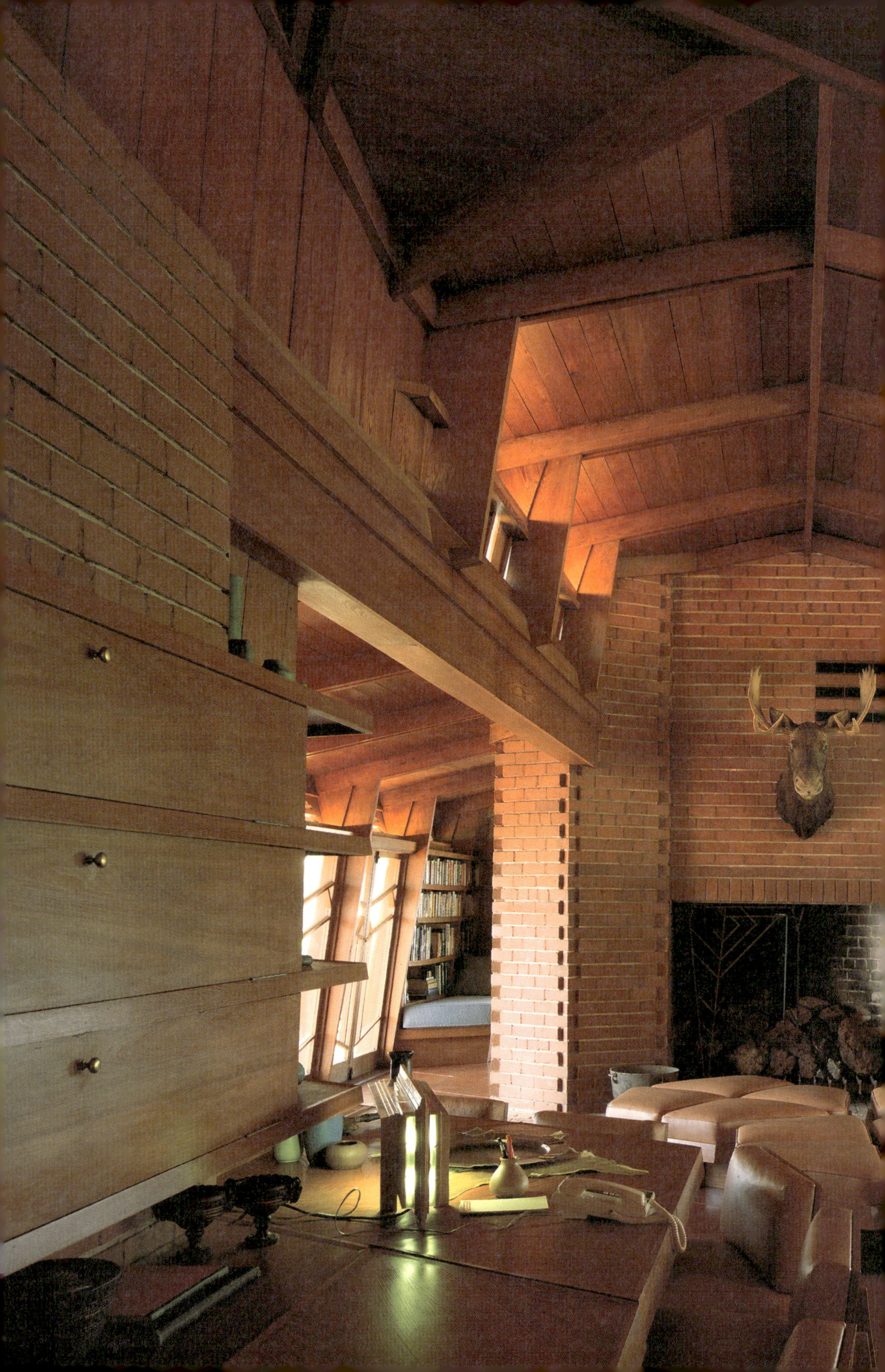

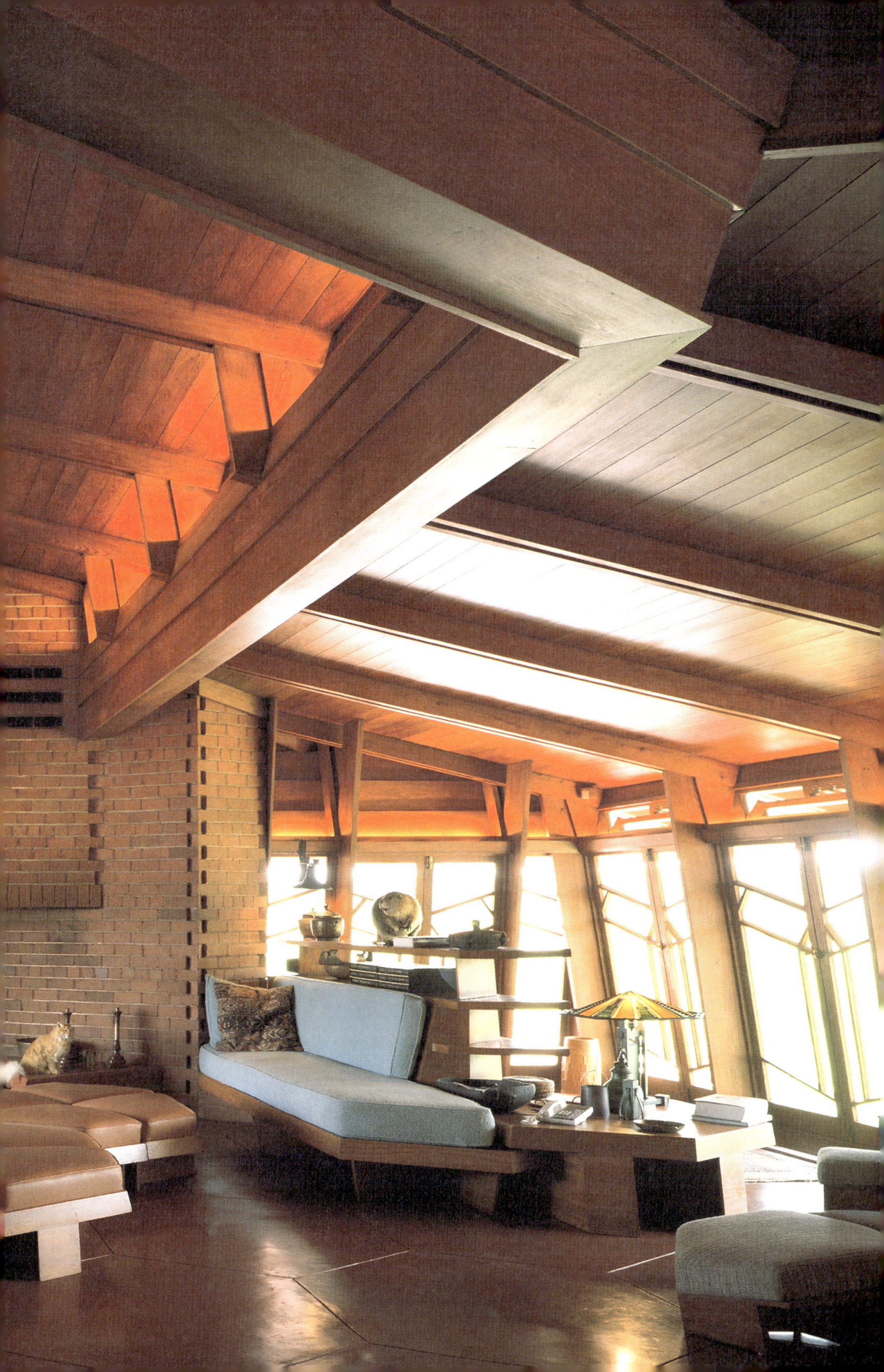

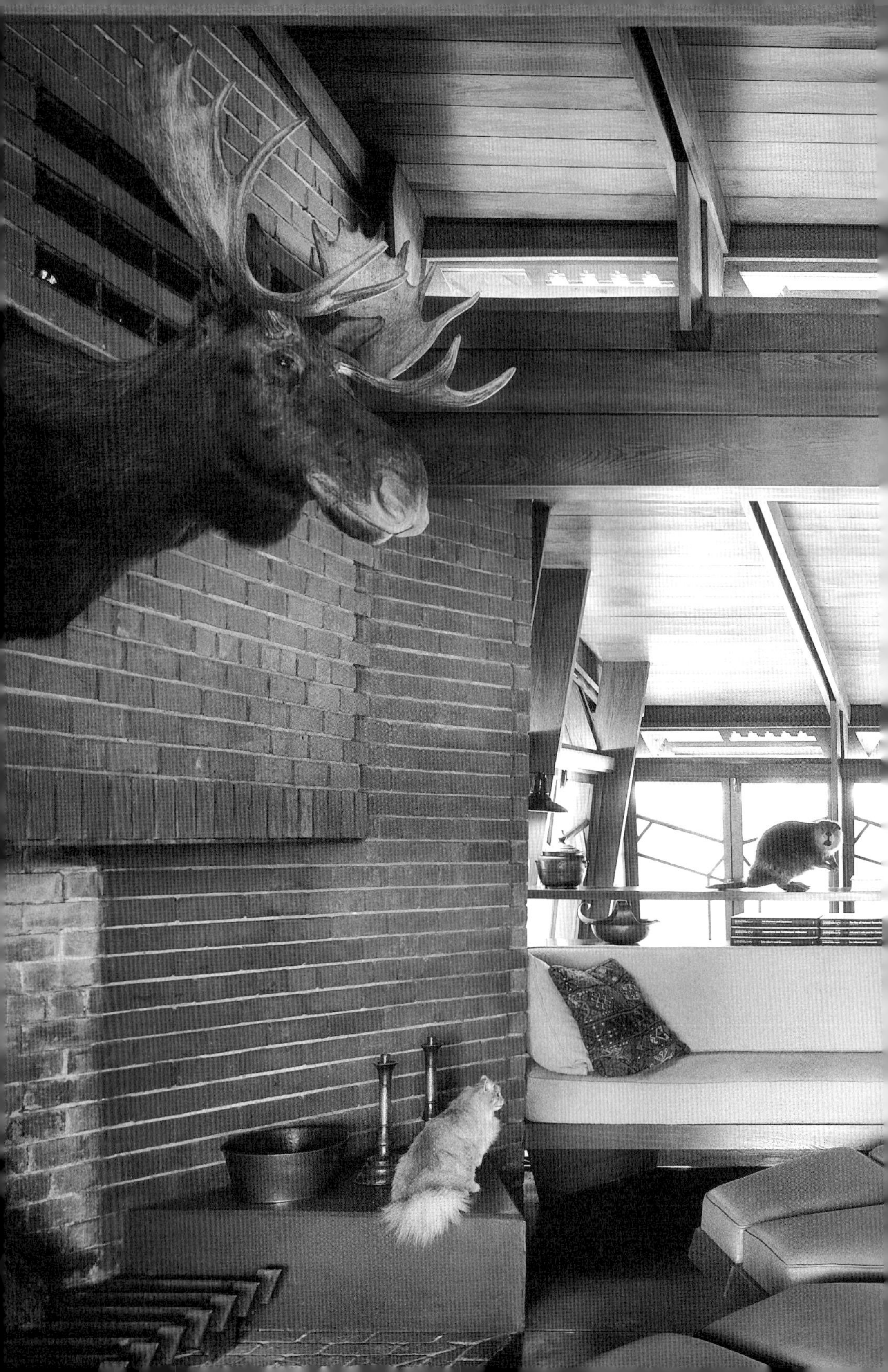

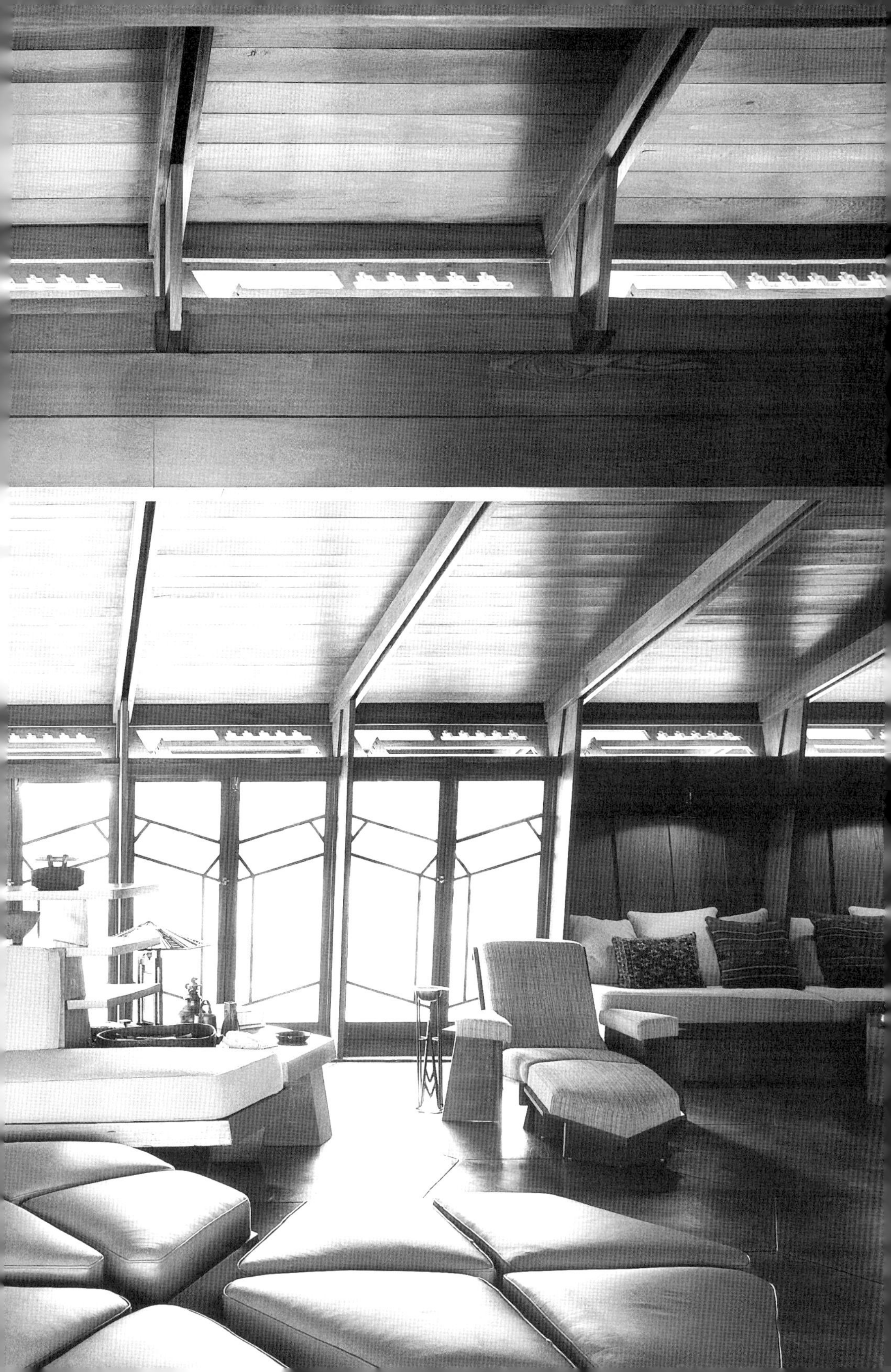

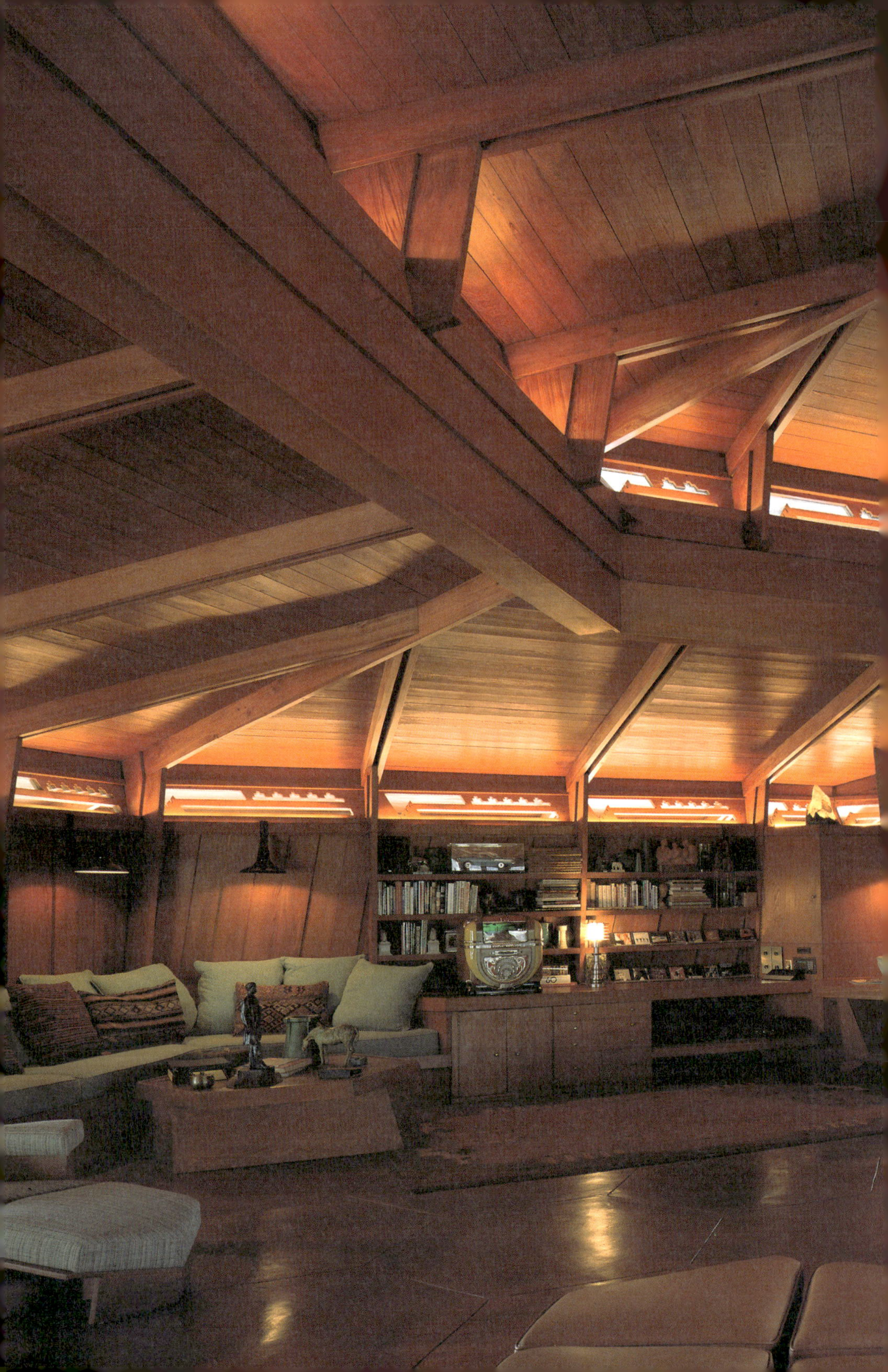

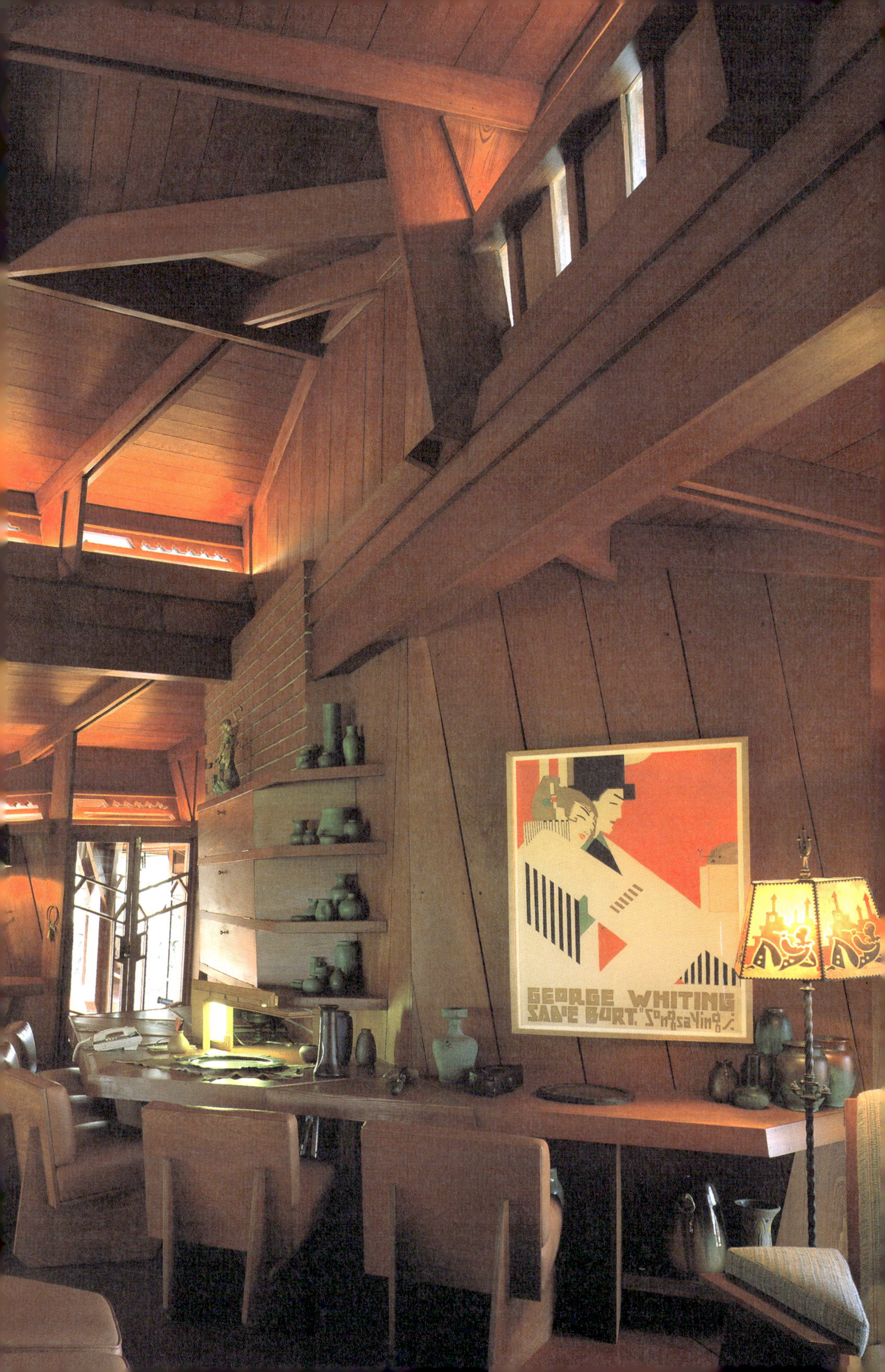
GEORGE WHITING
SADIE BURT.

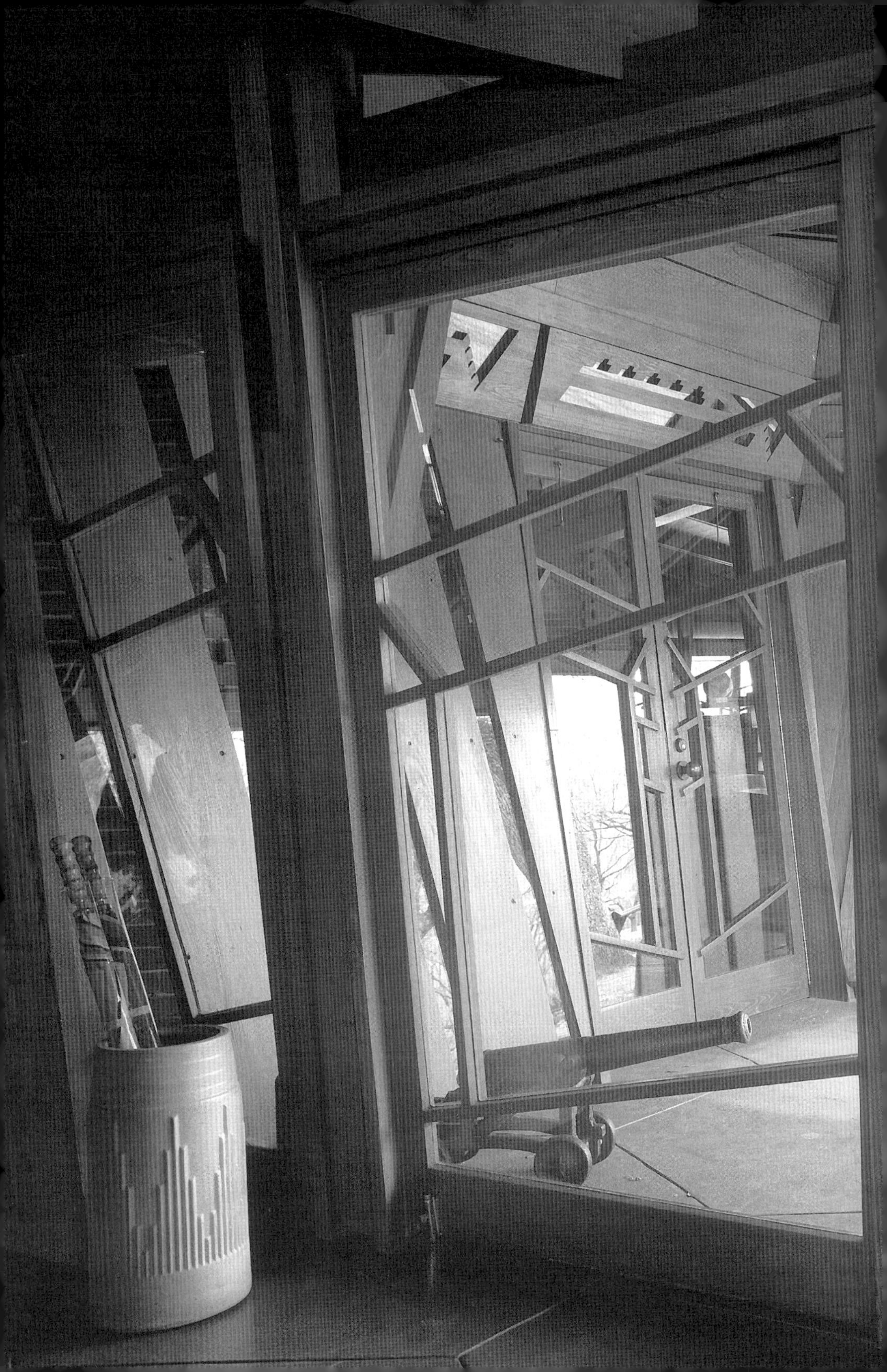

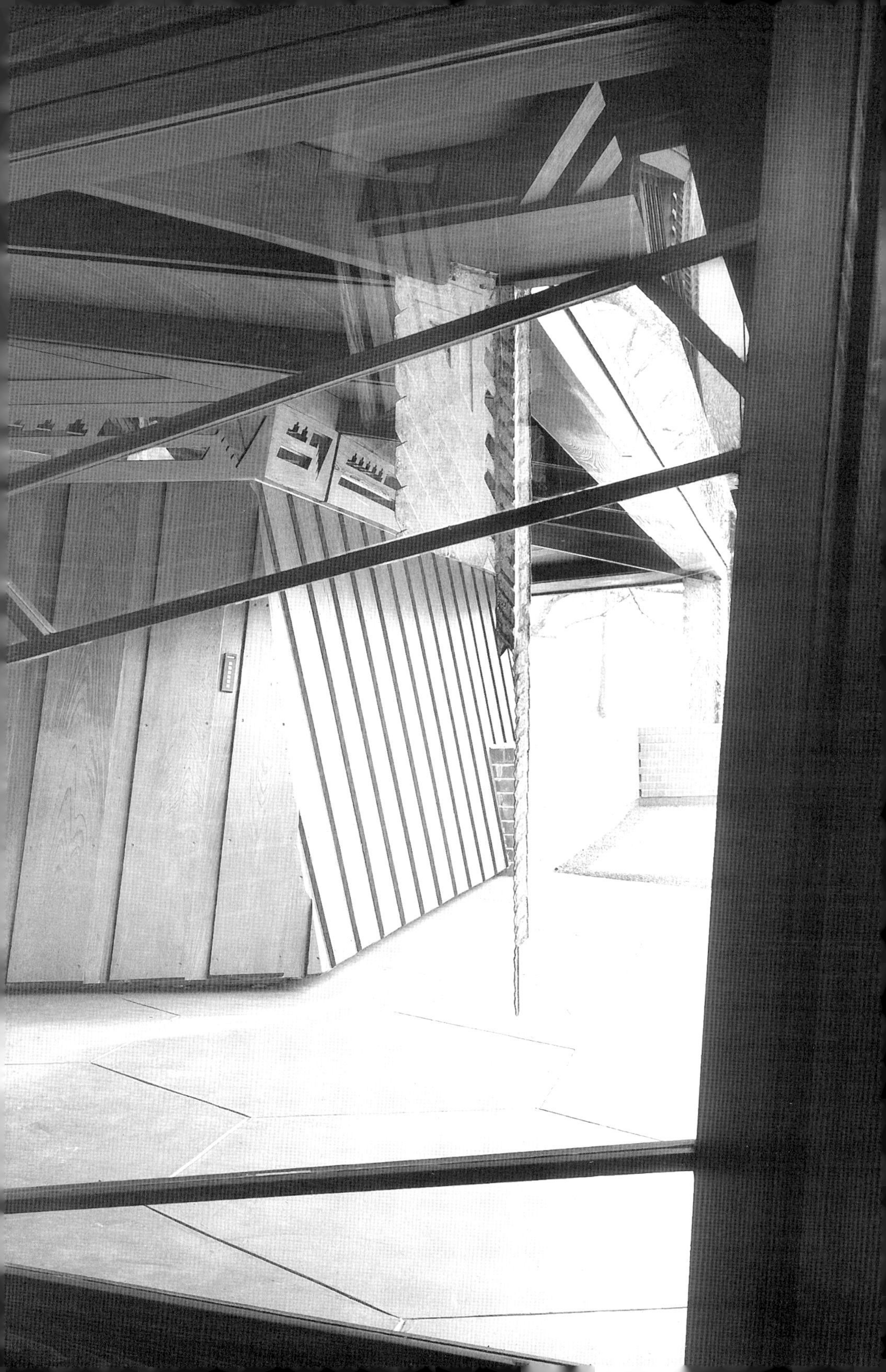

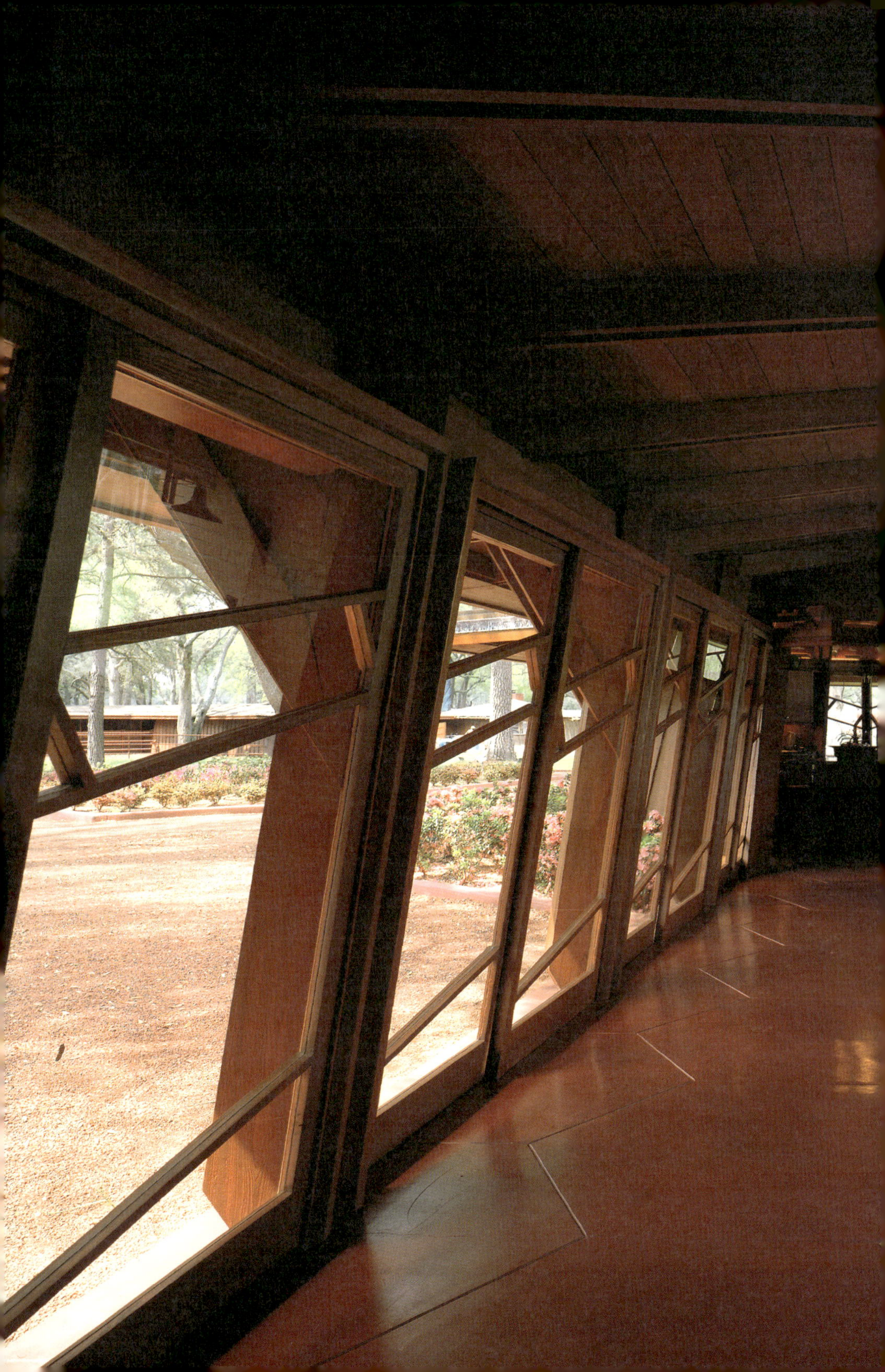

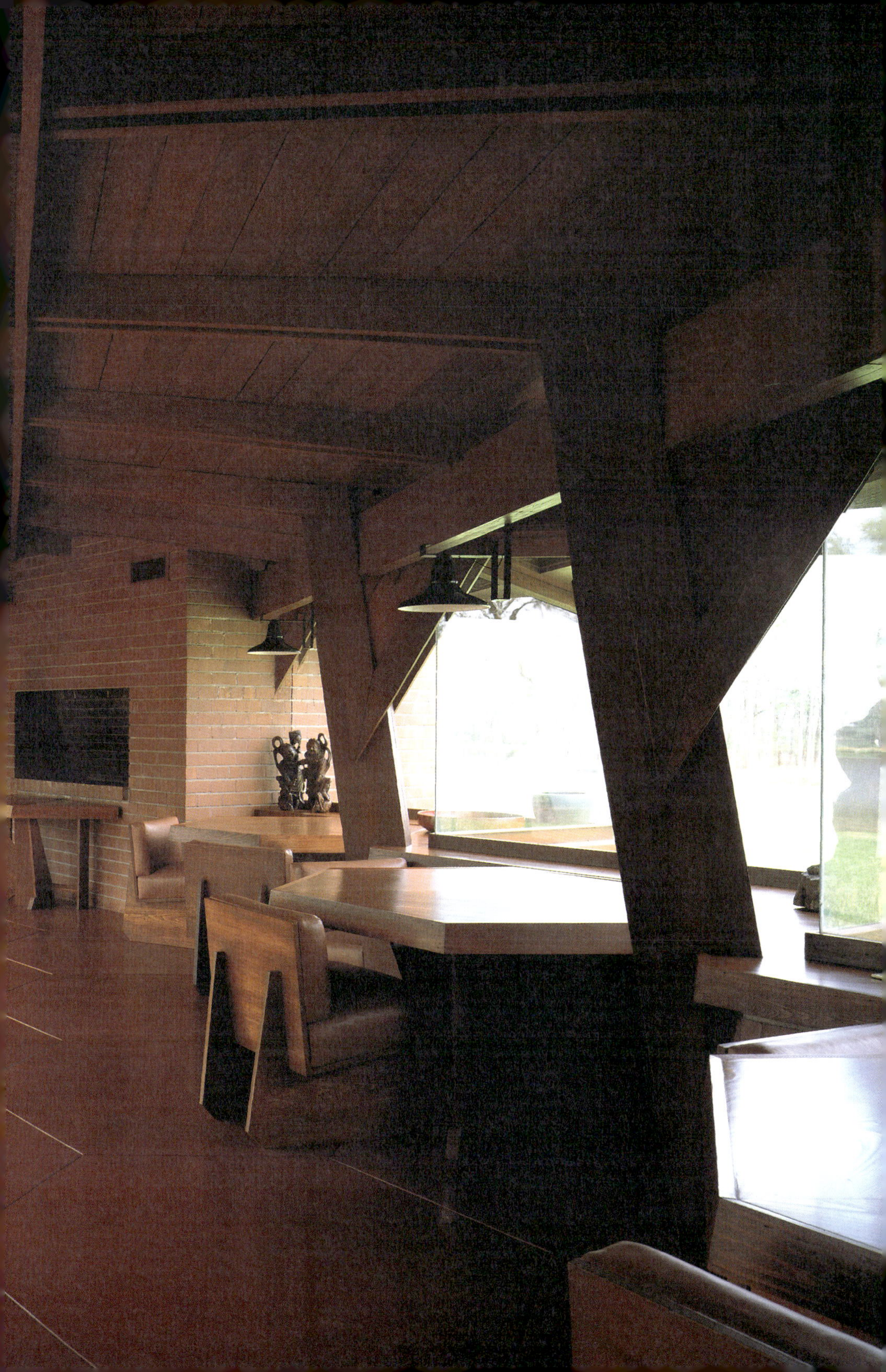

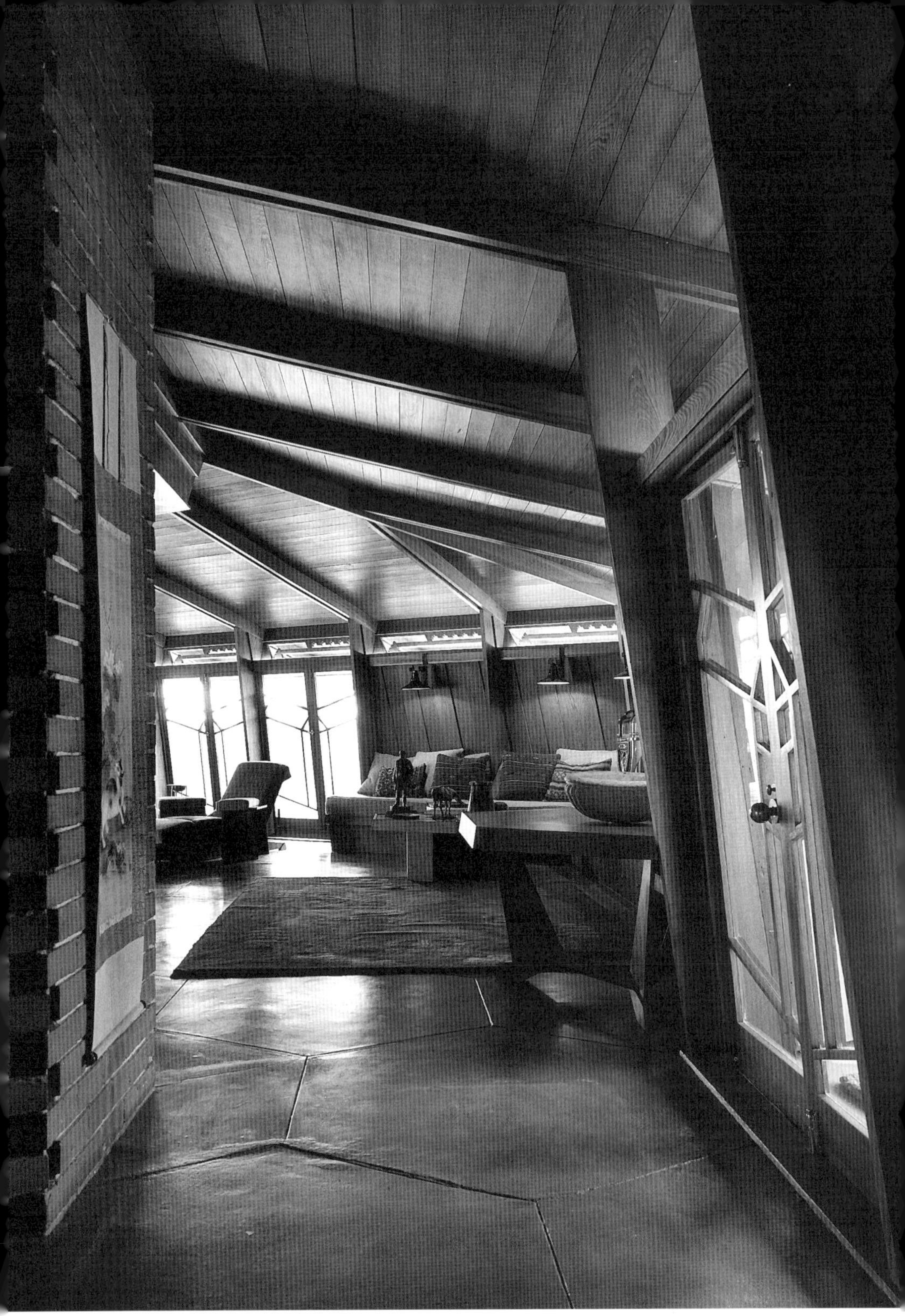

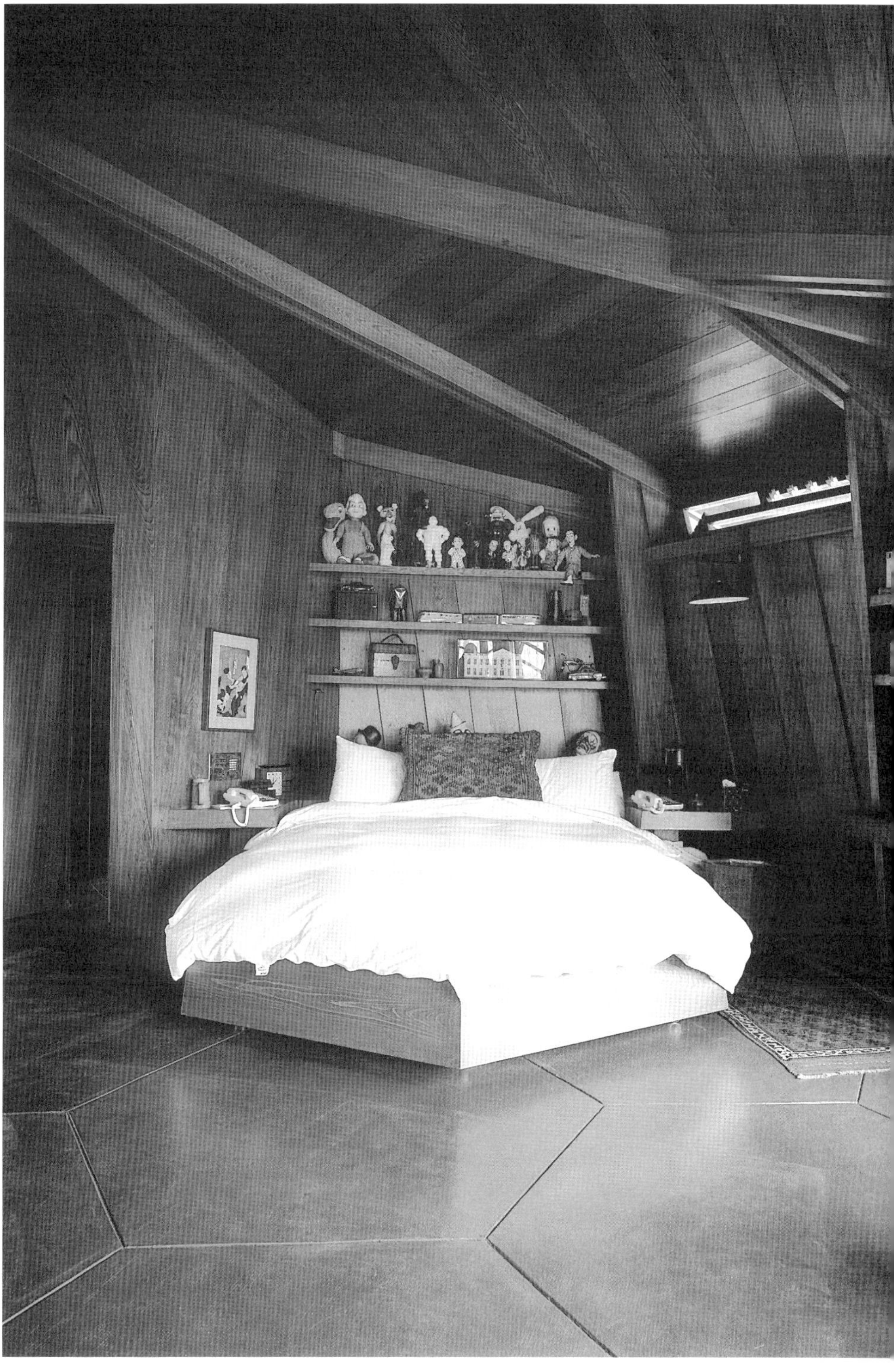

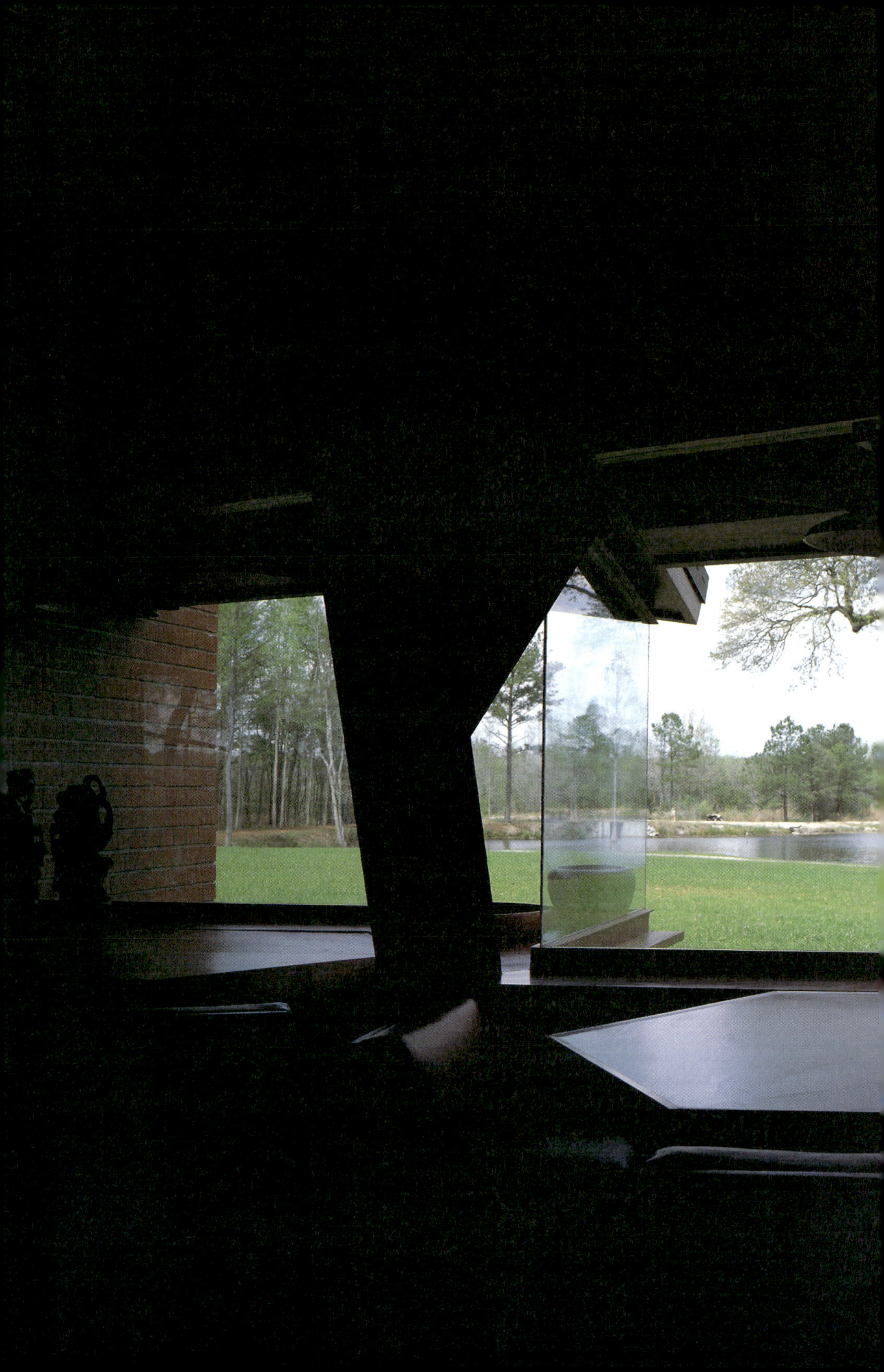

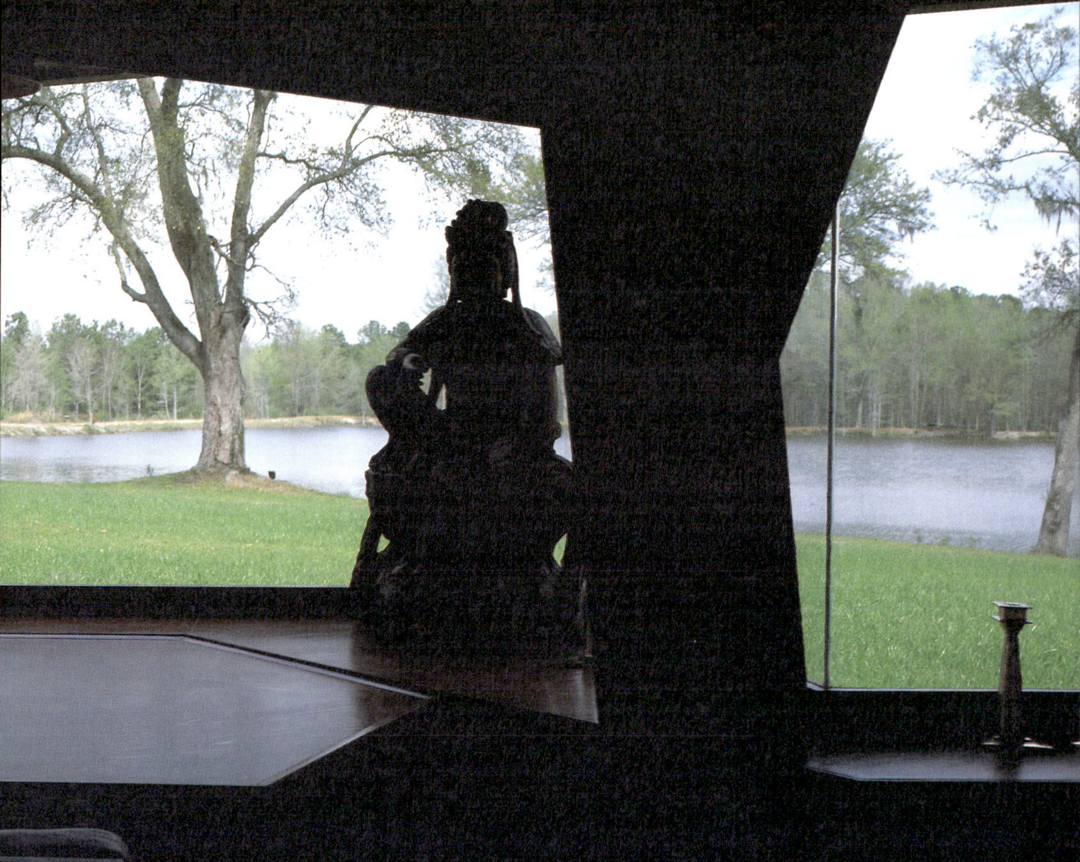

Lowell Walter House, "Cedar Rock"
Quasqueton, Iowa, 1945

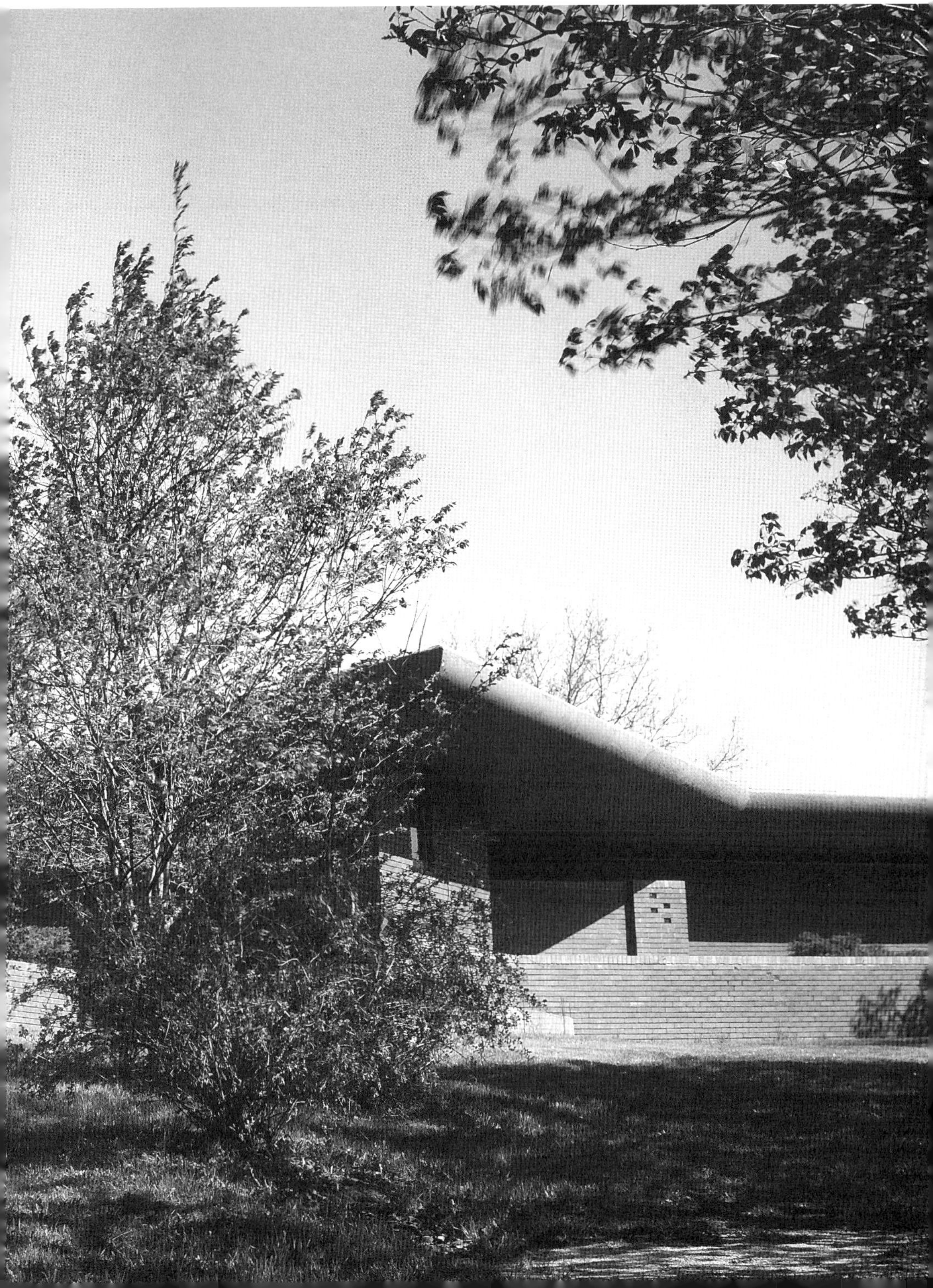

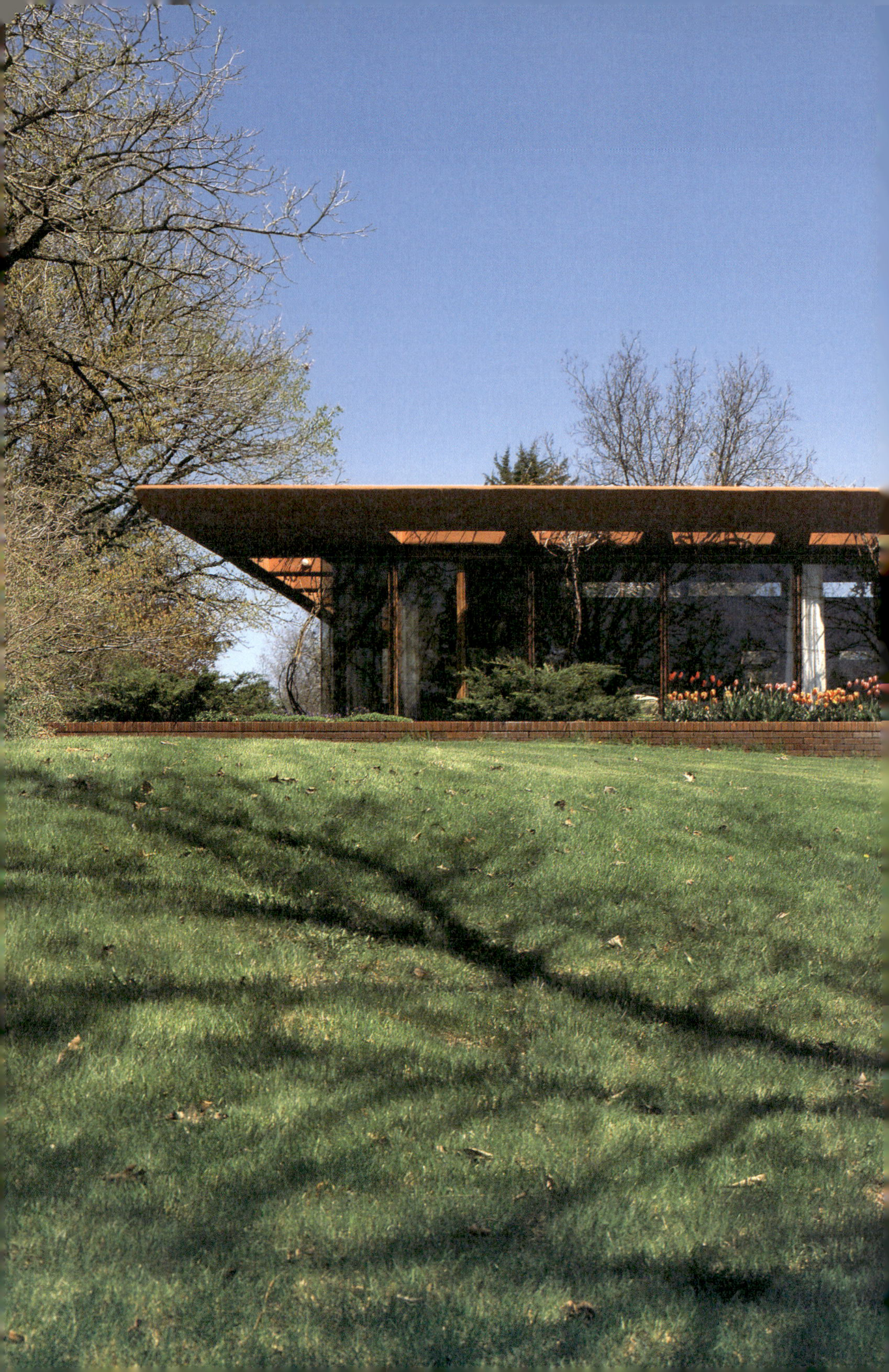

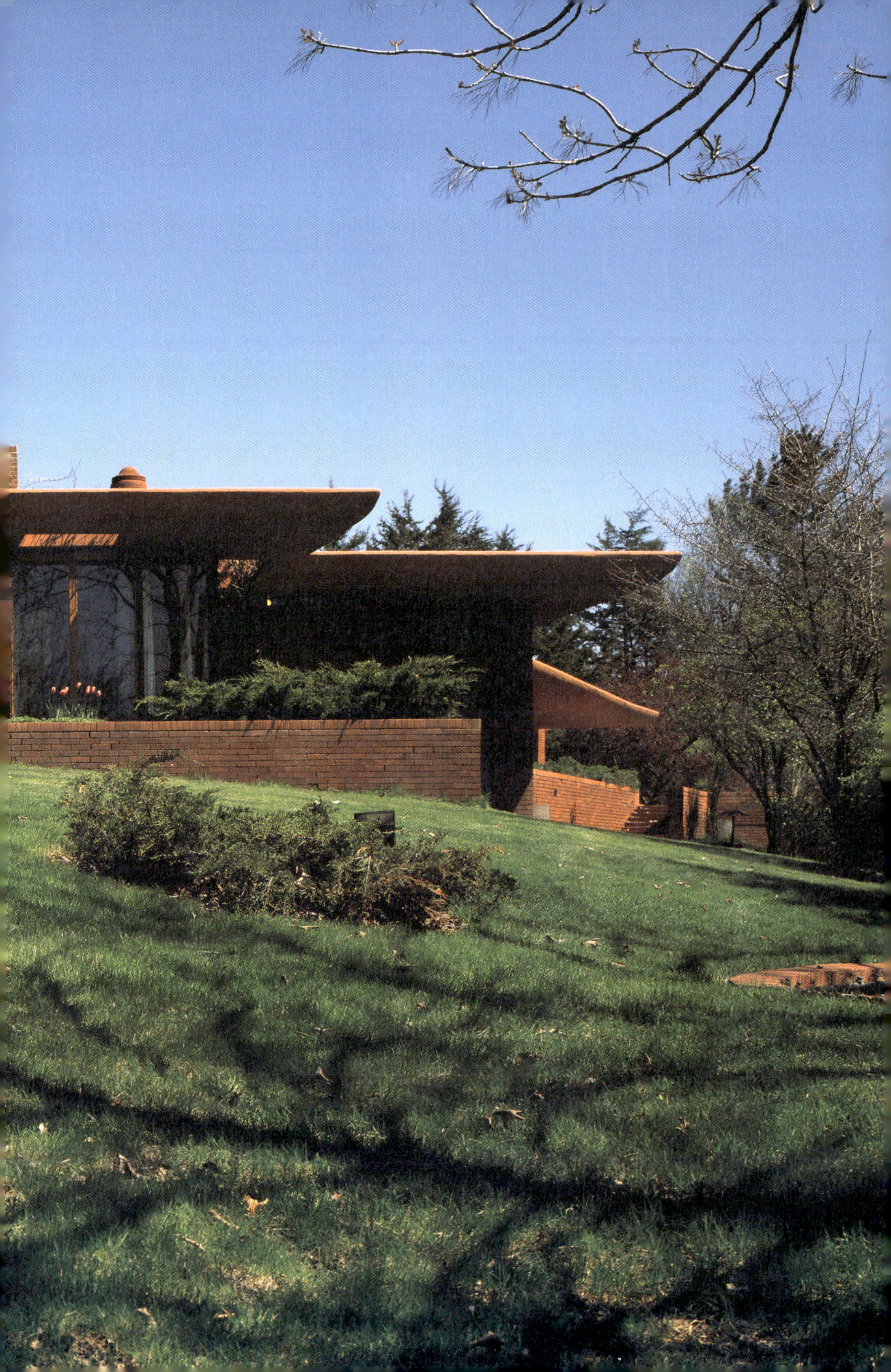

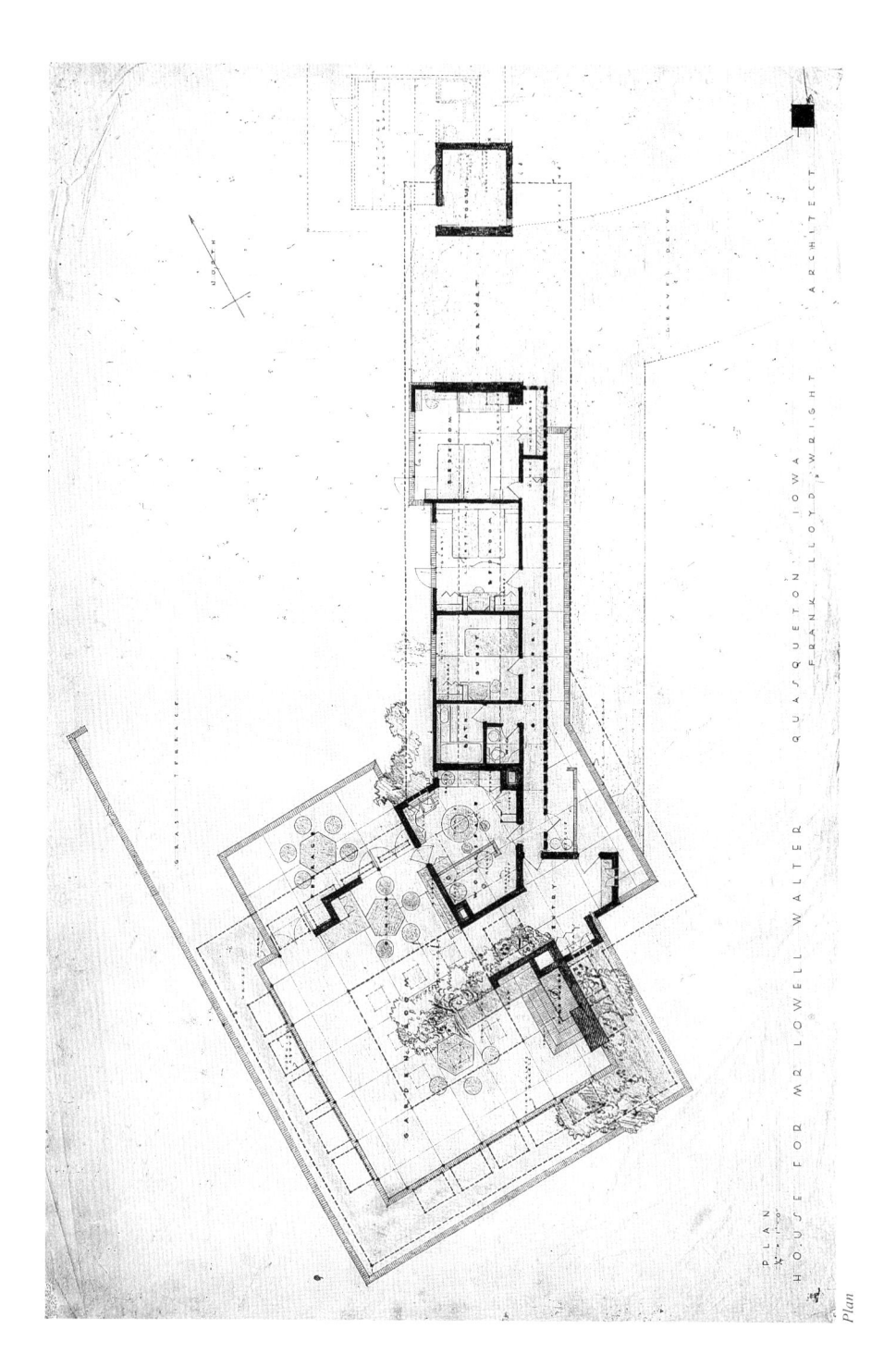

Plan

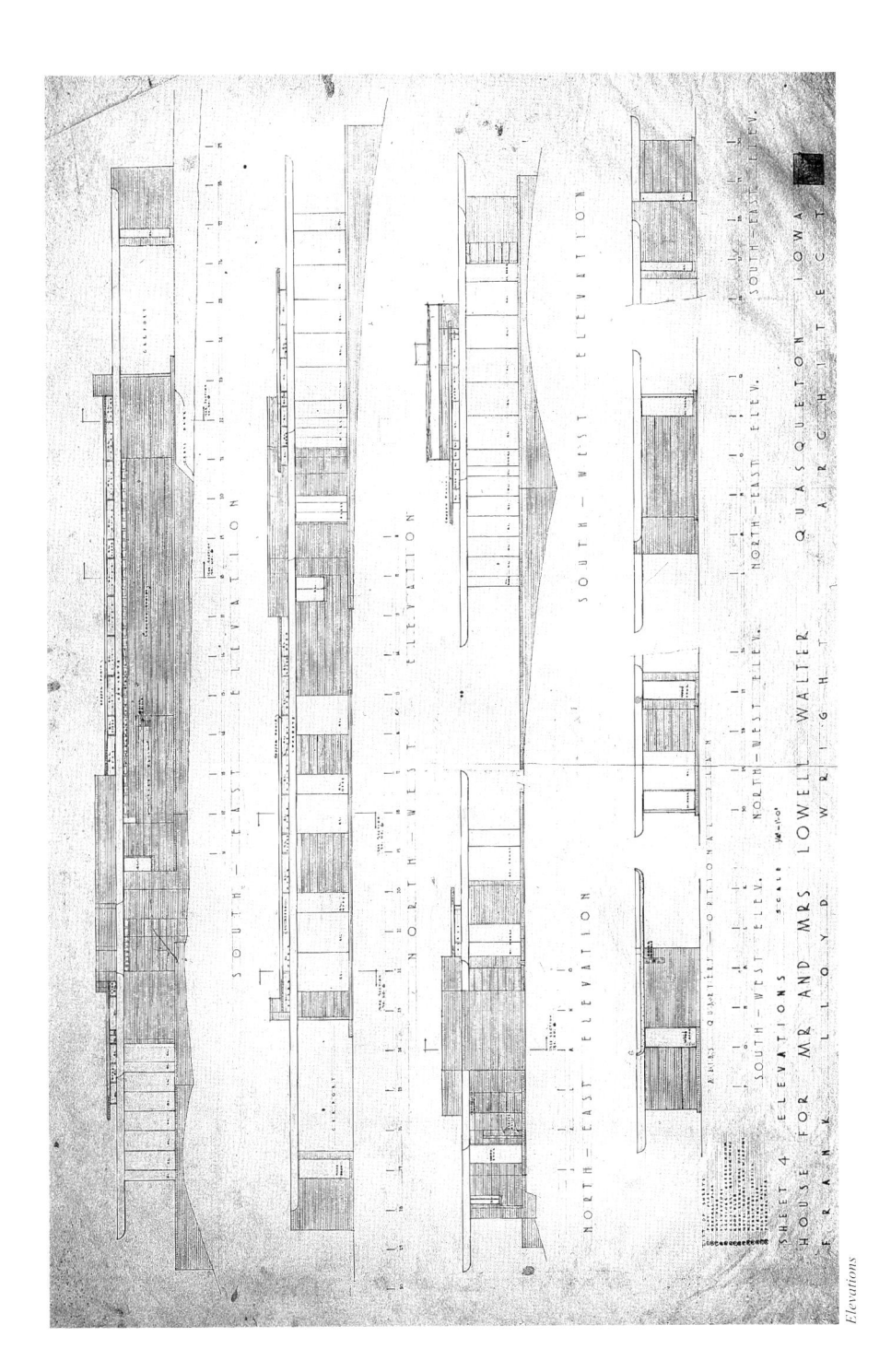

Elevations

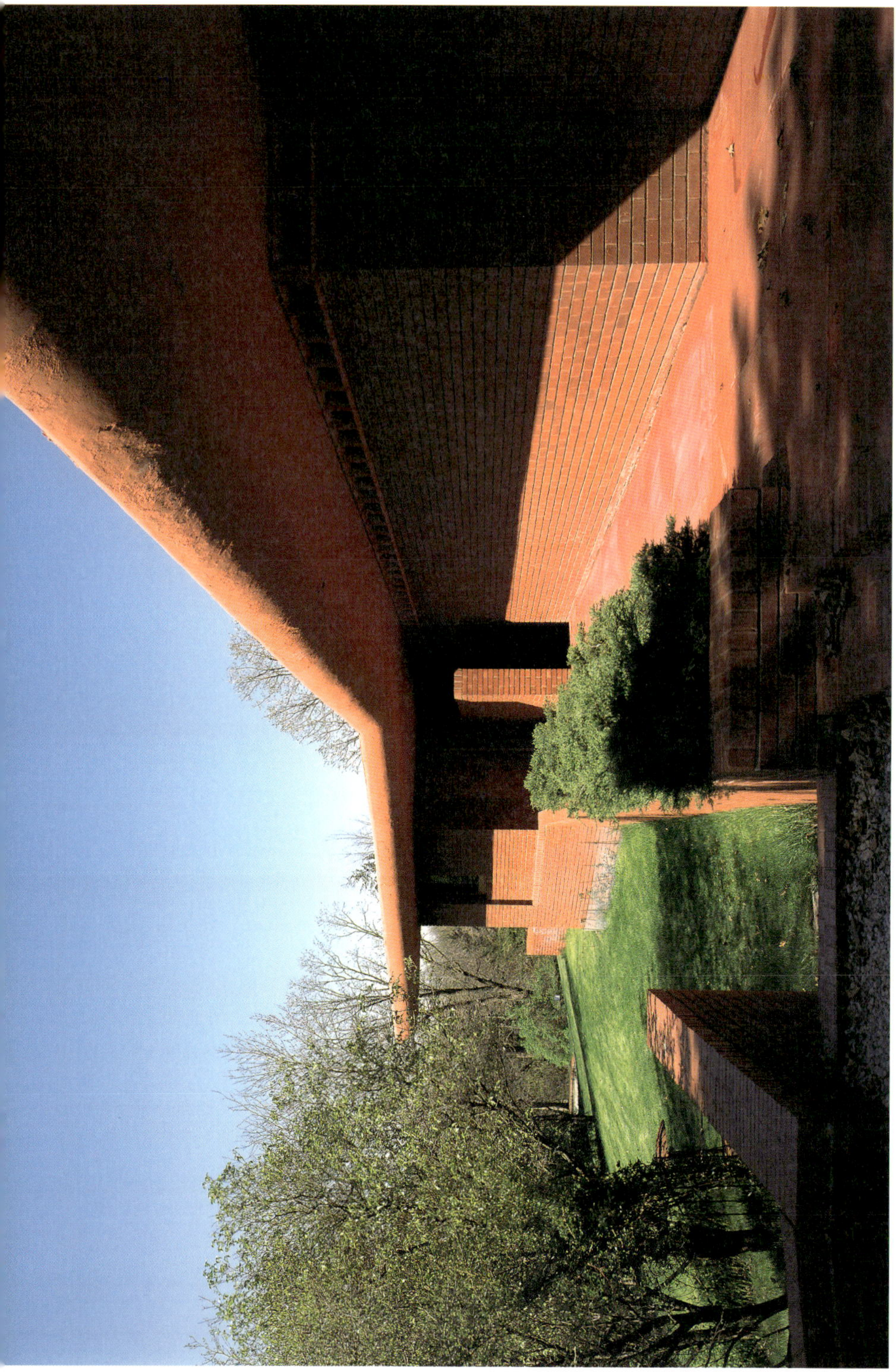

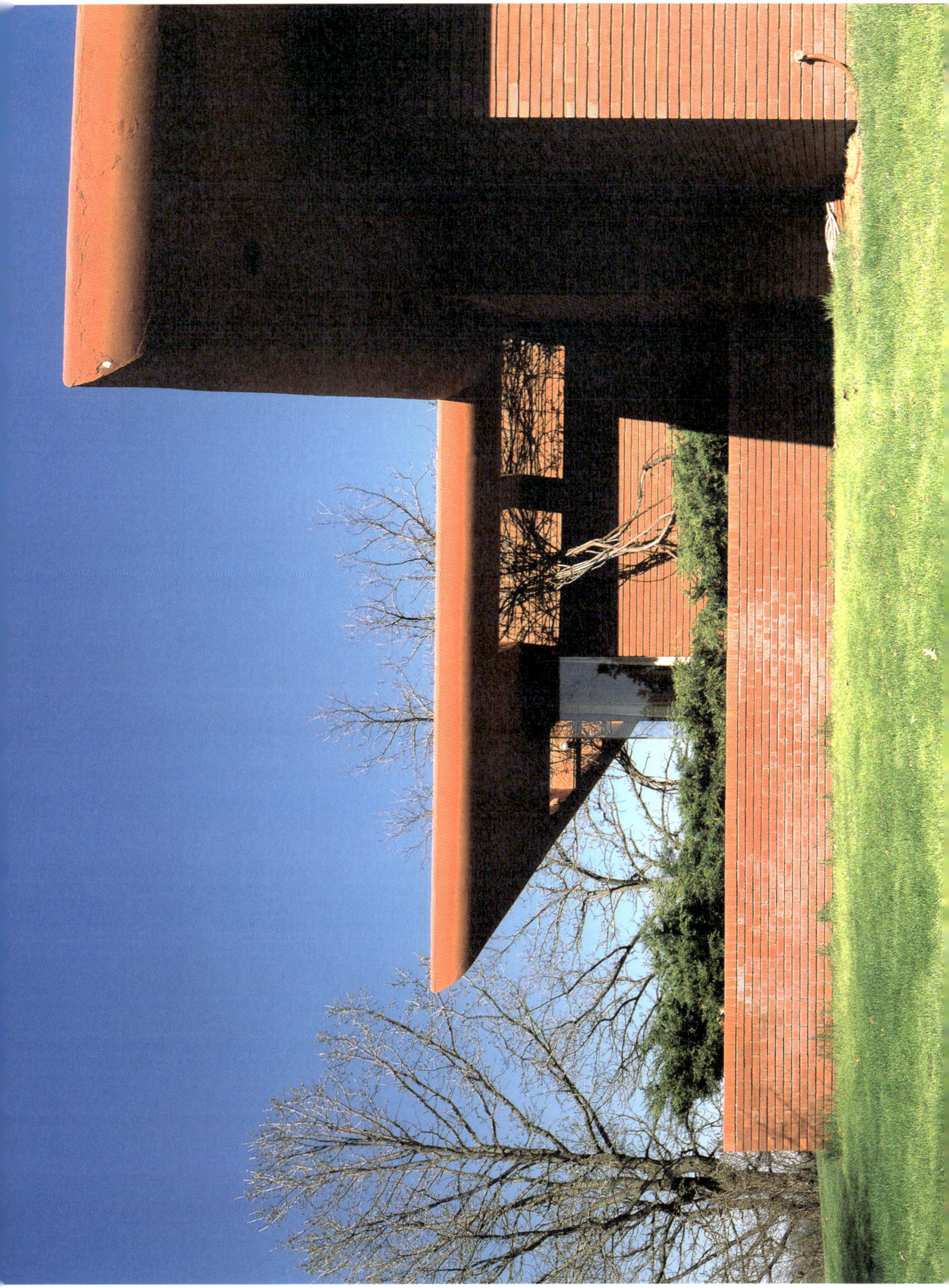

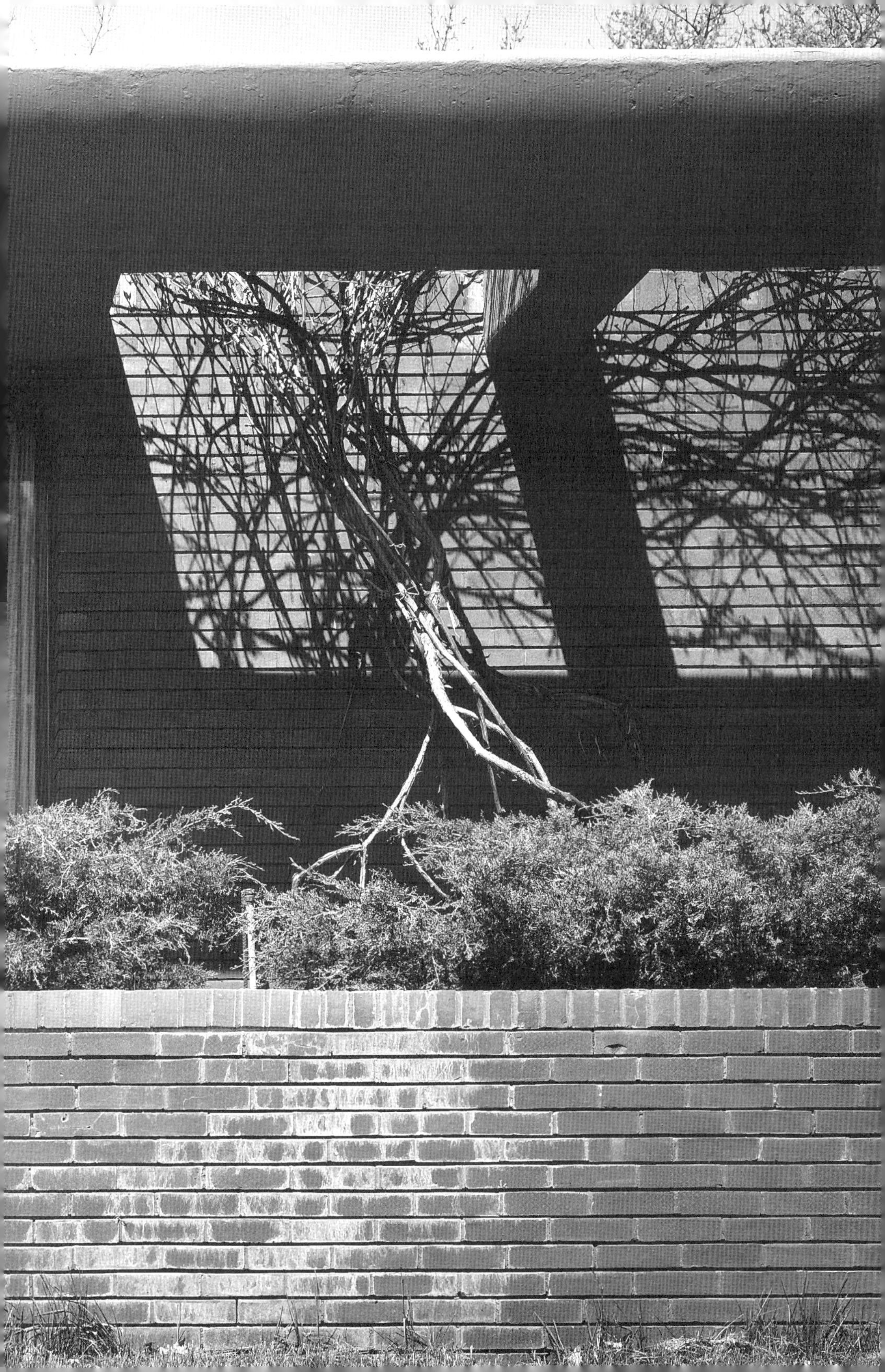

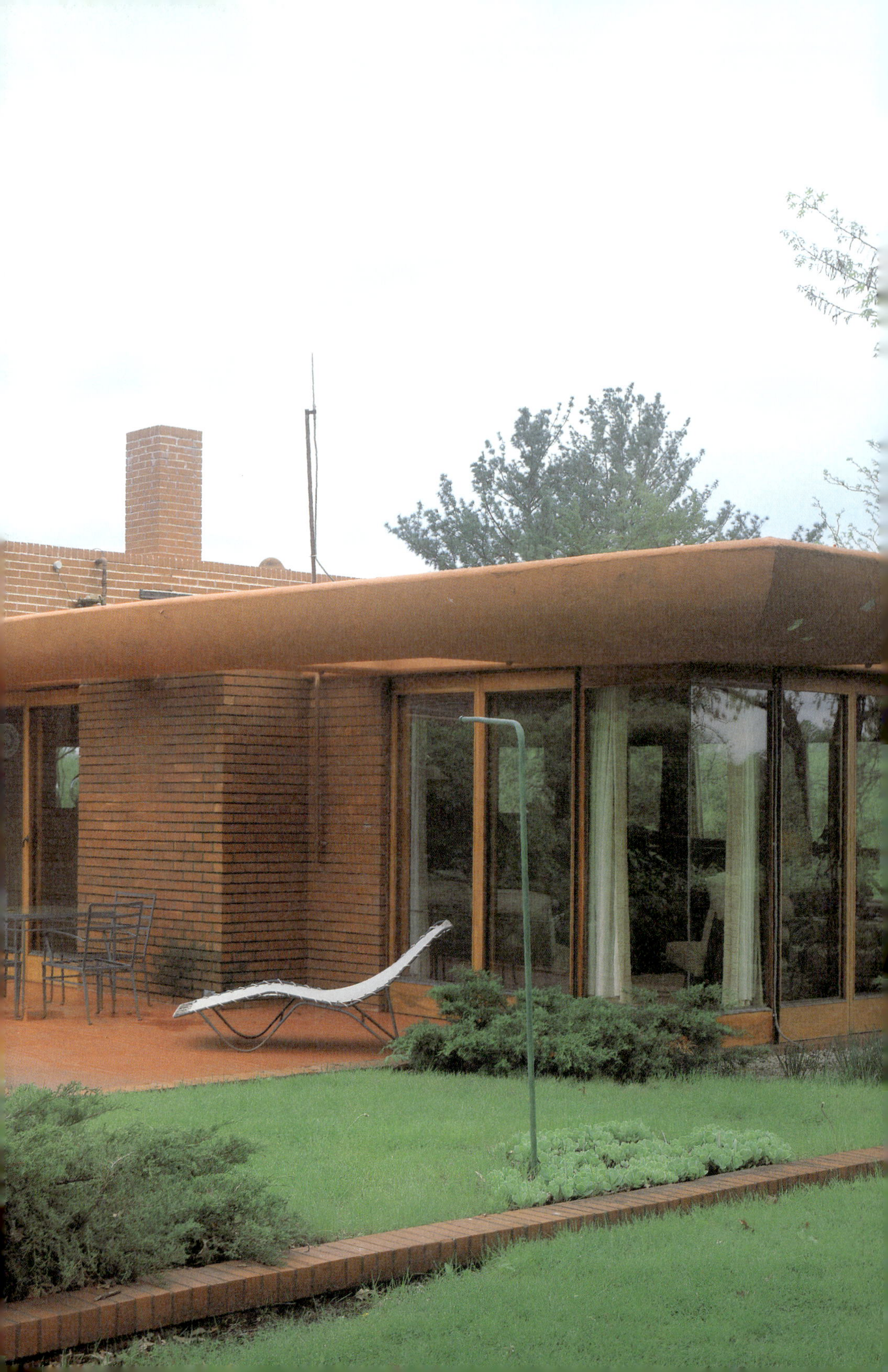

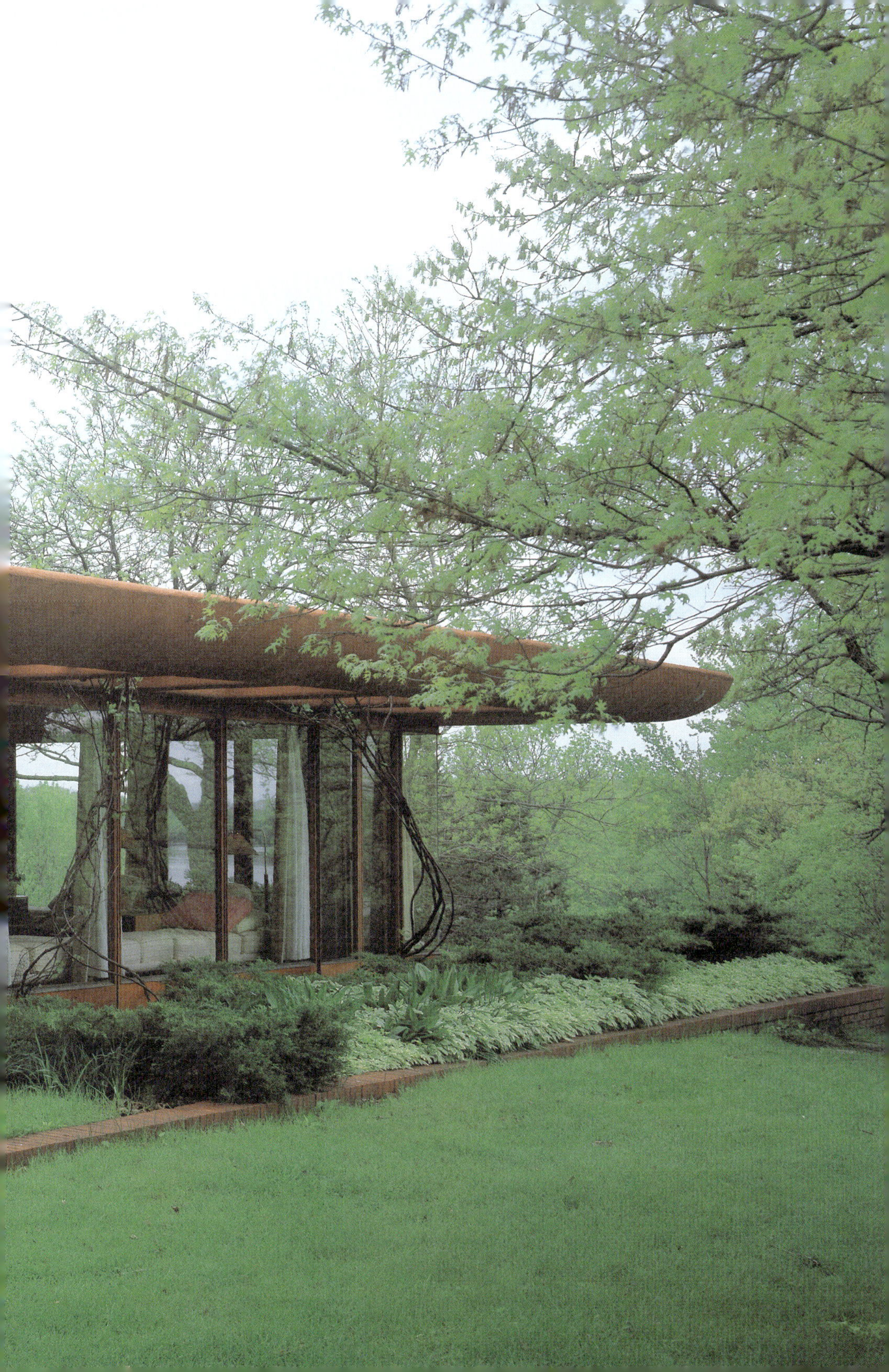

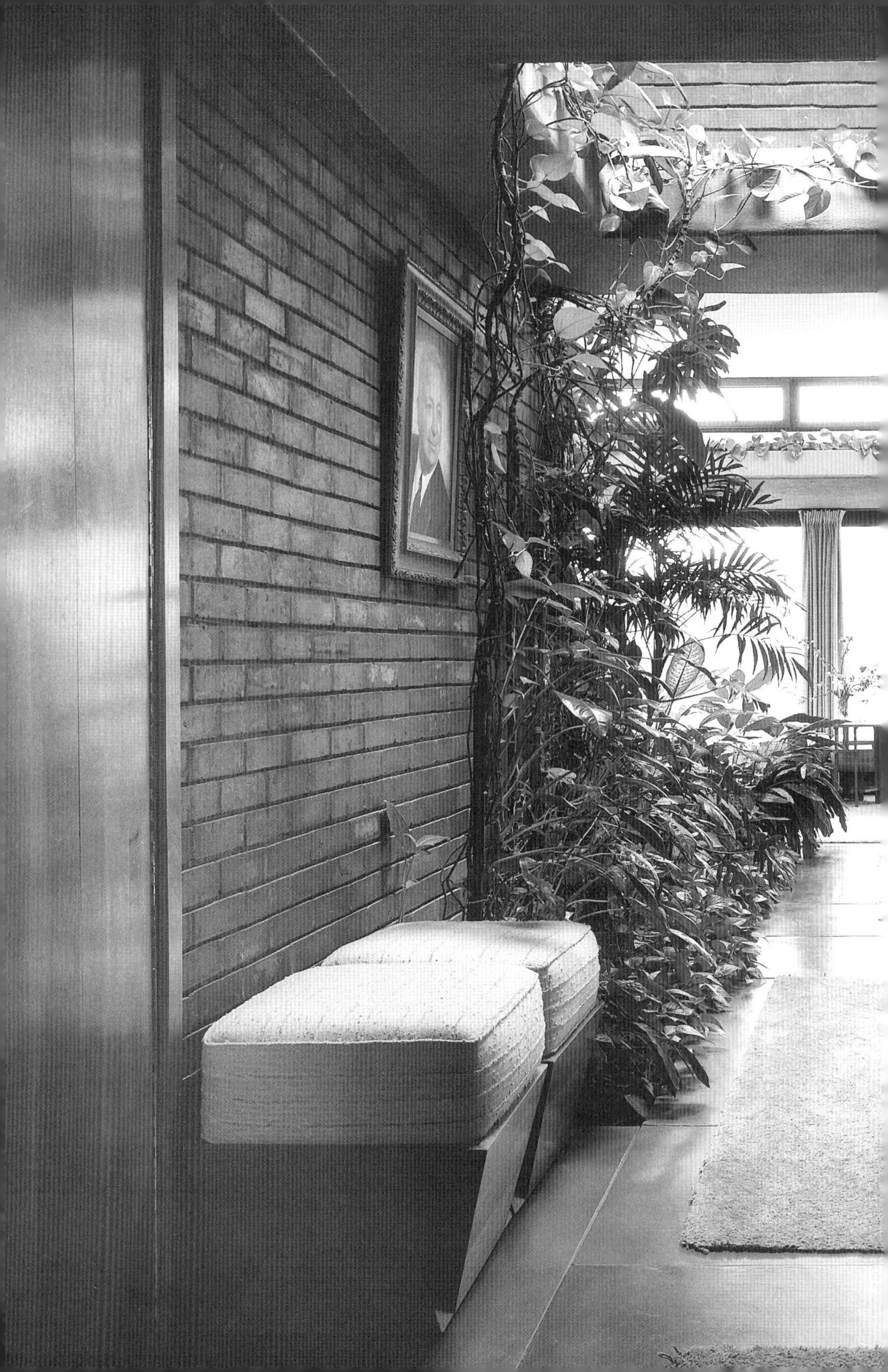

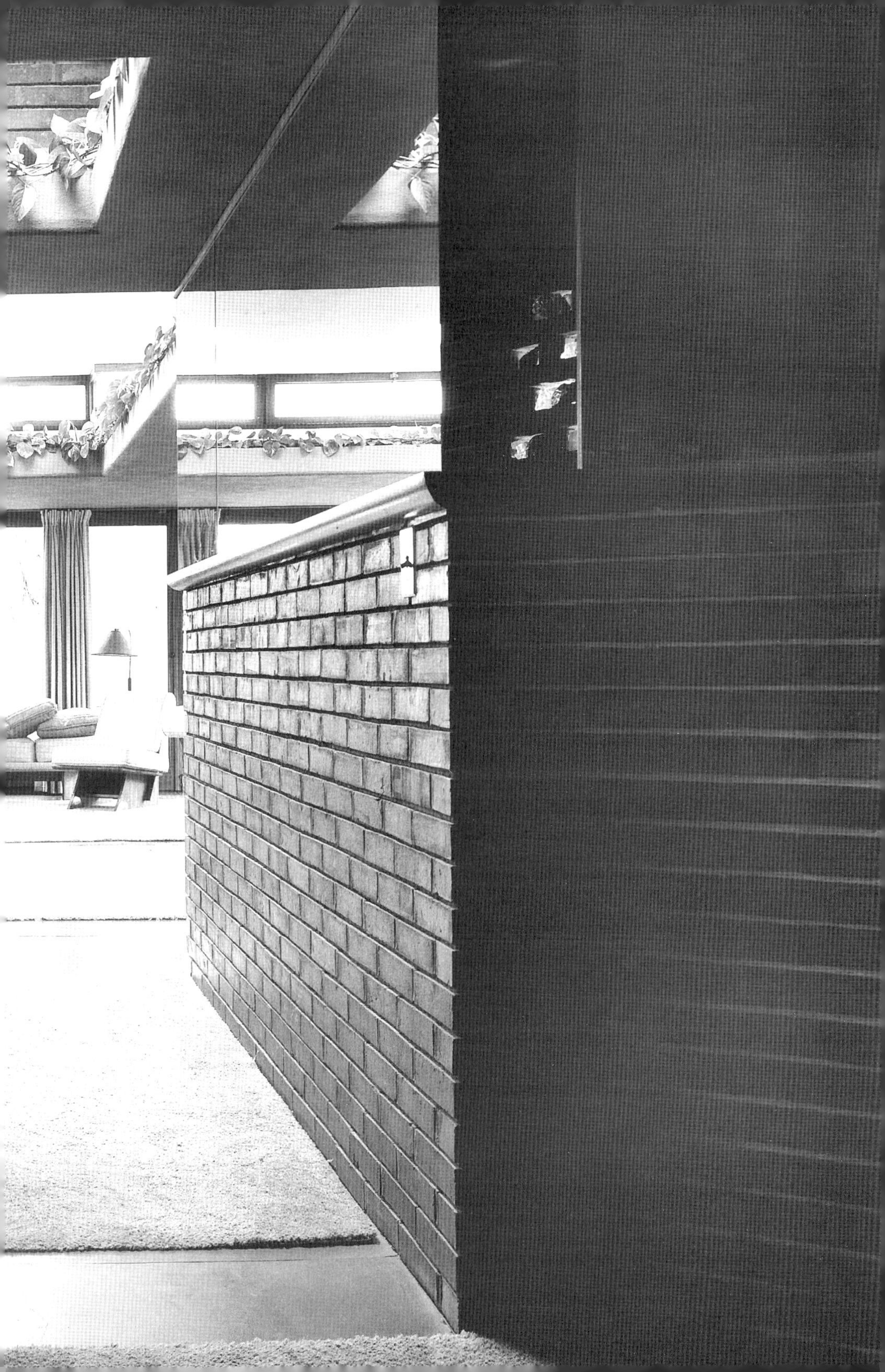

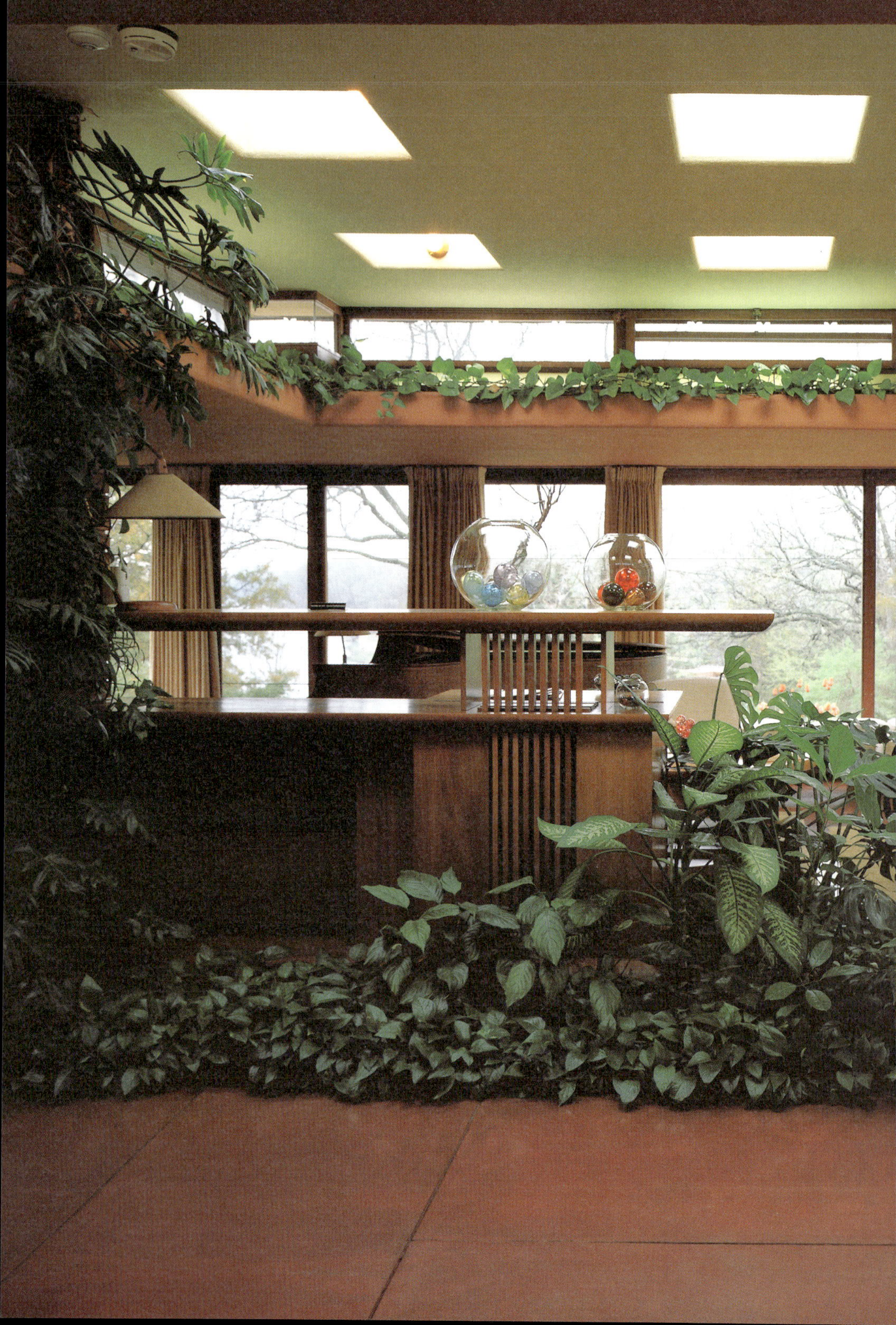

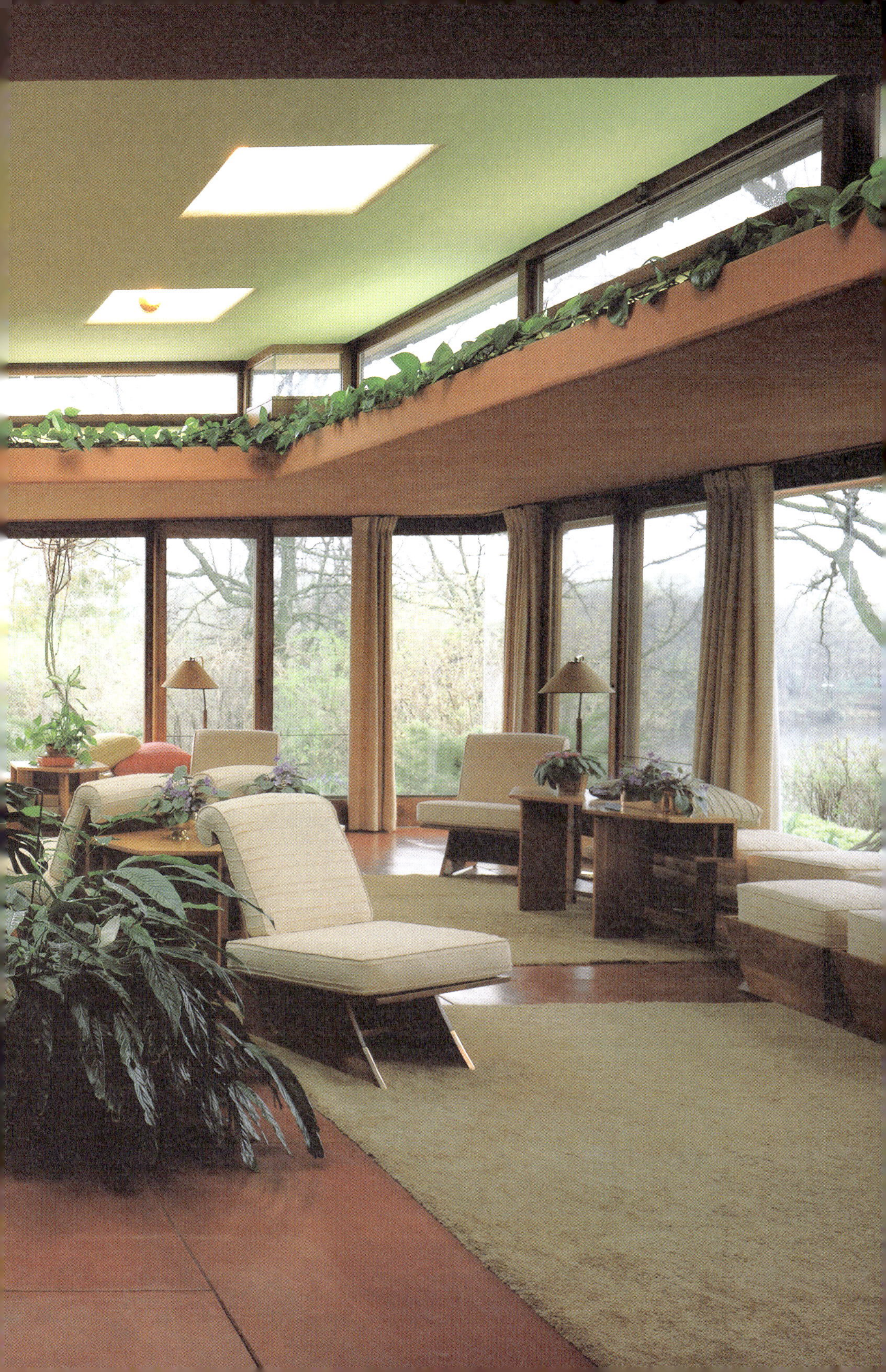

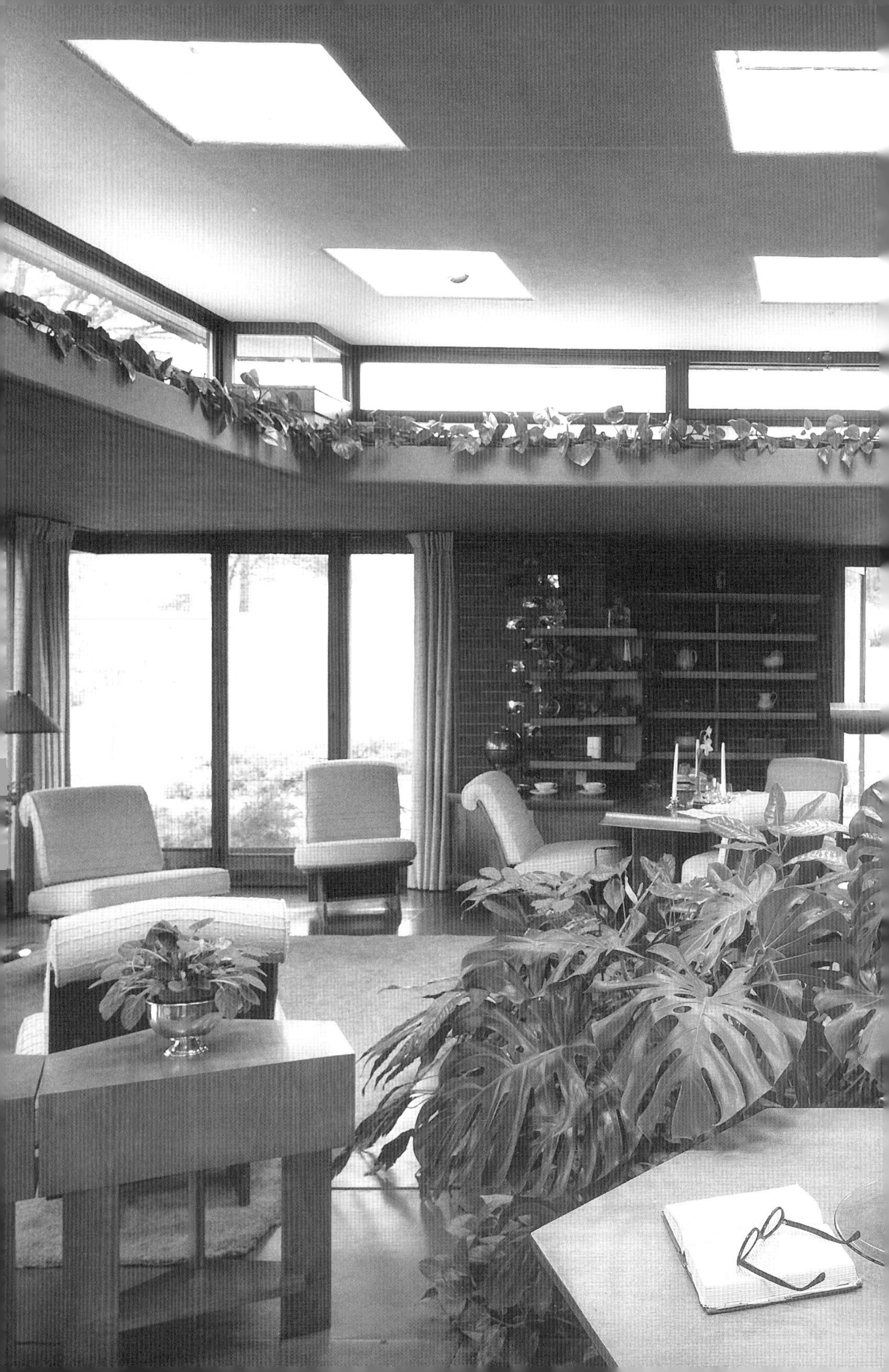

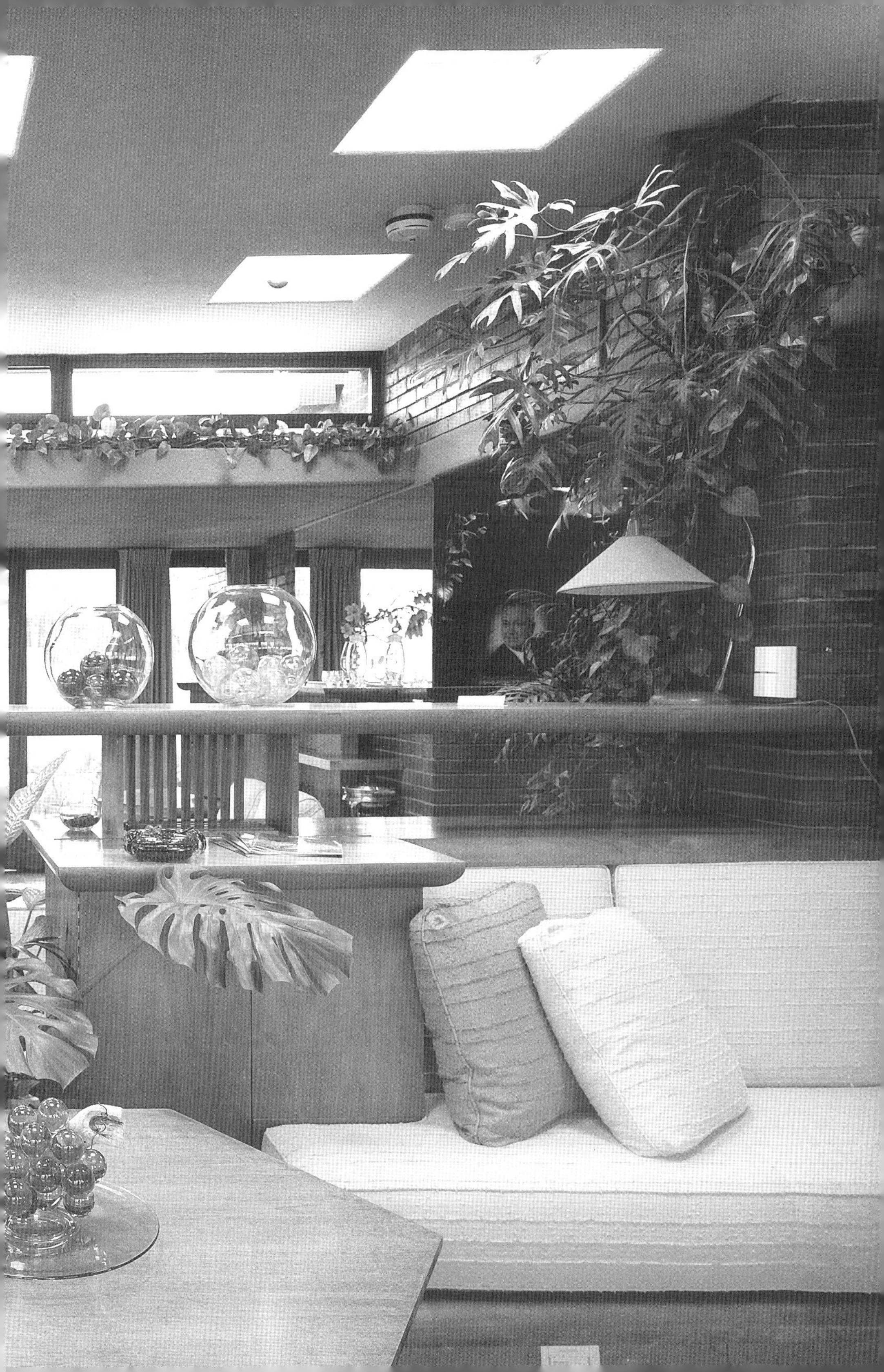

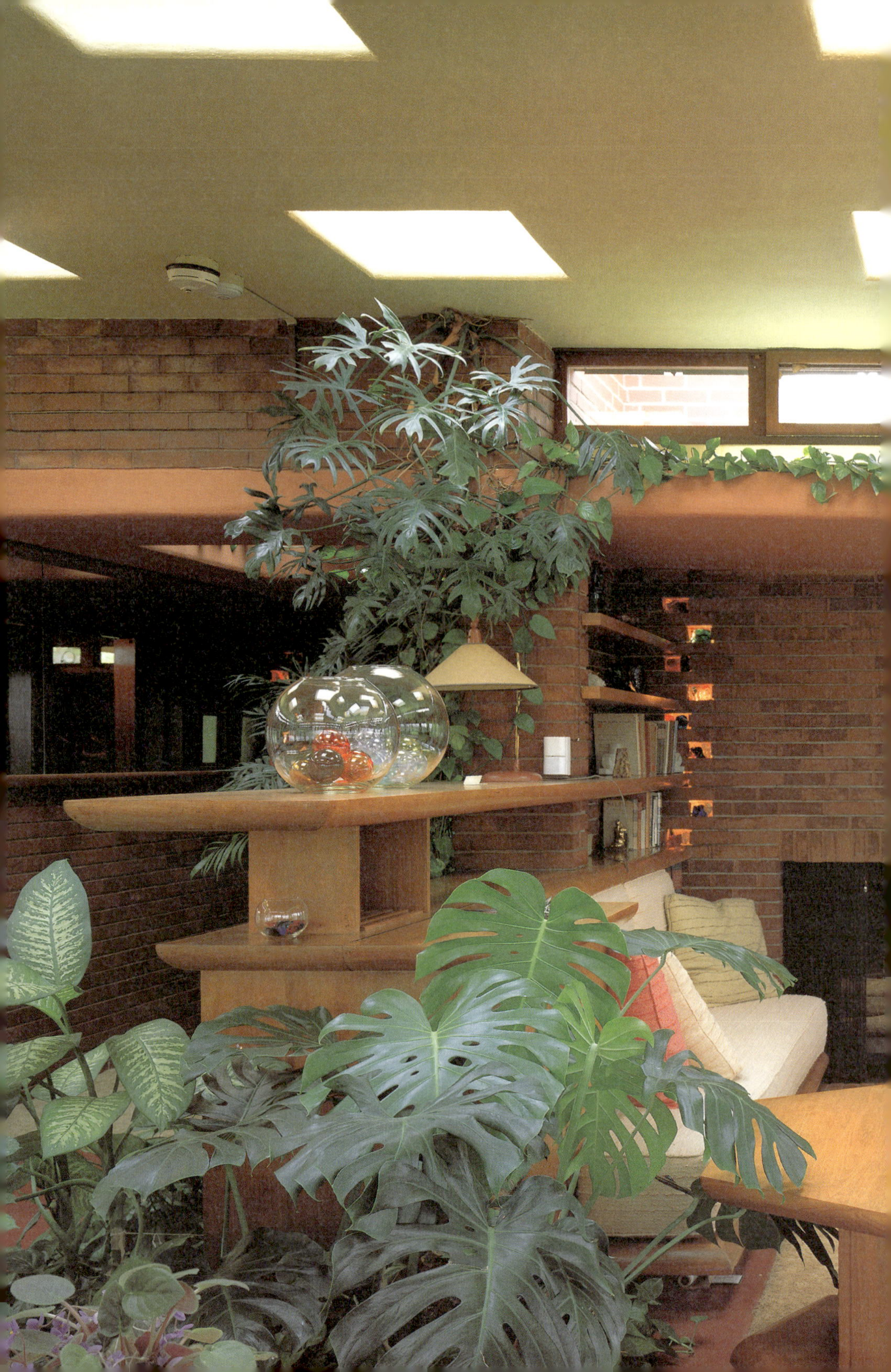

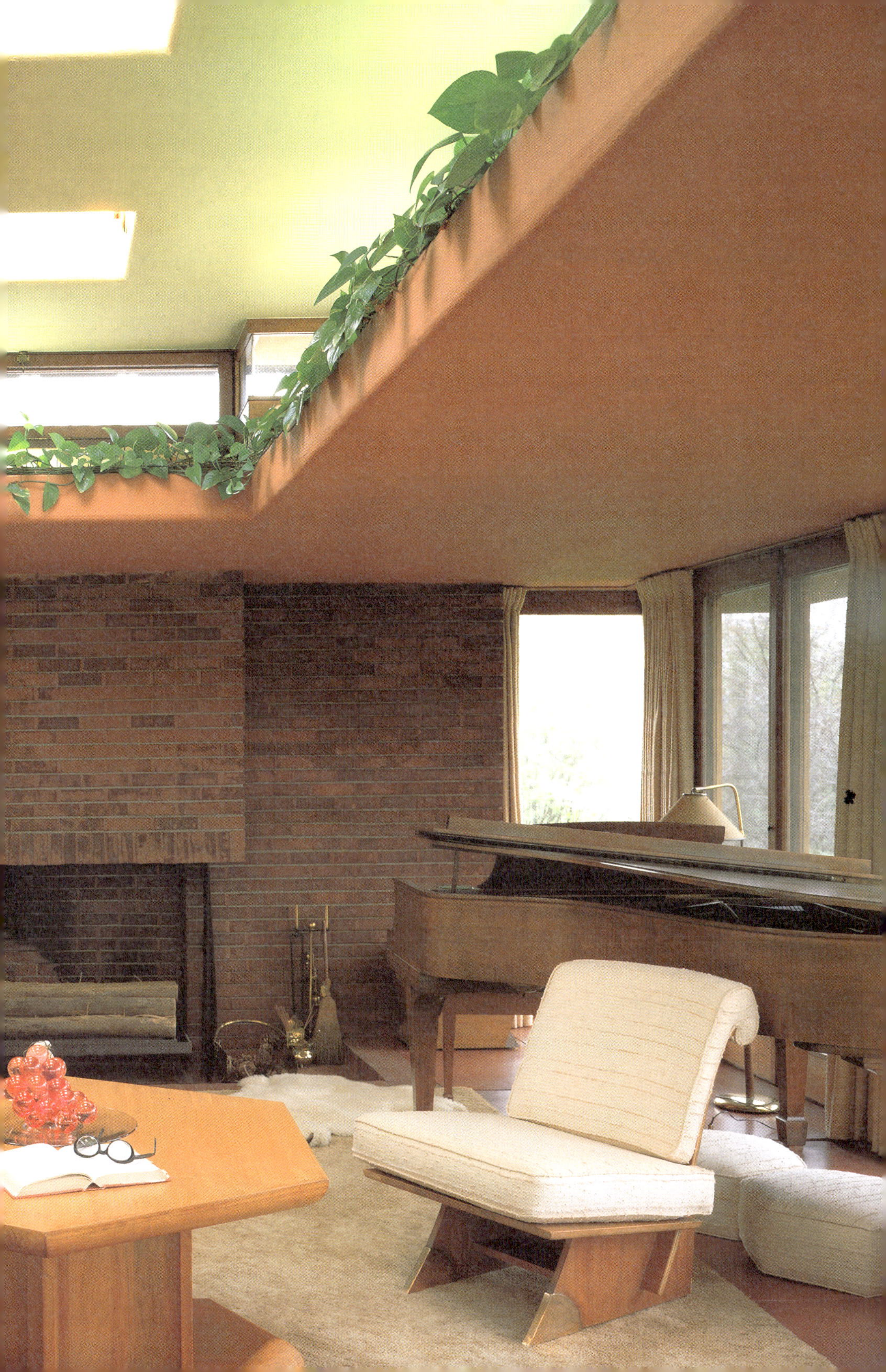

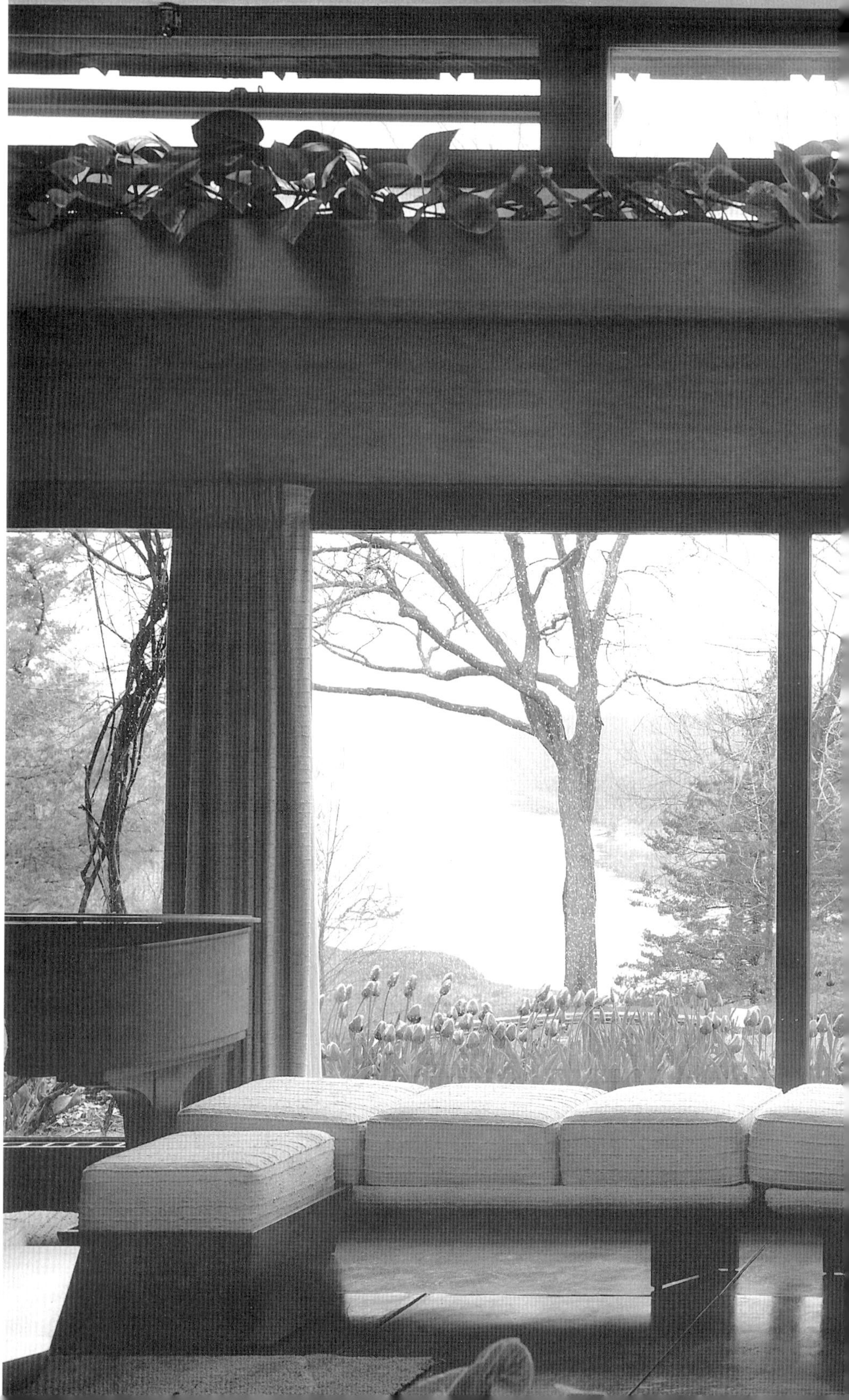

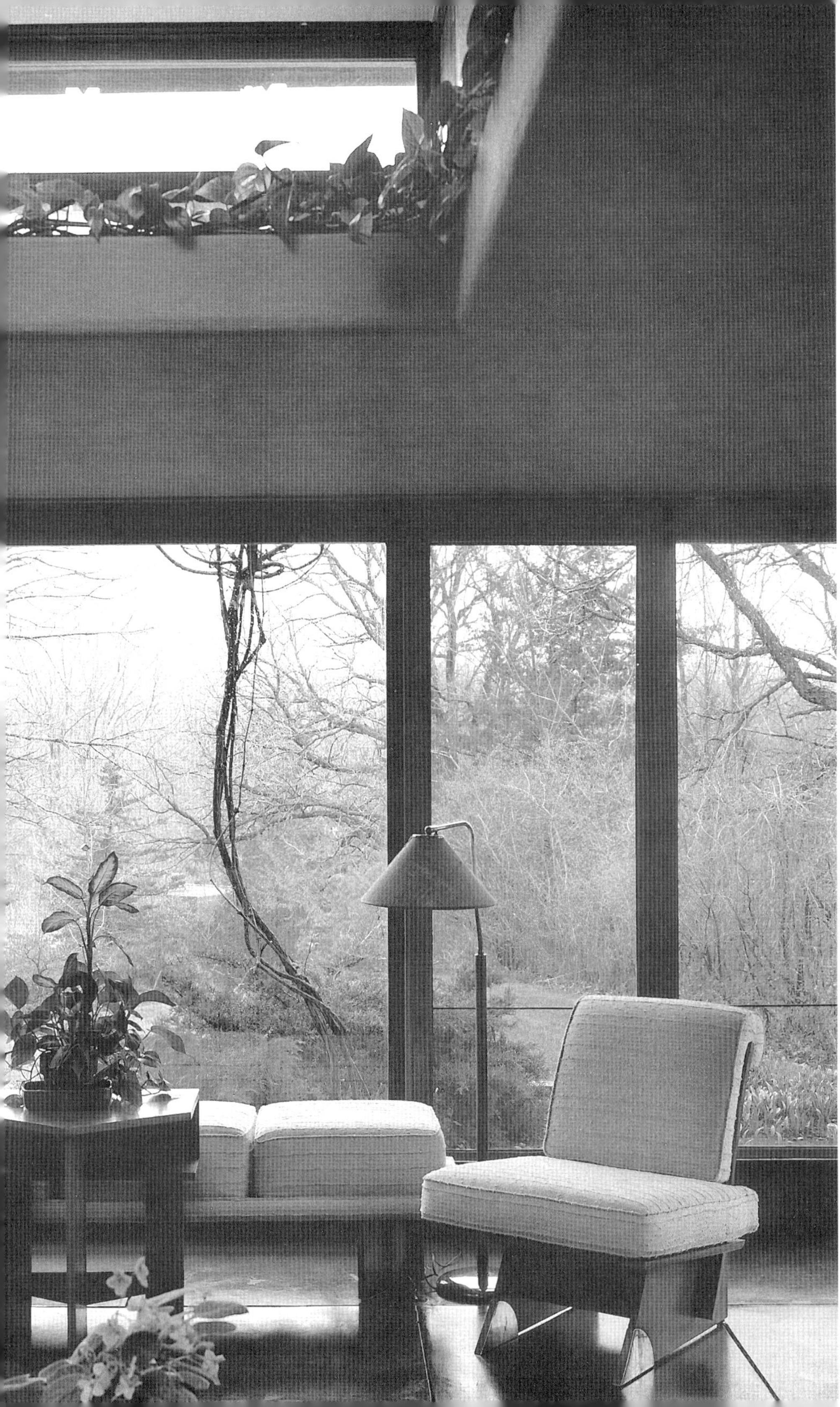

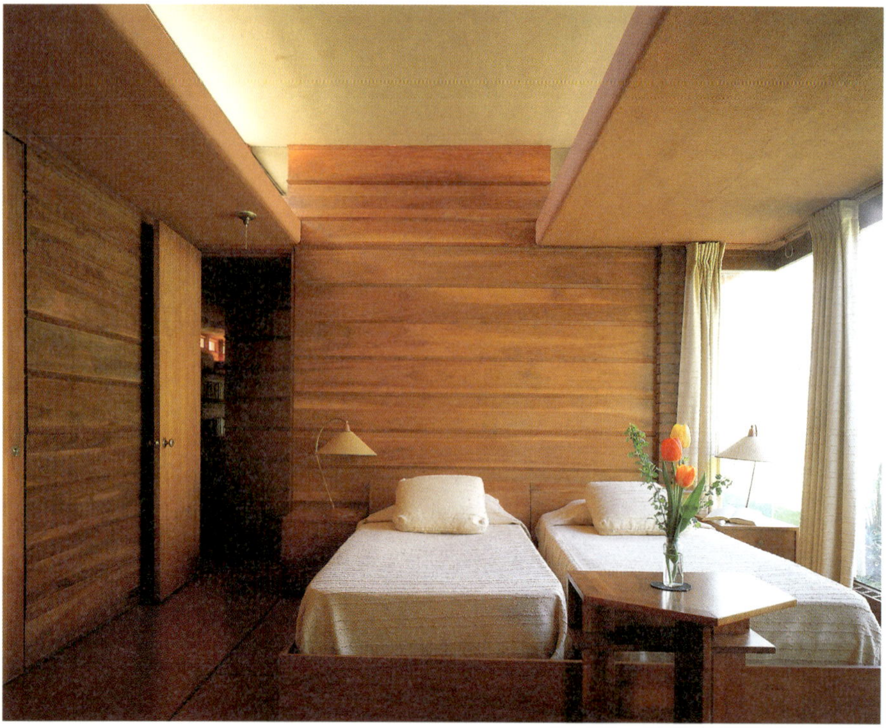

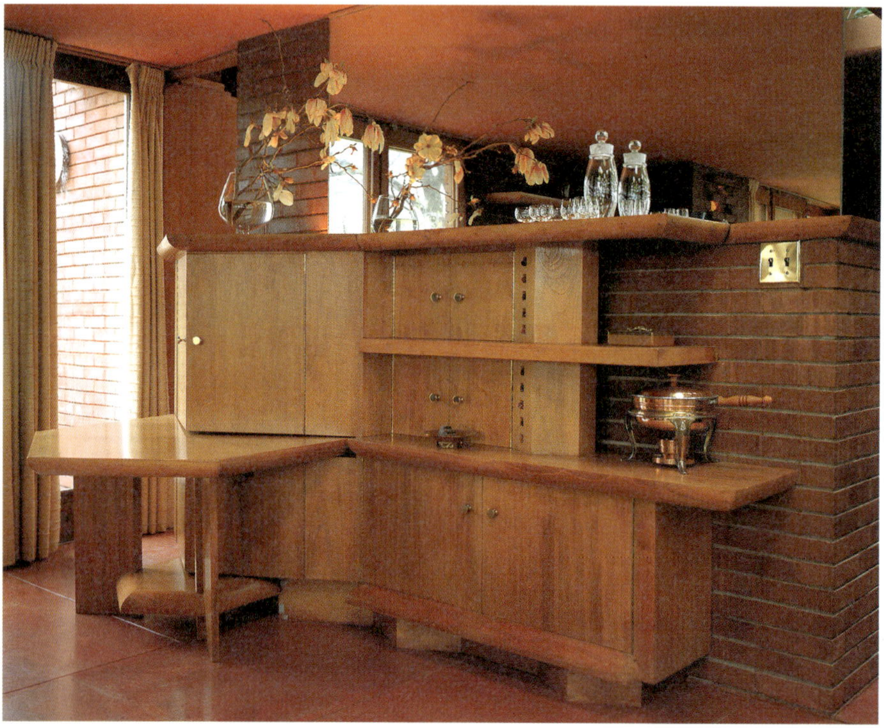

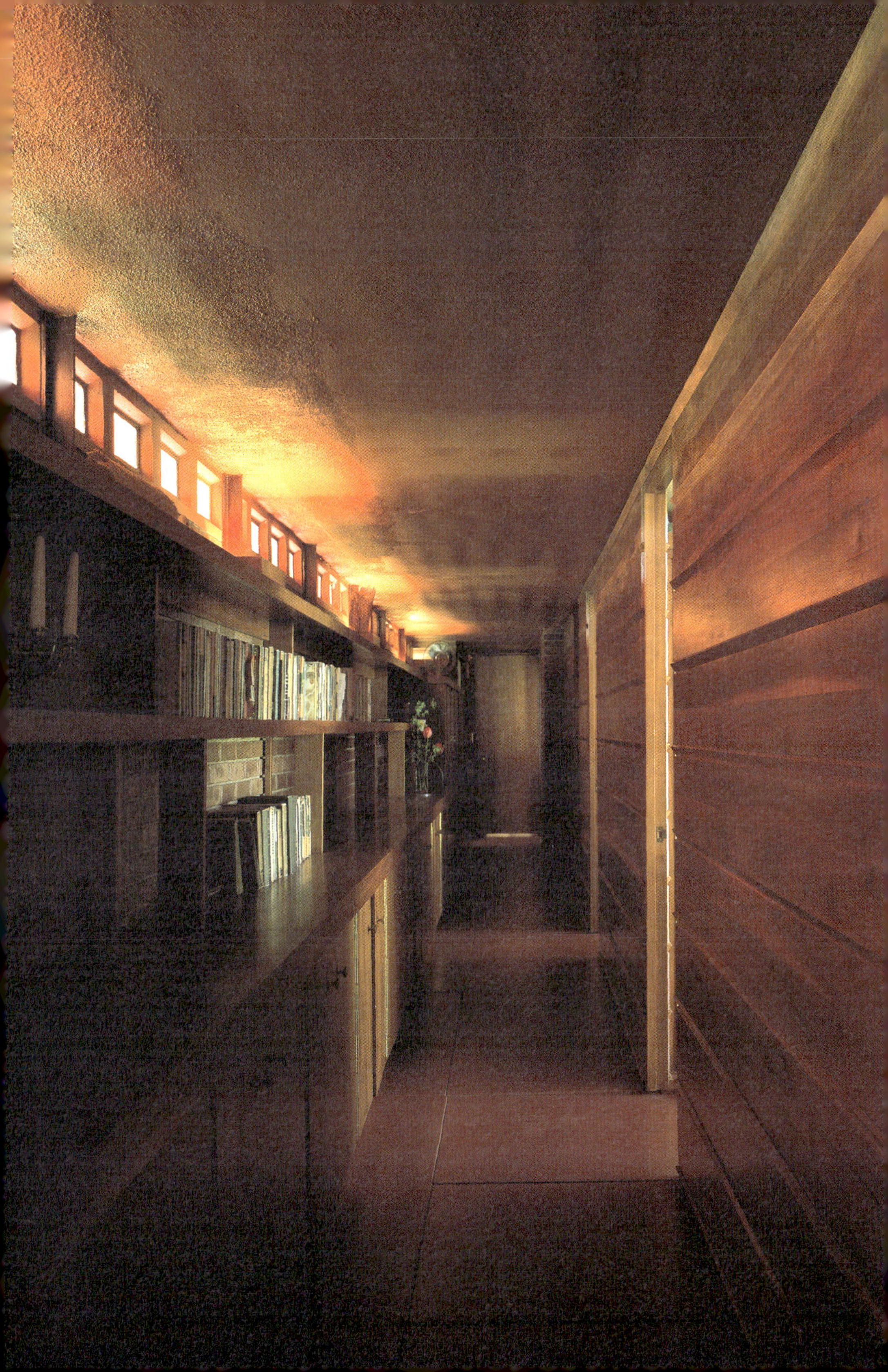

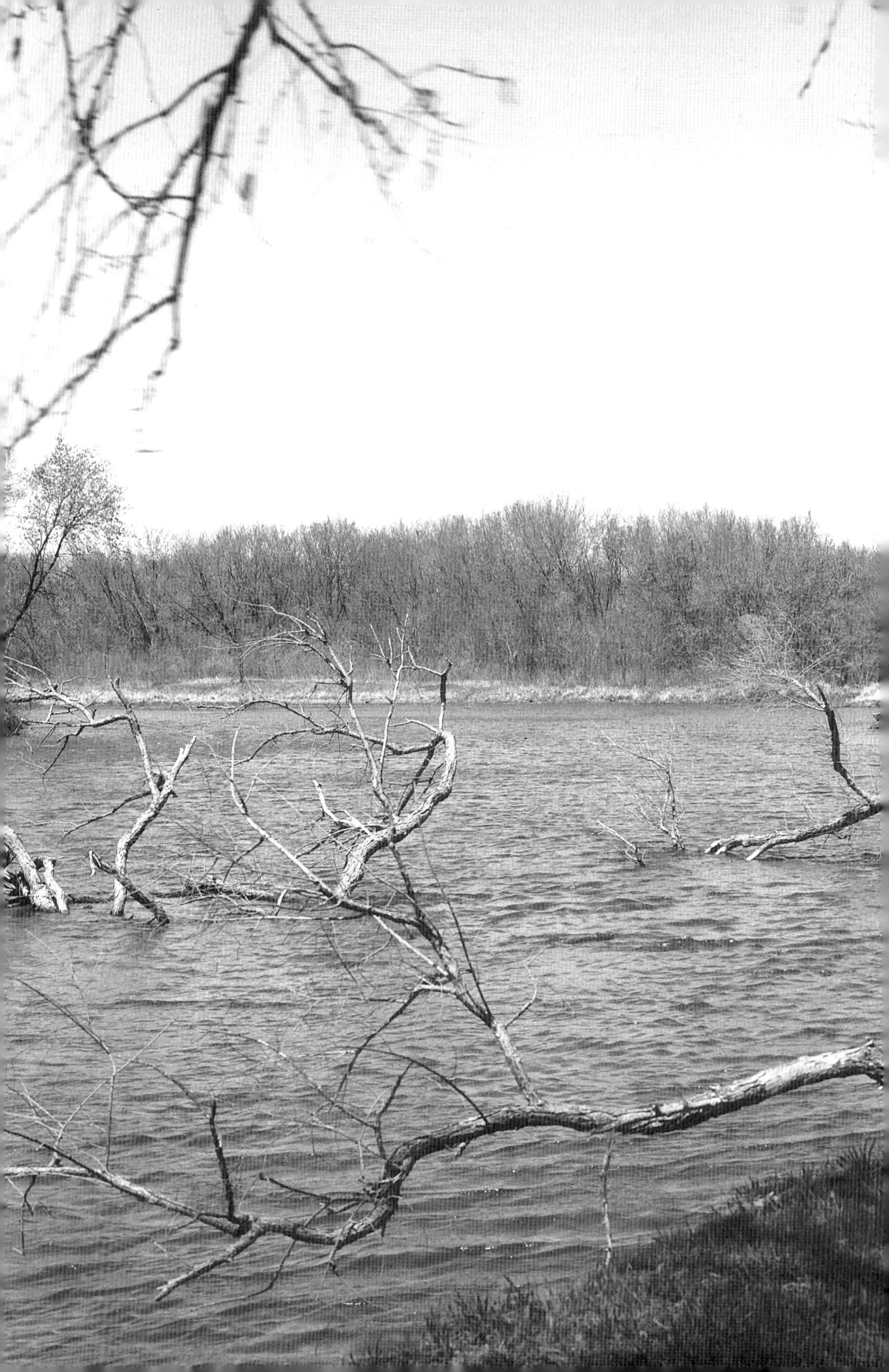

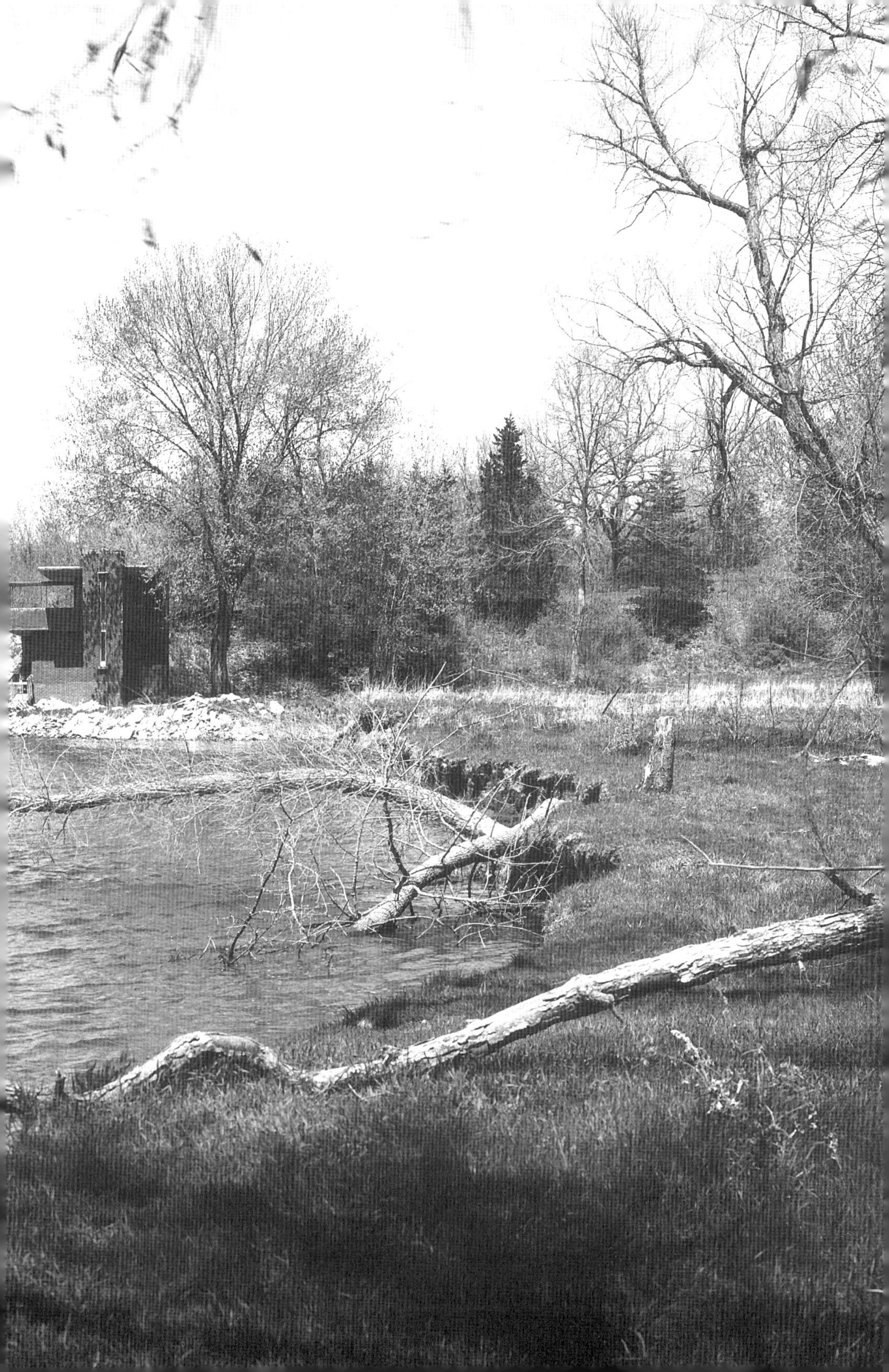

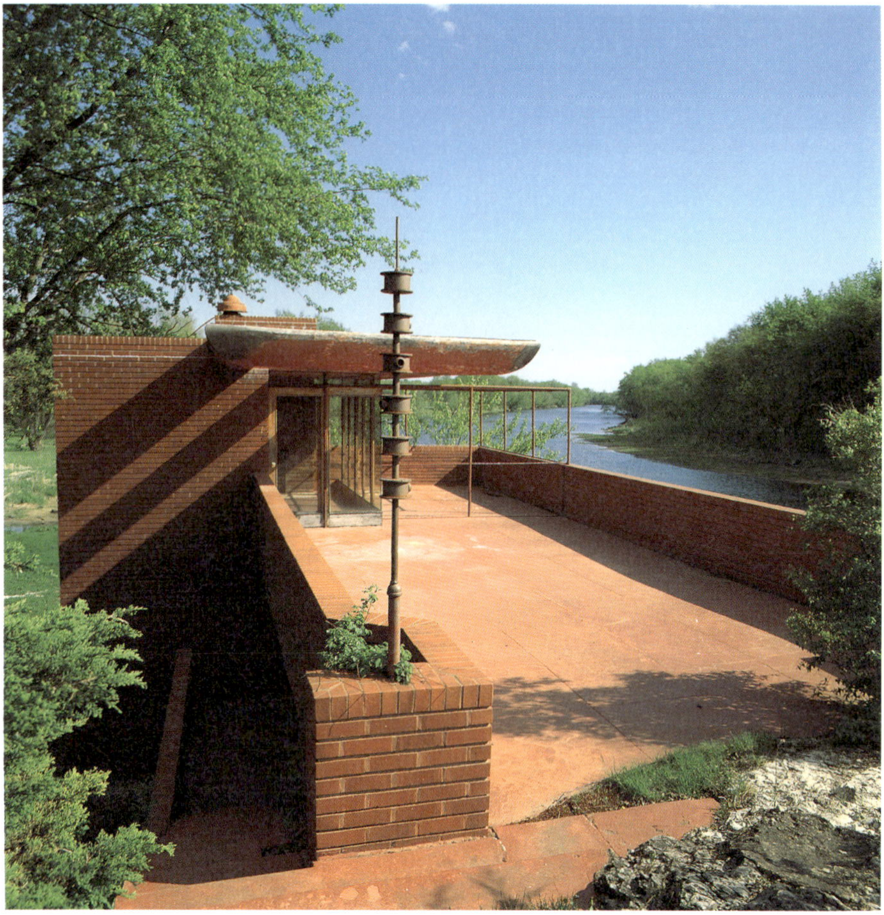

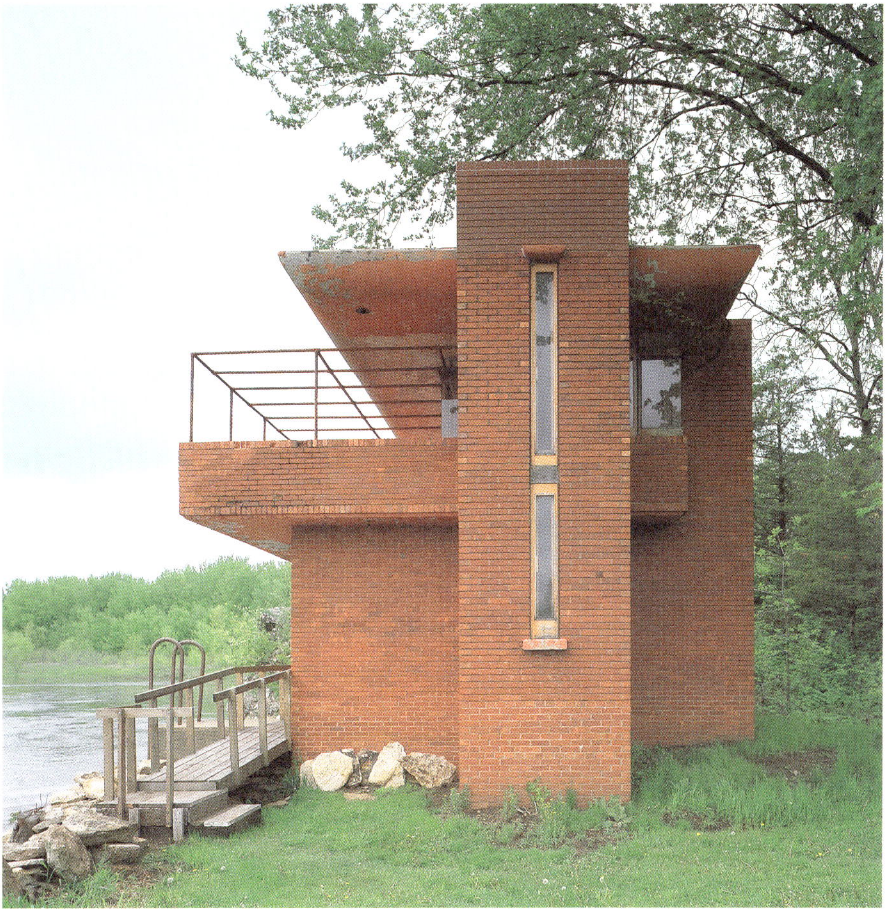

Herman T. Mossberg House
South Bend, Indiana, 1946

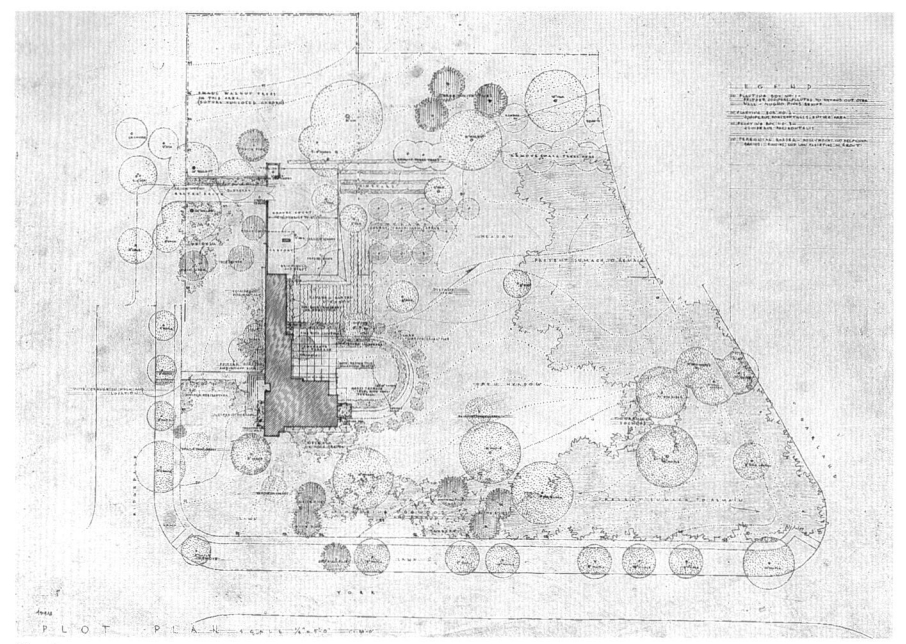

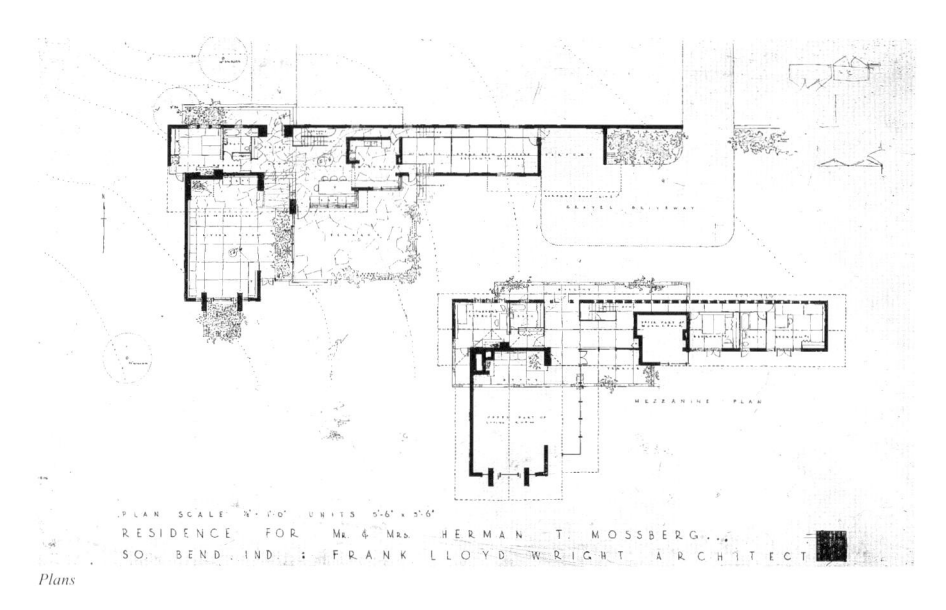

Site plan

Plans

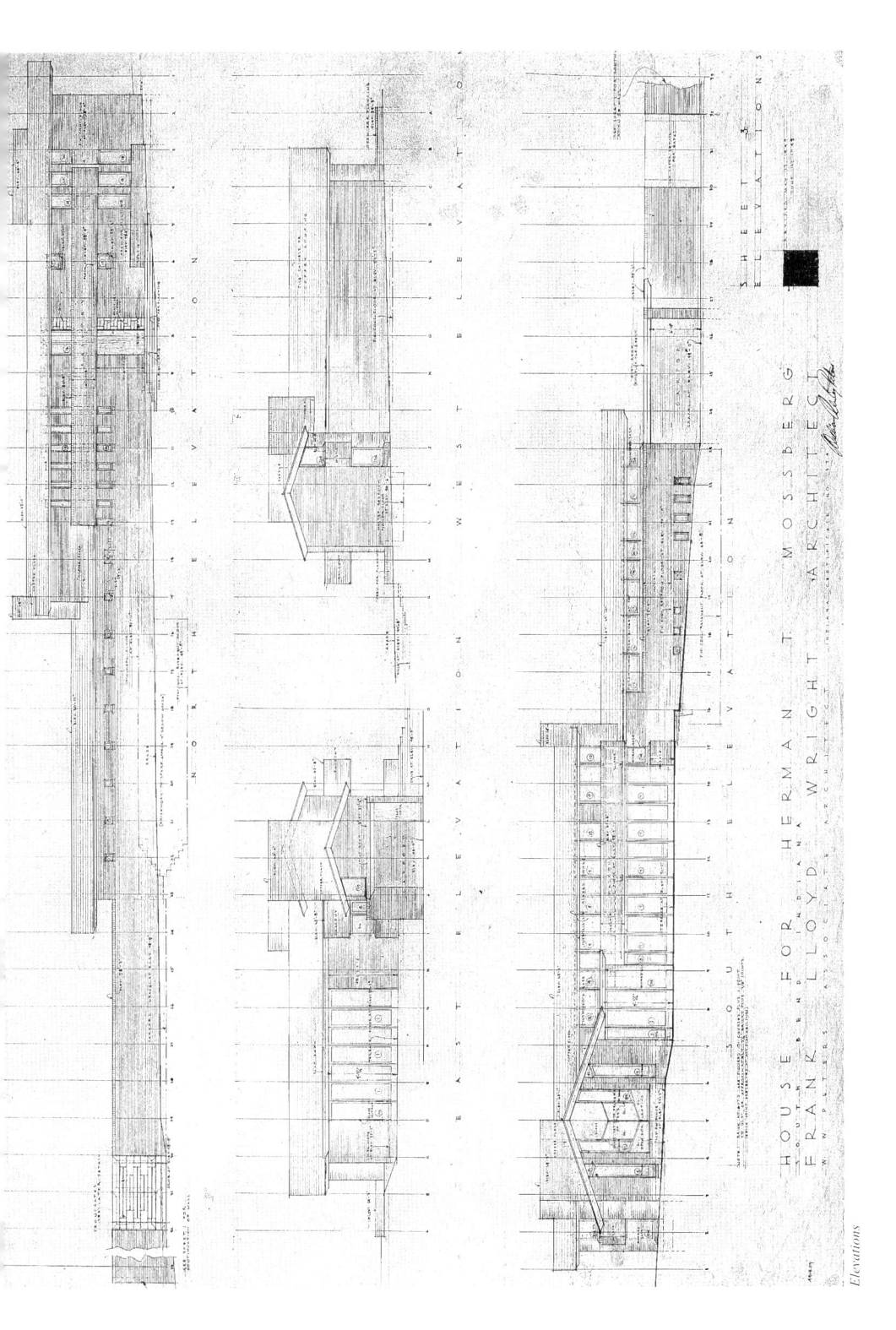

Elevations

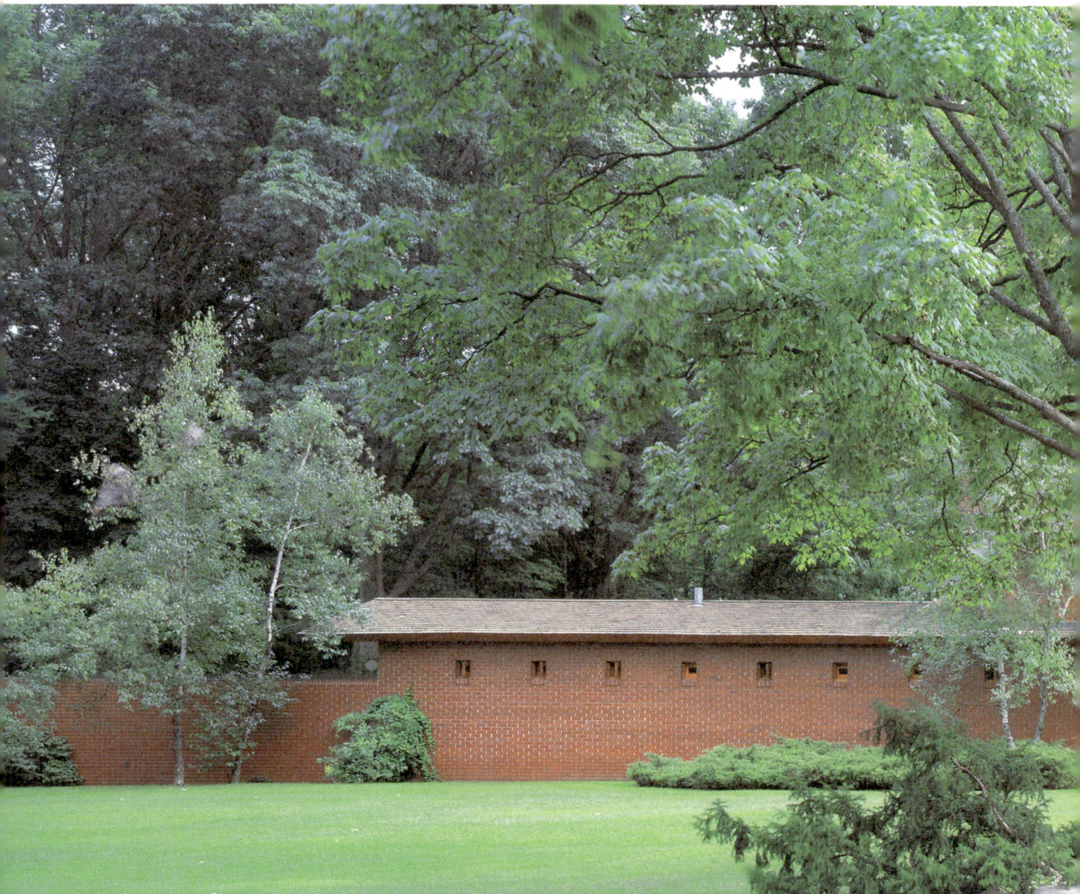

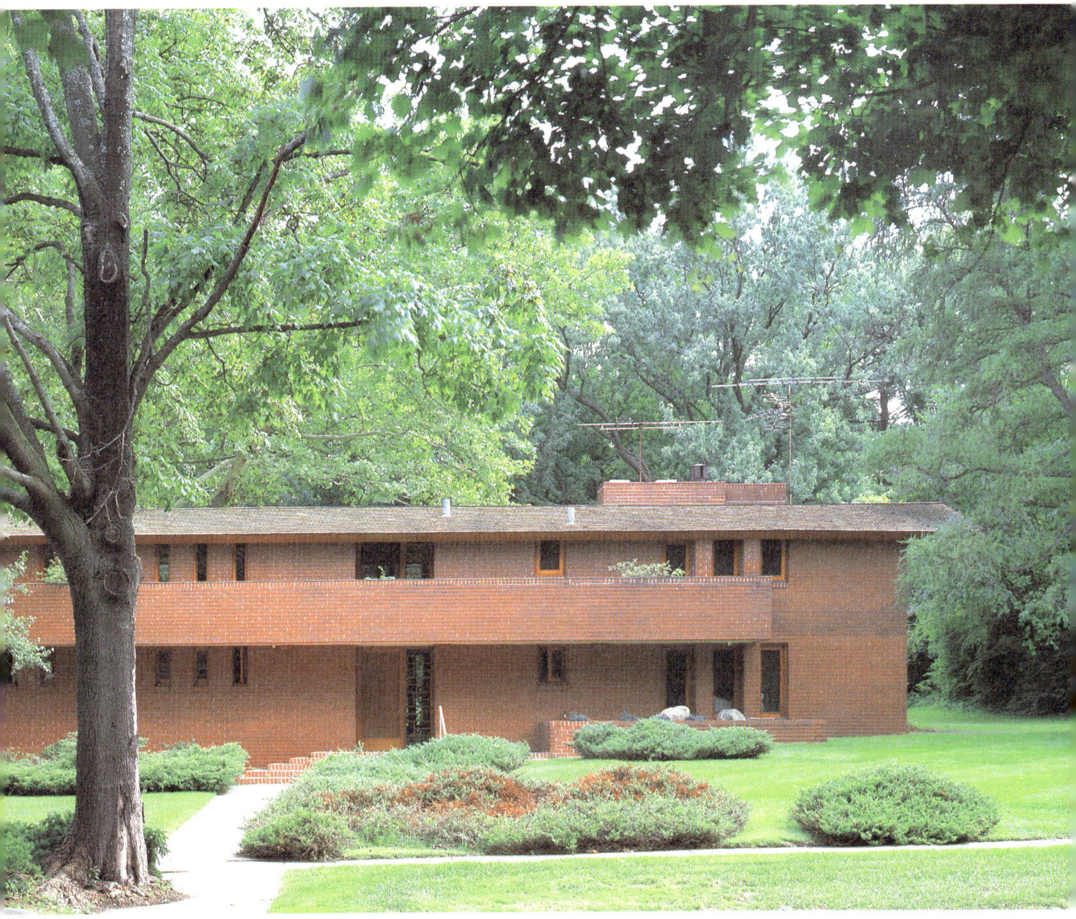

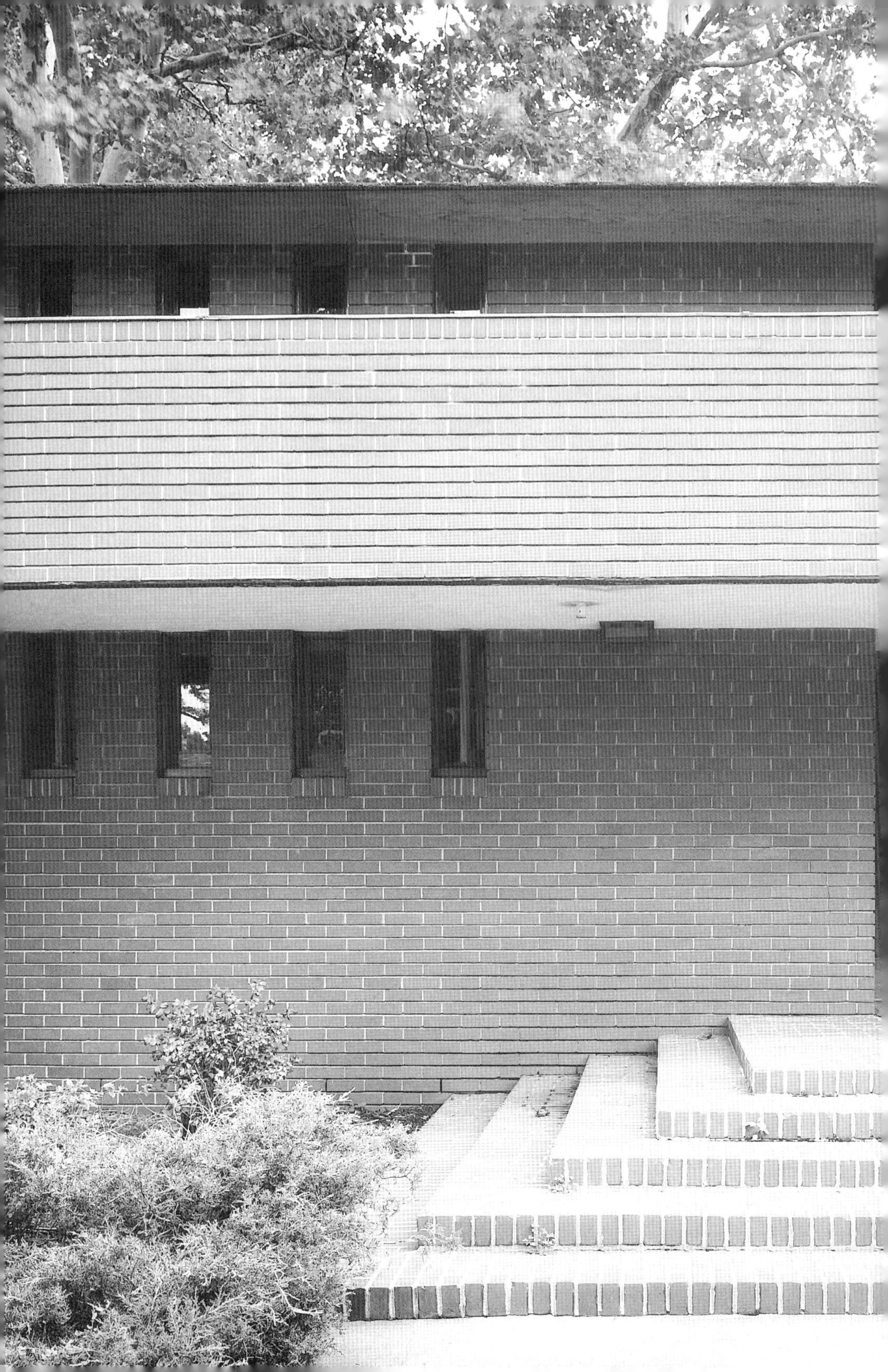

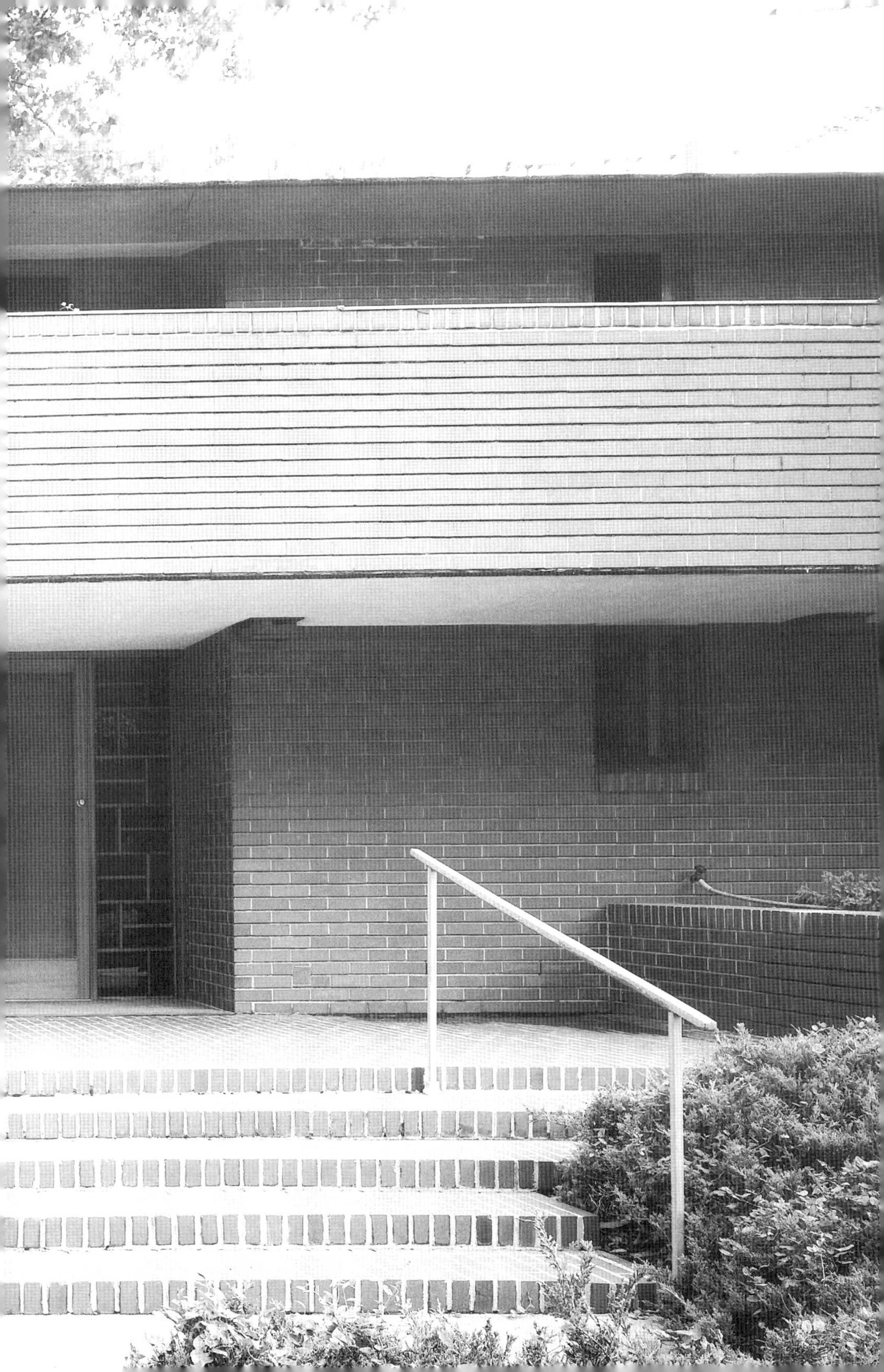

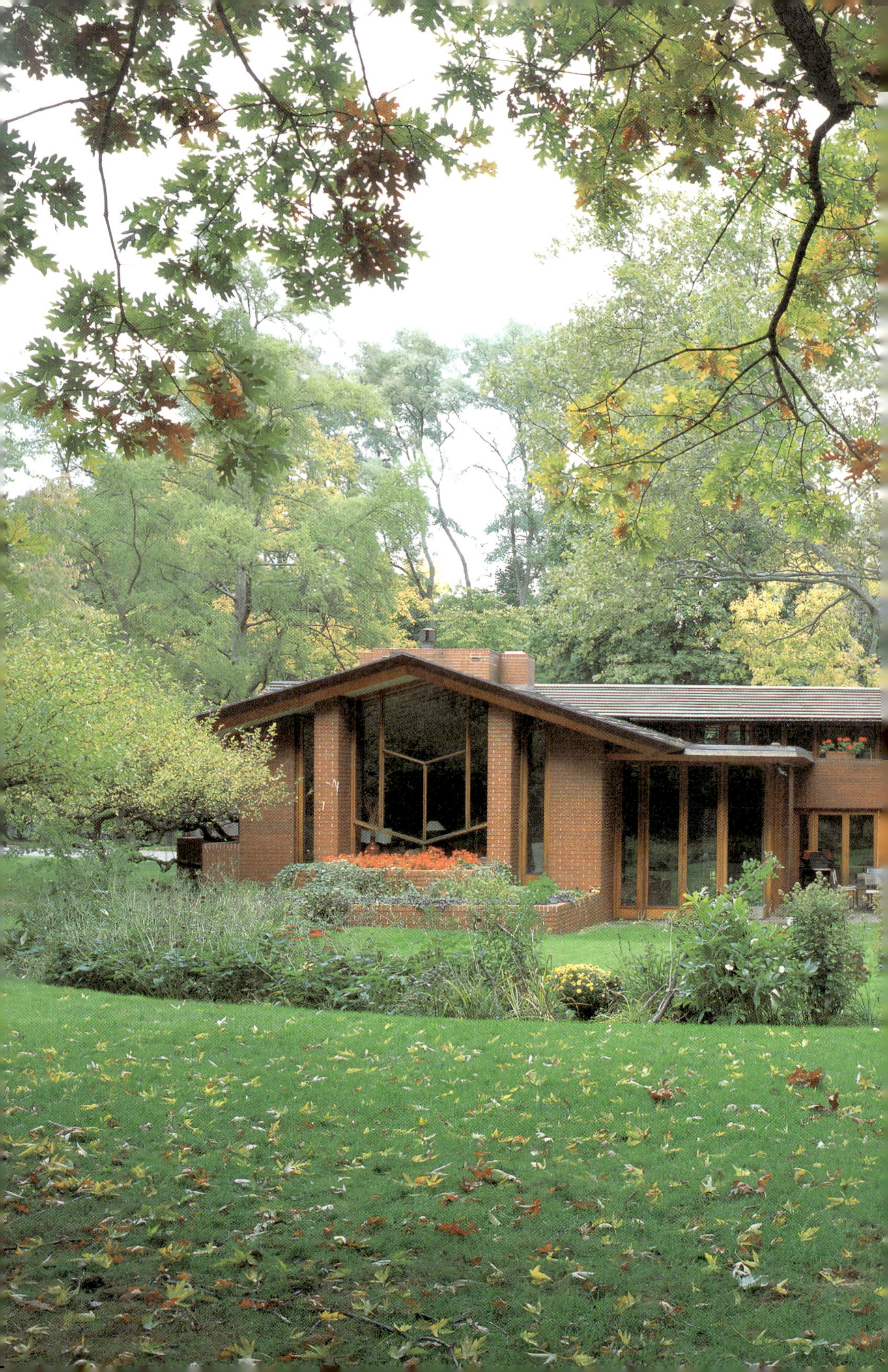

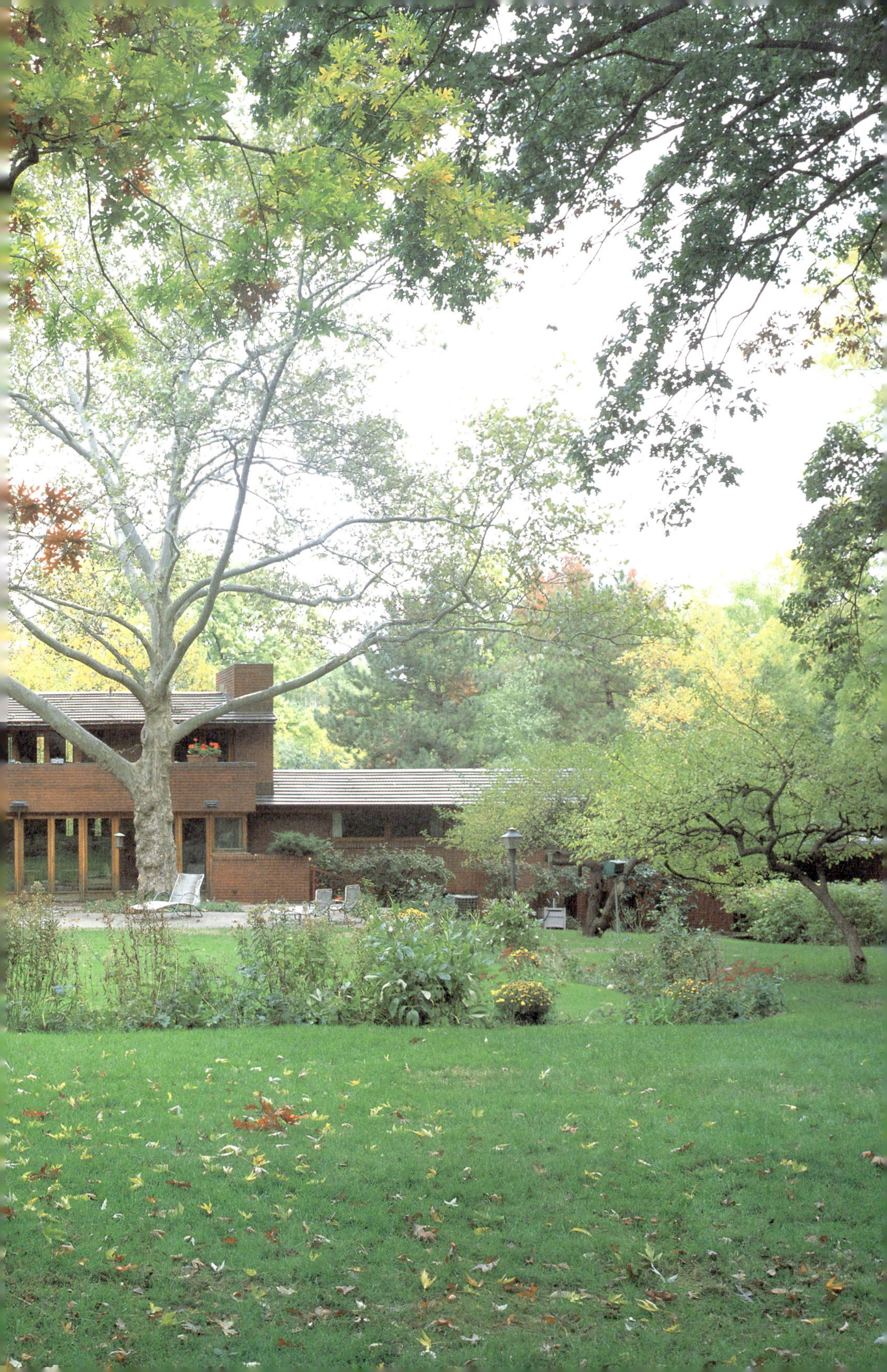

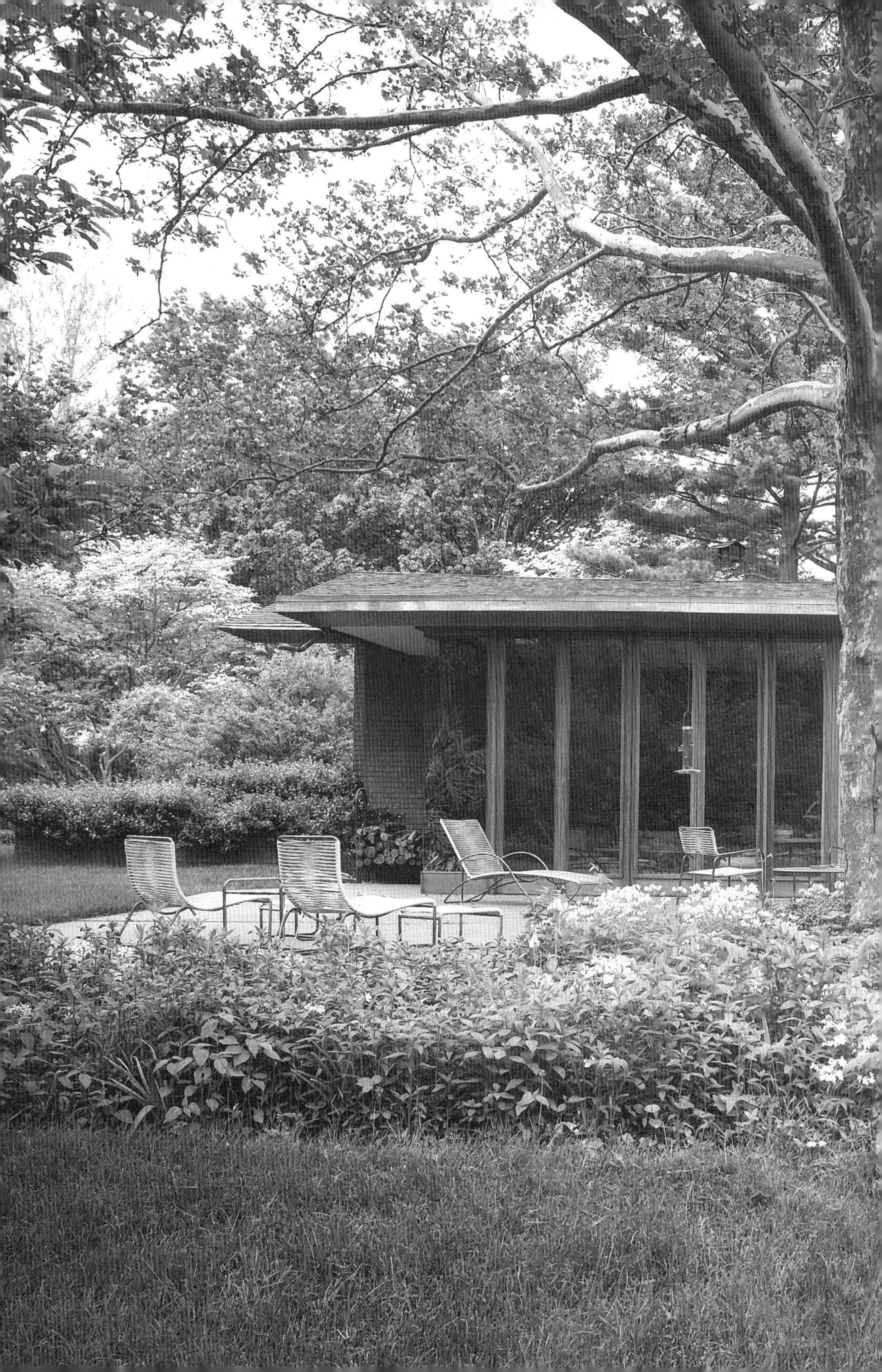

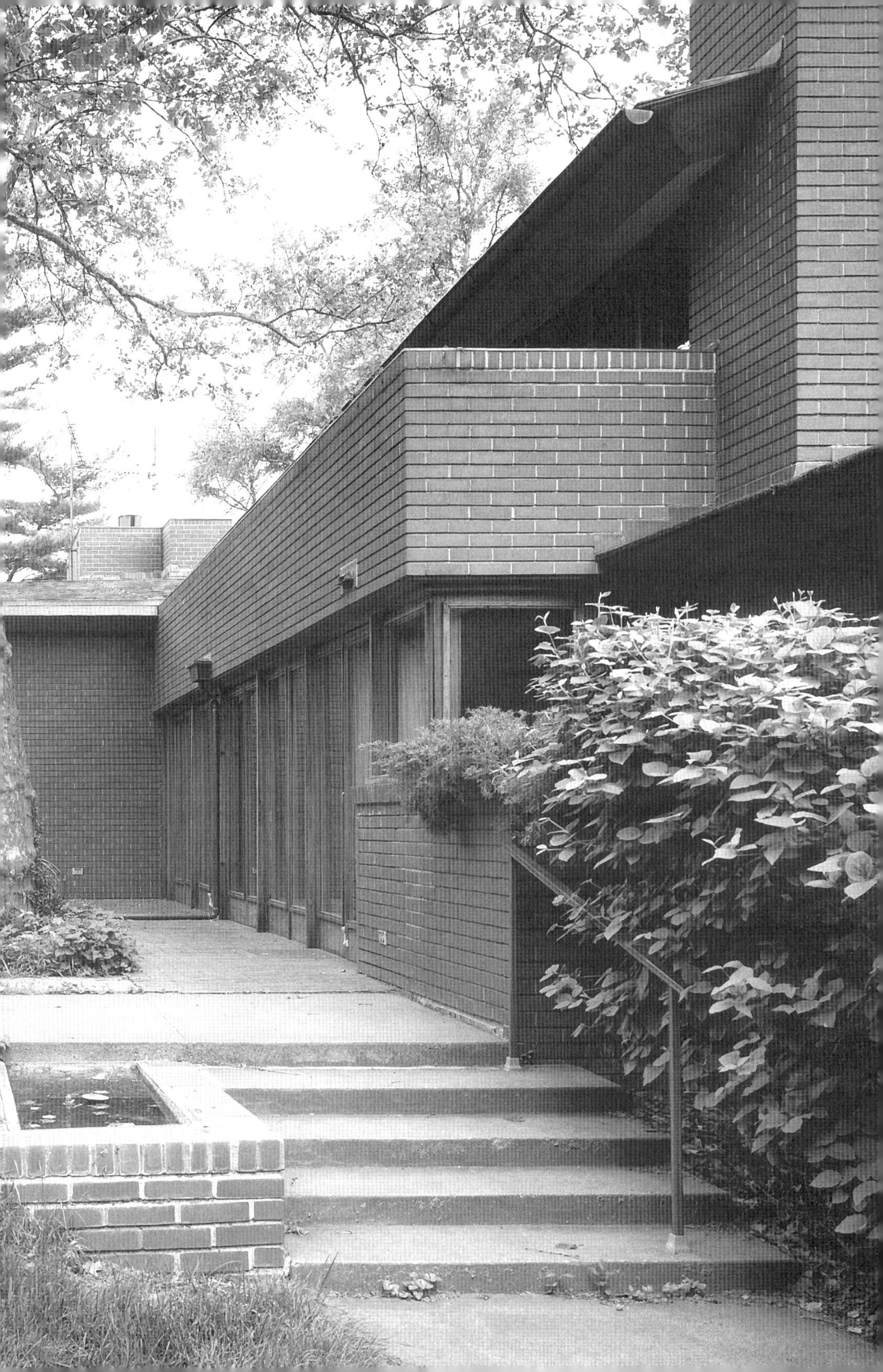

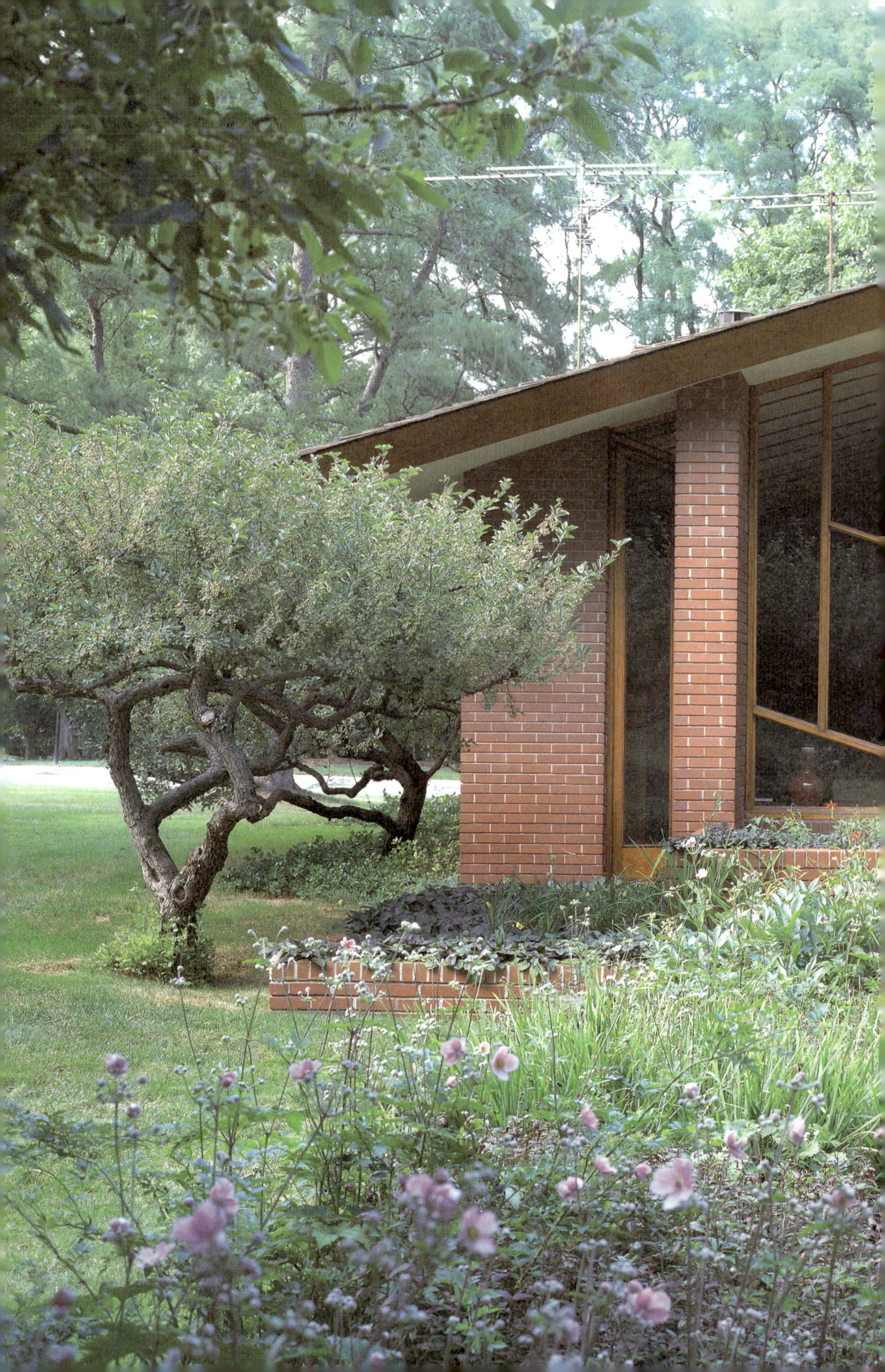

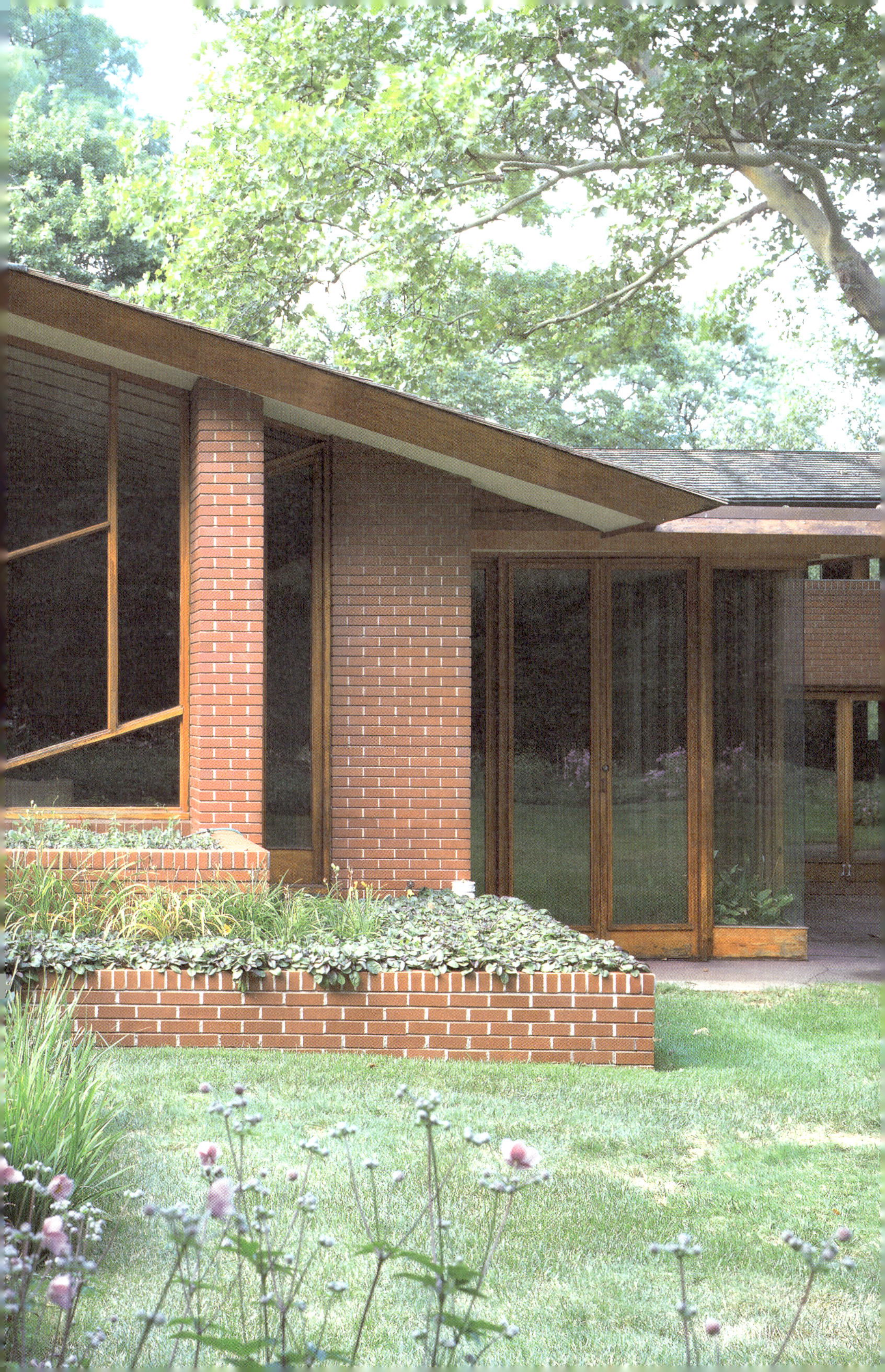

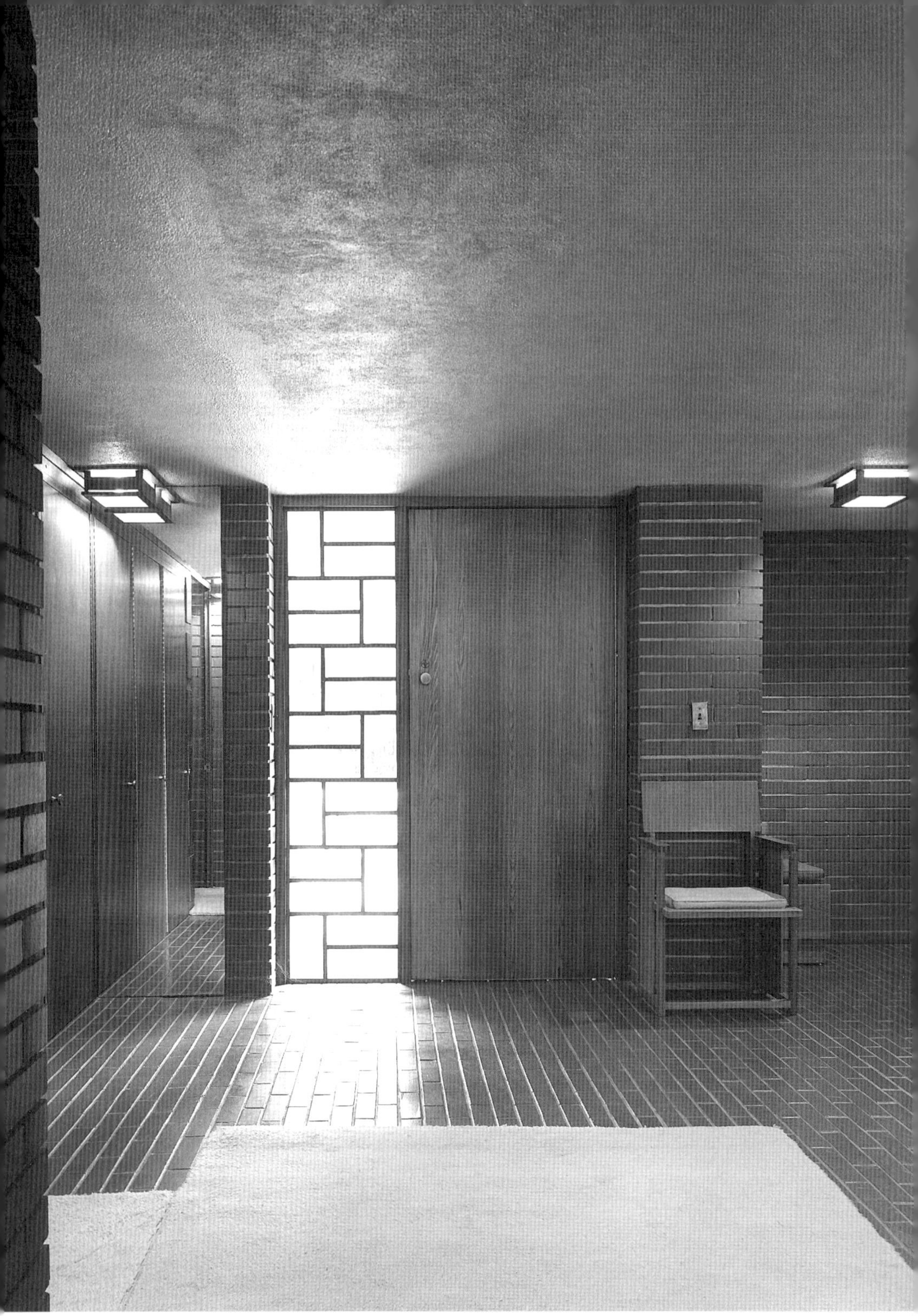

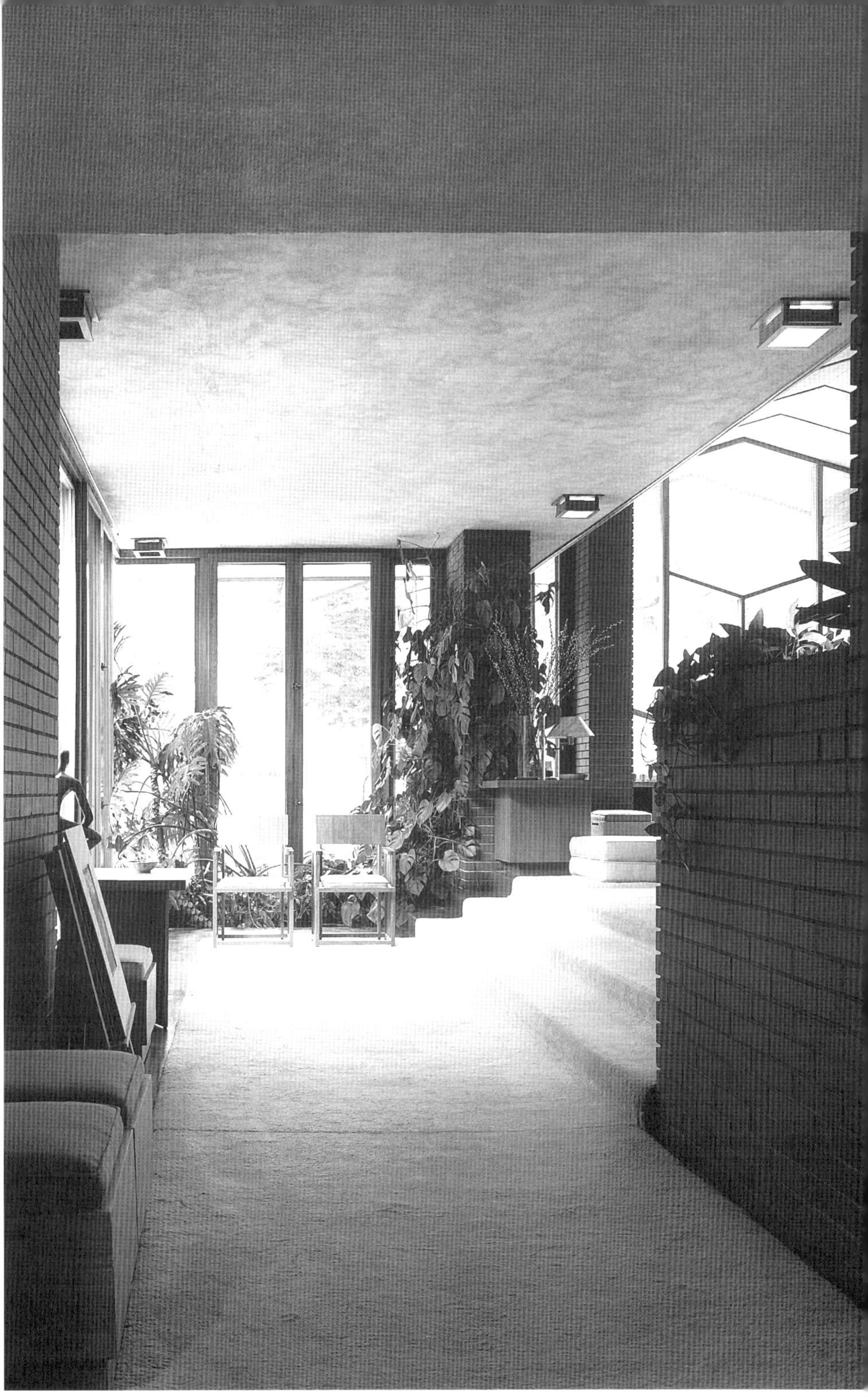

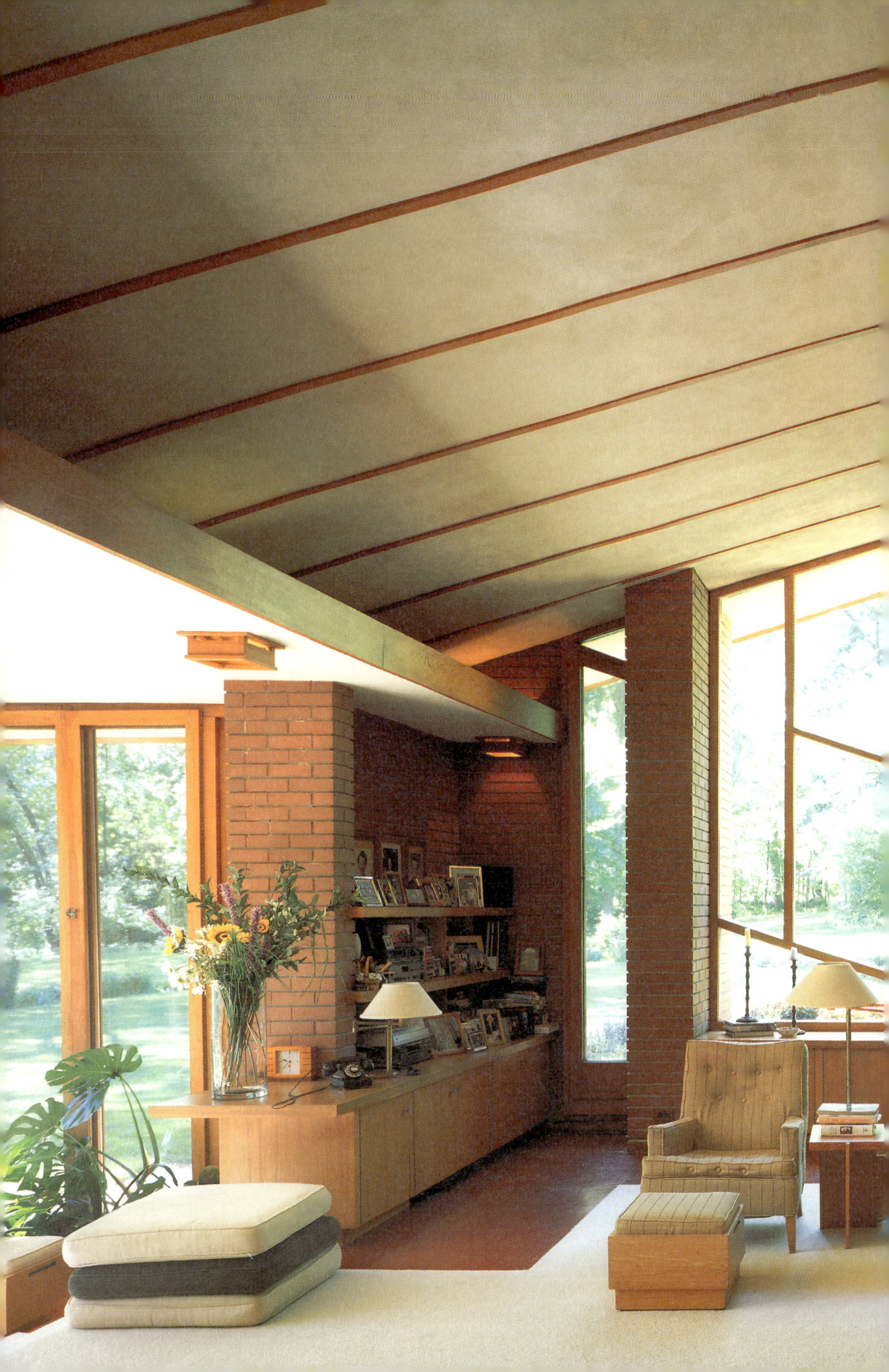

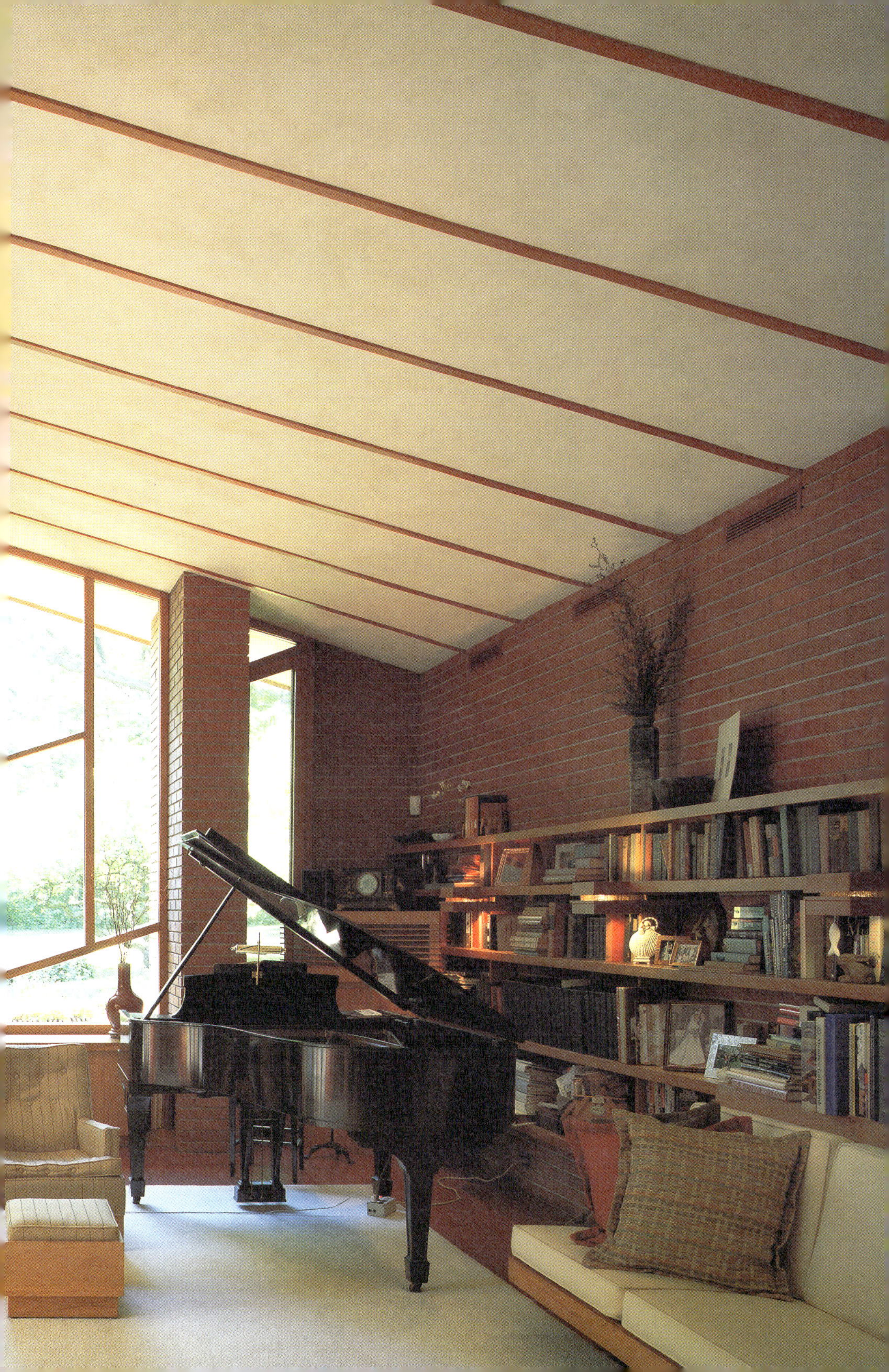

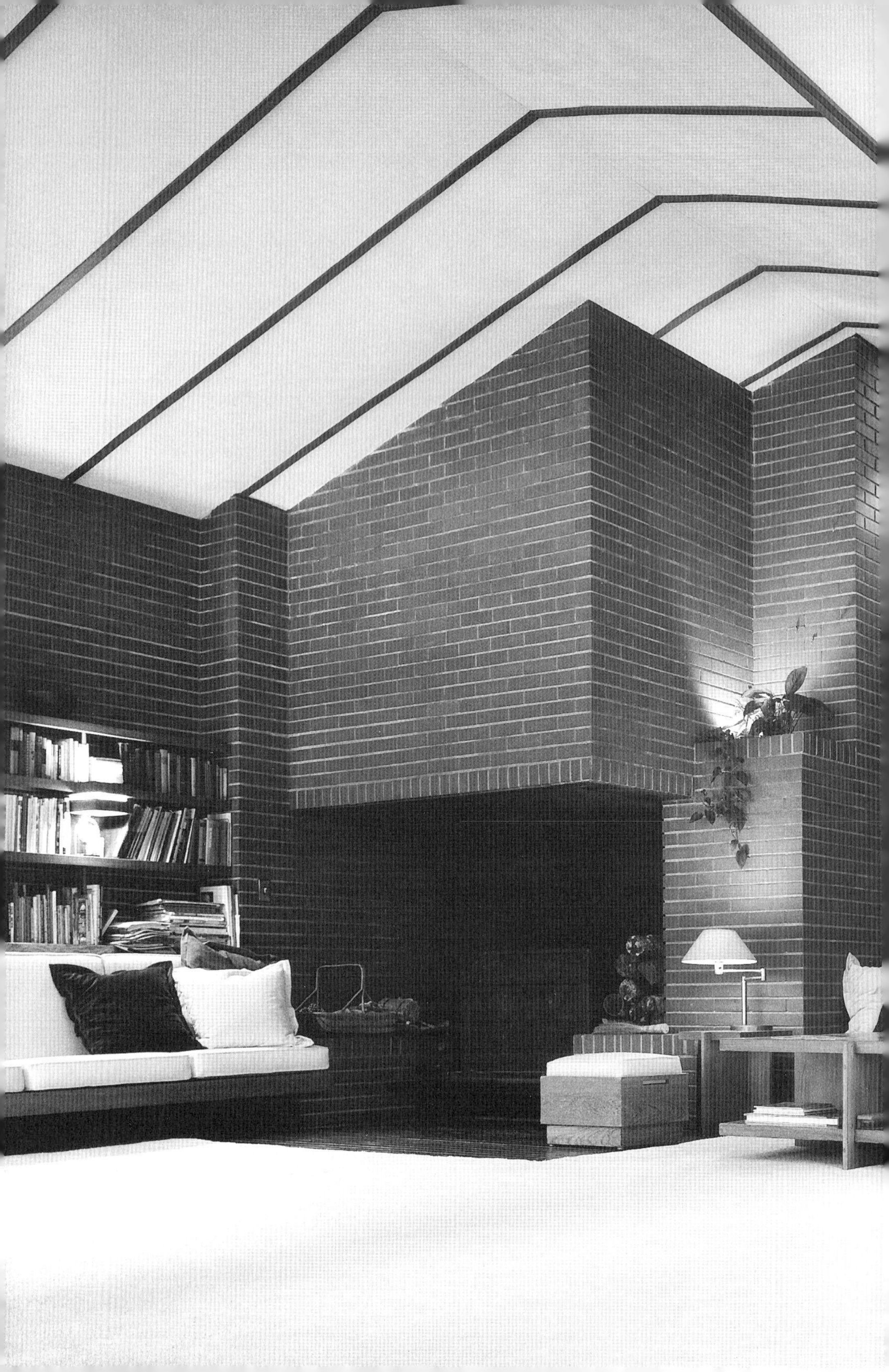

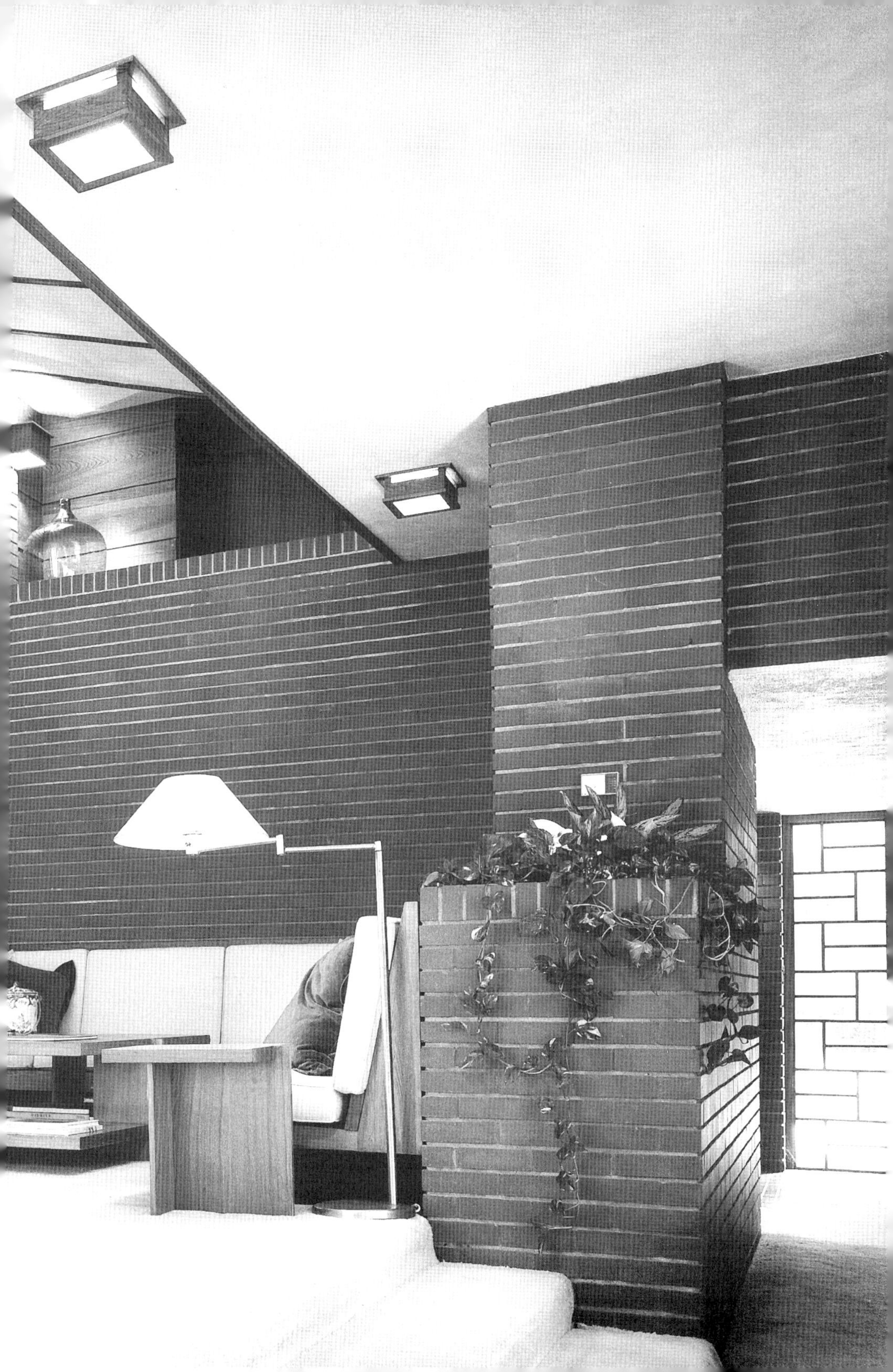

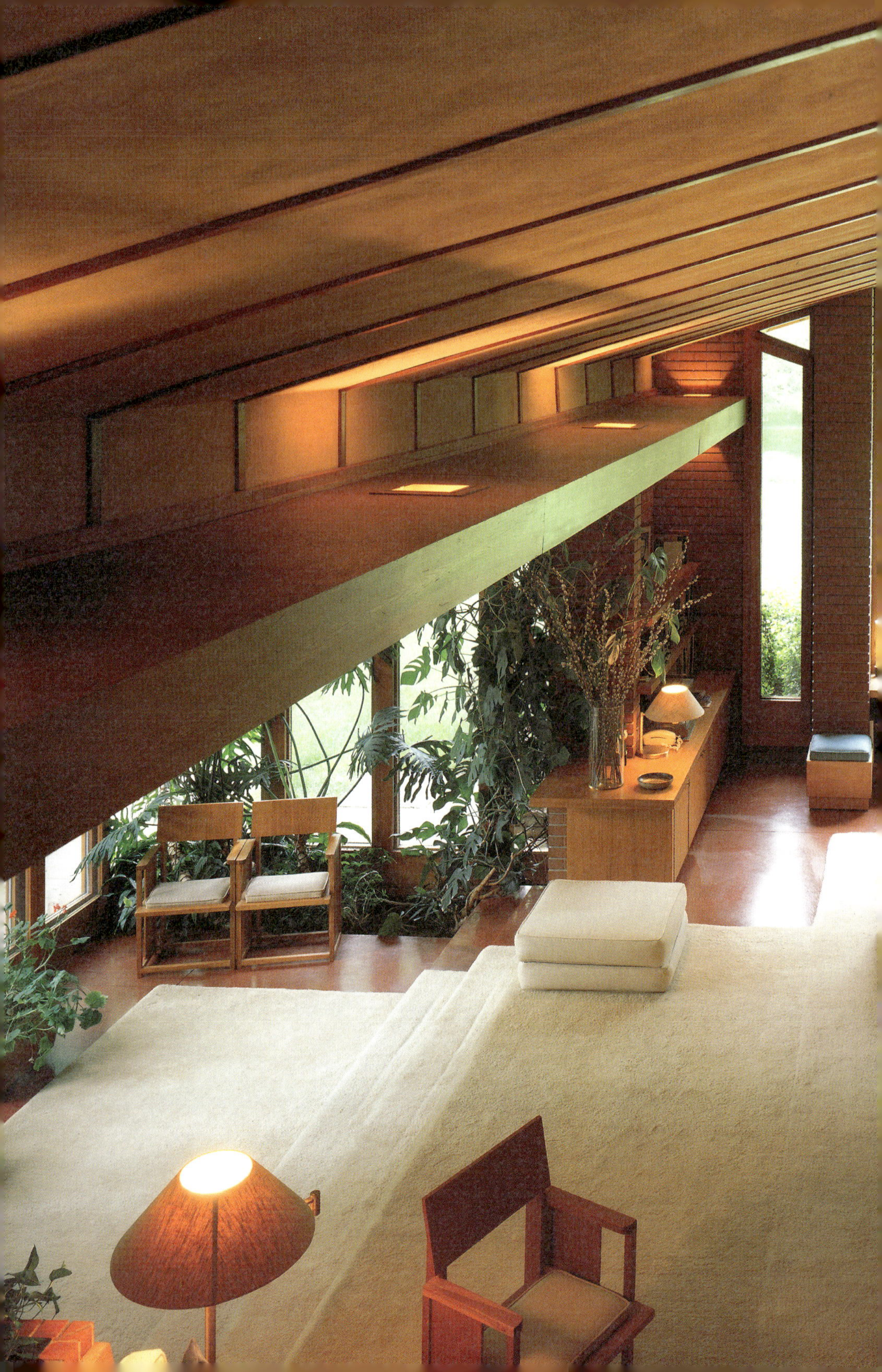

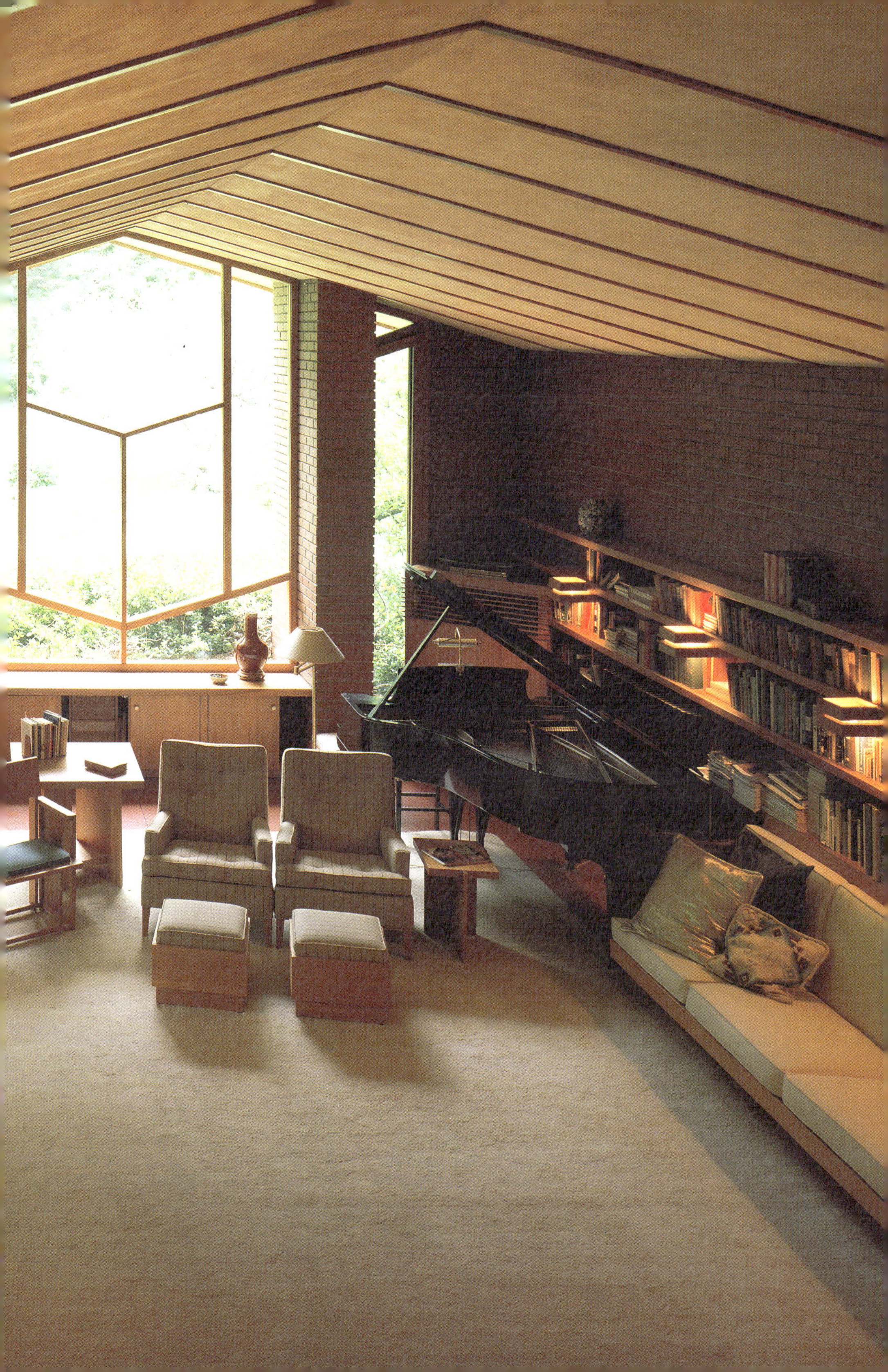

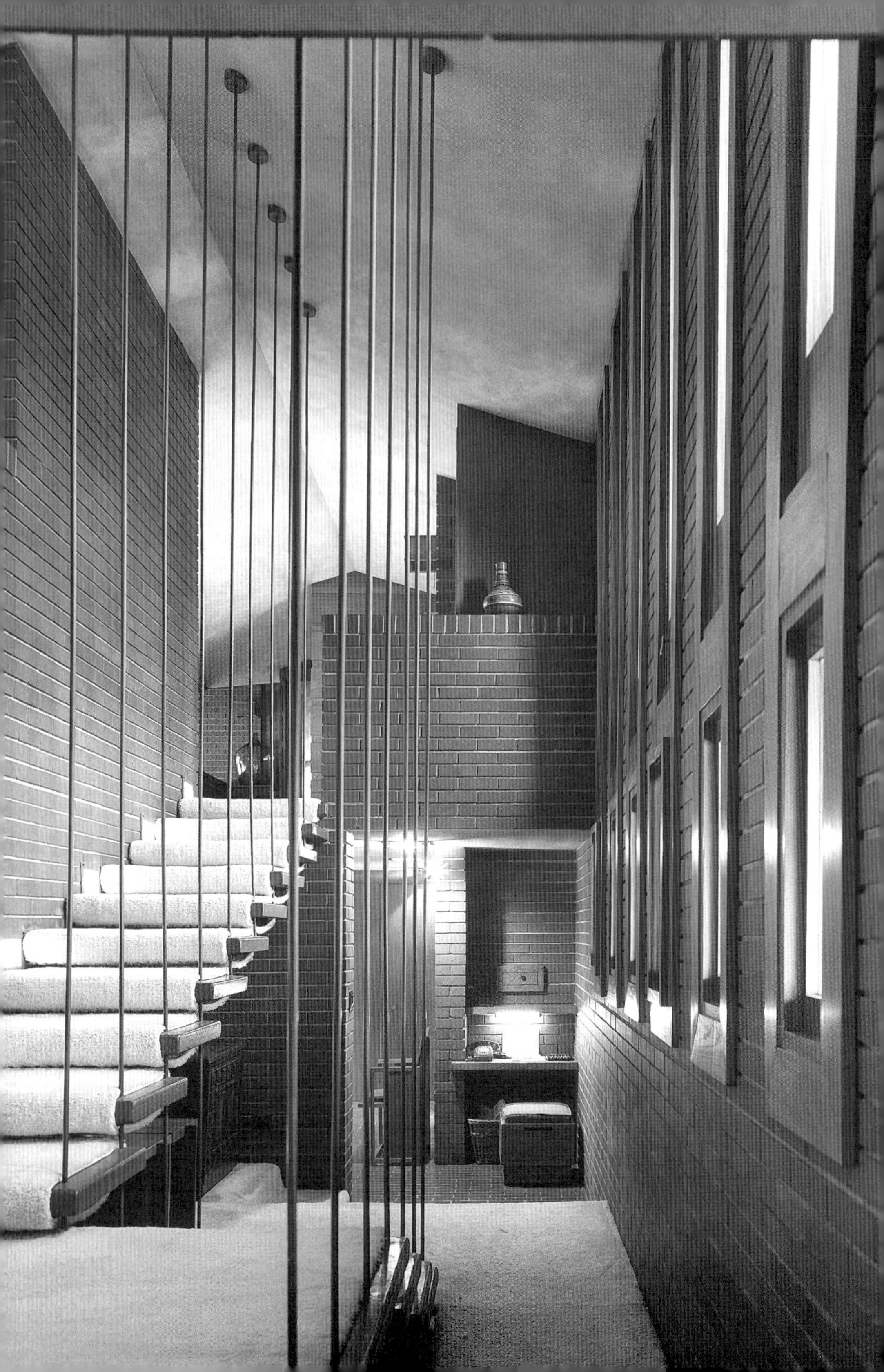

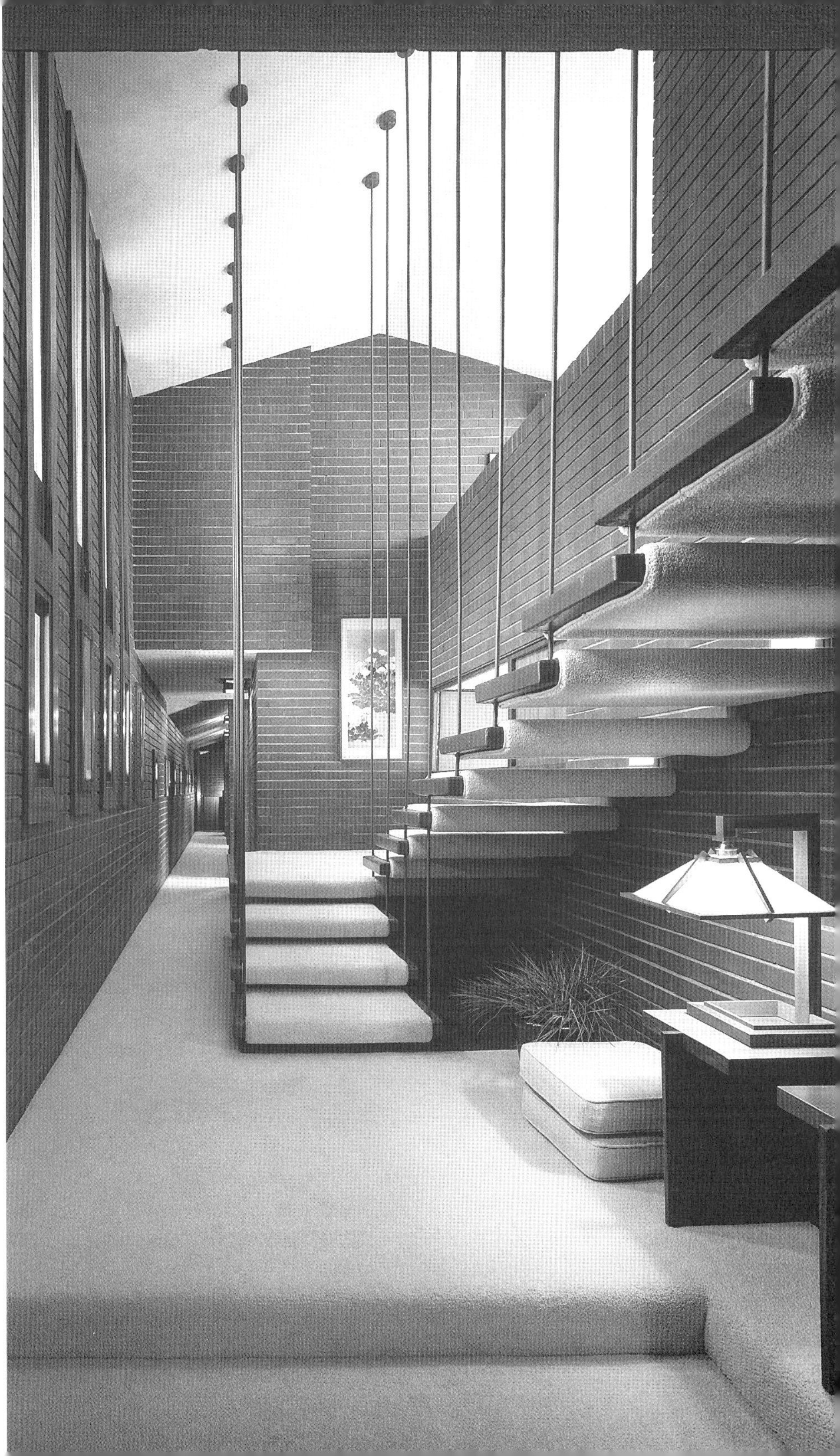

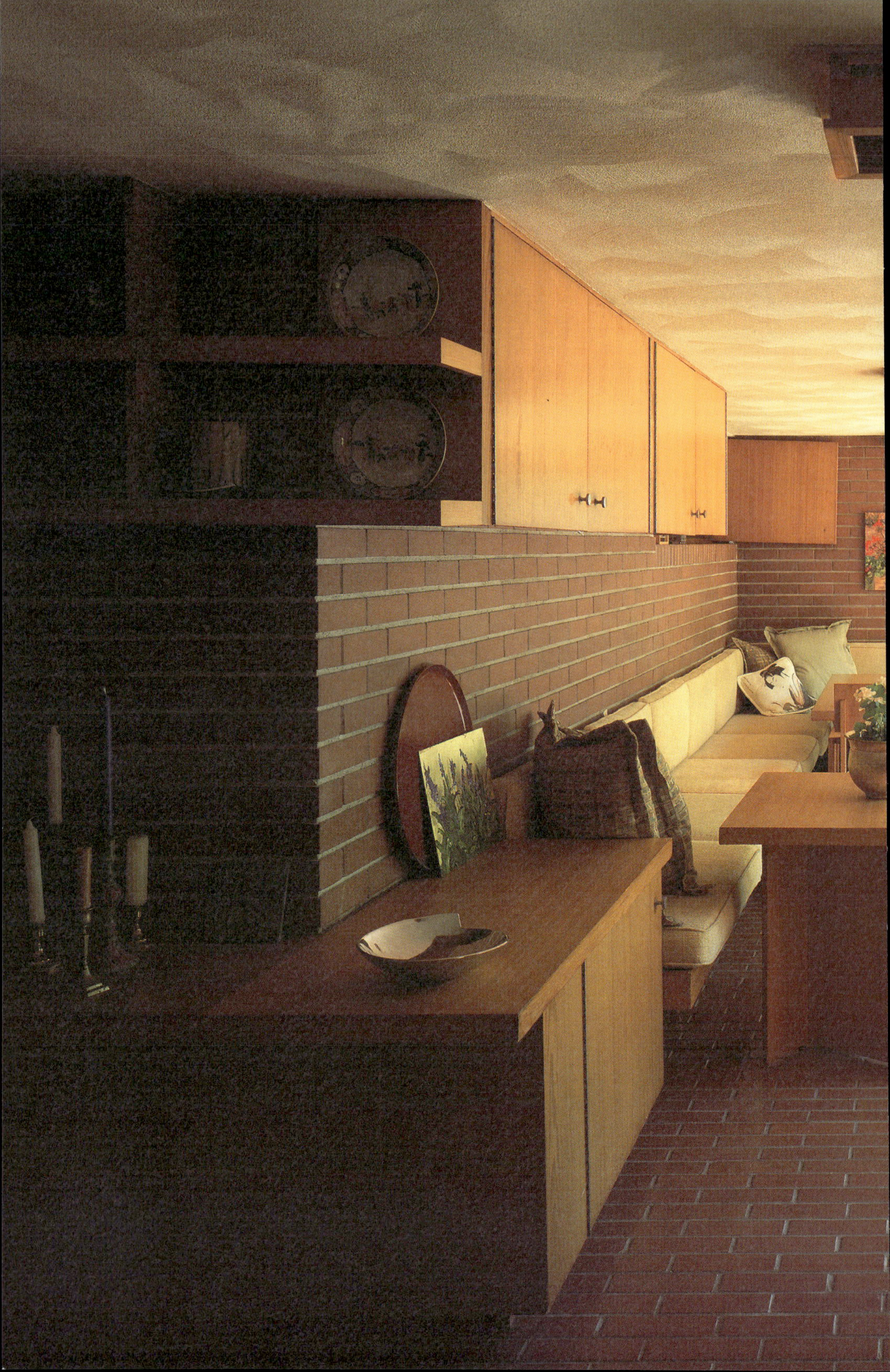

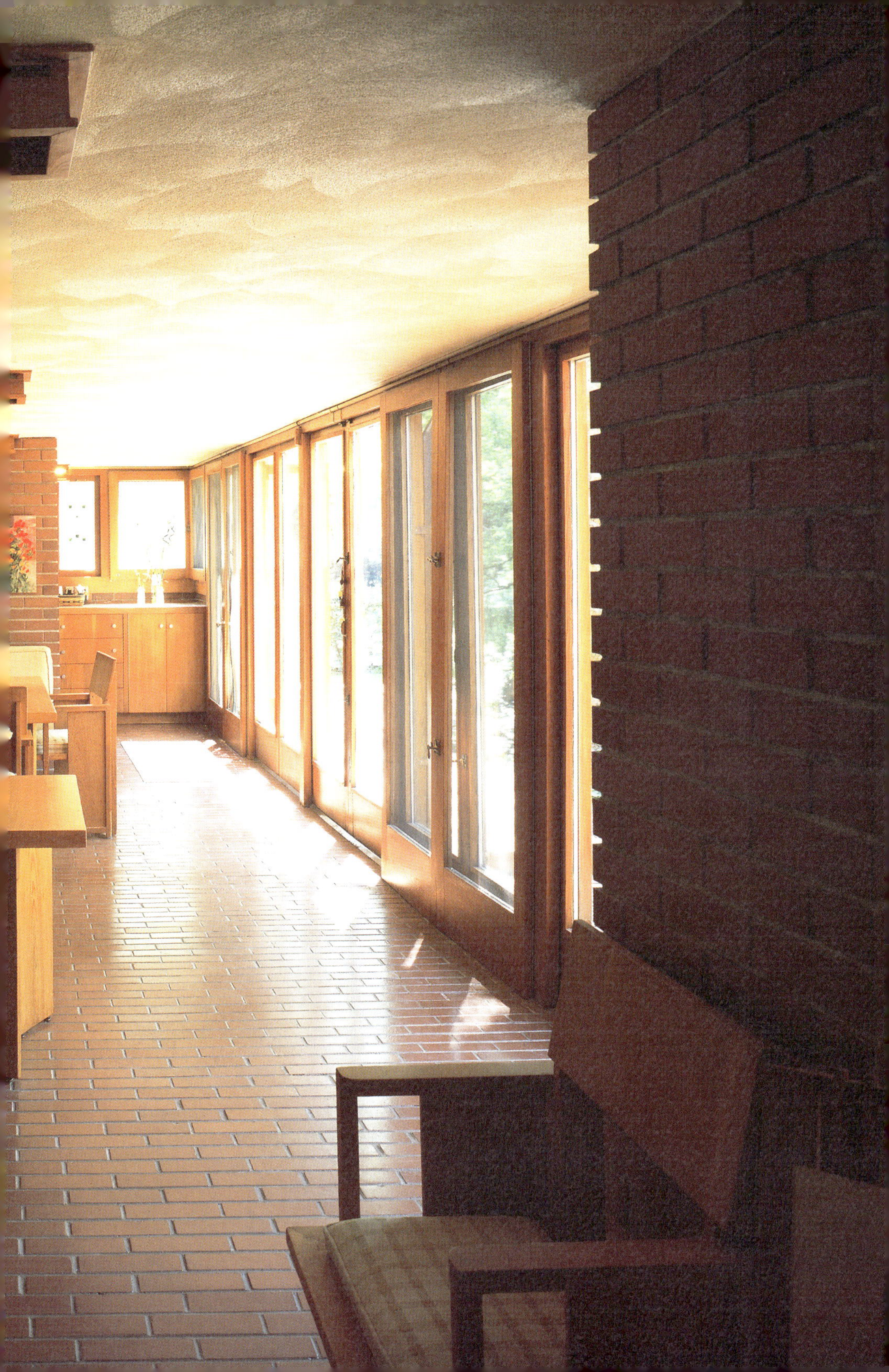

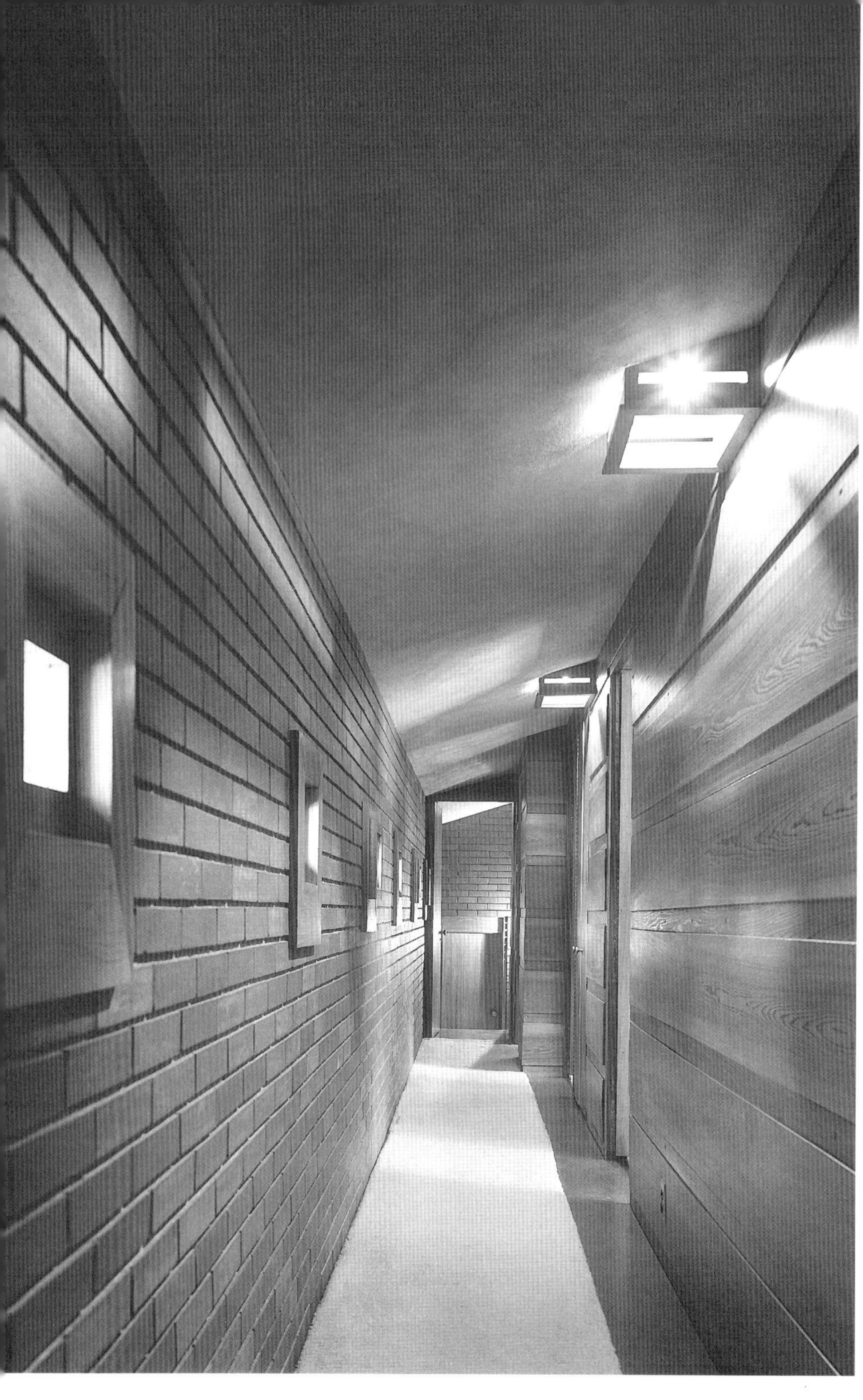

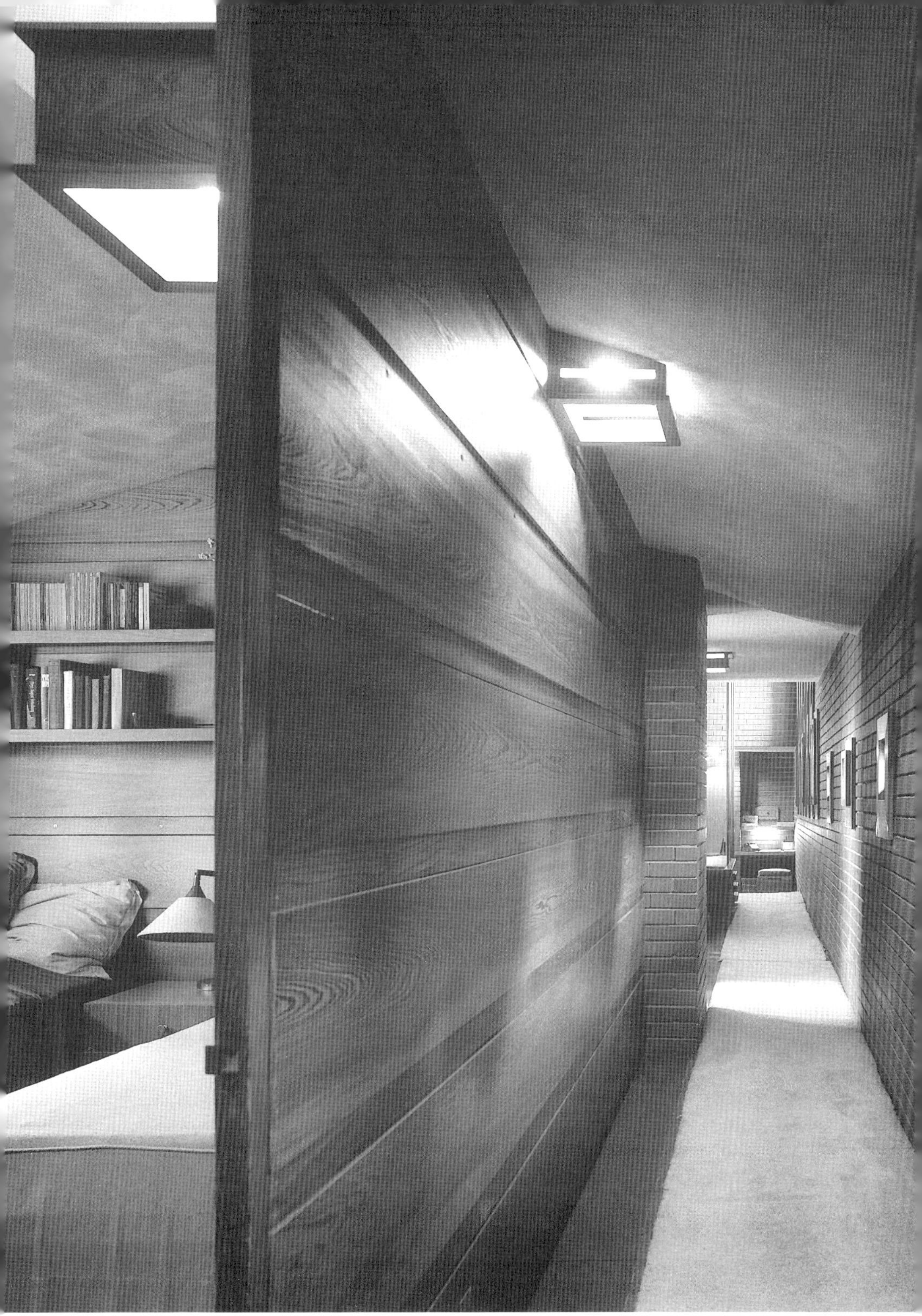

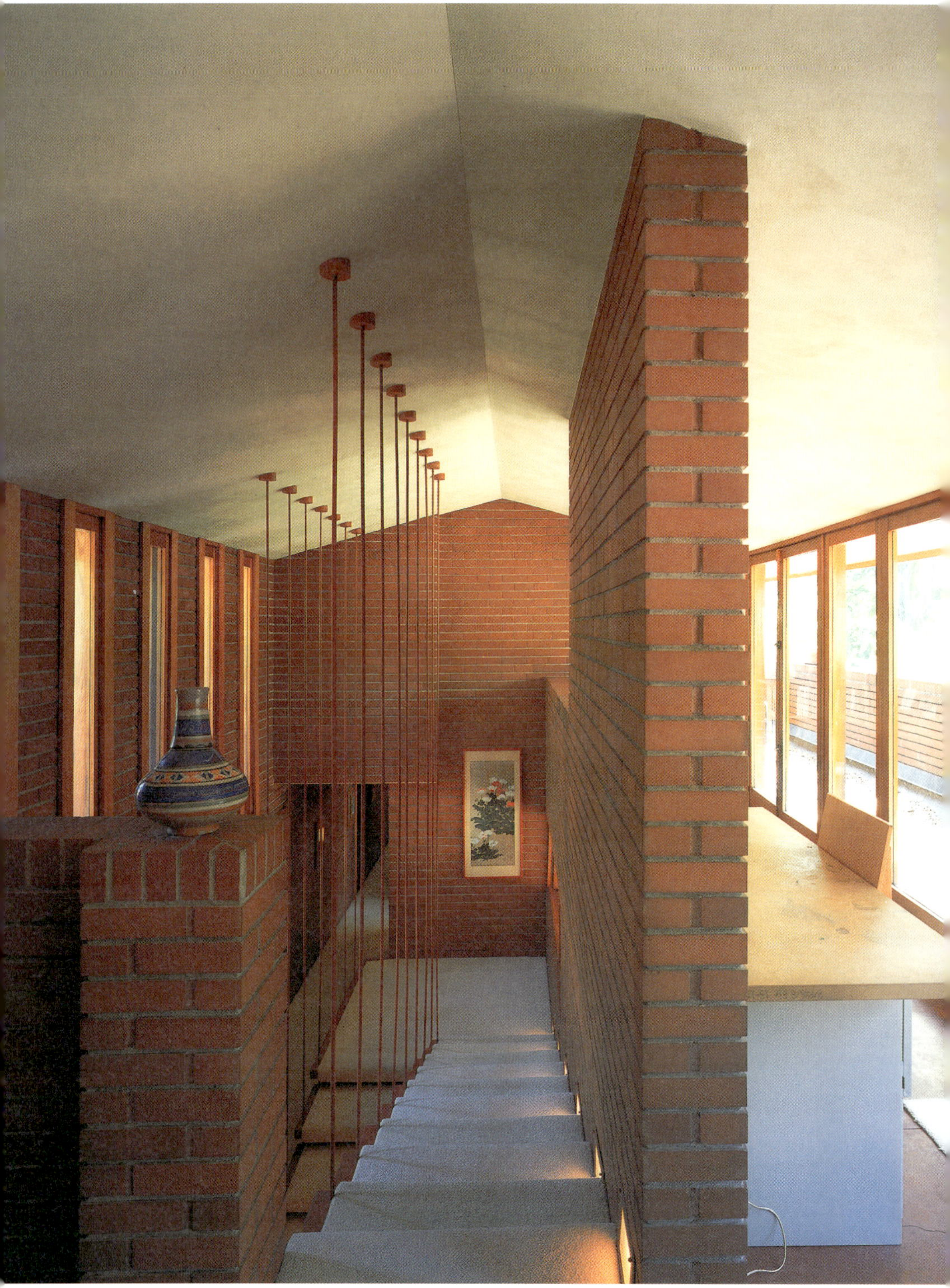

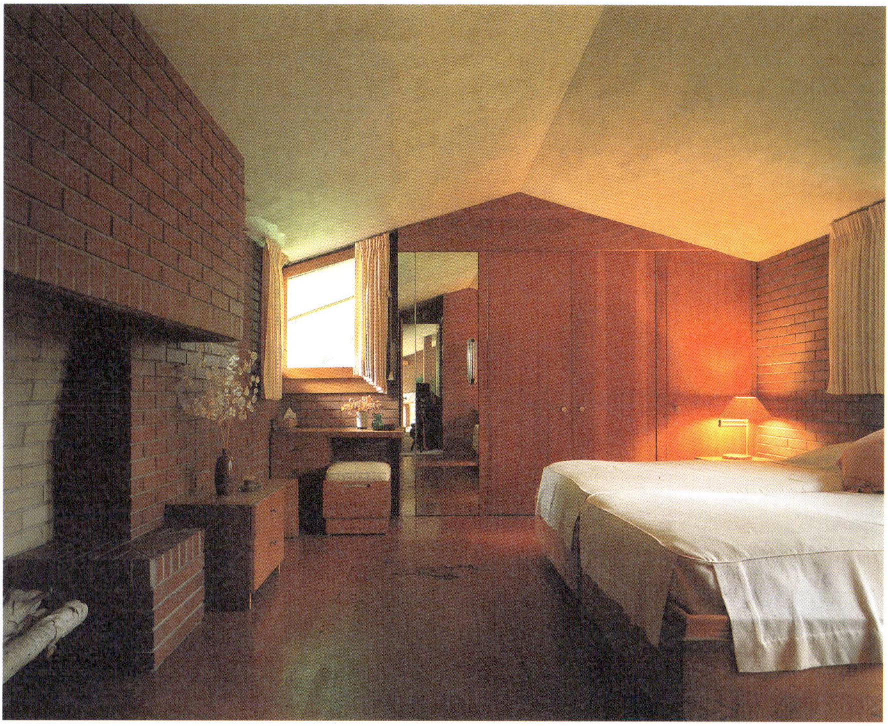

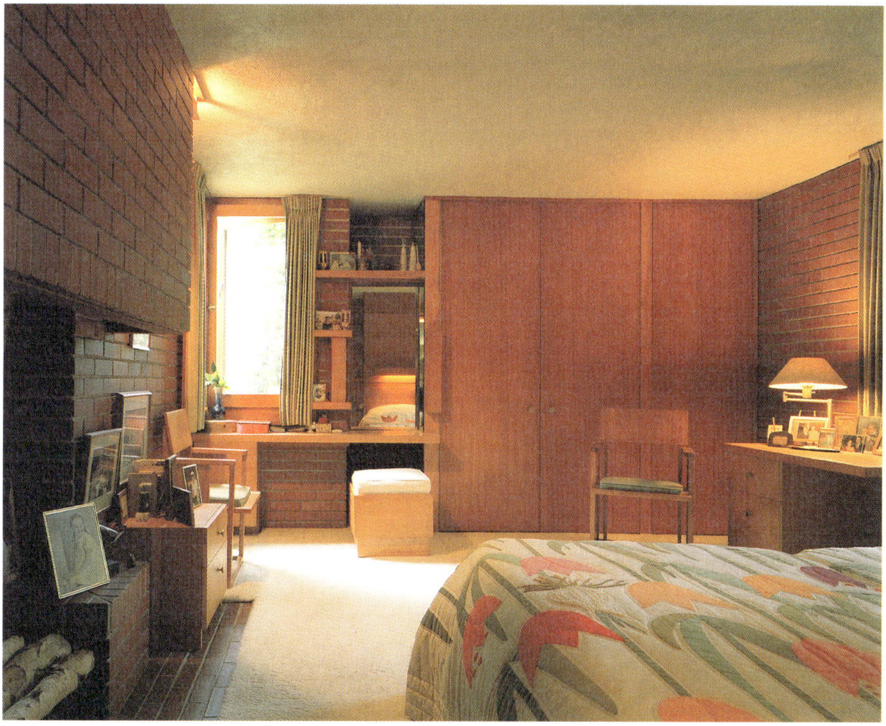

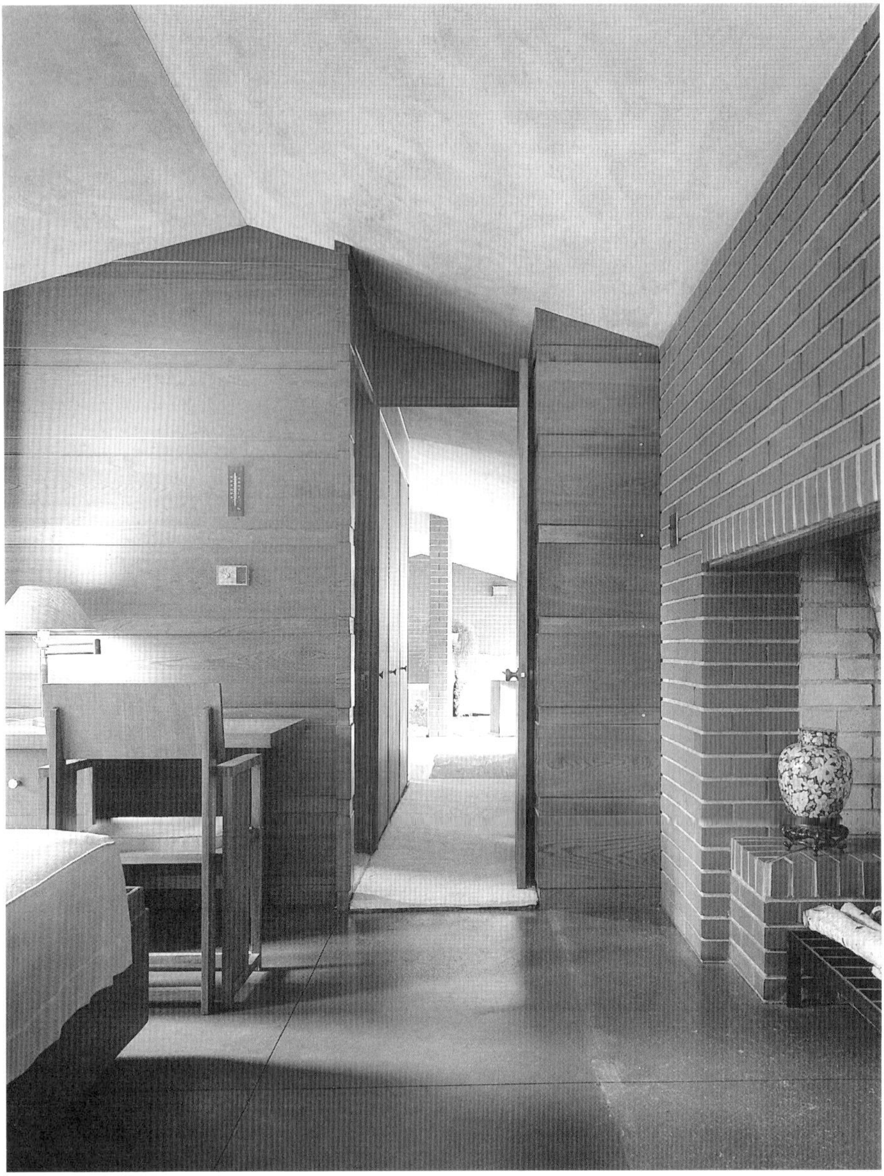

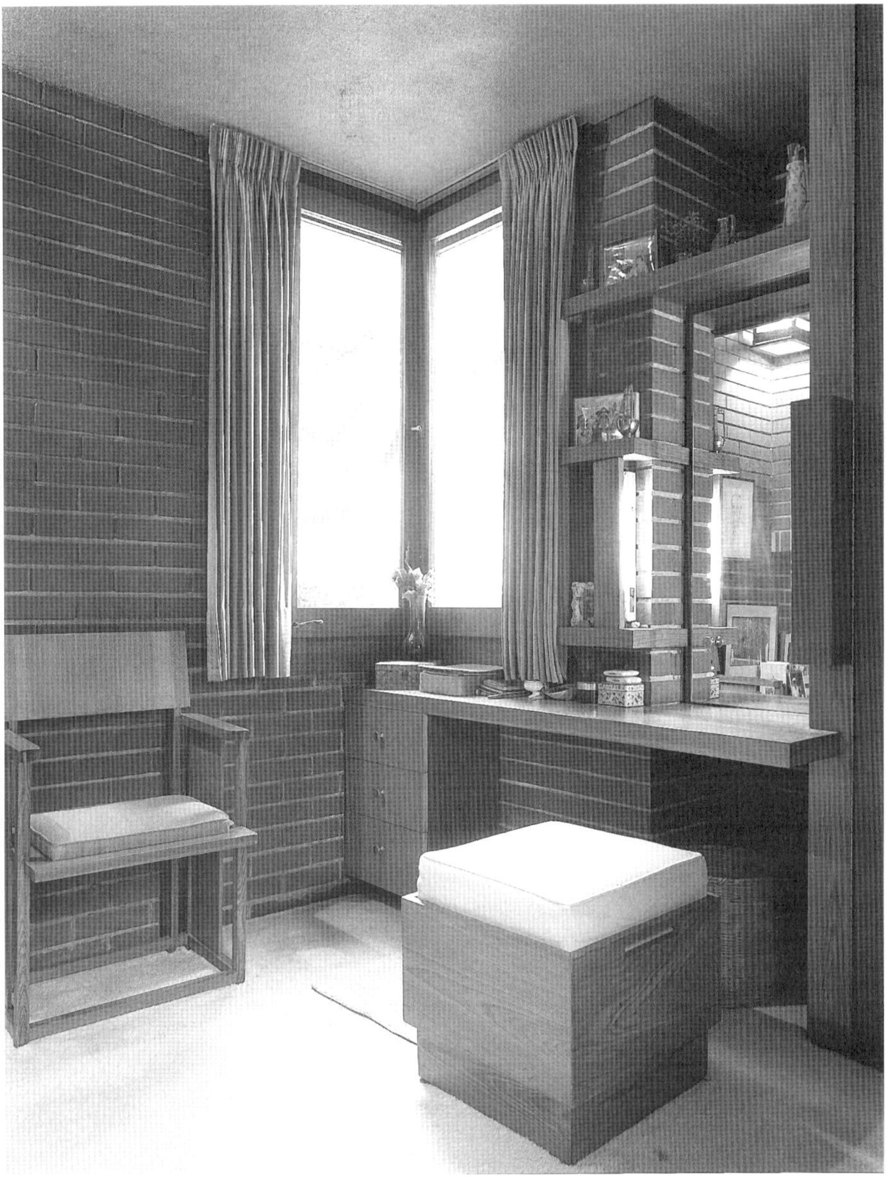

Kenneth Laurent House
Rockford, Illinois, 1949

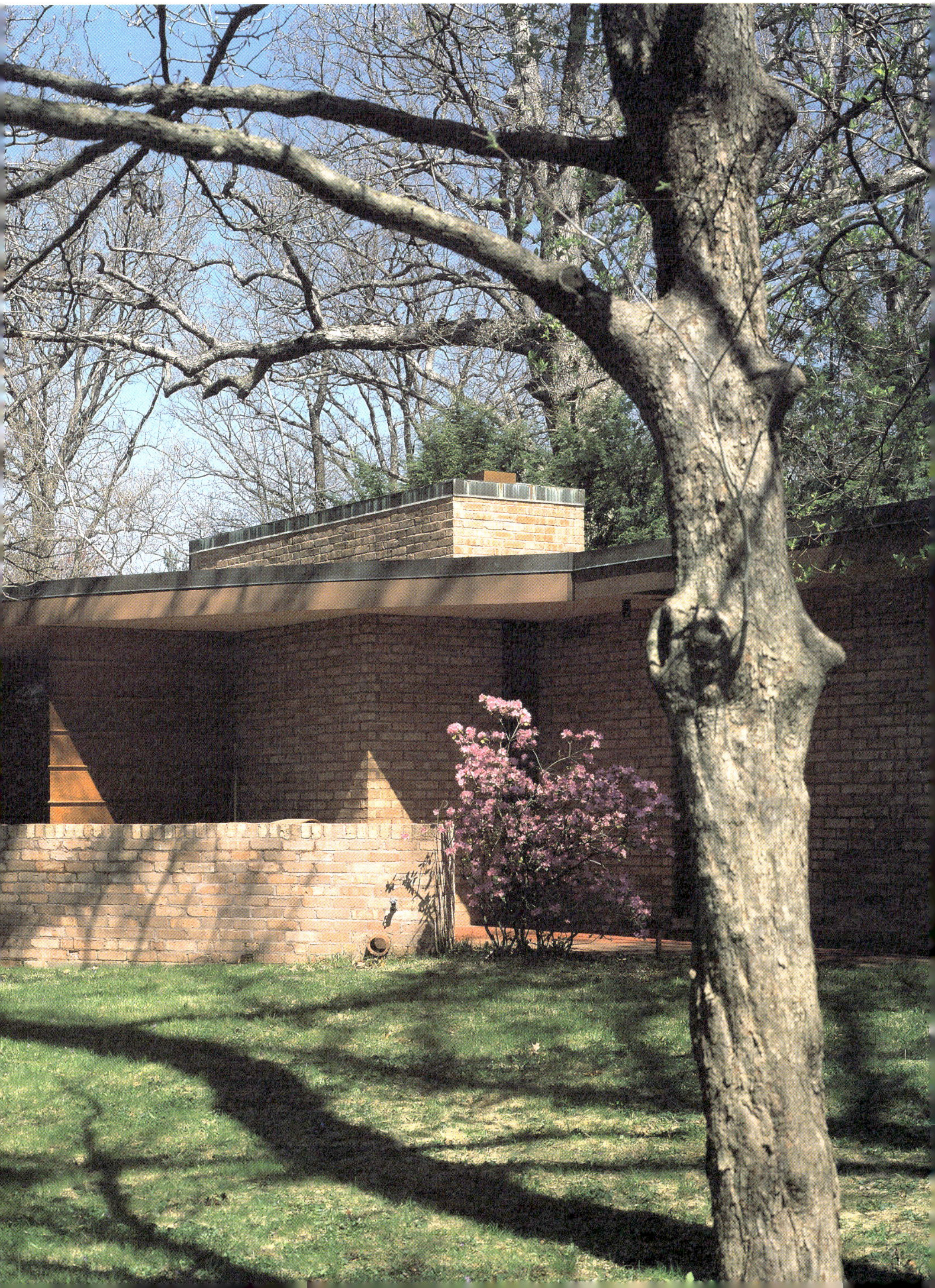

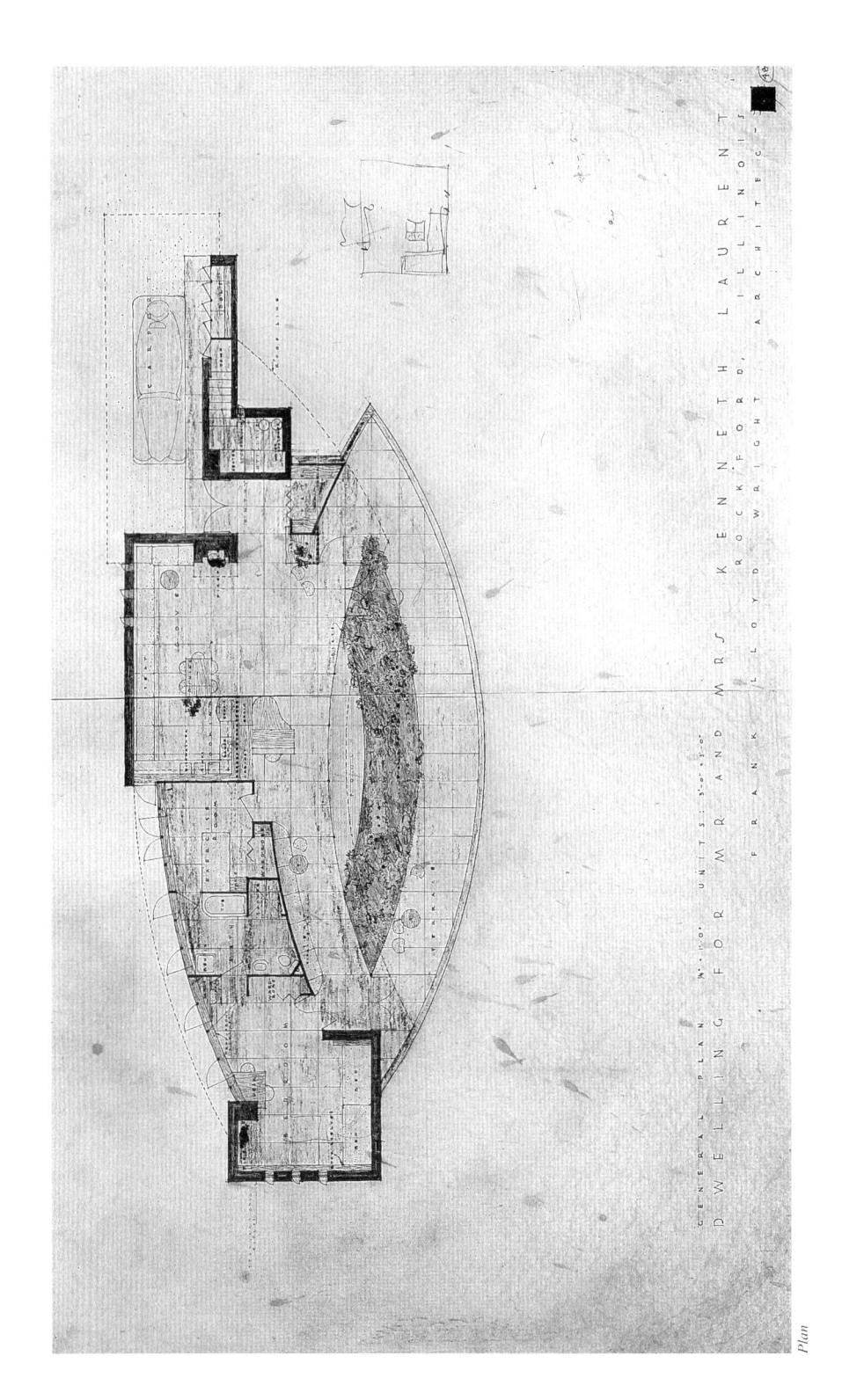

Plan

Elevations

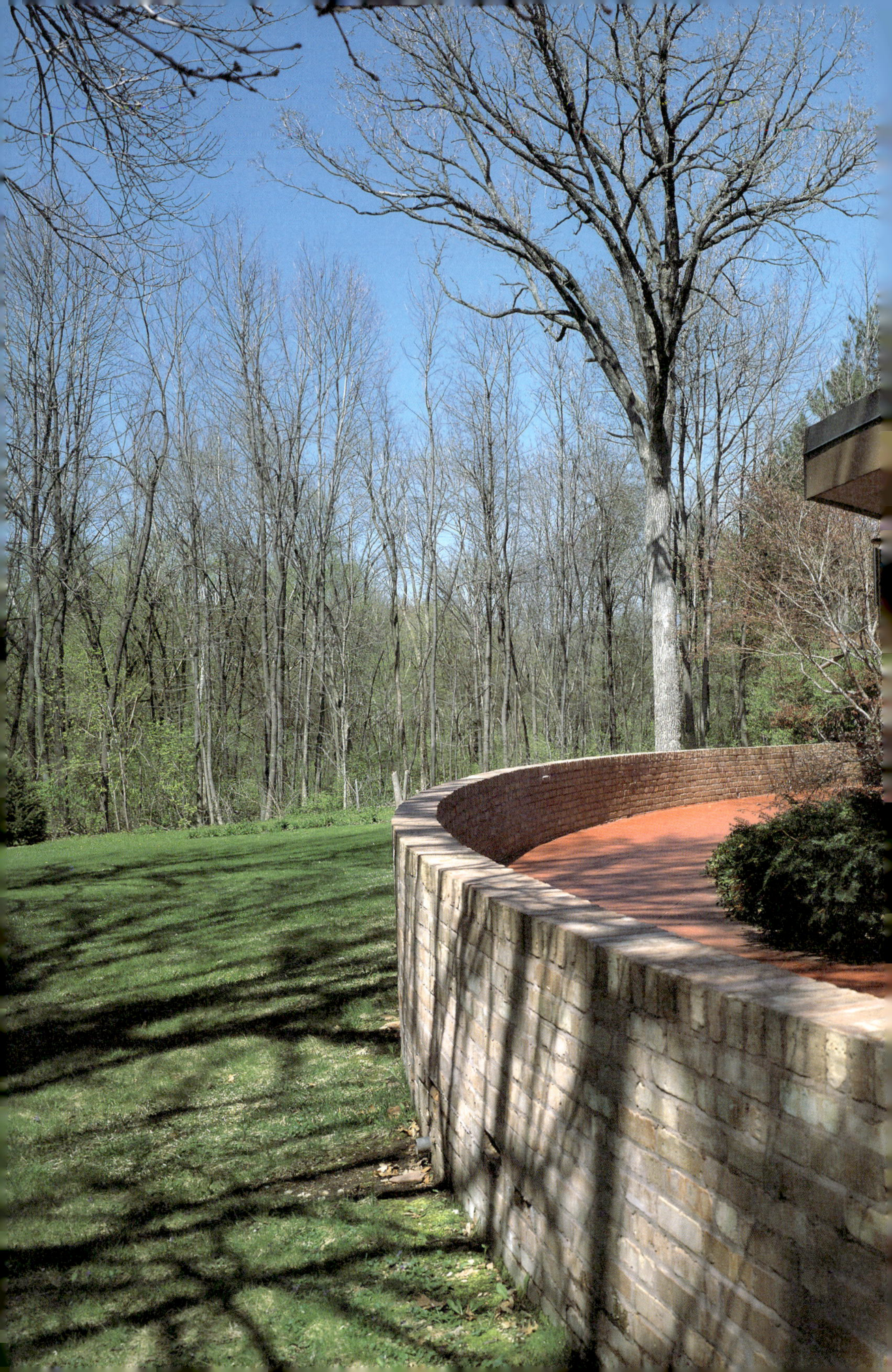

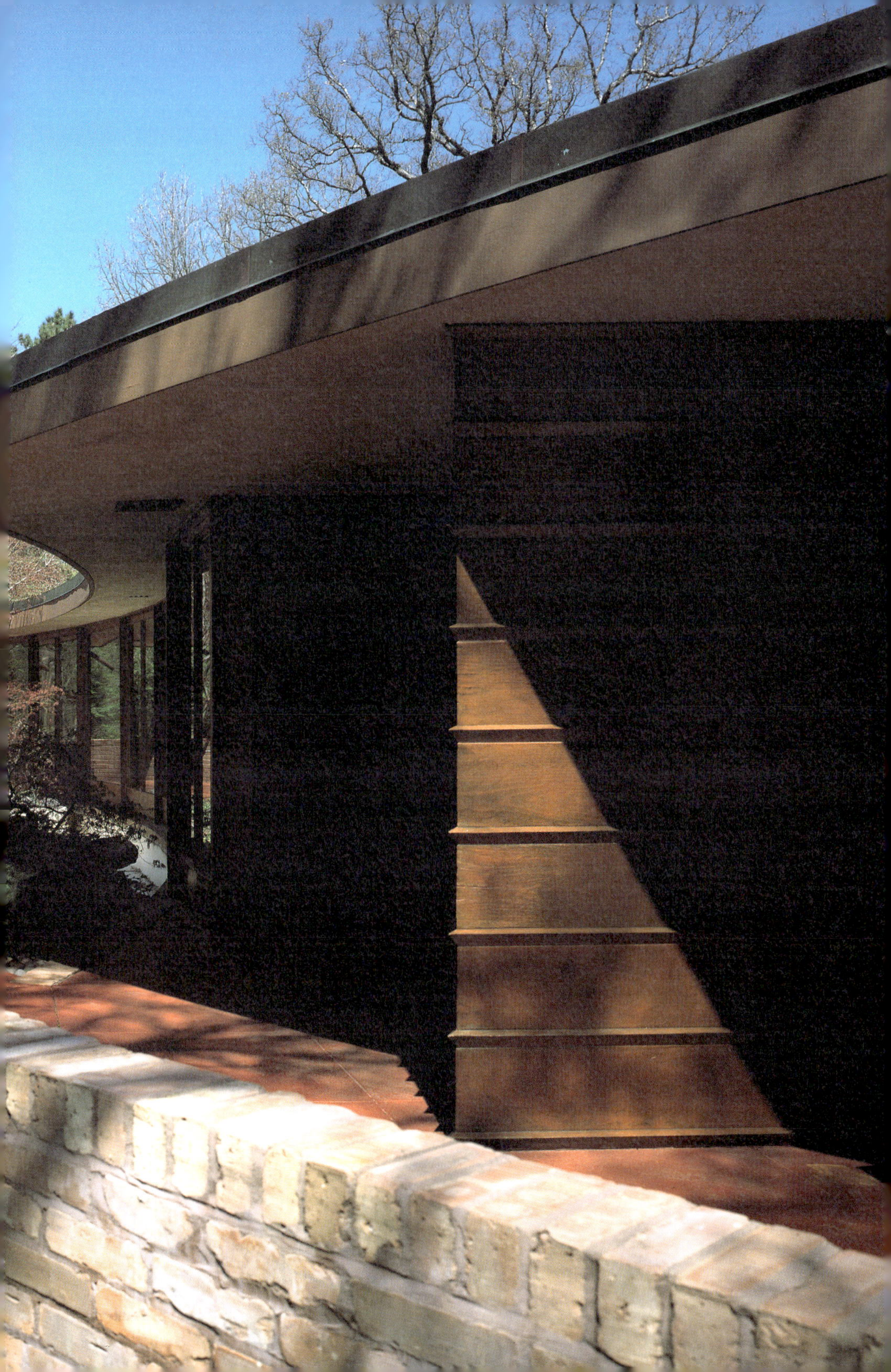

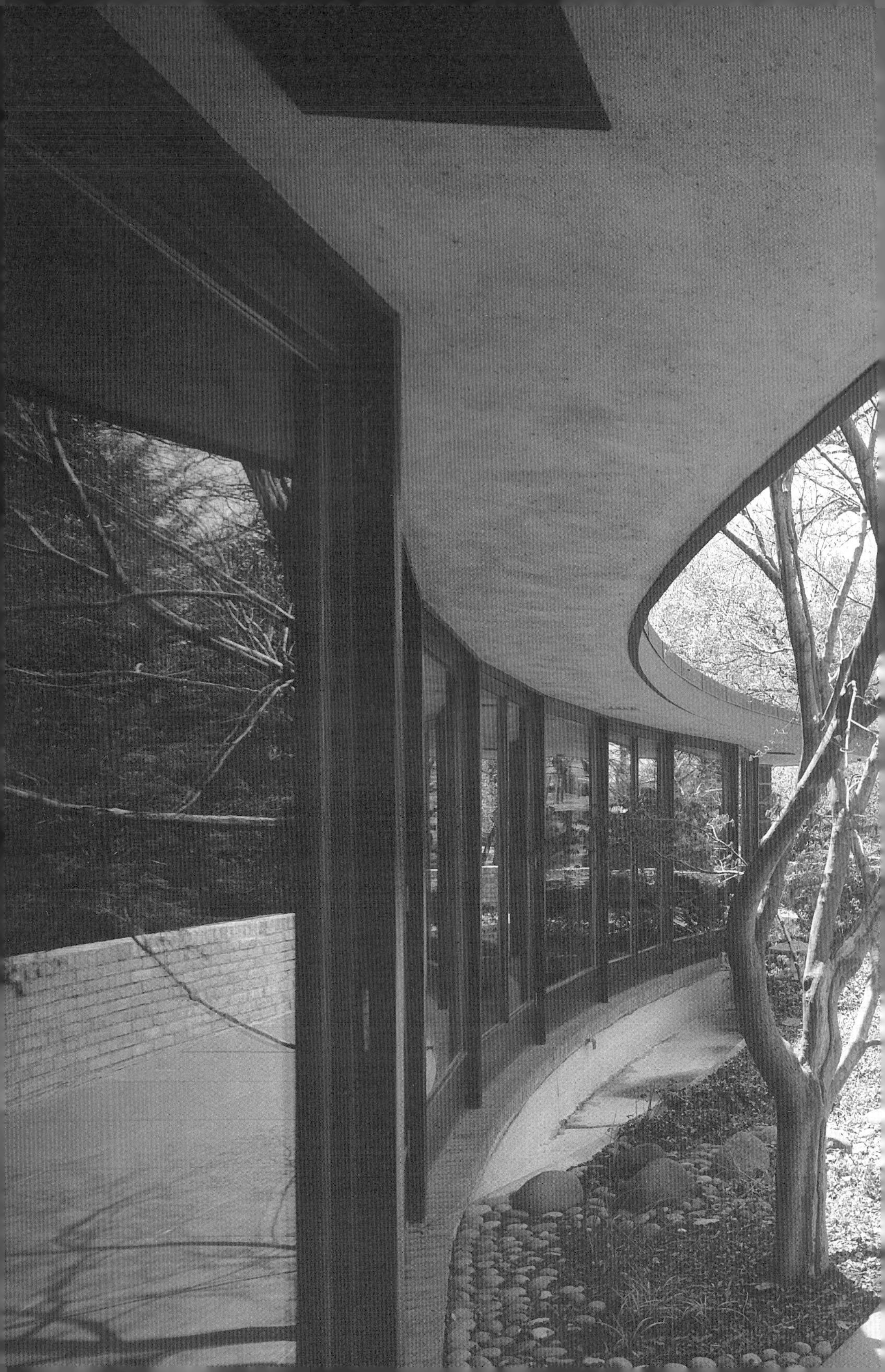

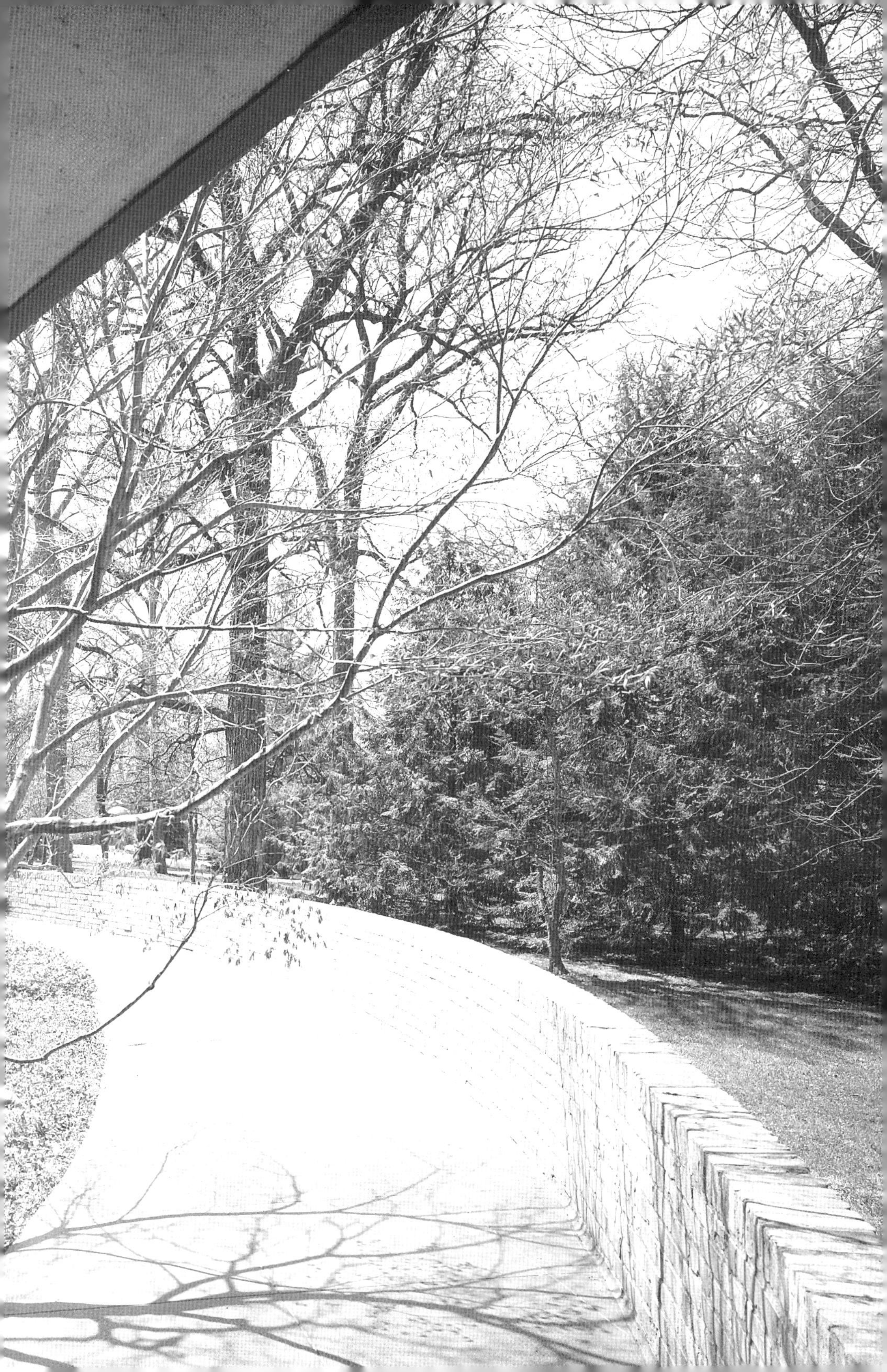

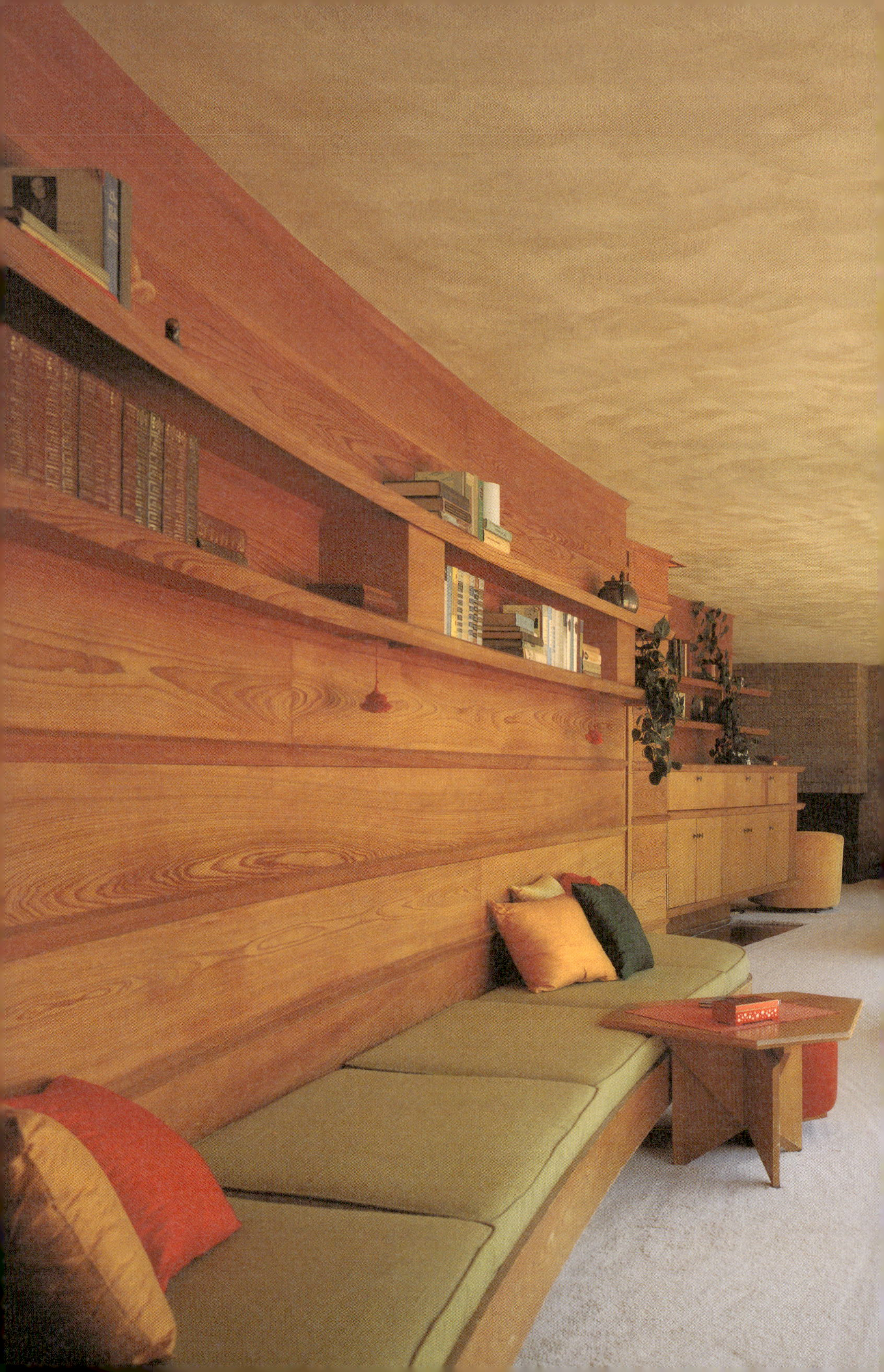

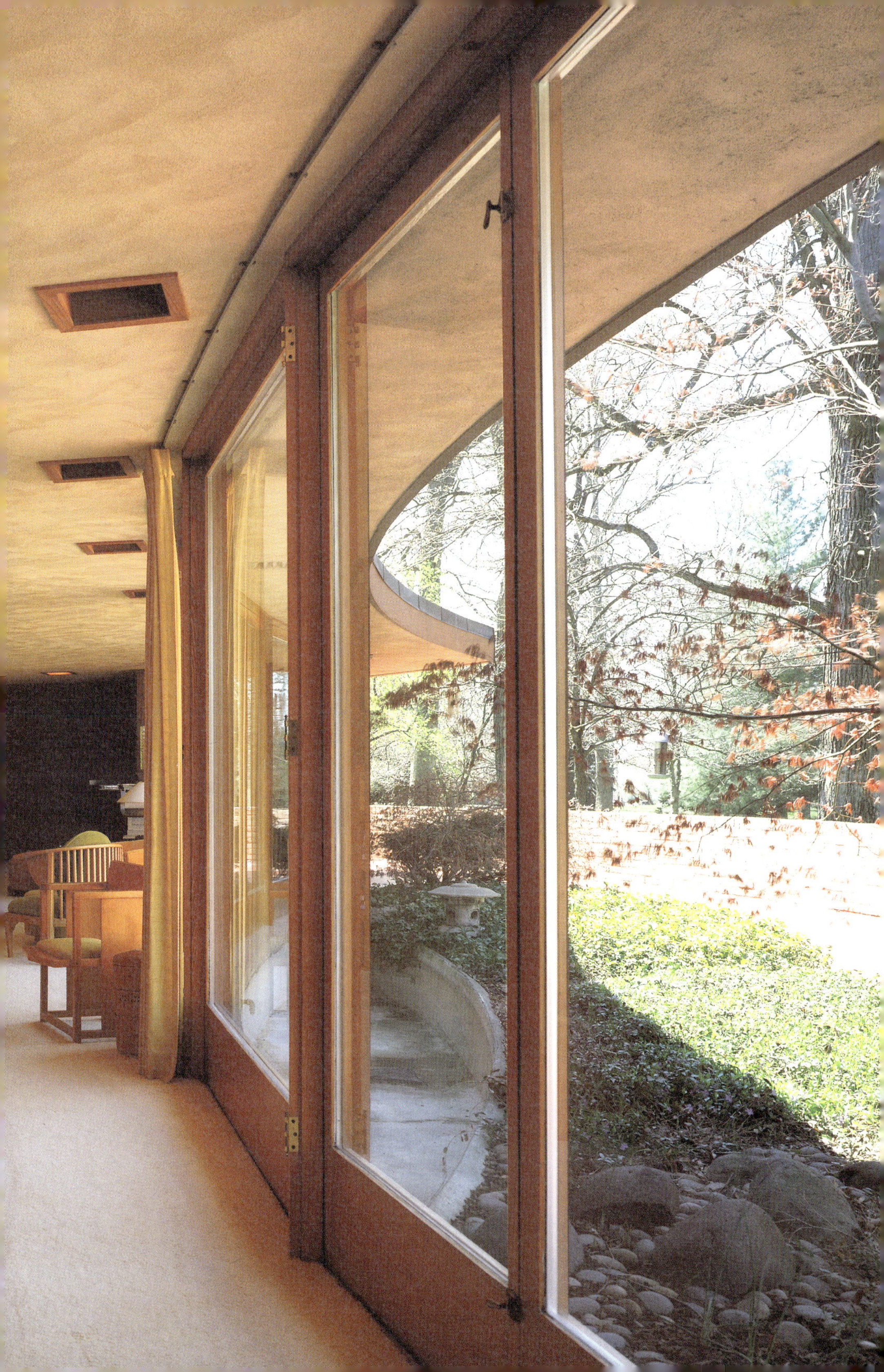

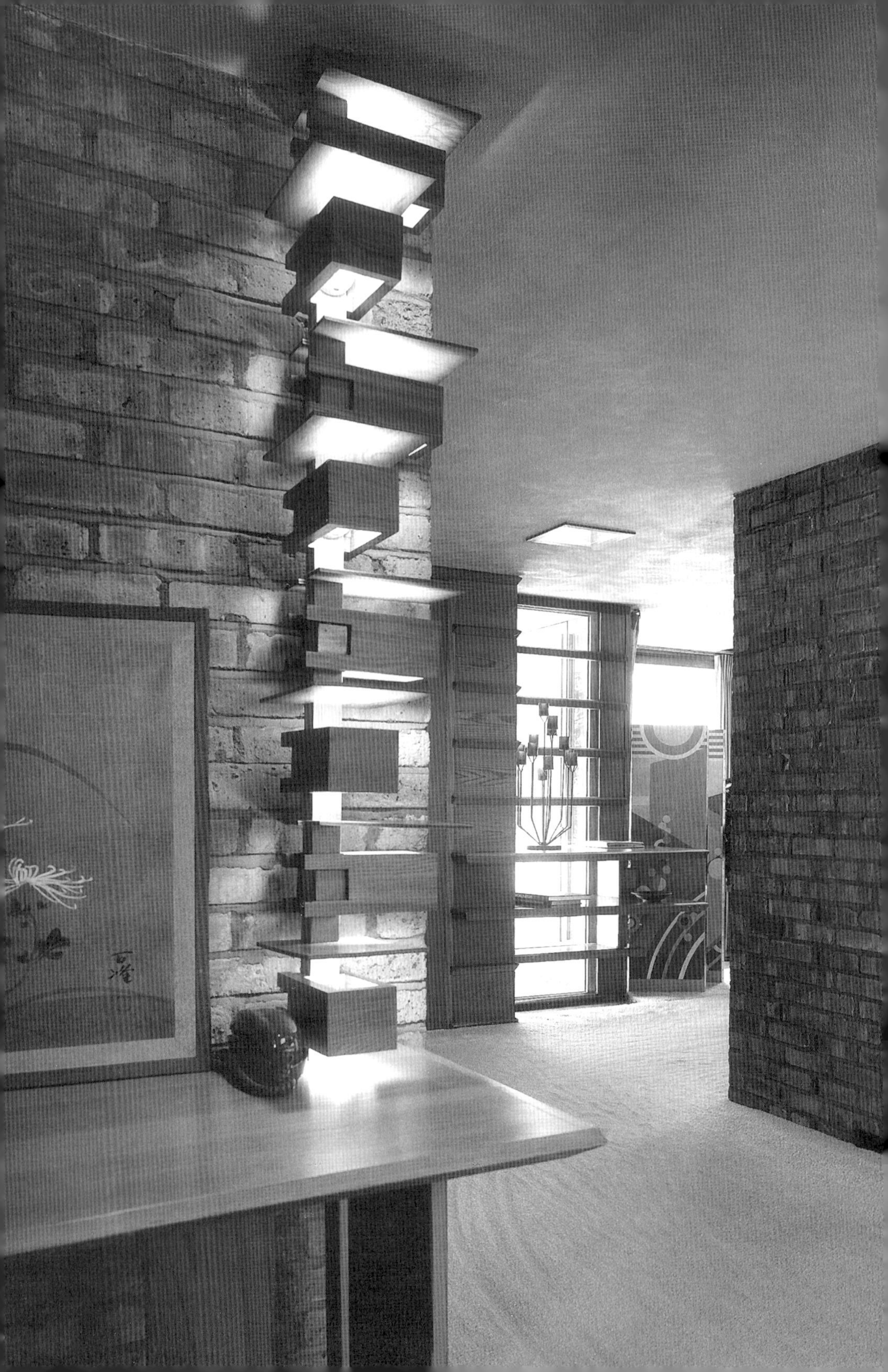

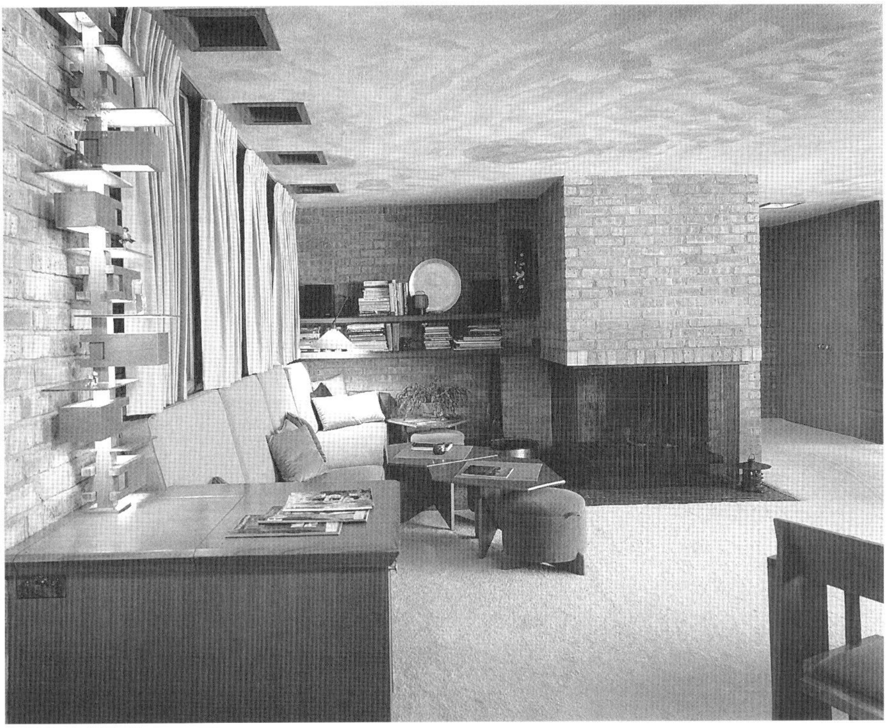

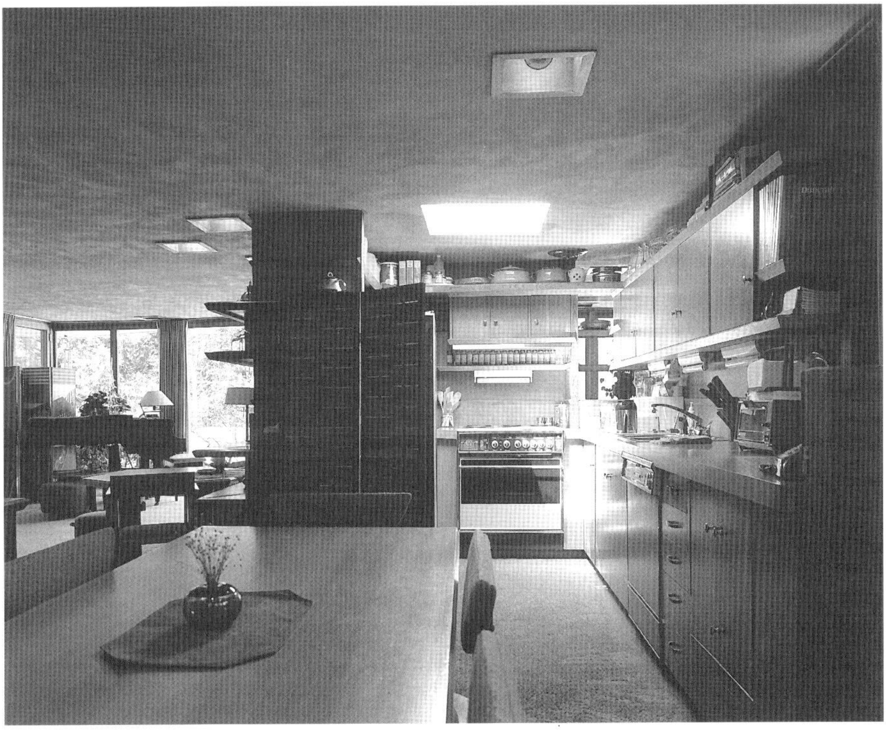

174

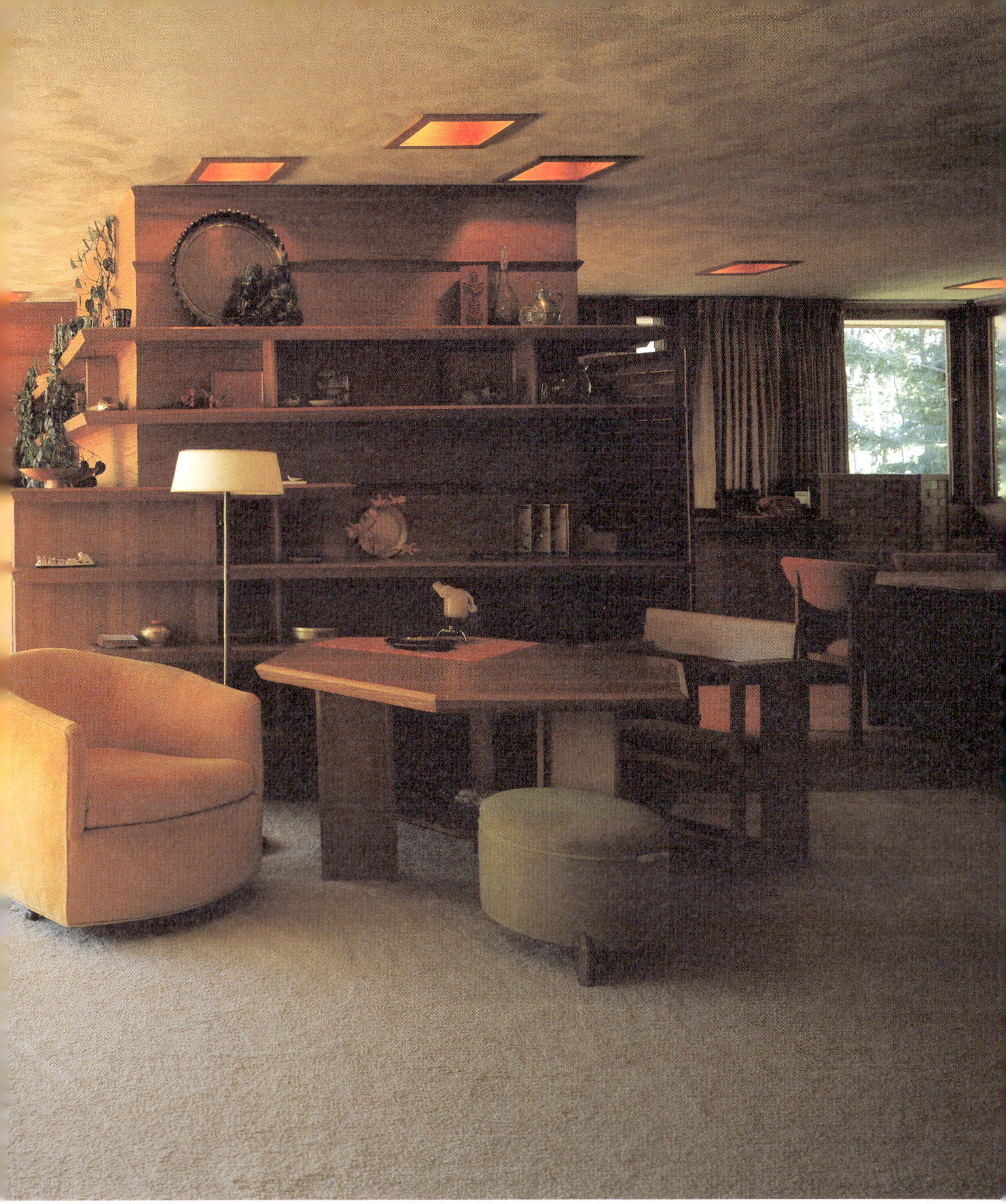

David Wright House
Phoenix, Arizona, 1950

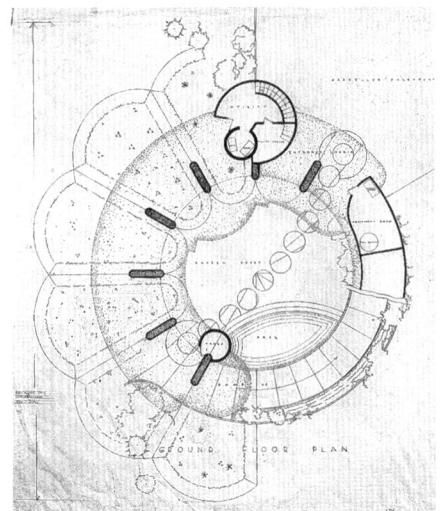

Ground floor plan

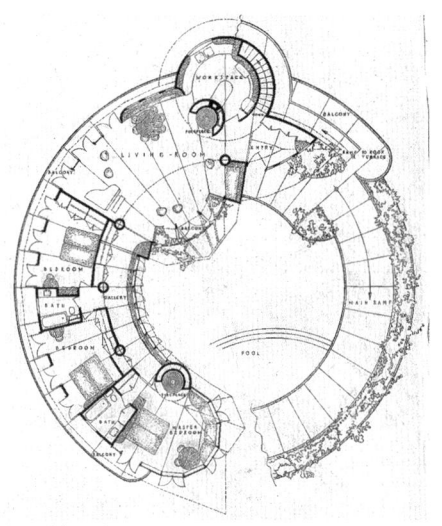

Second floor plan

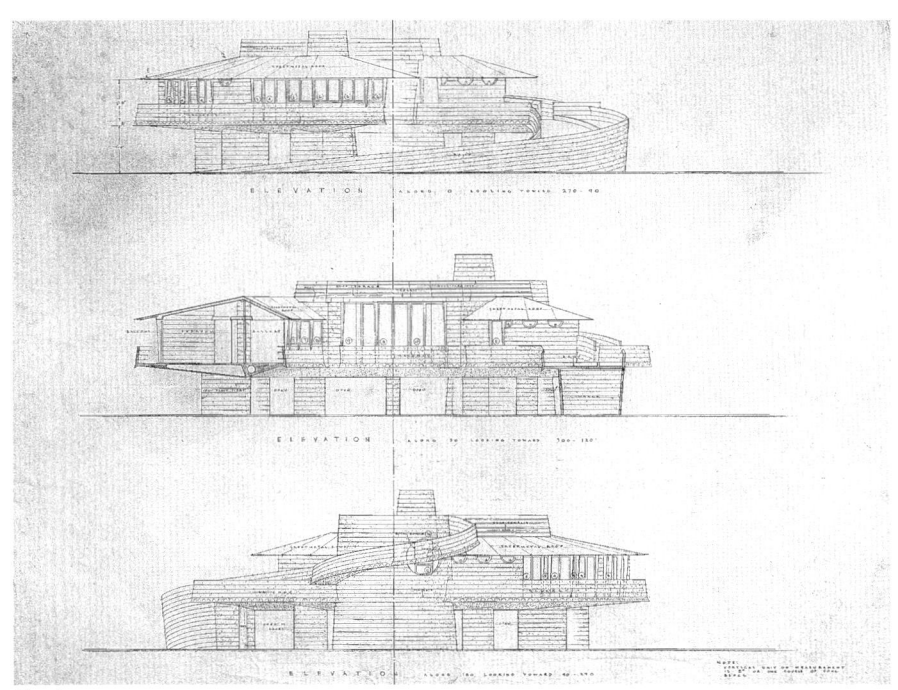

Elevations

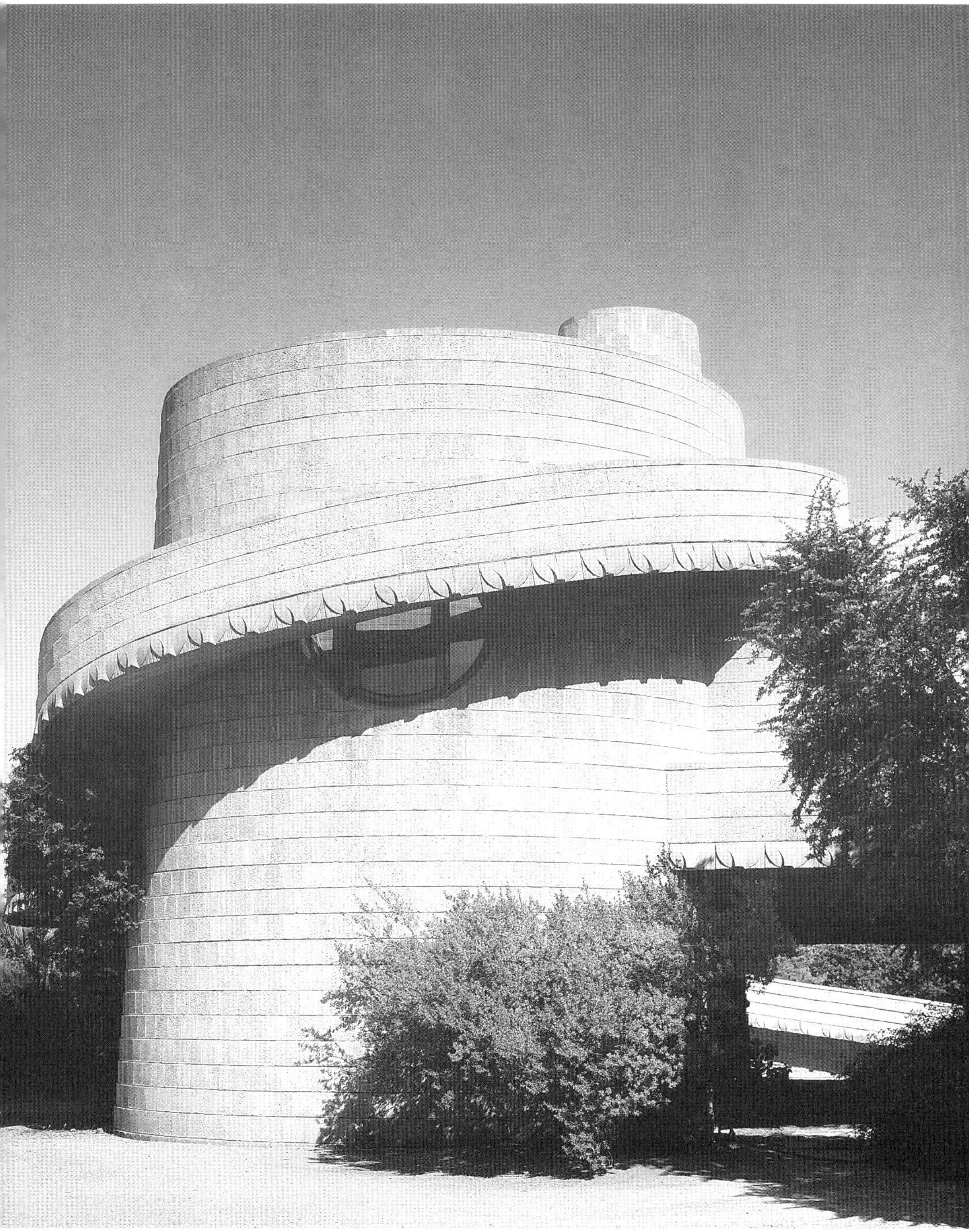

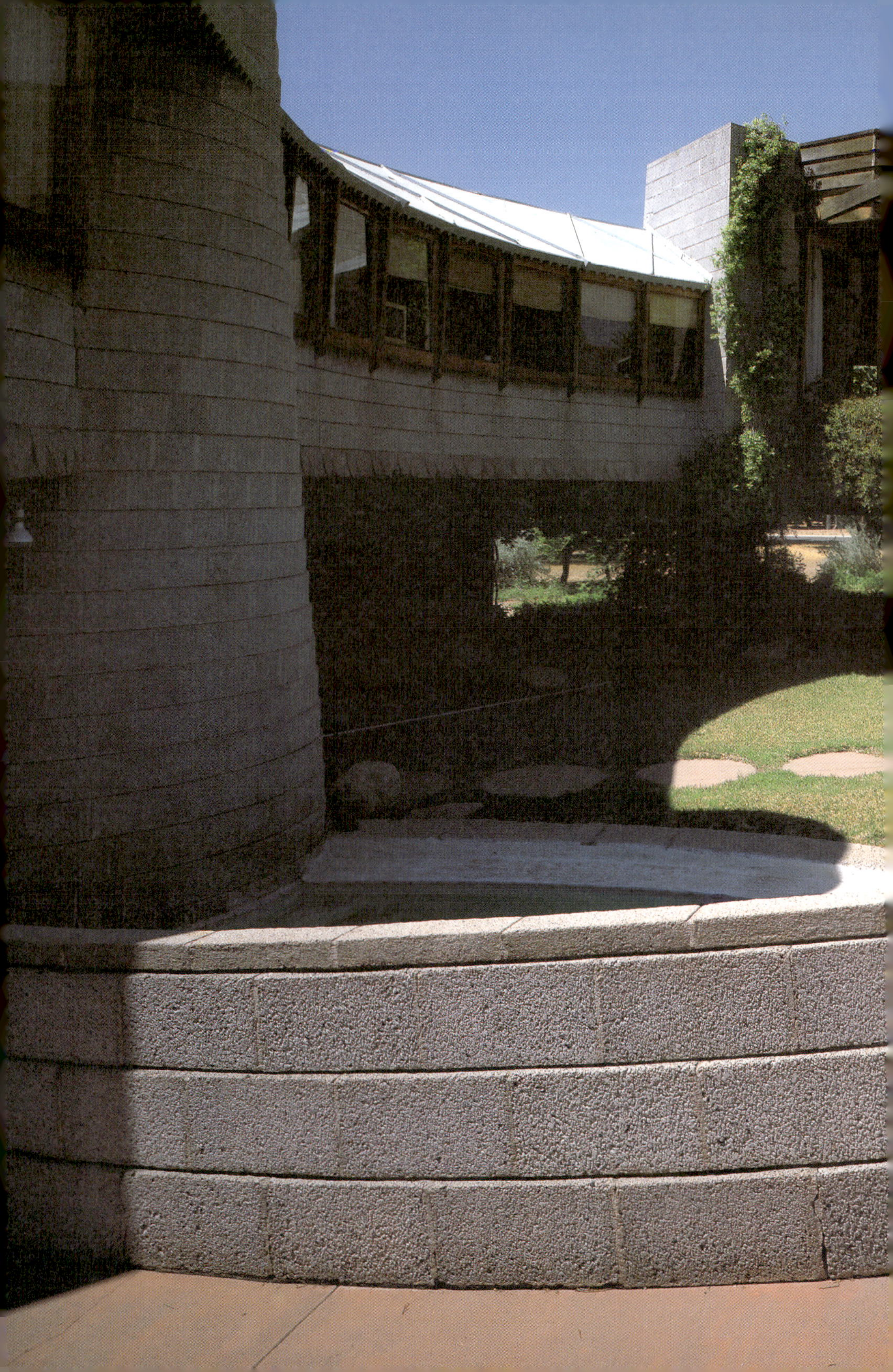

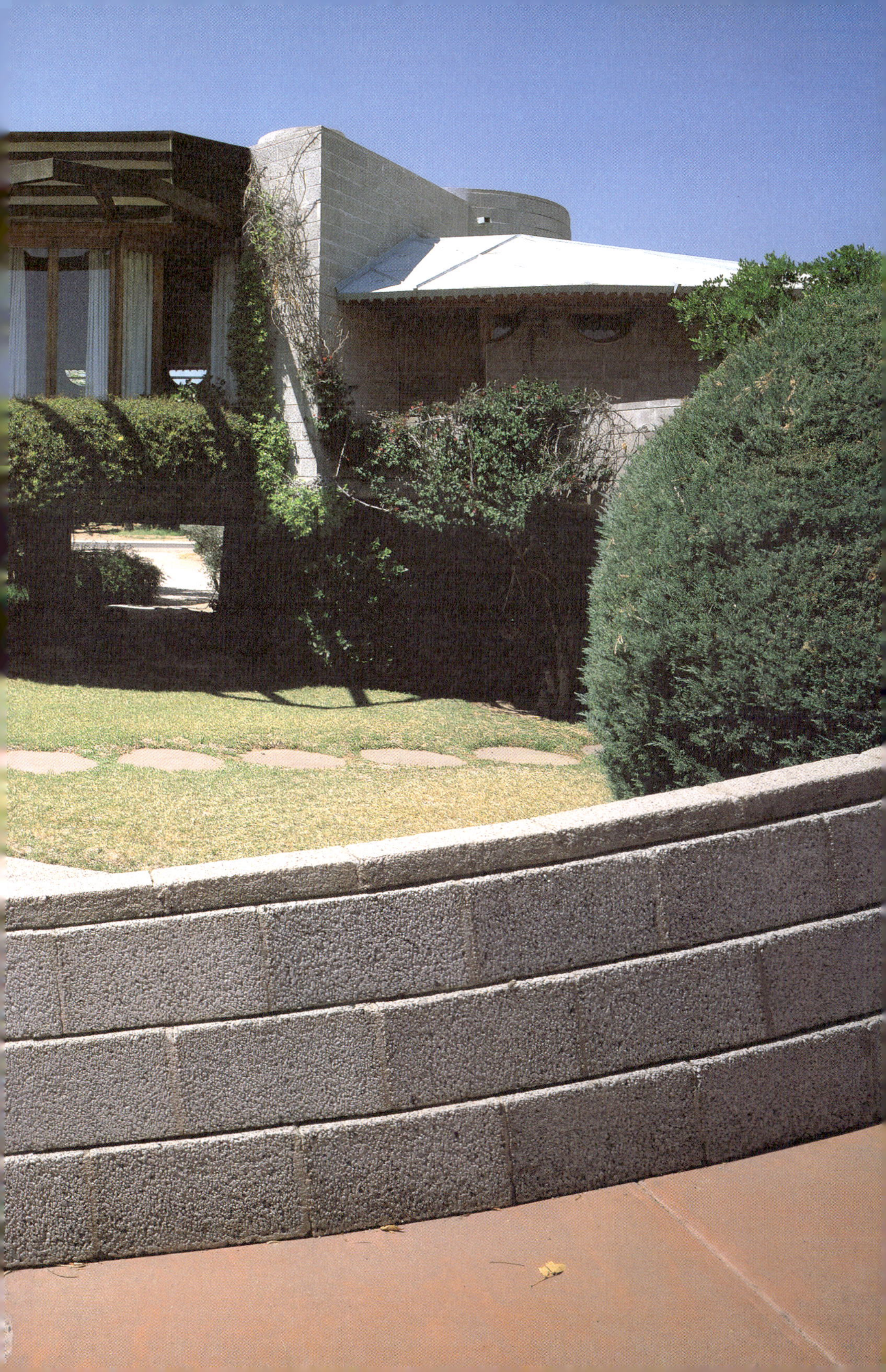

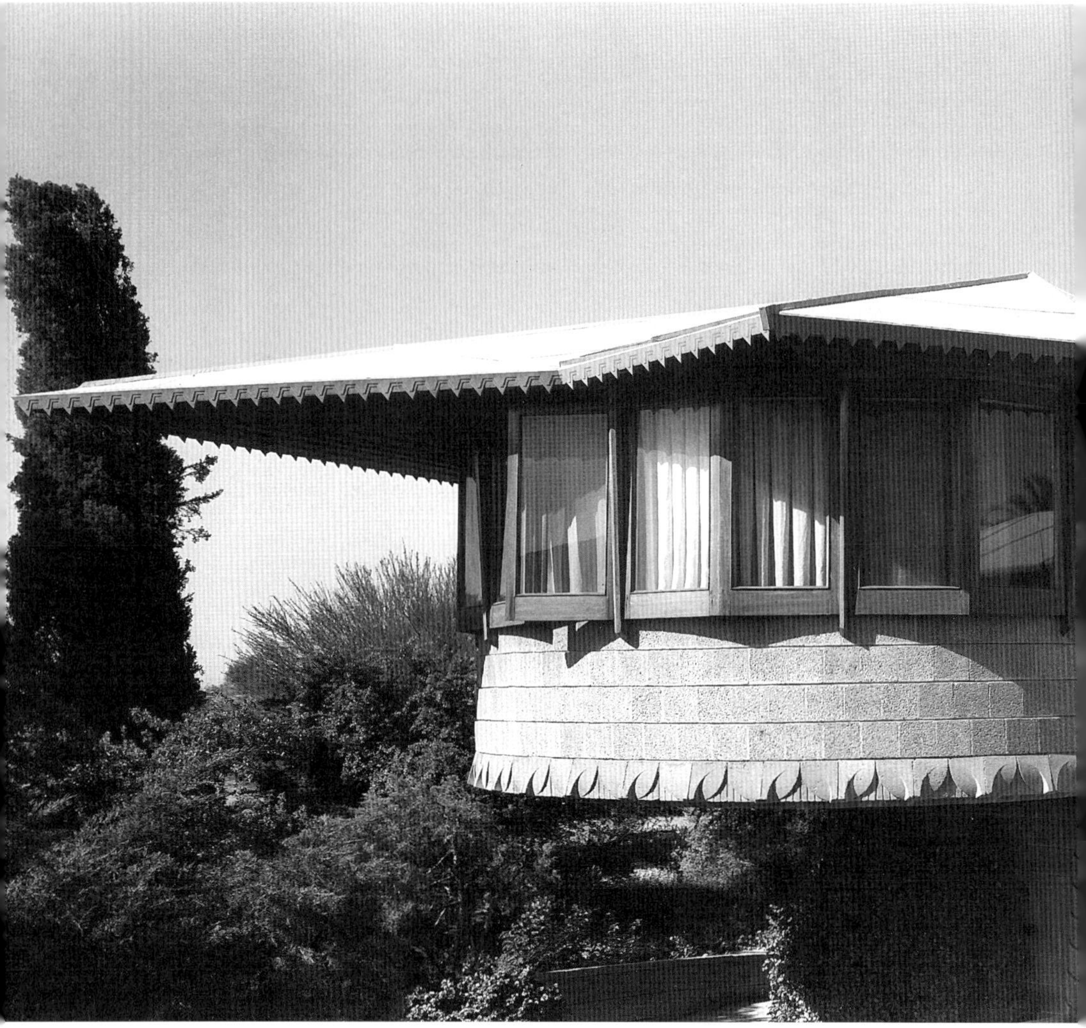

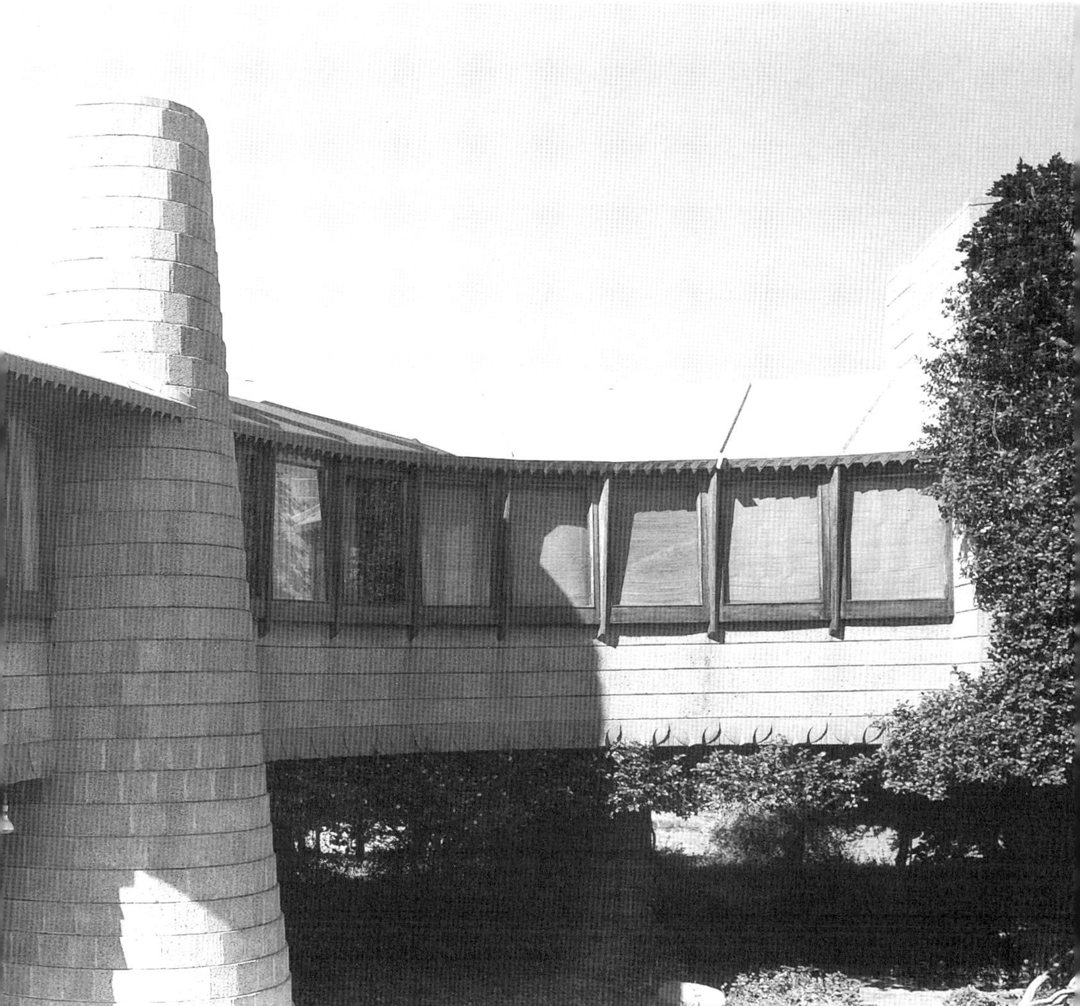

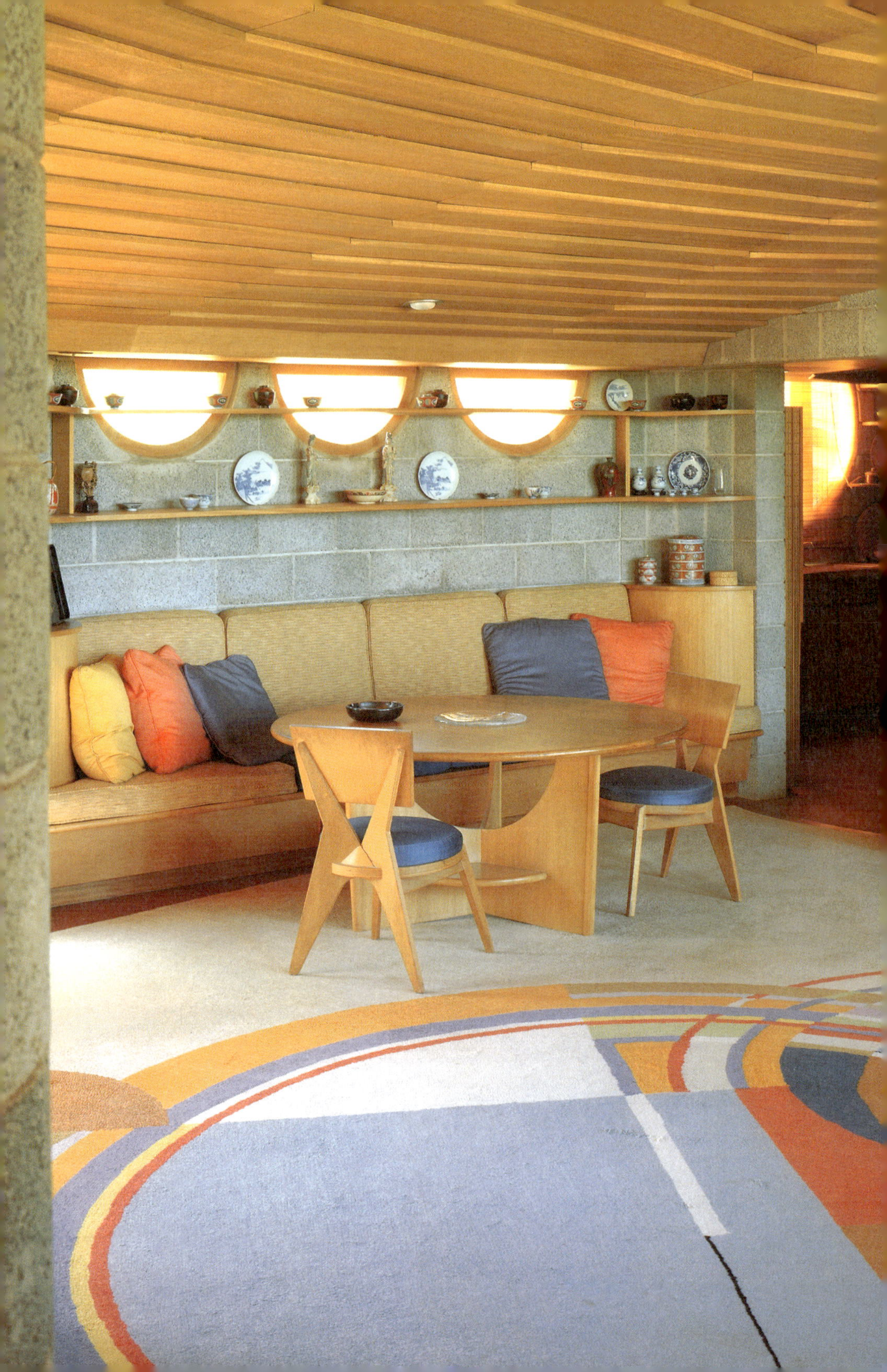

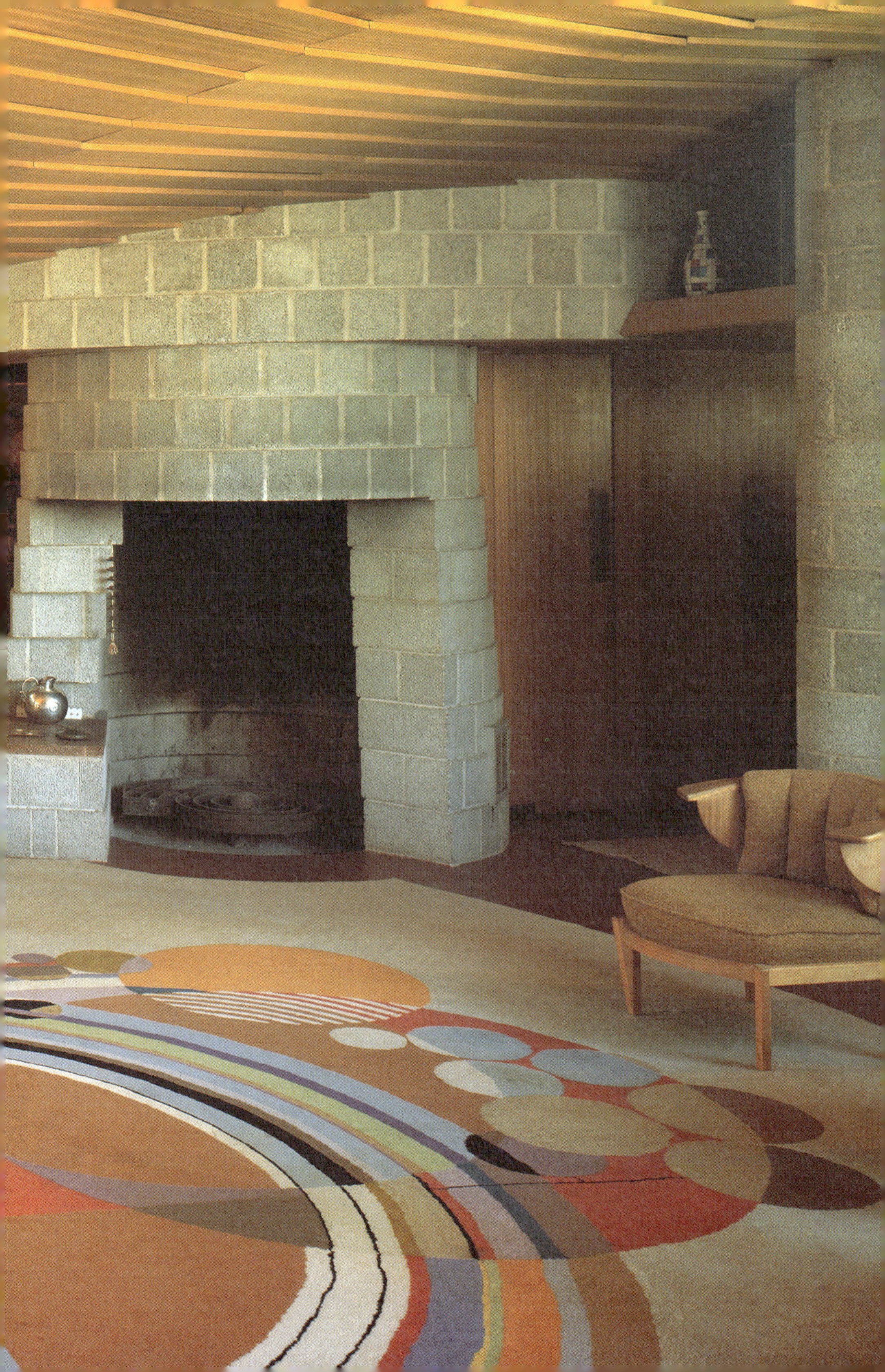

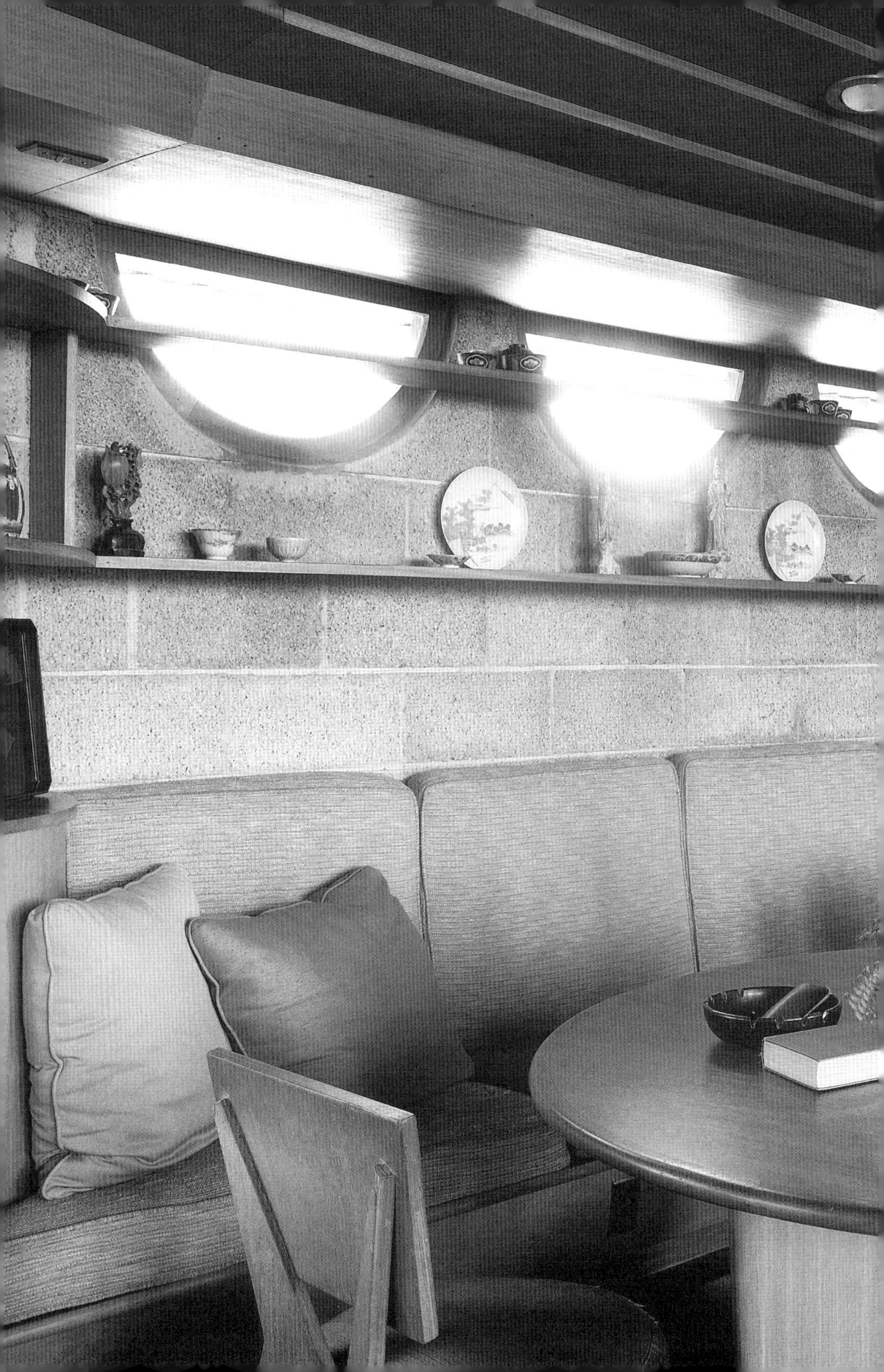

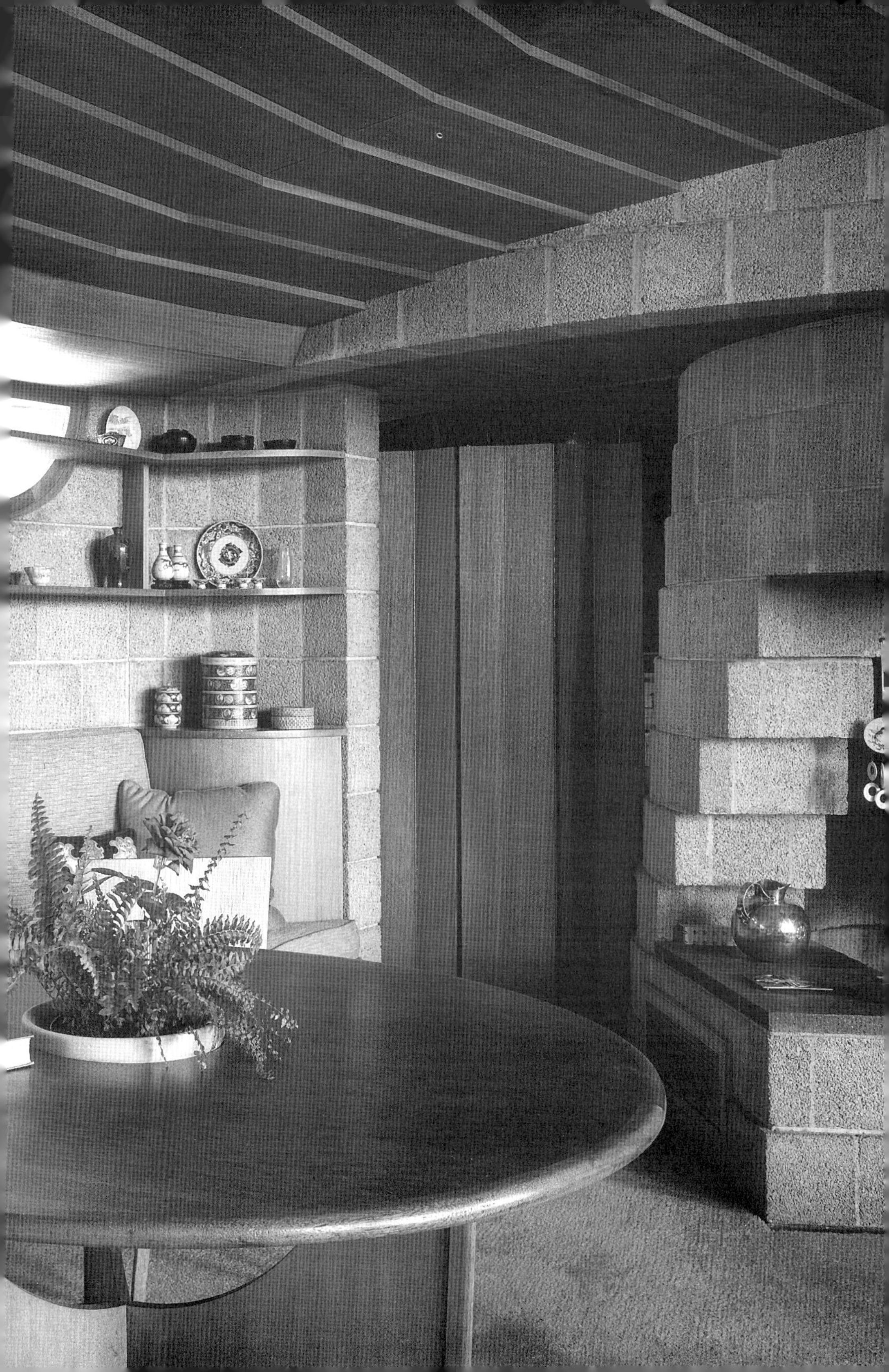

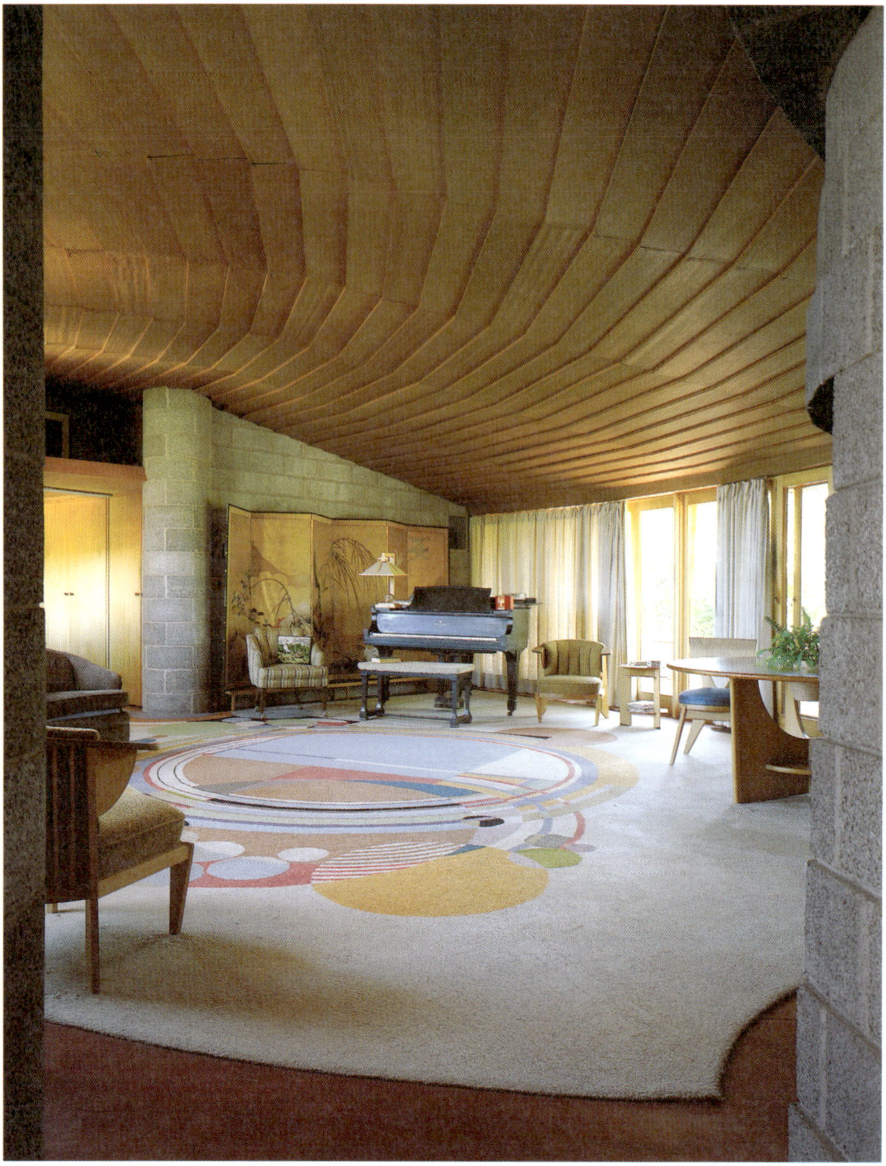

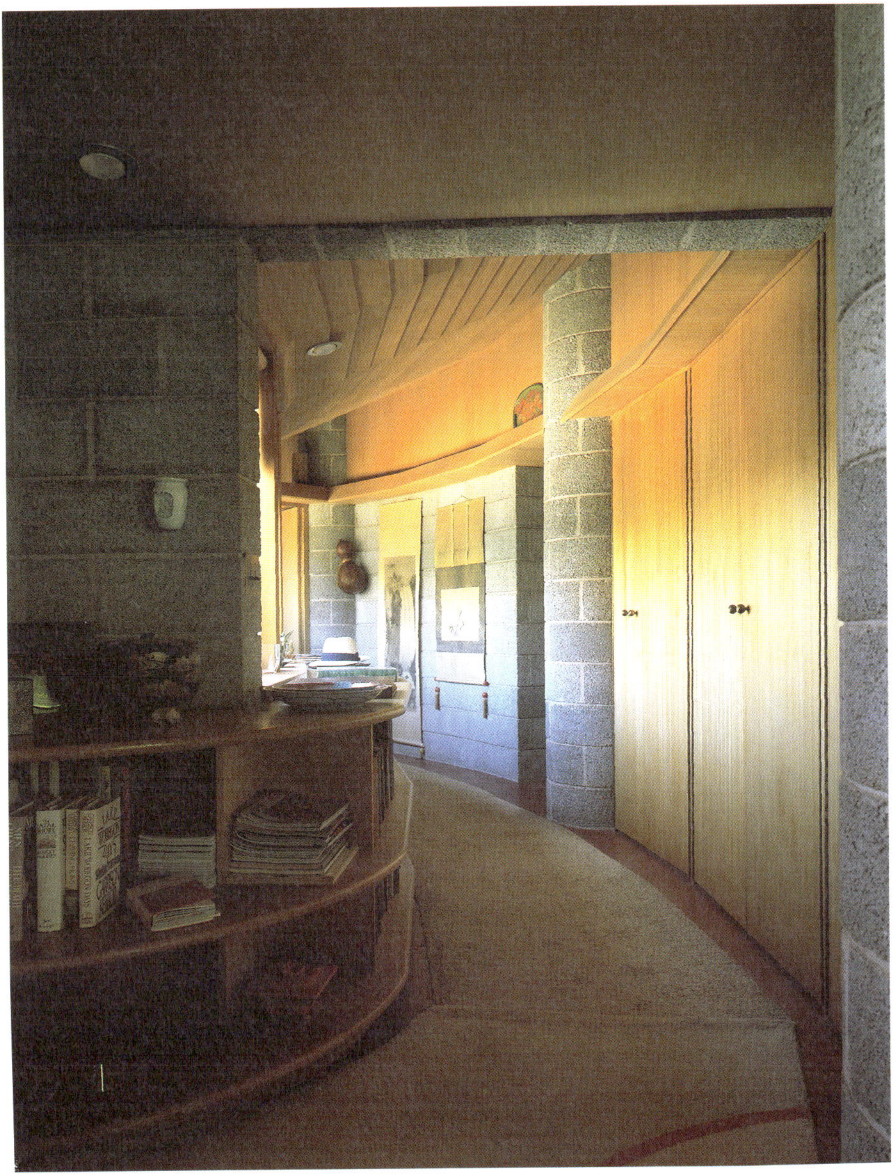

William Palmer House
Ann Arbor, Michigan, 1950

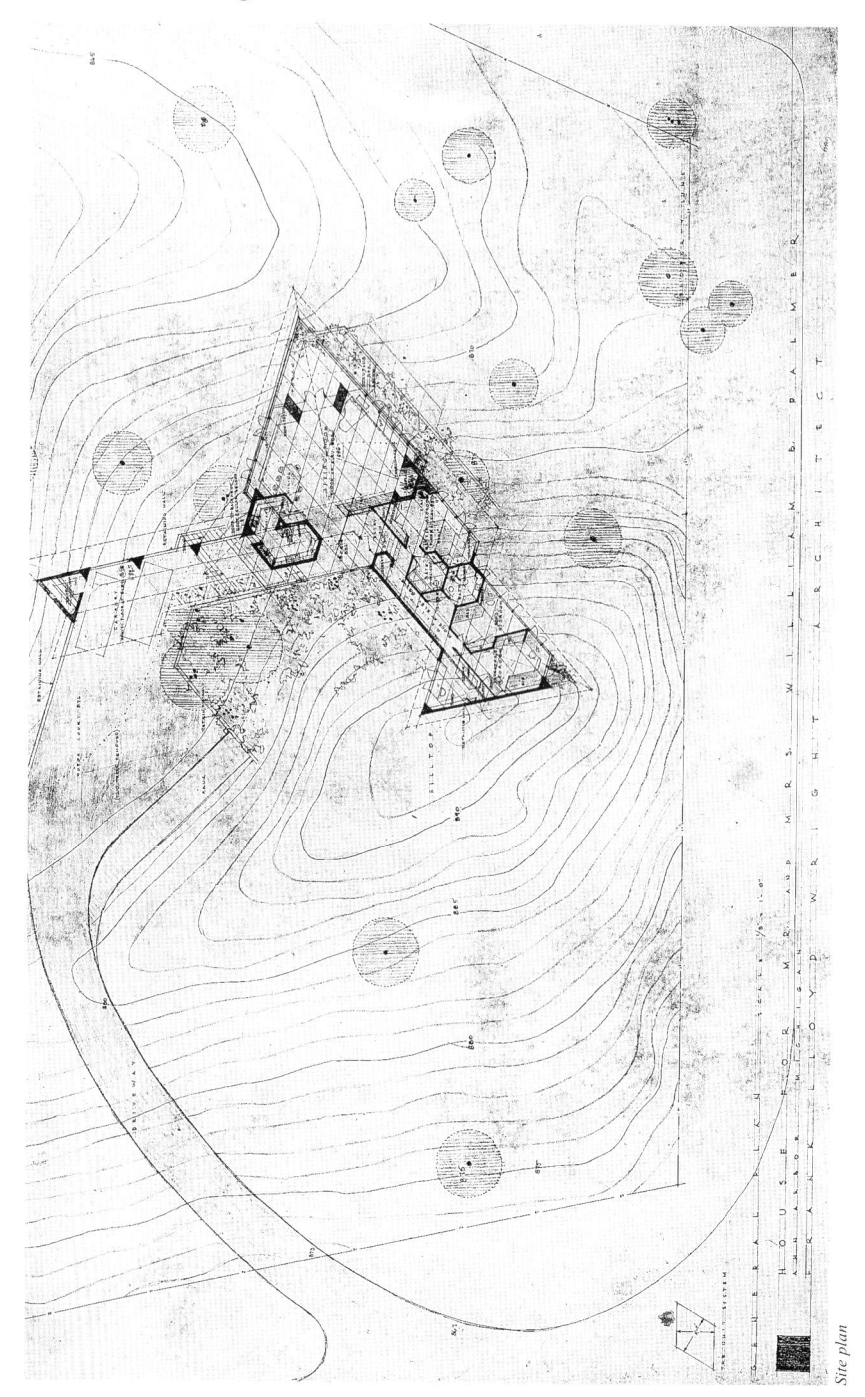

Site plan

Elevations

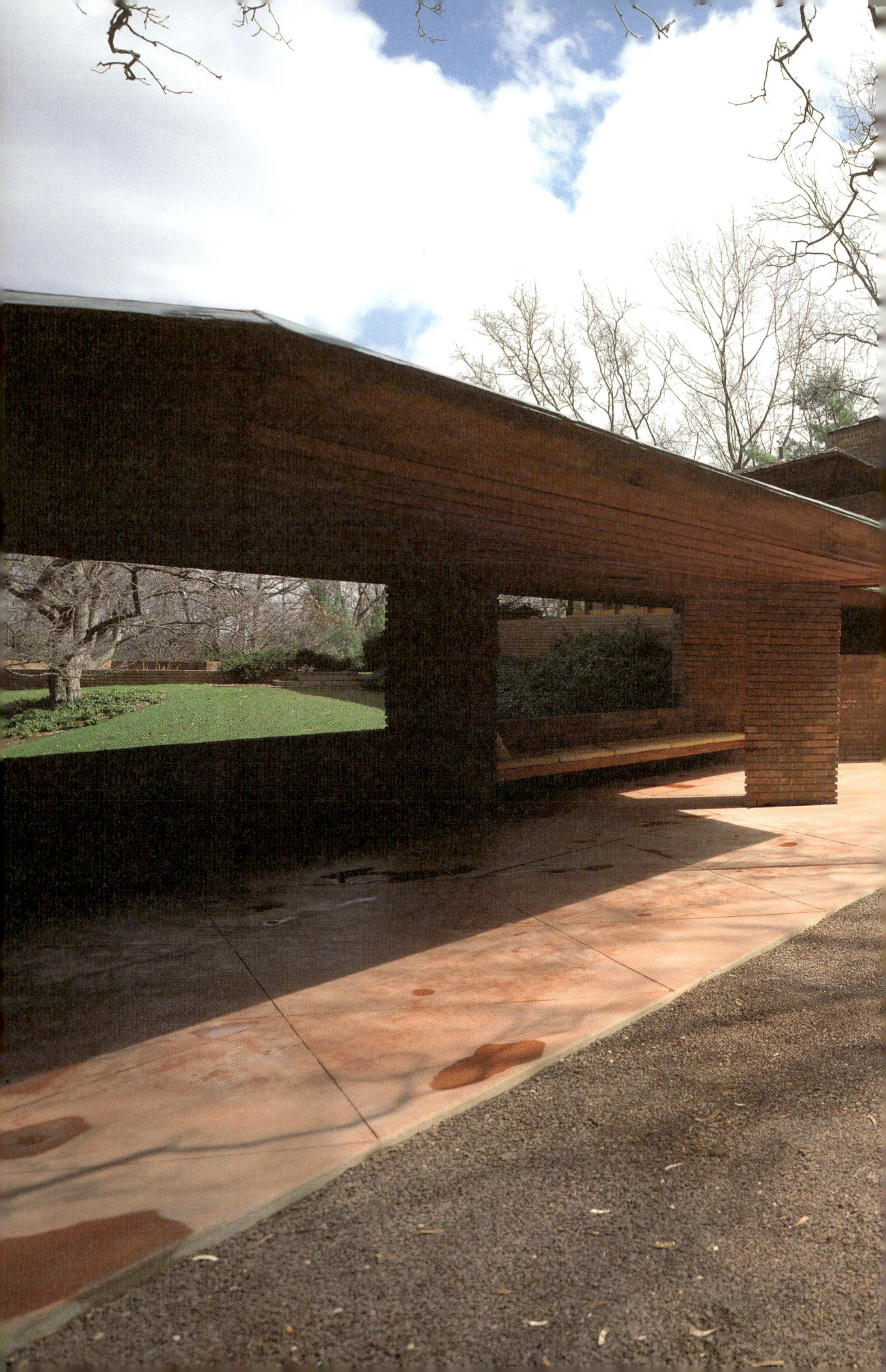

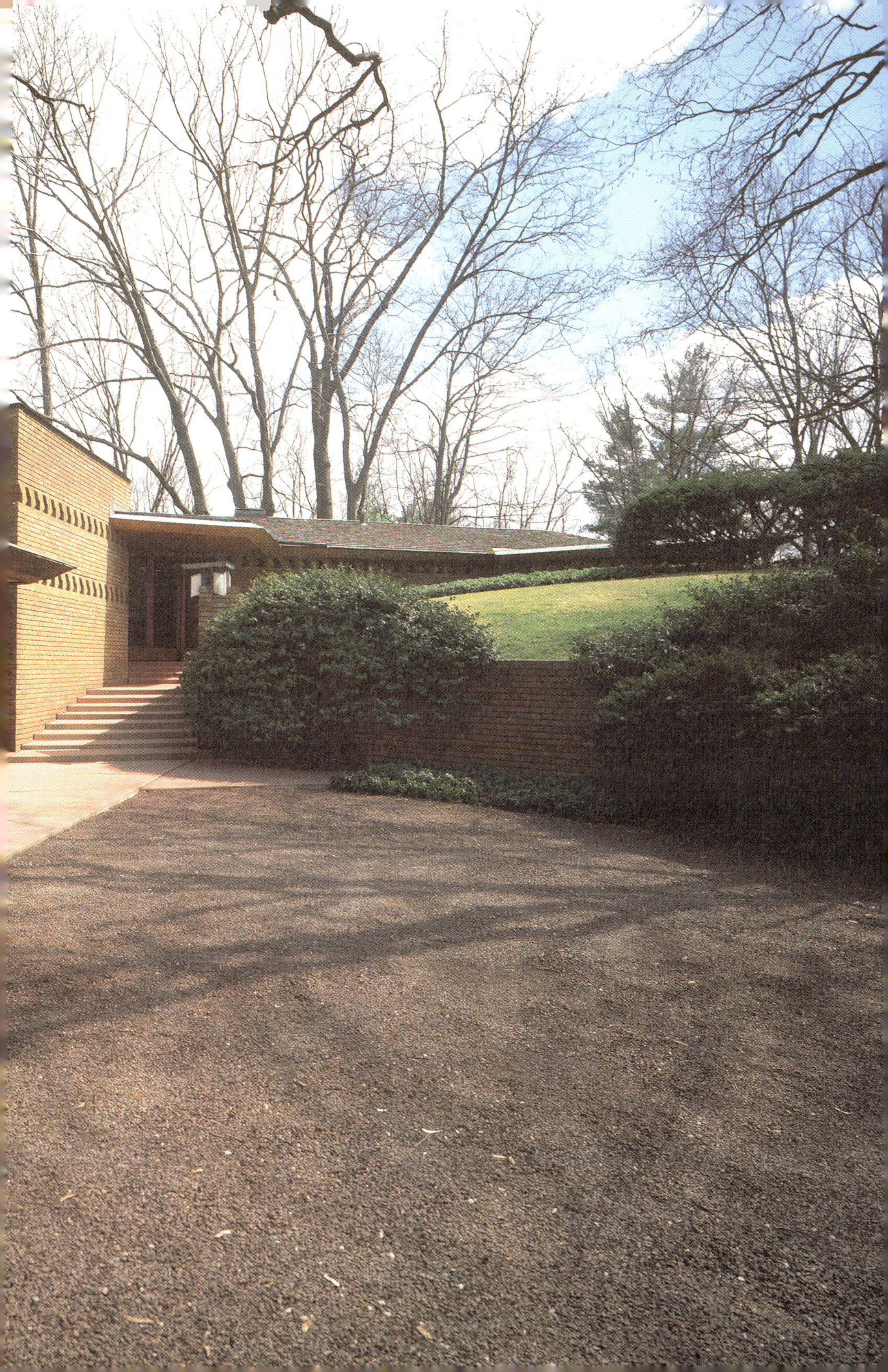

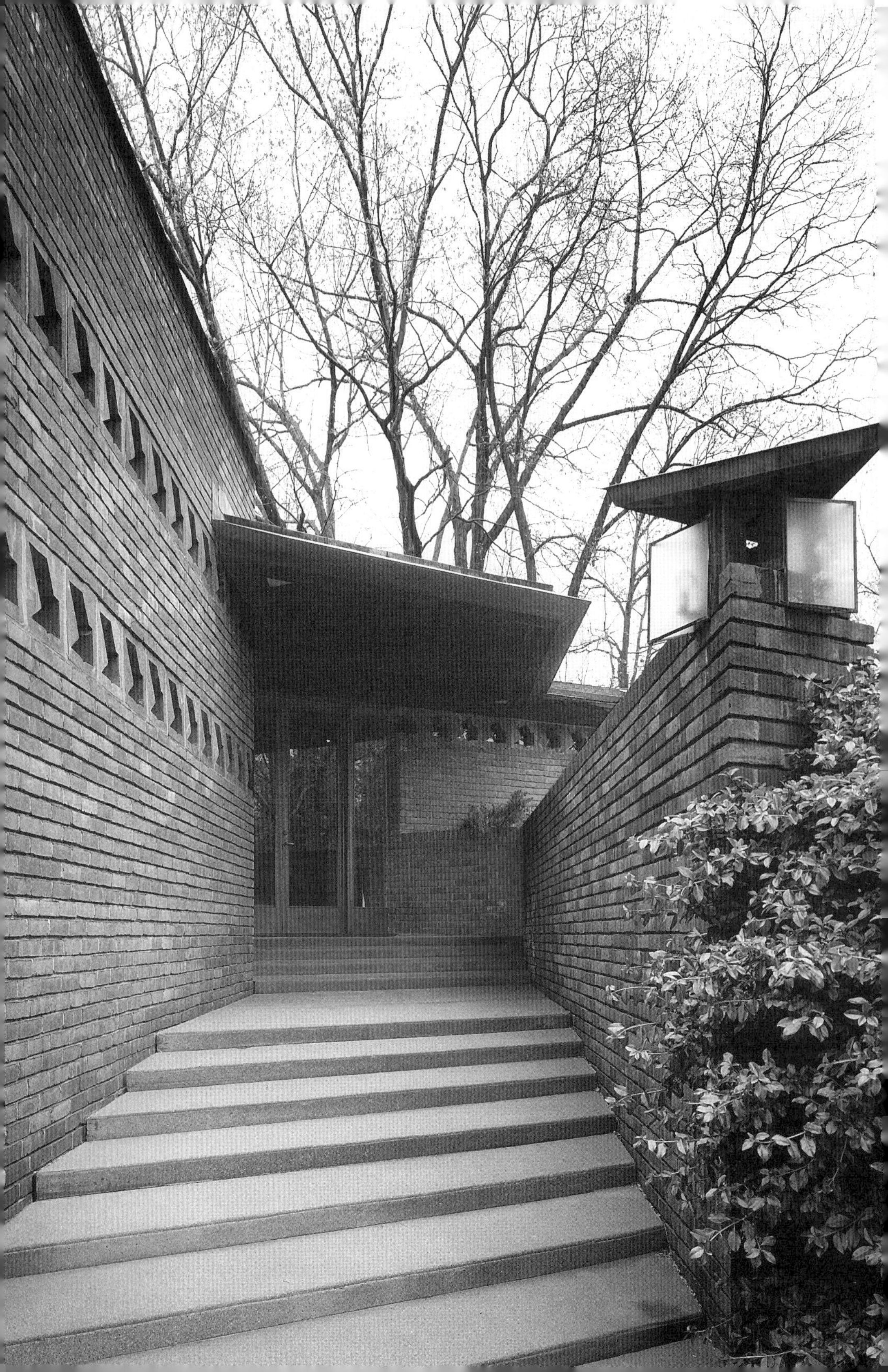

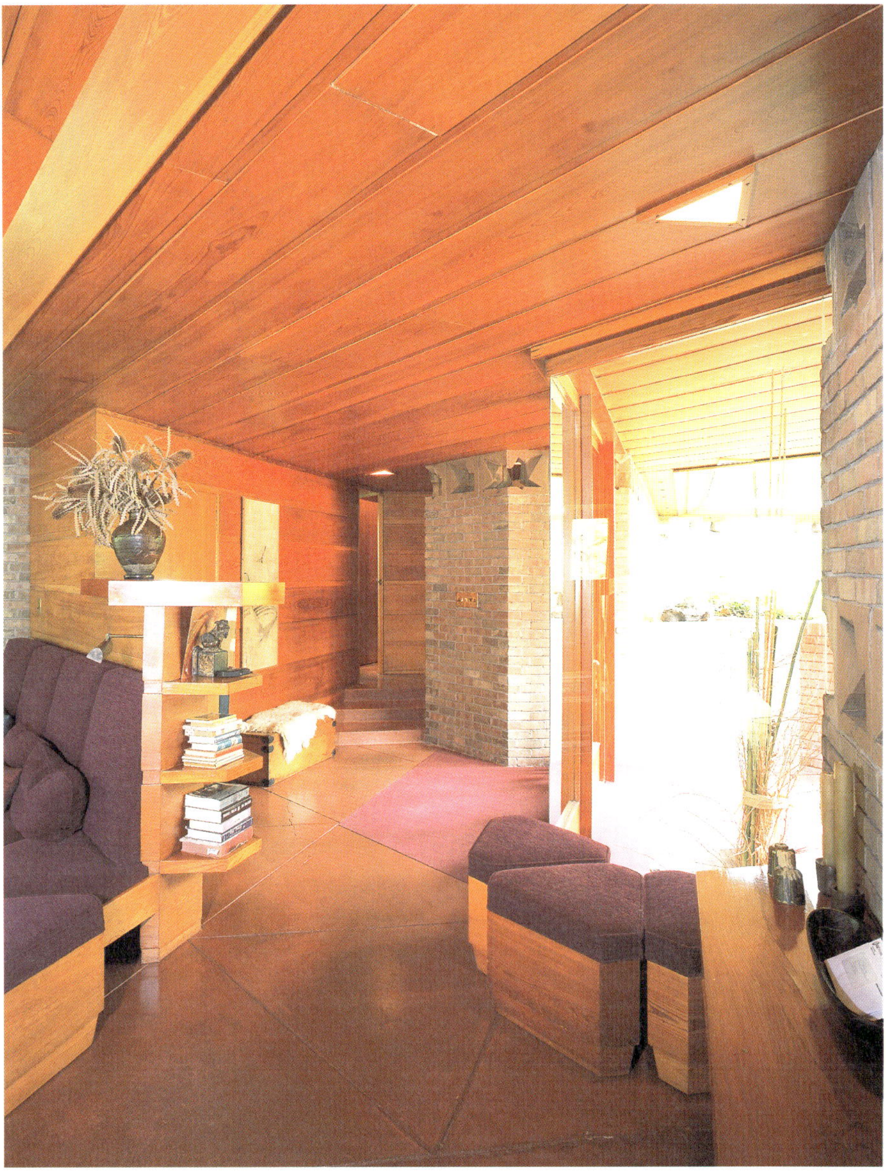

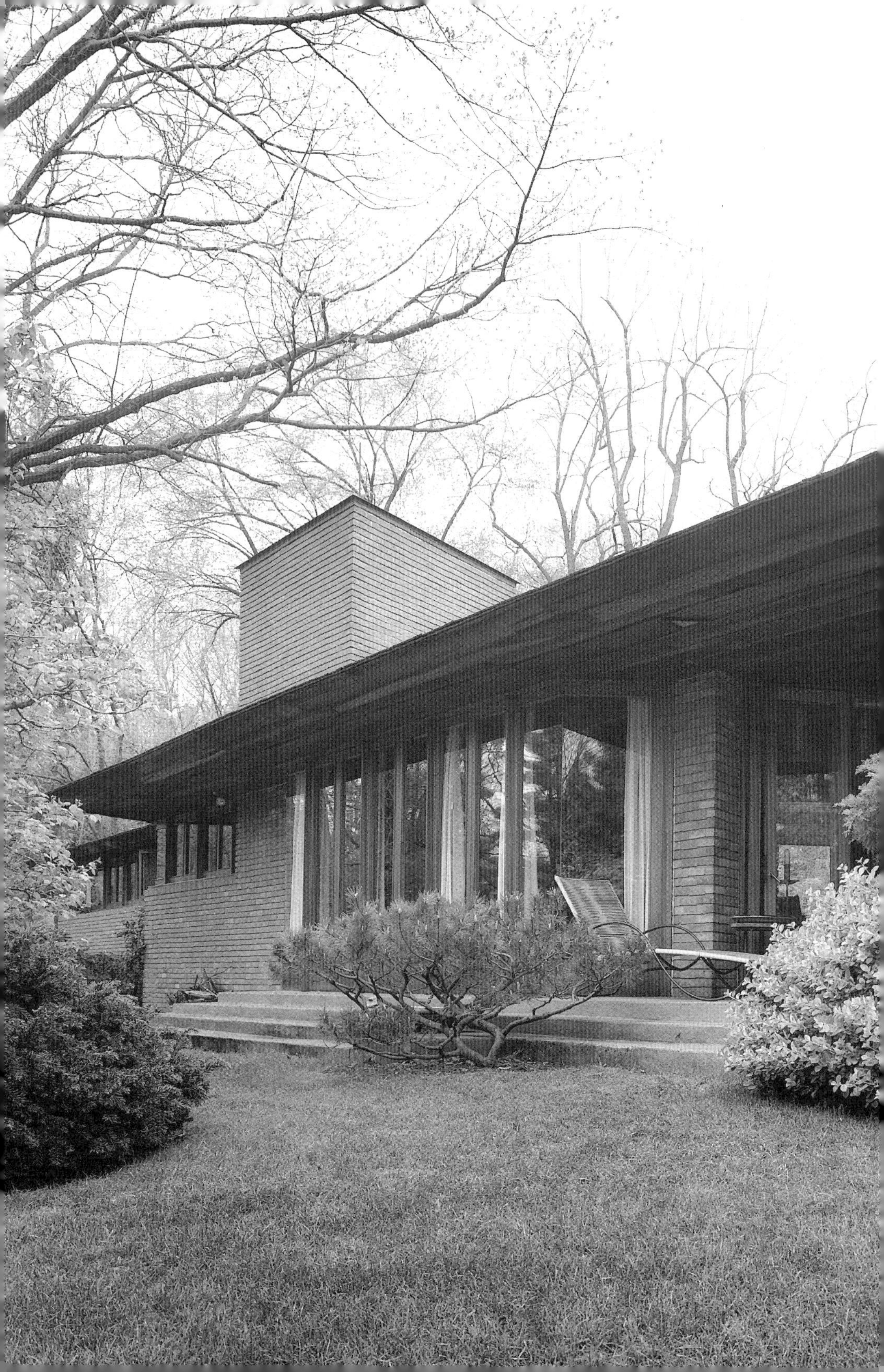

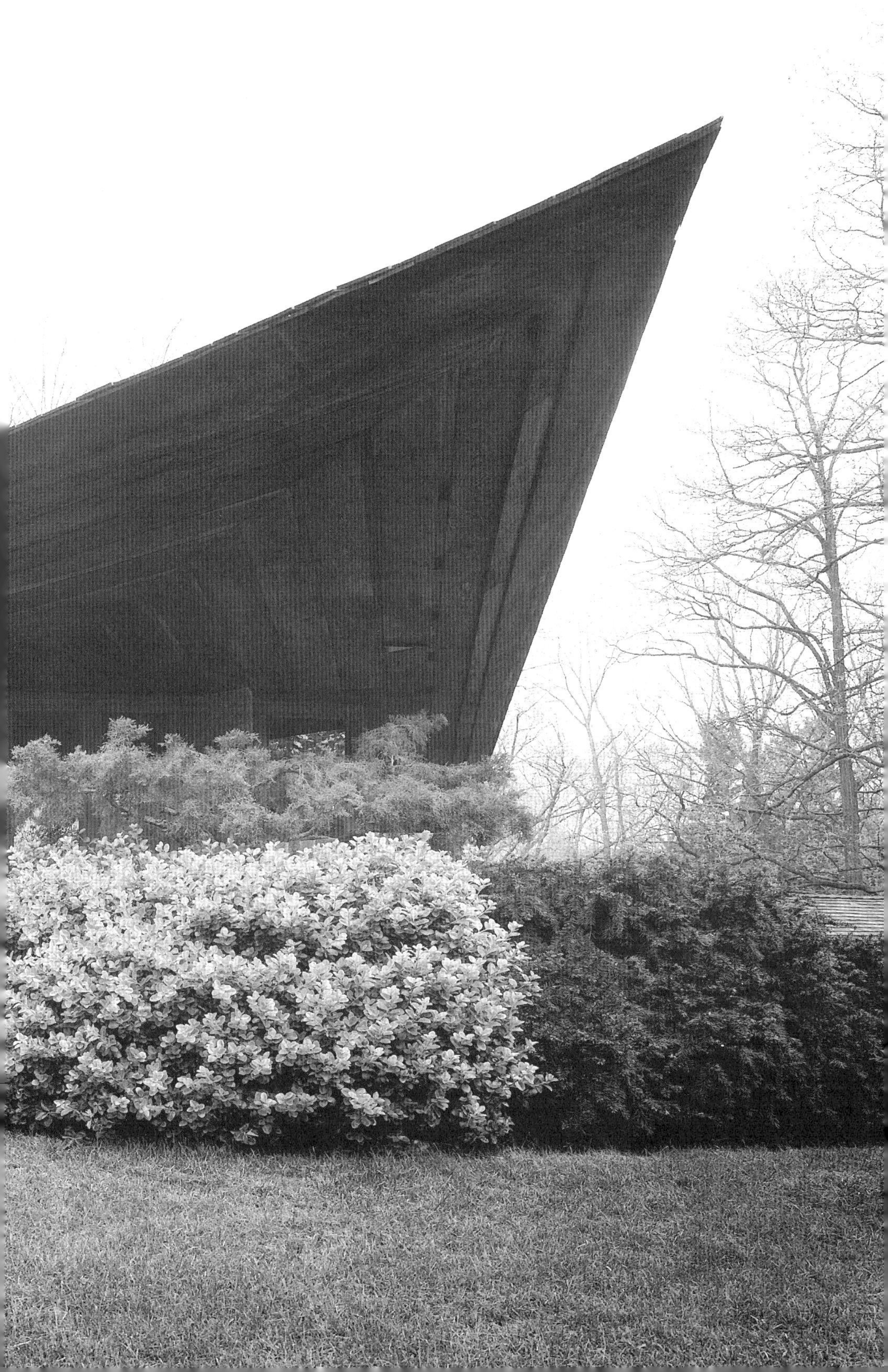

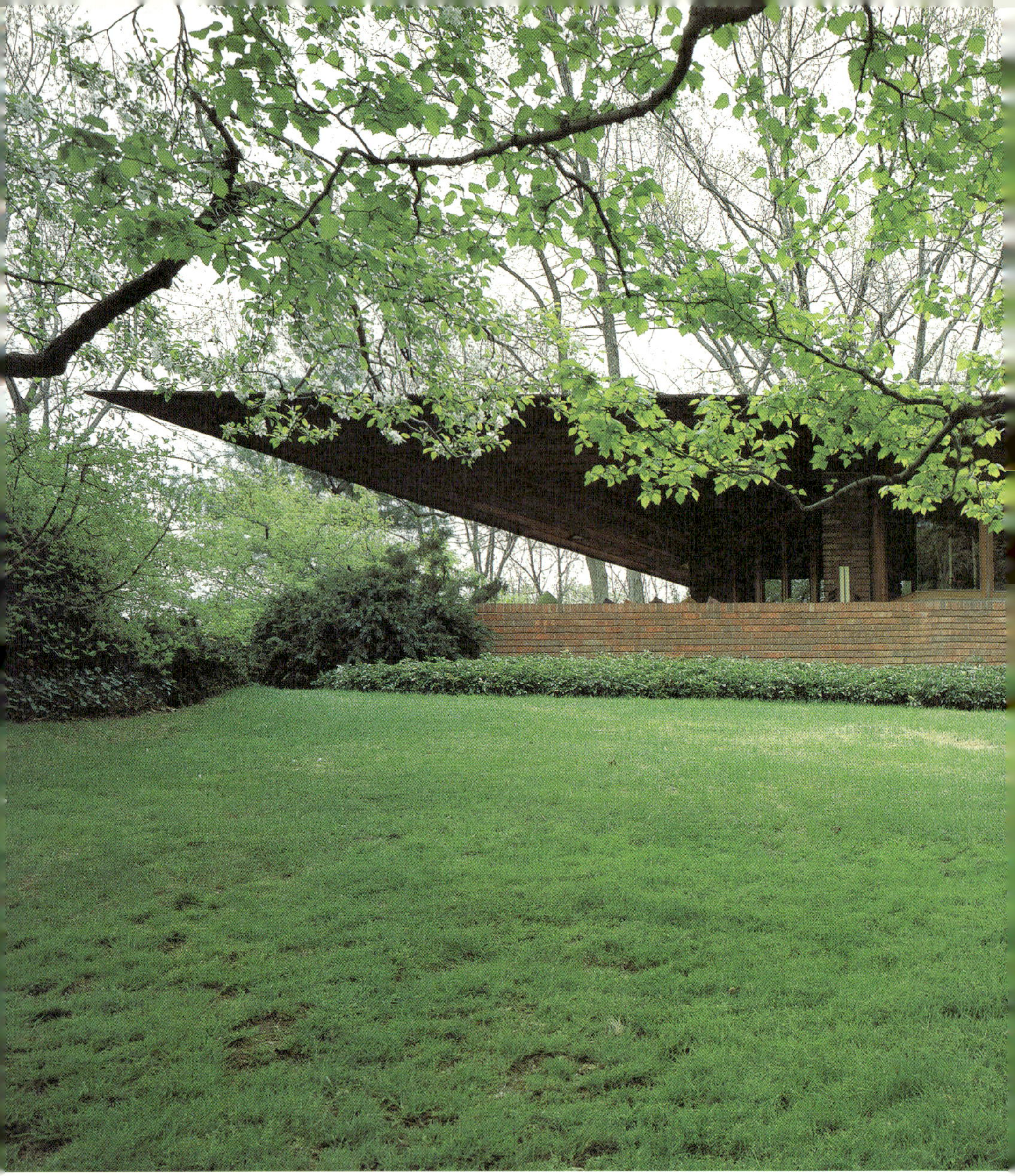

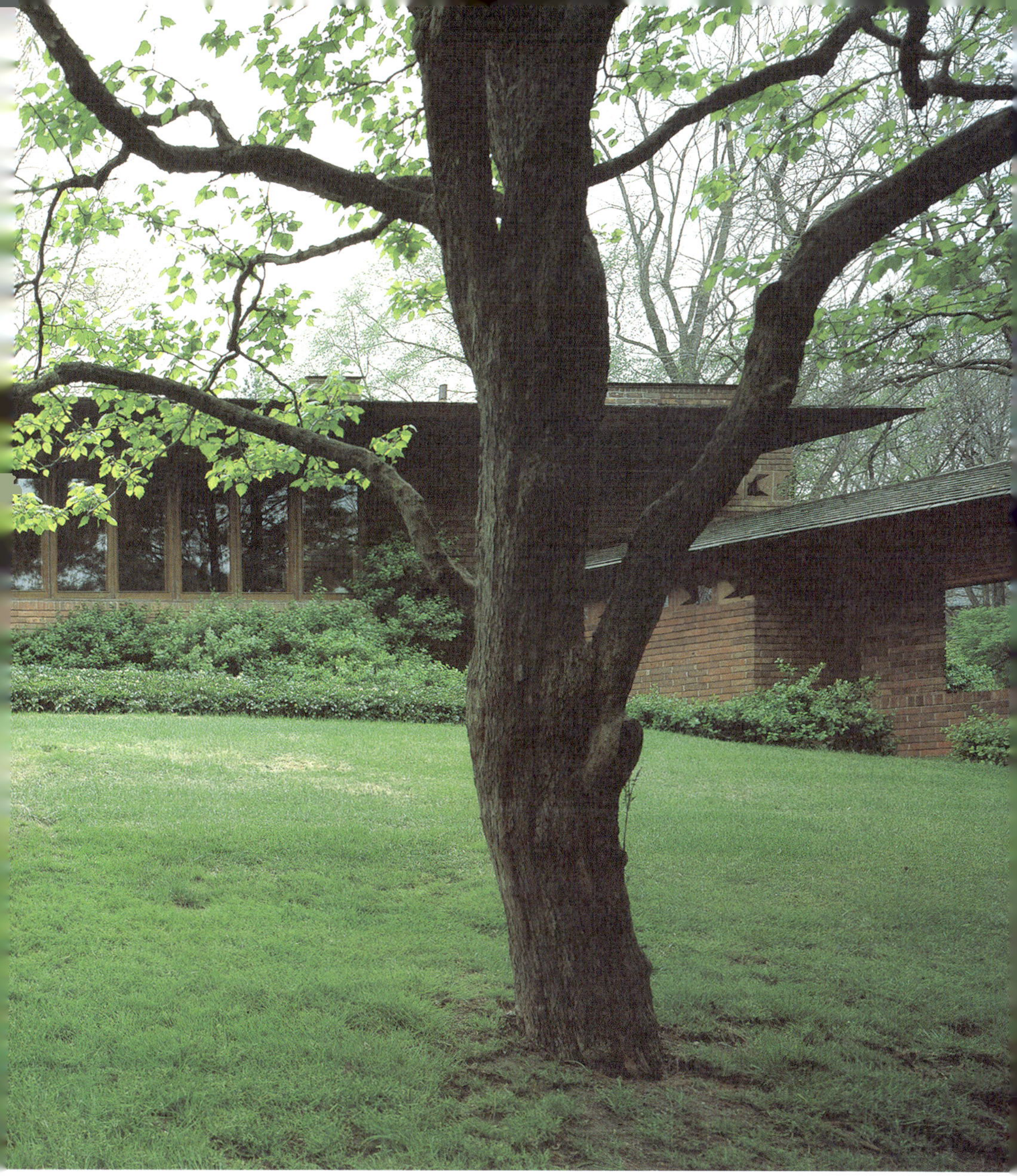

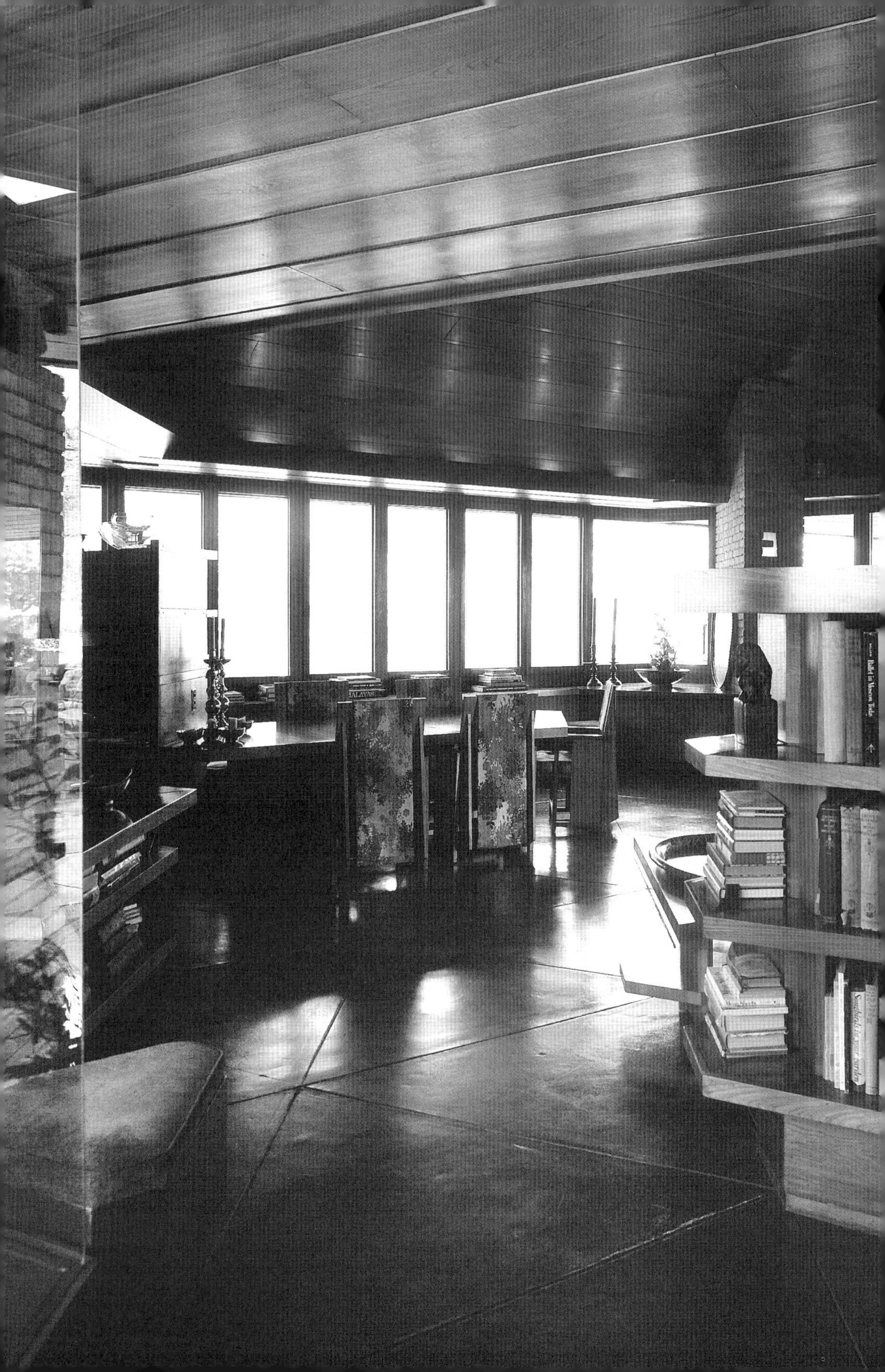
Ballet in Moscow Today
Songbirds in your garden

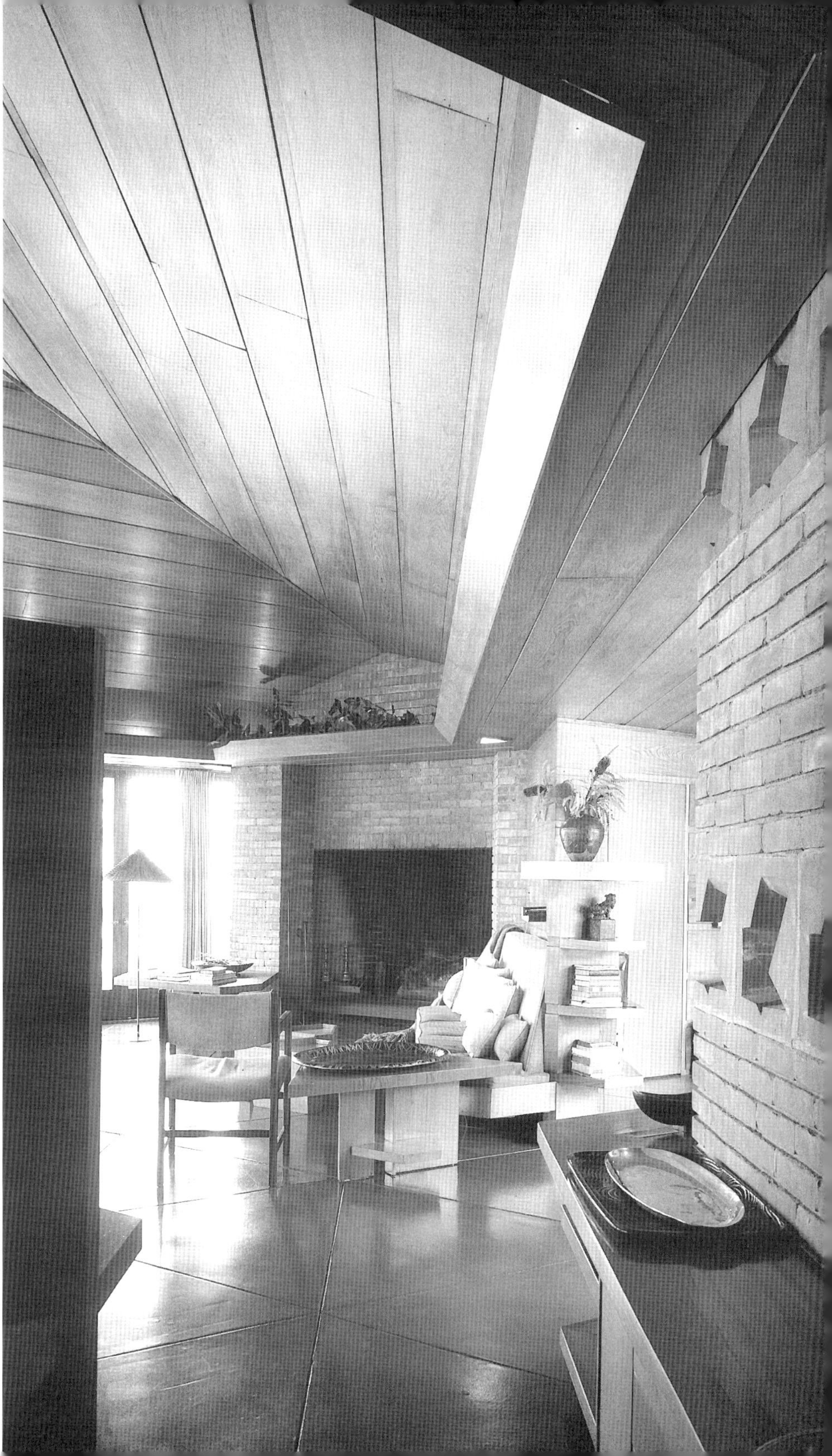

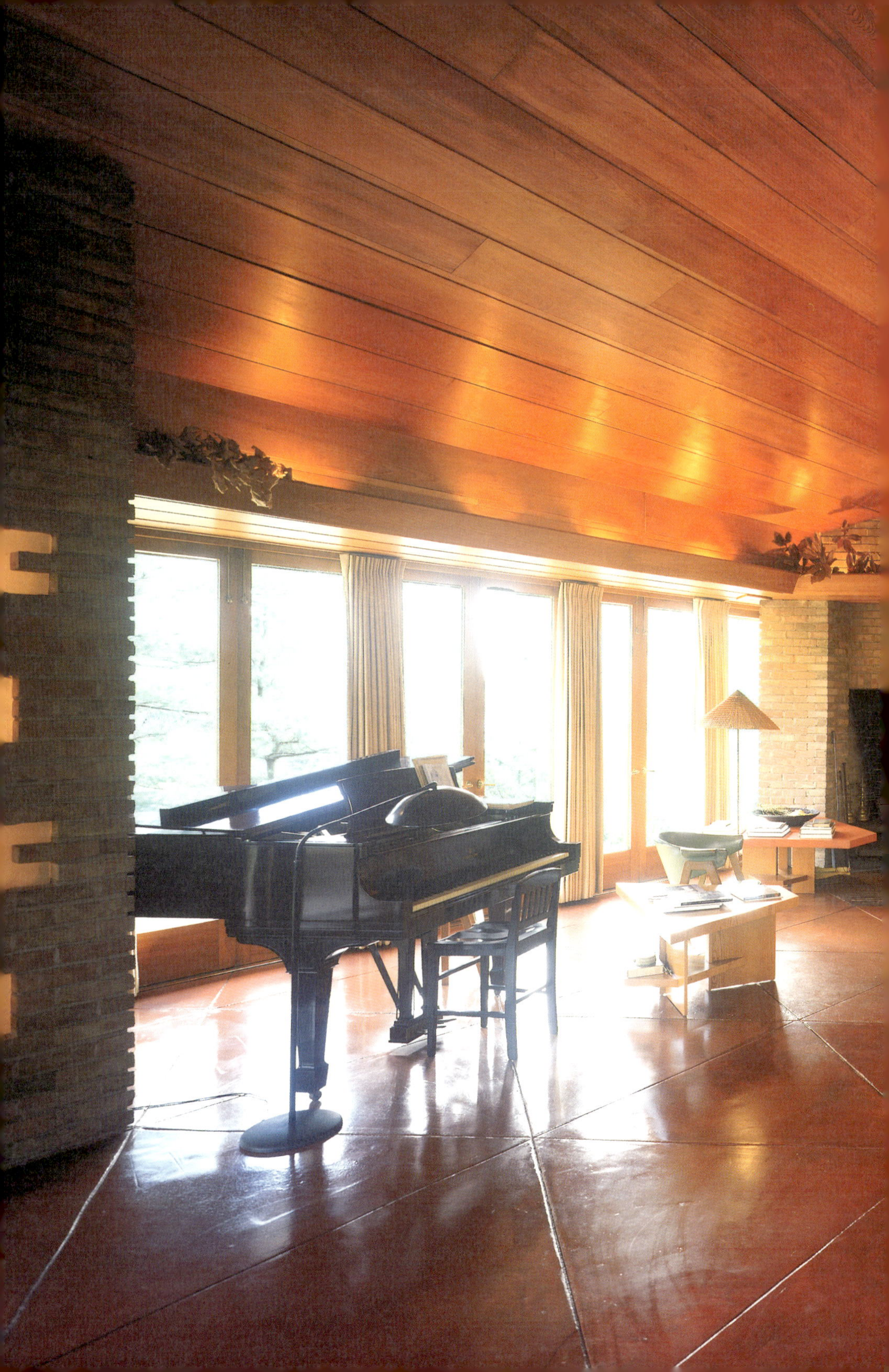

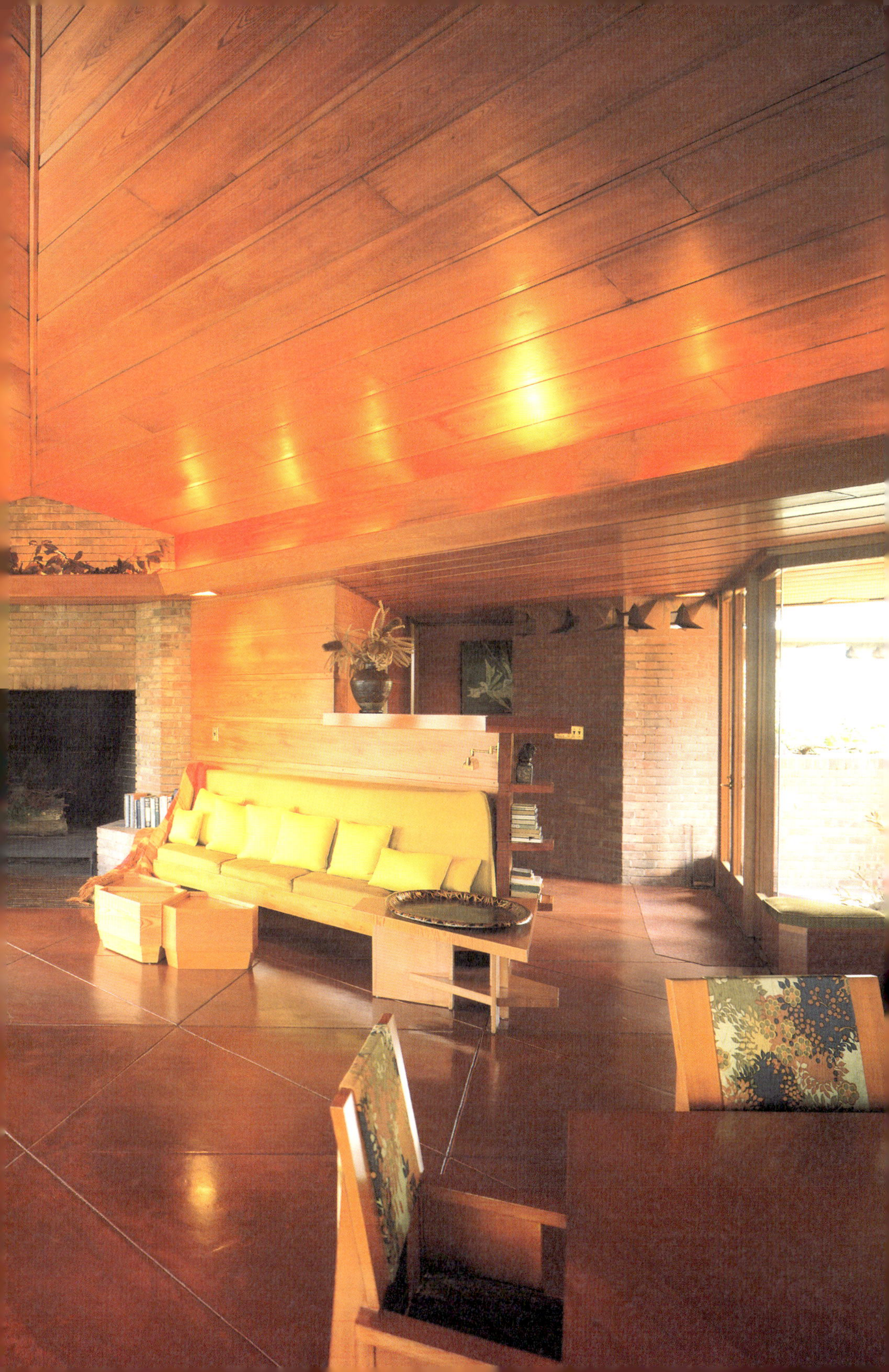

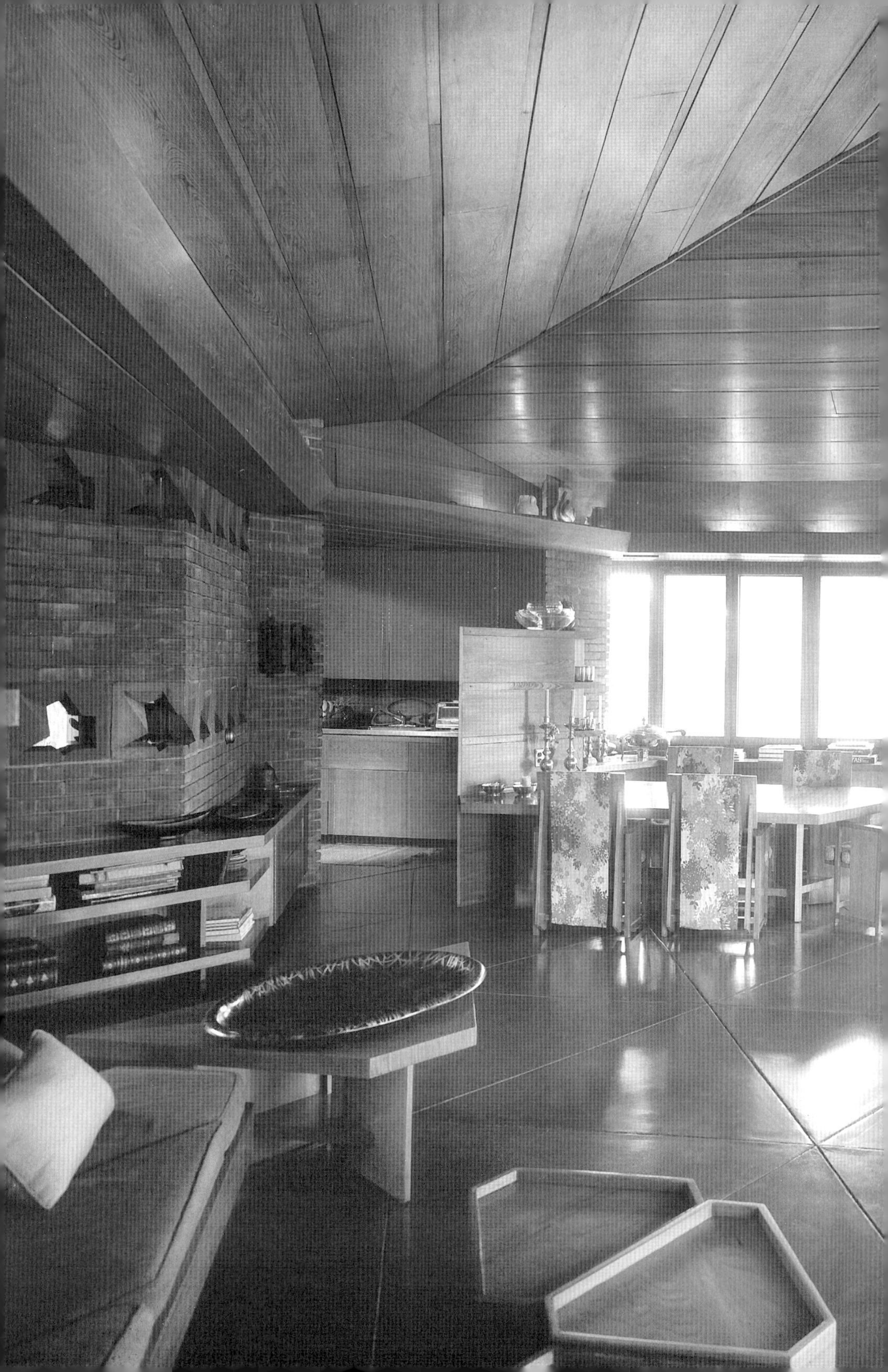

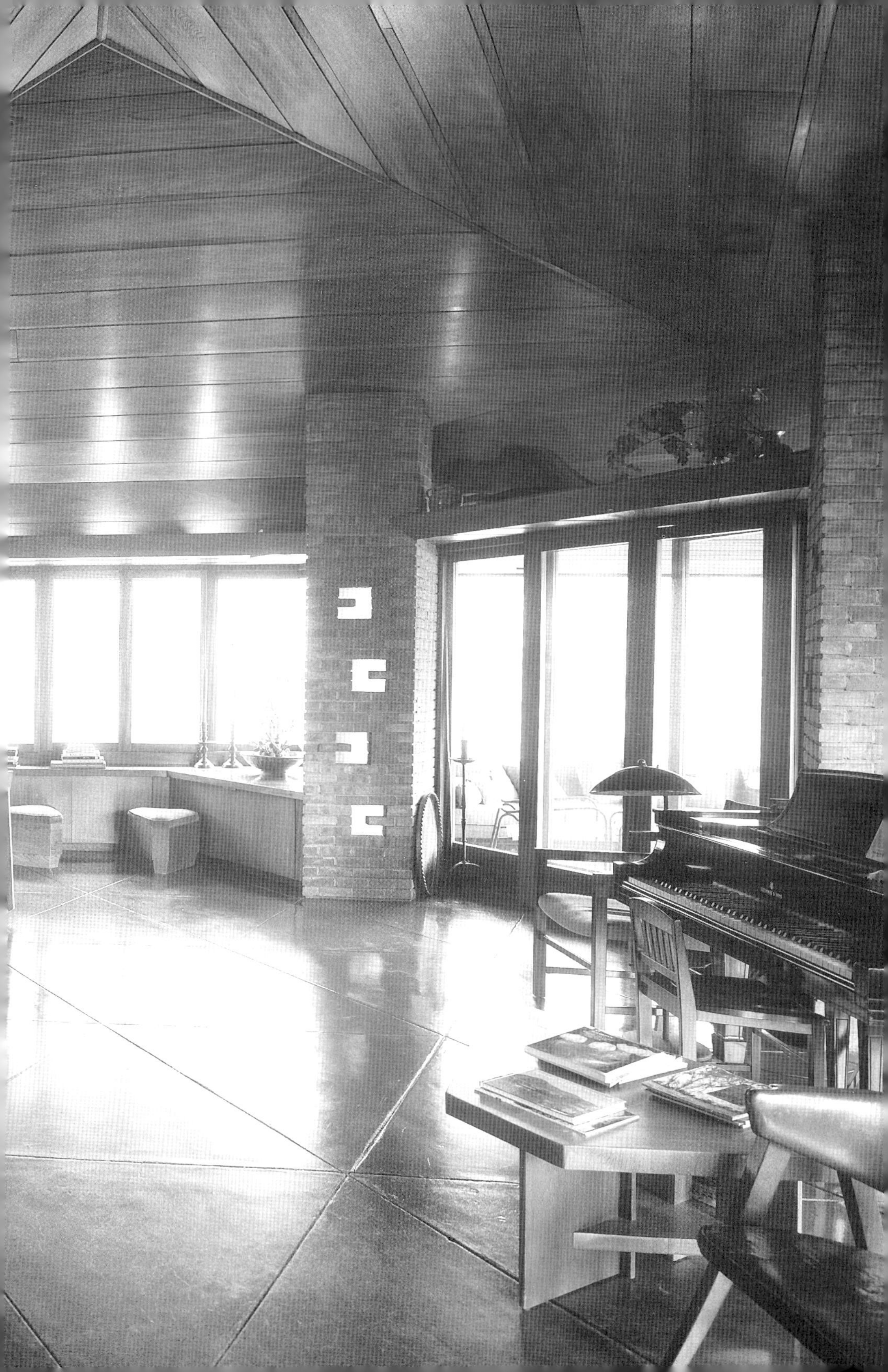

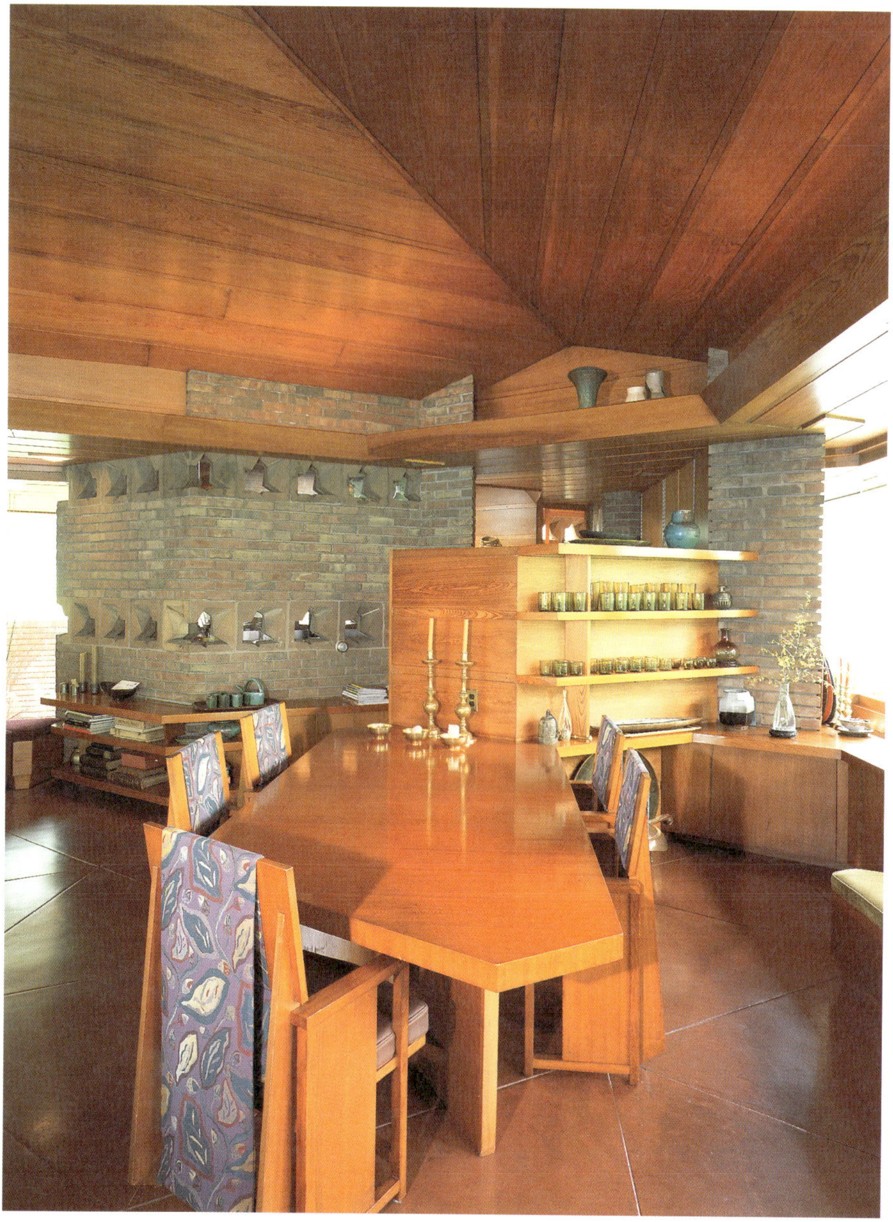

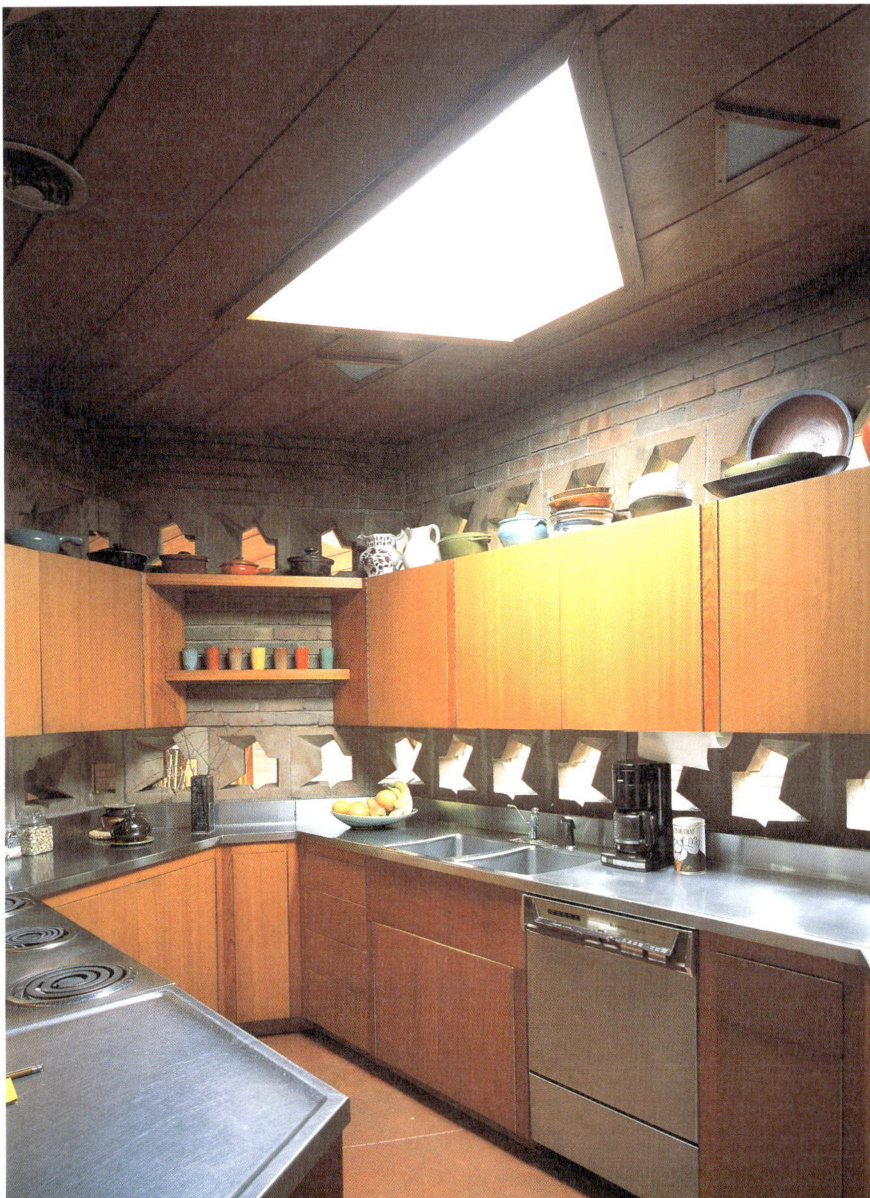

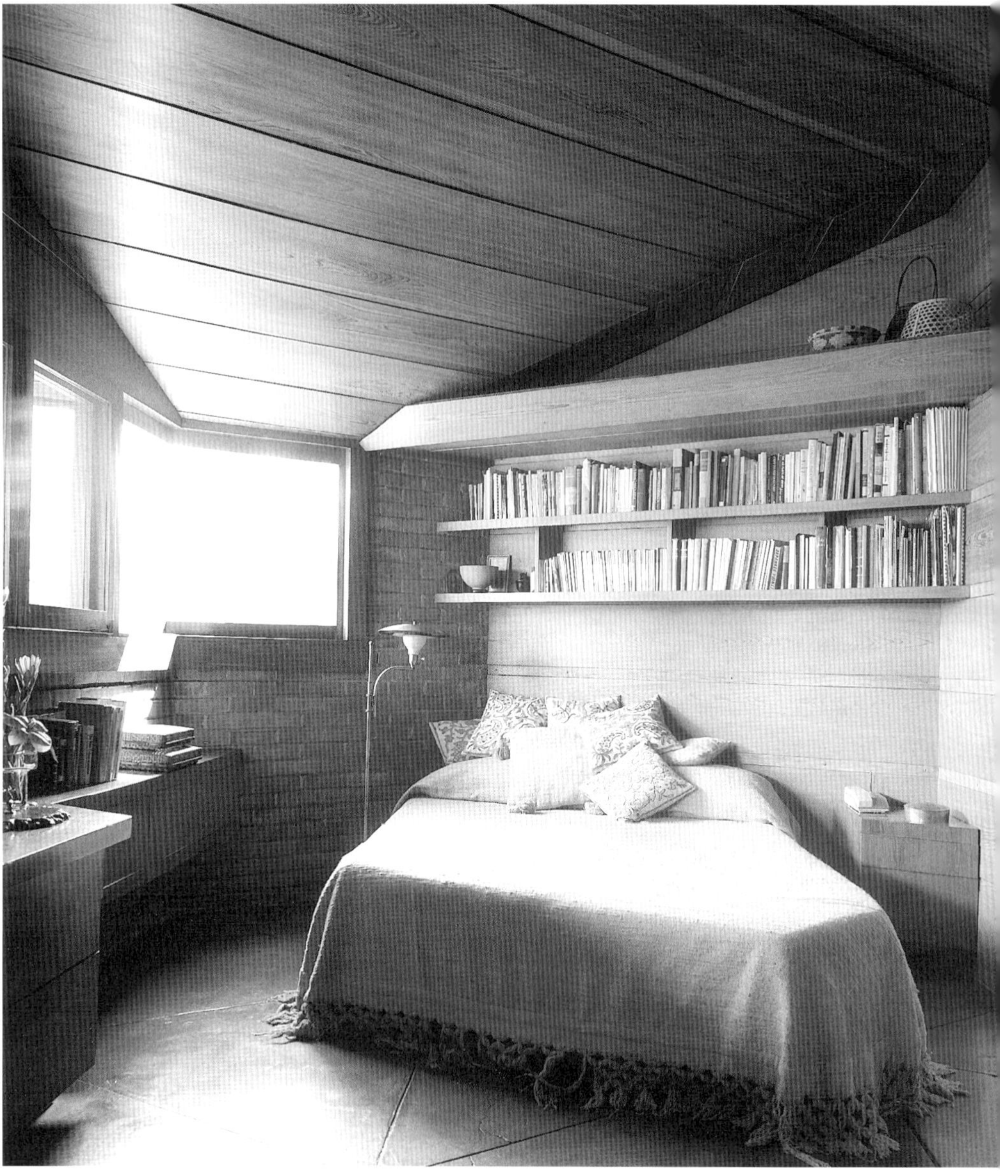

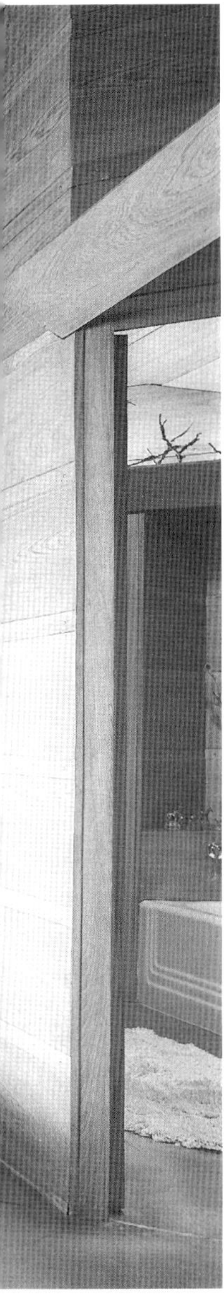

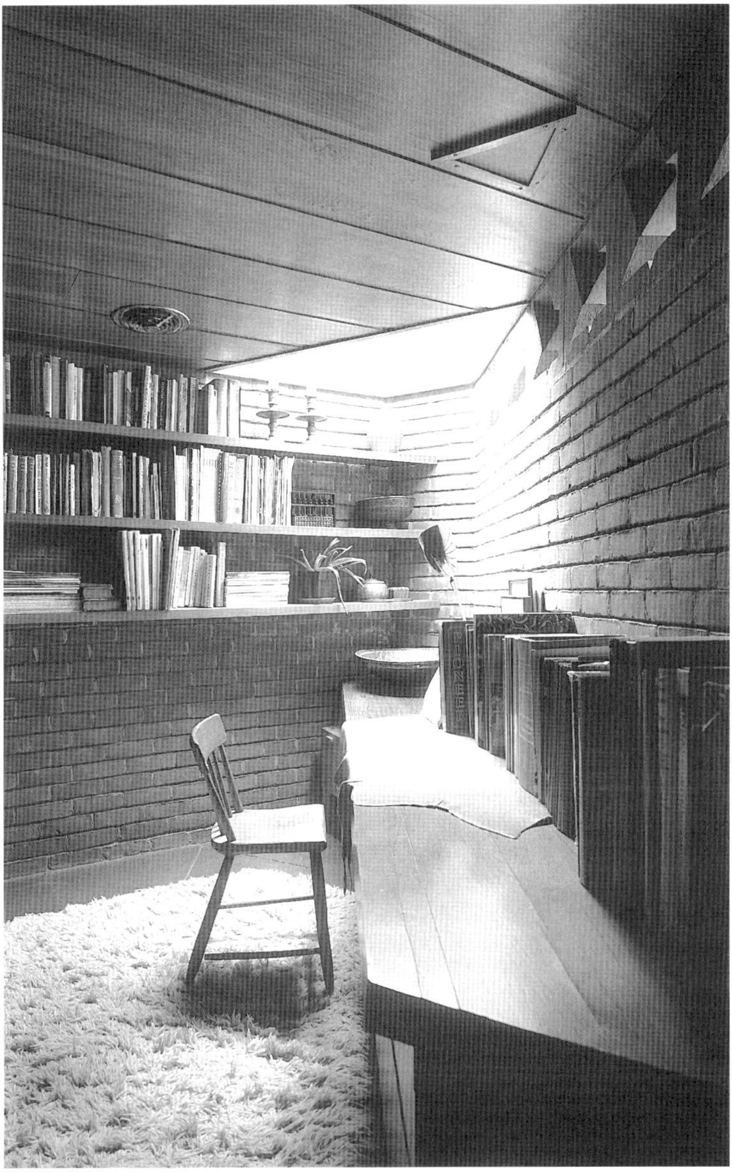

Isadore J. Zimmerman House
Manchester, New Hampshire, 1950

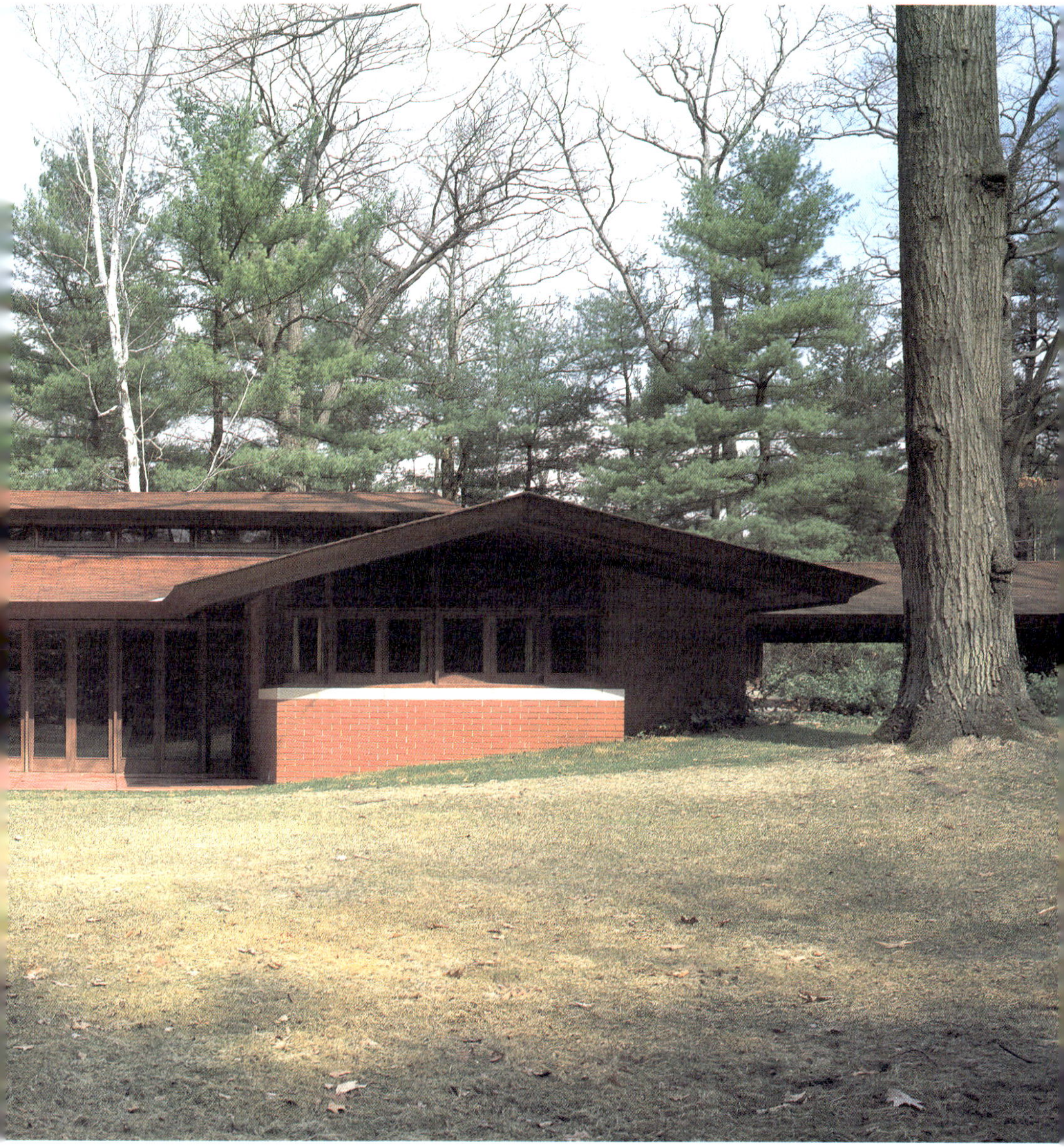

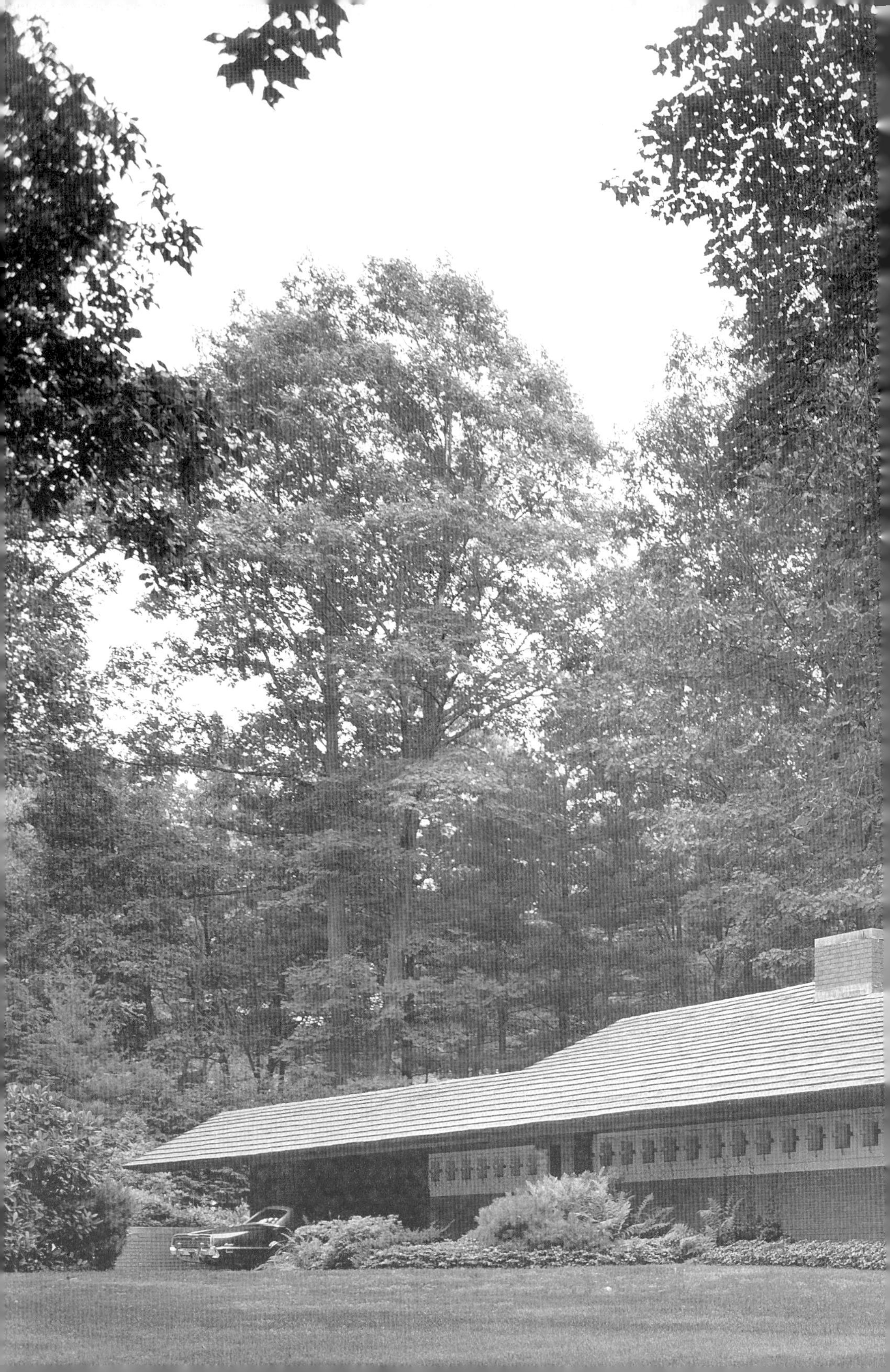

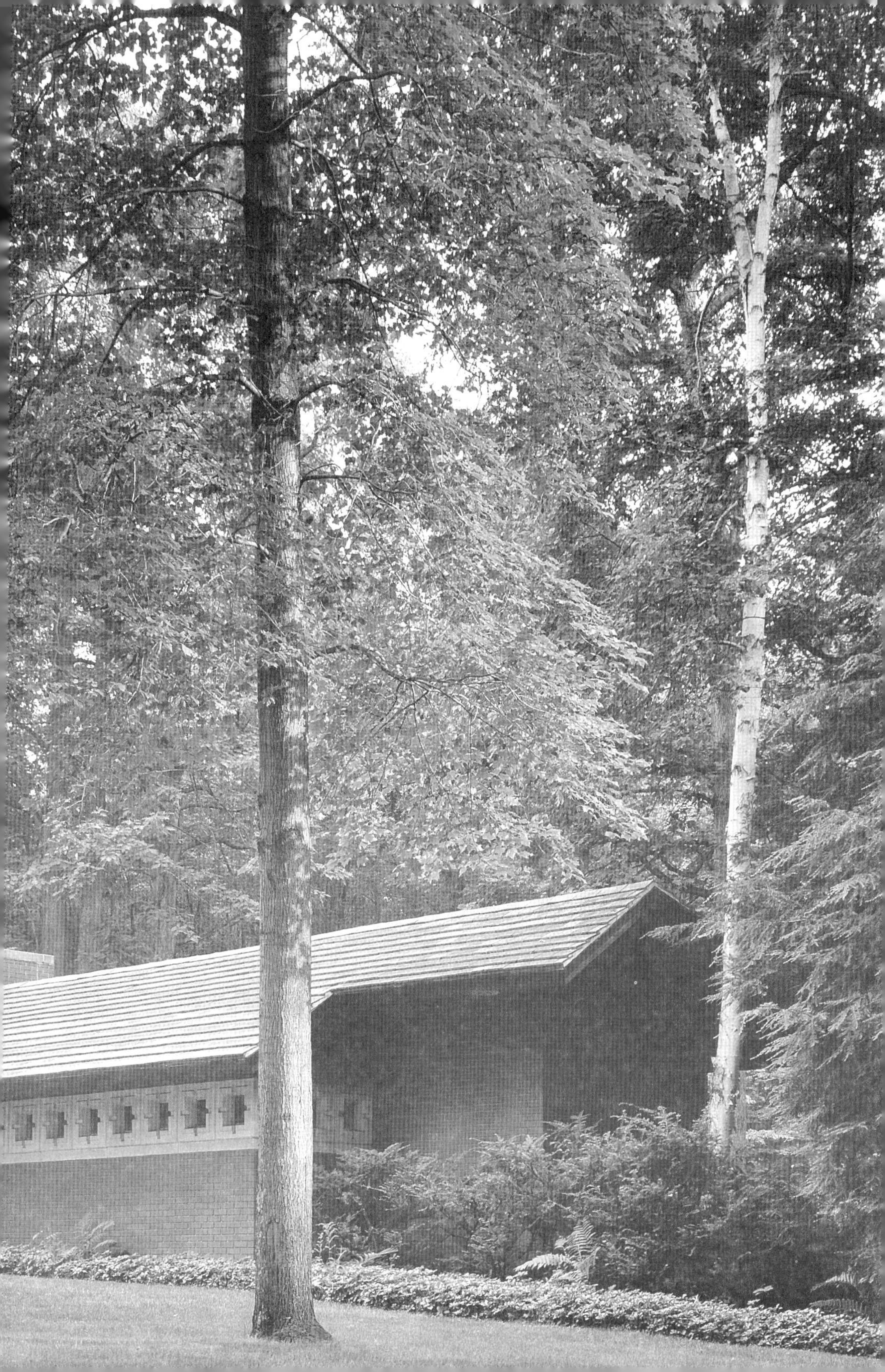

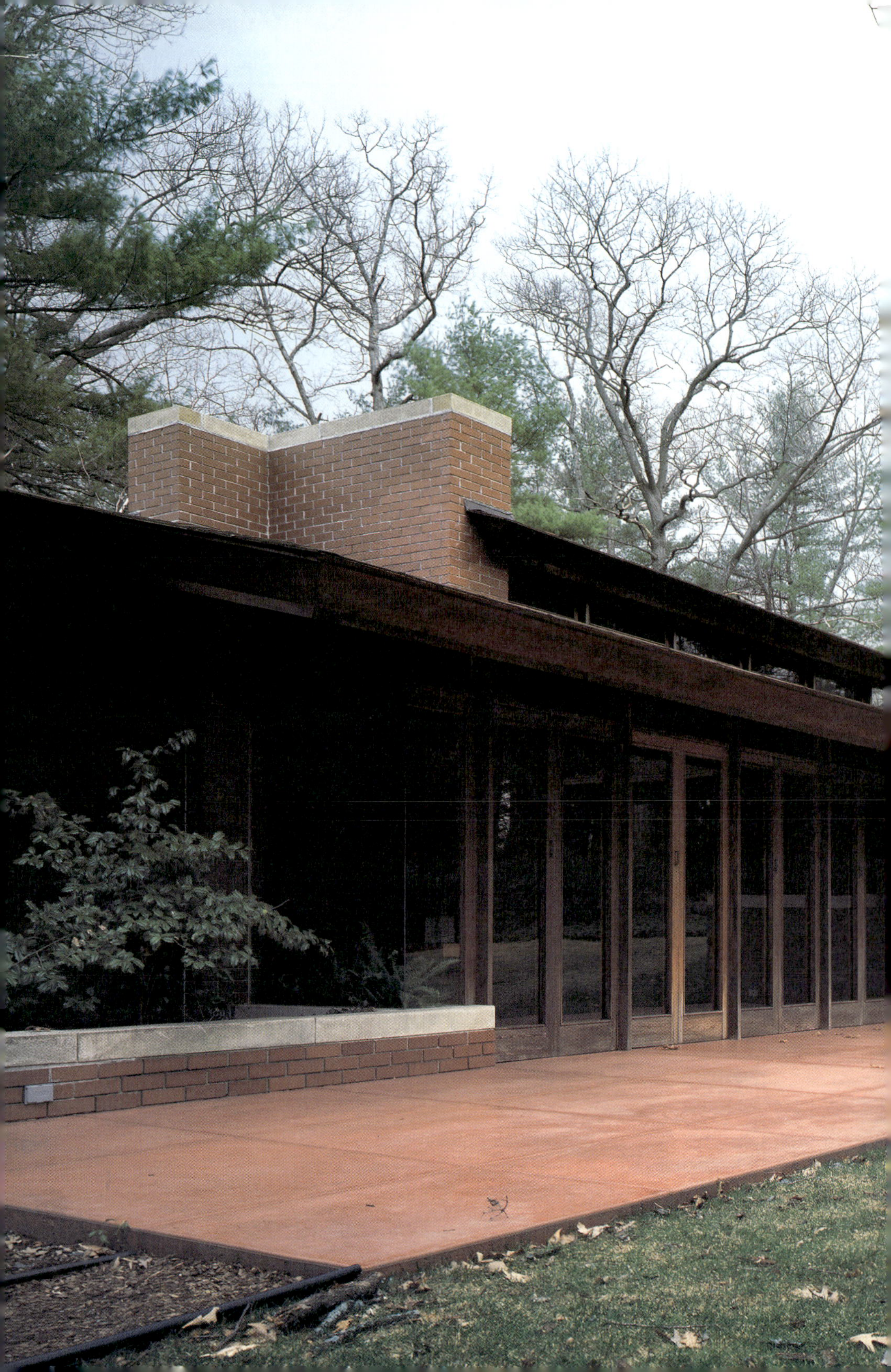

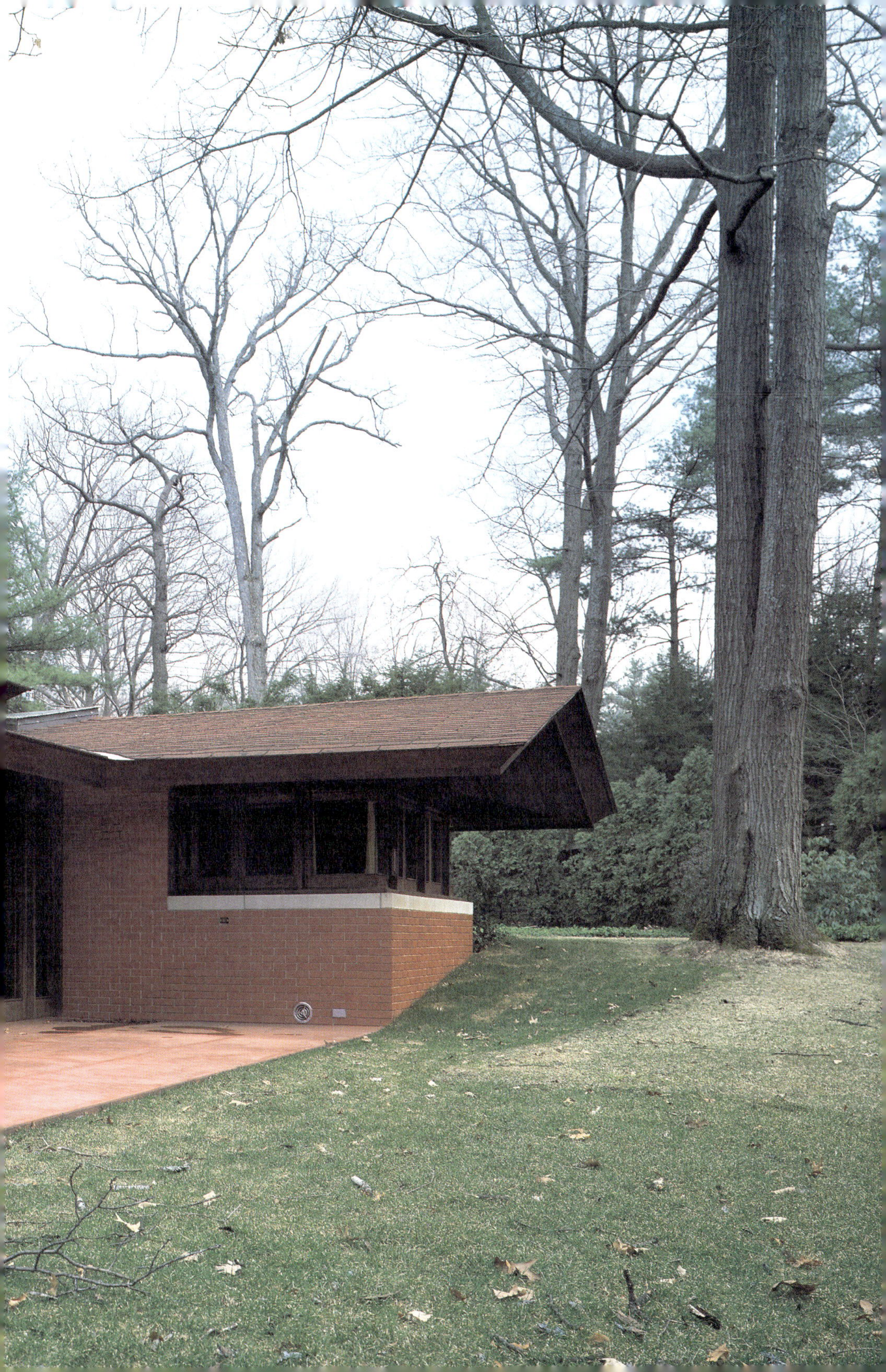

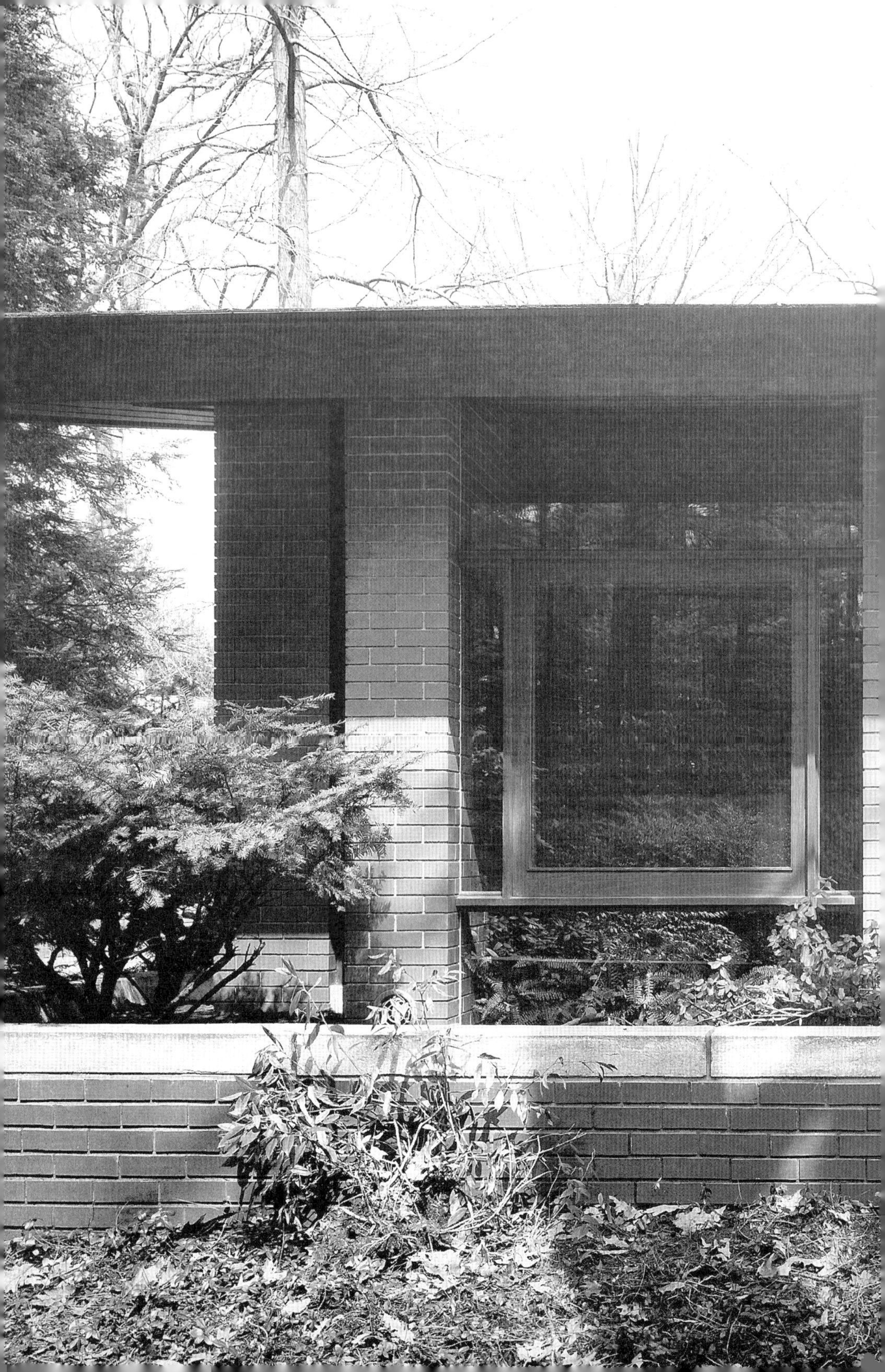

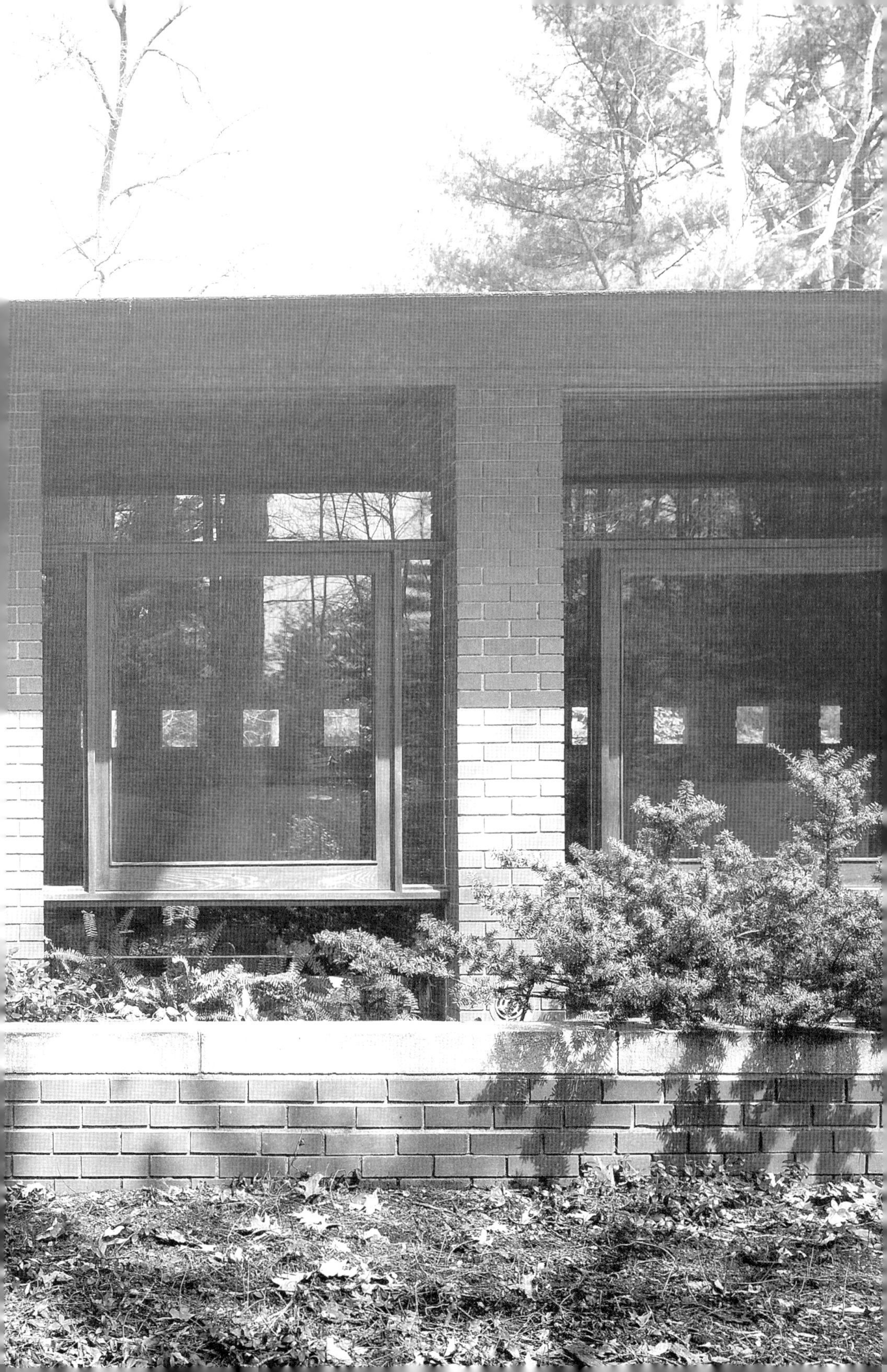

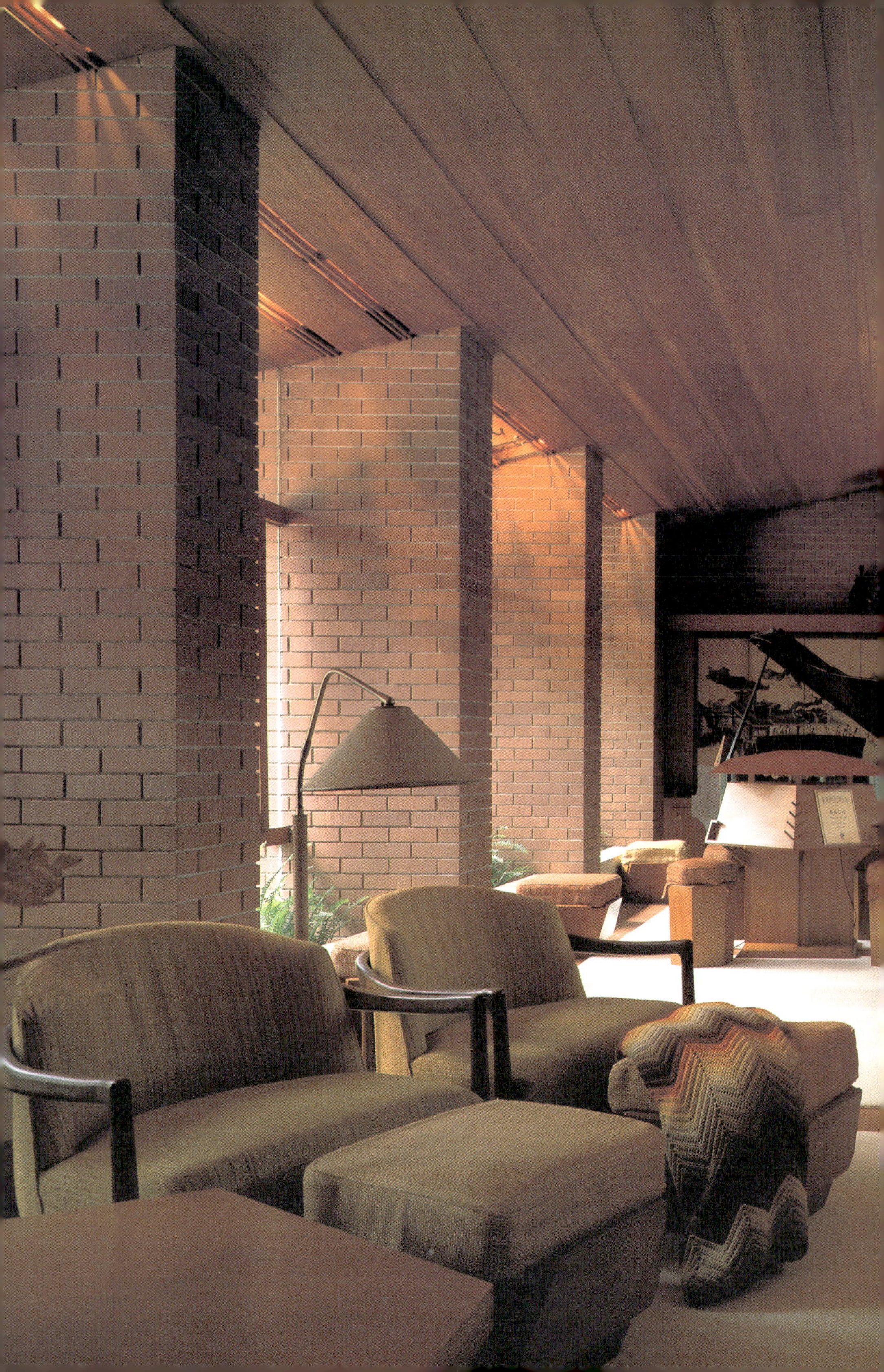
BACH

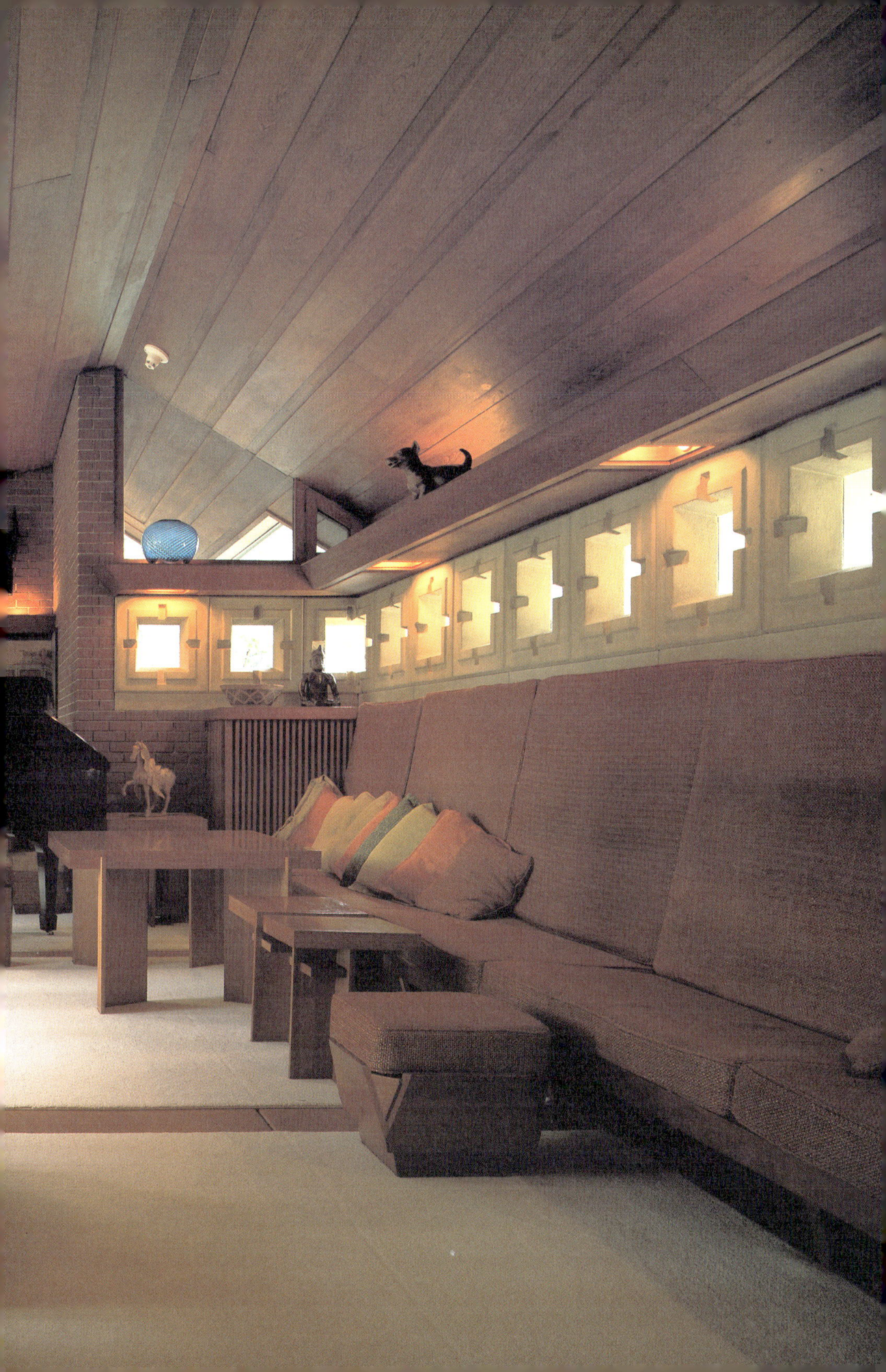

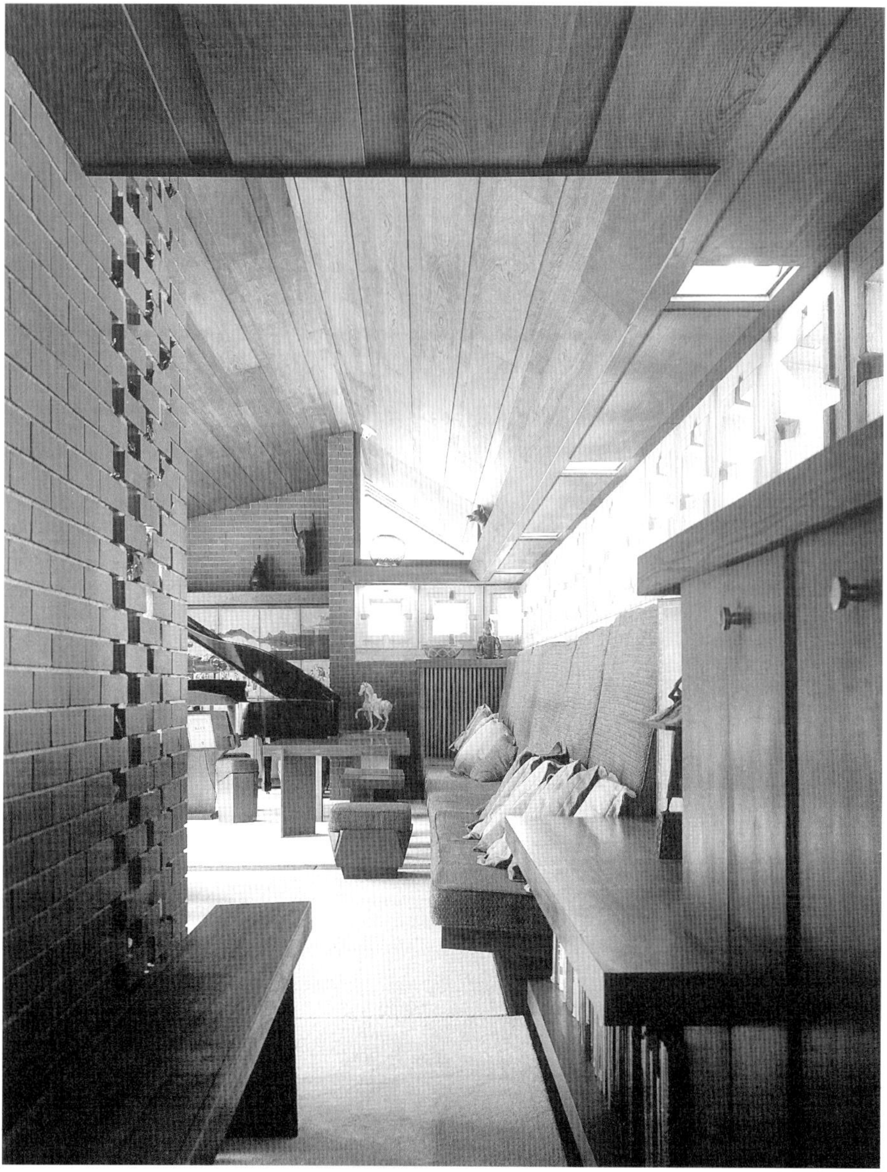

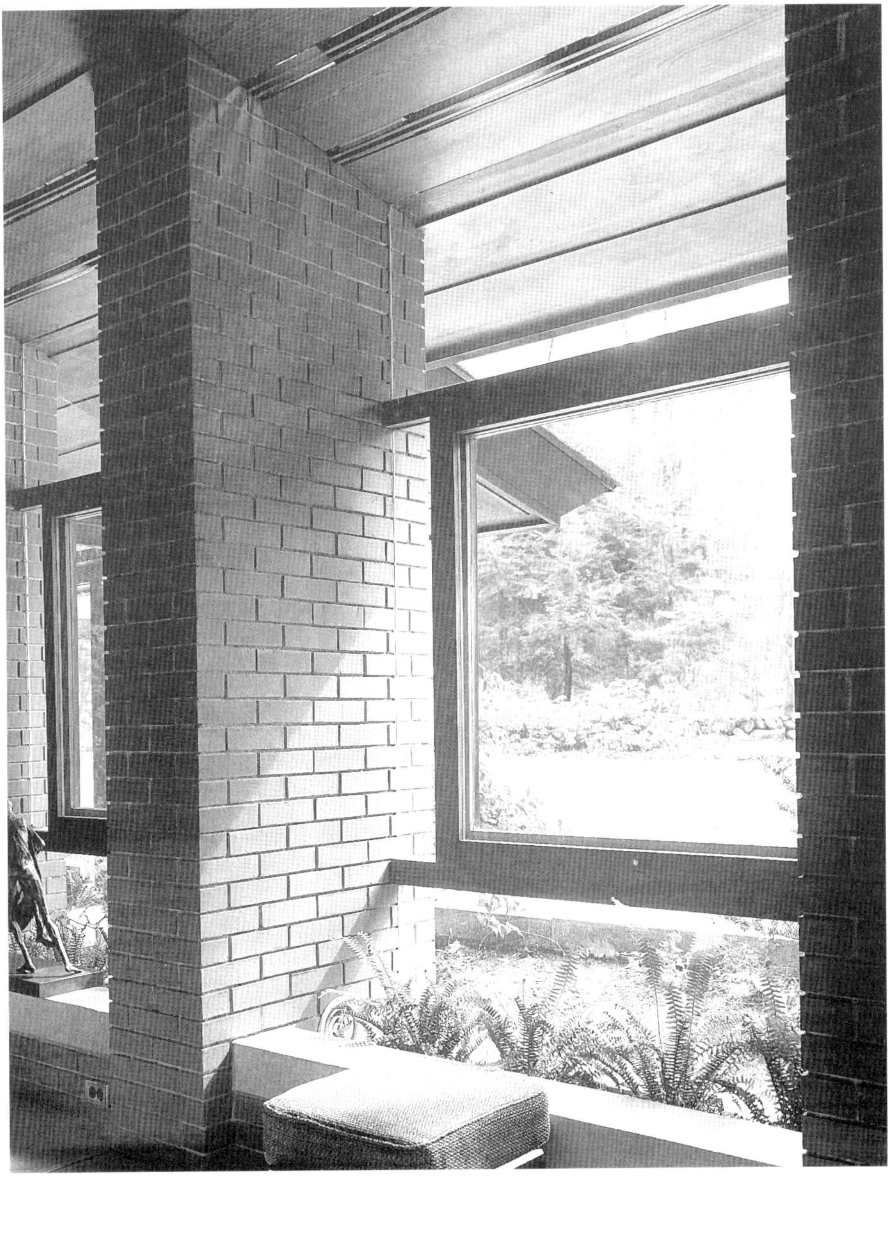

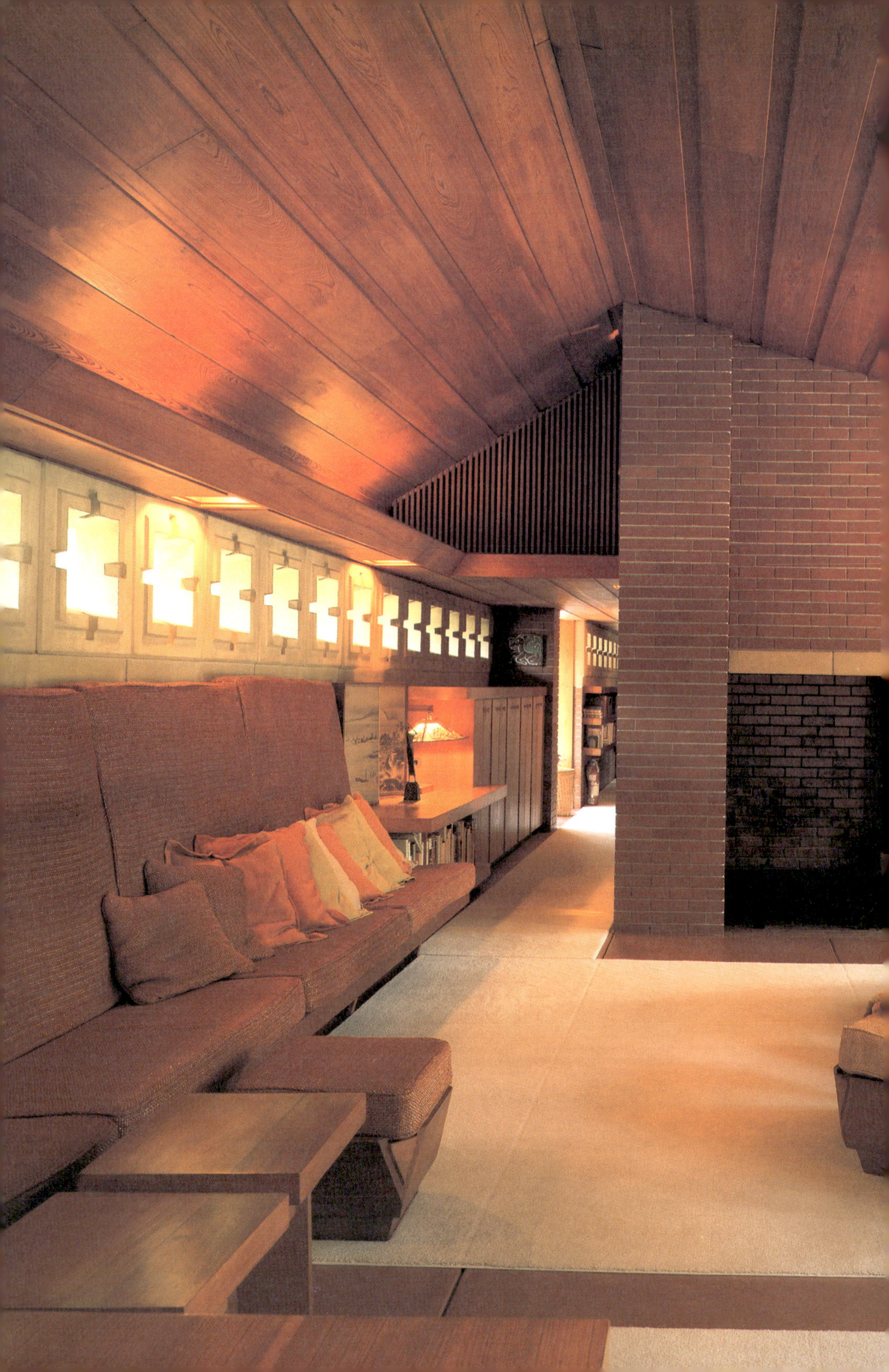

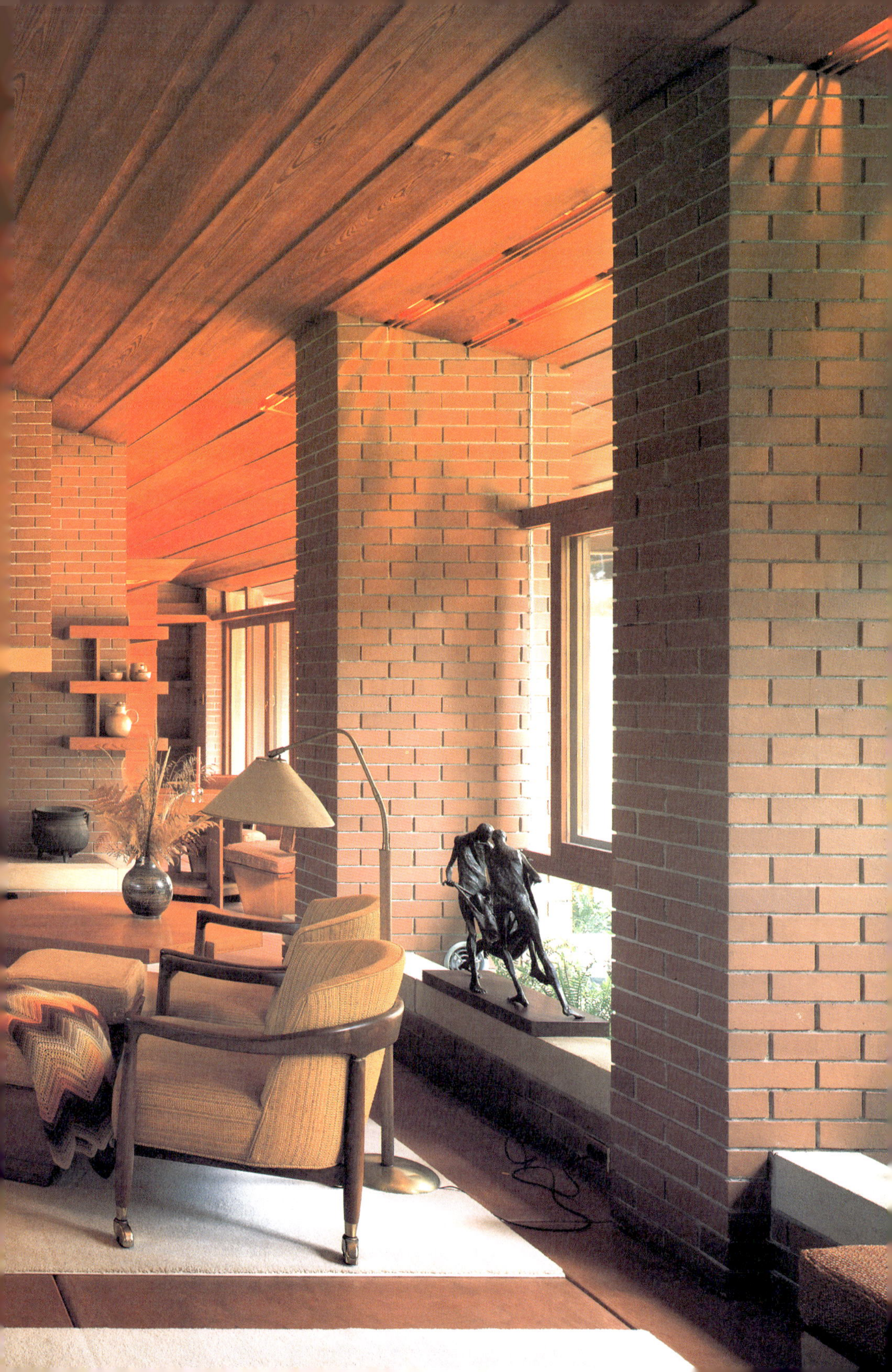

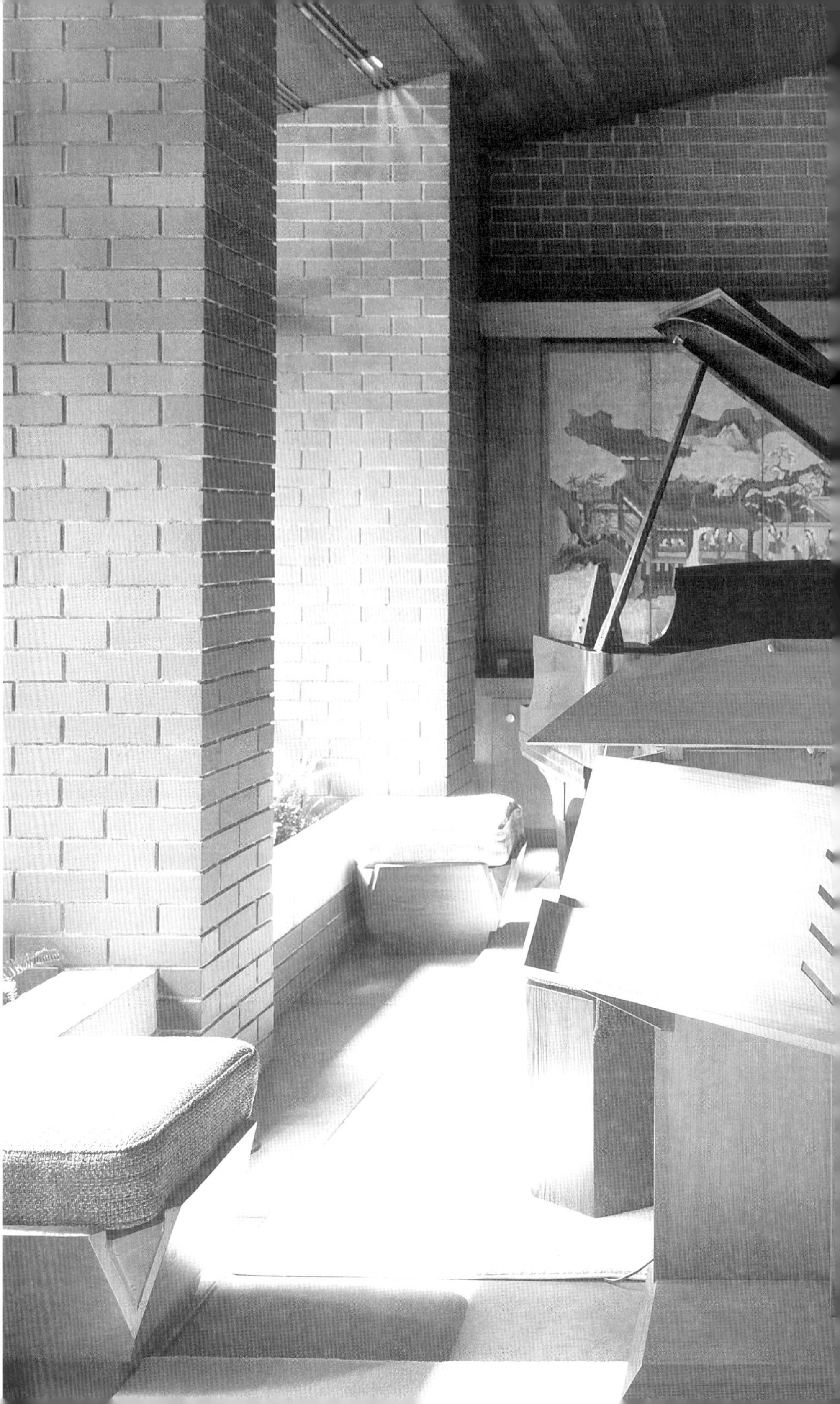

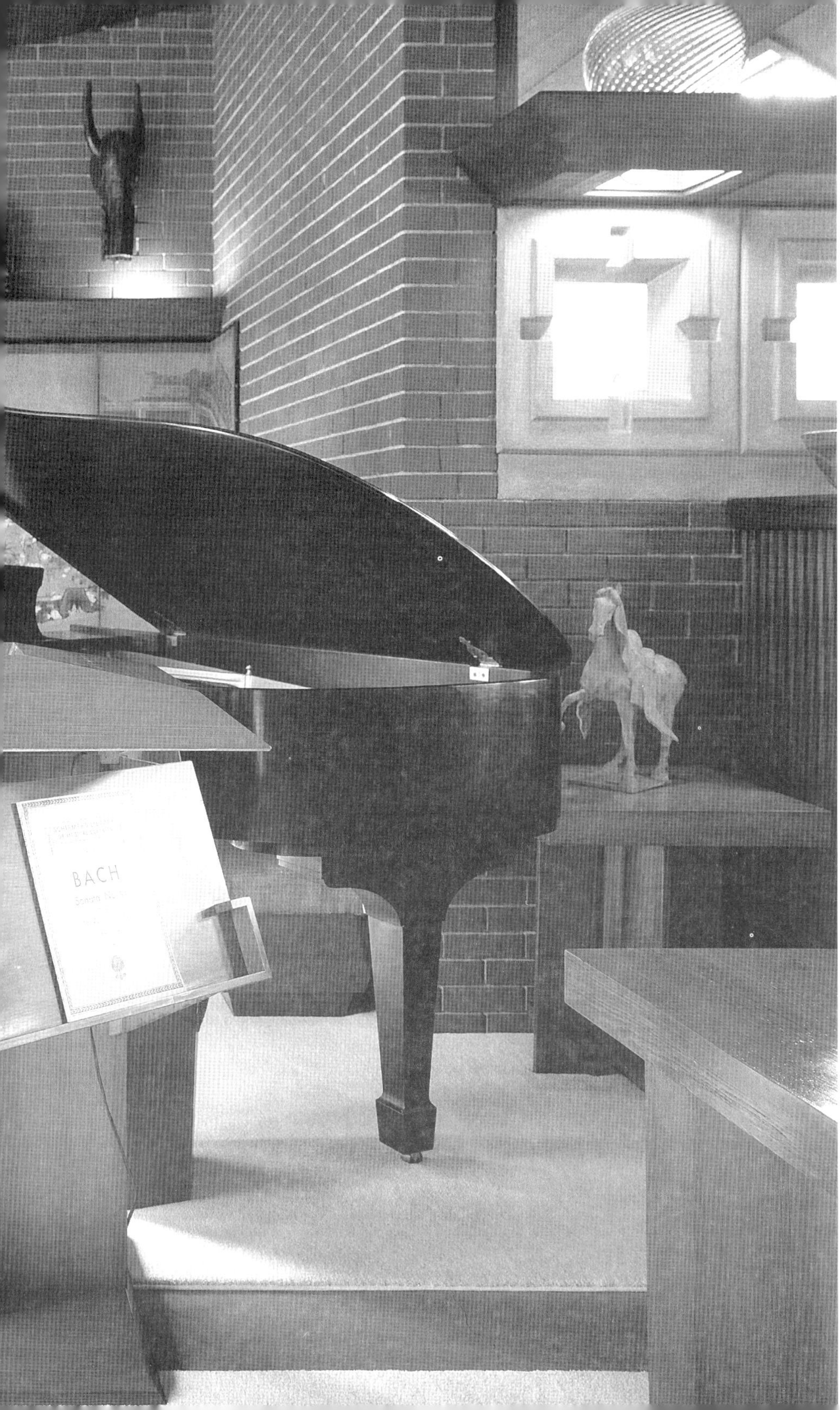
BACH

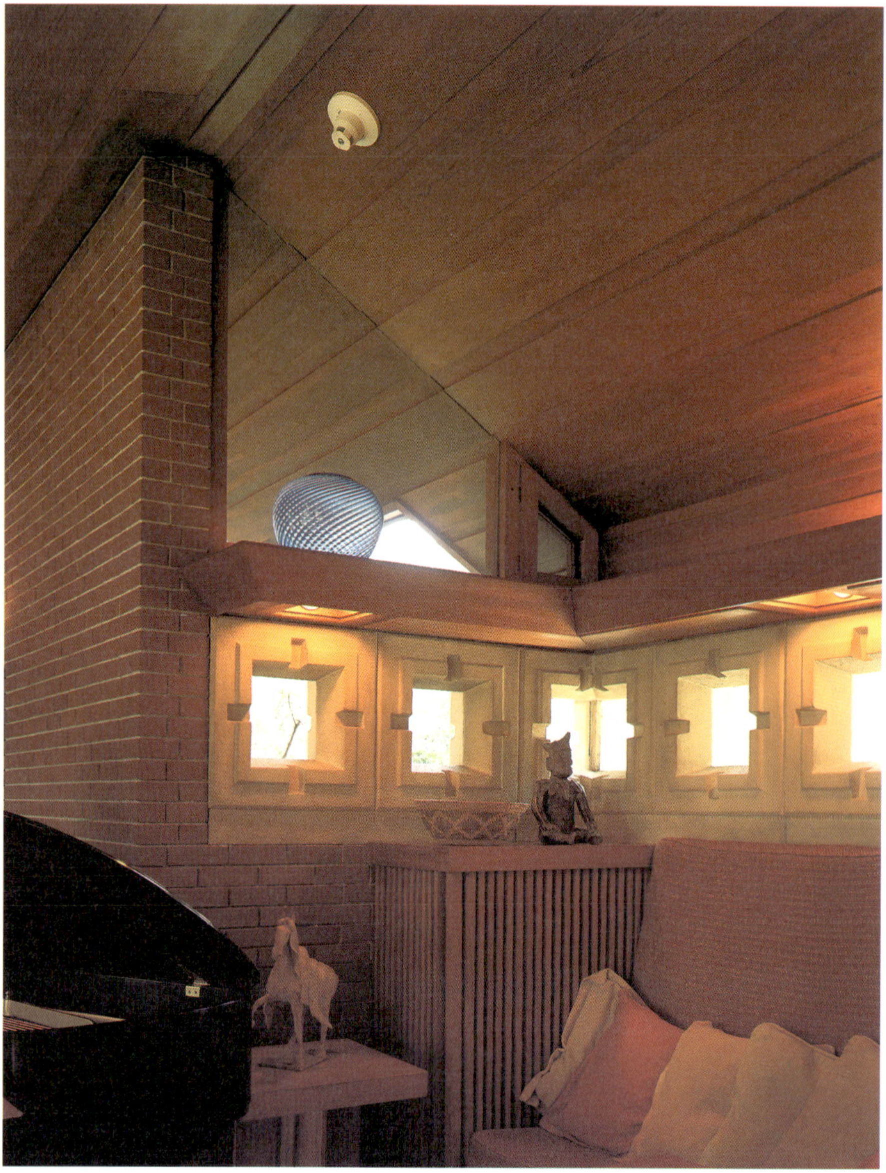

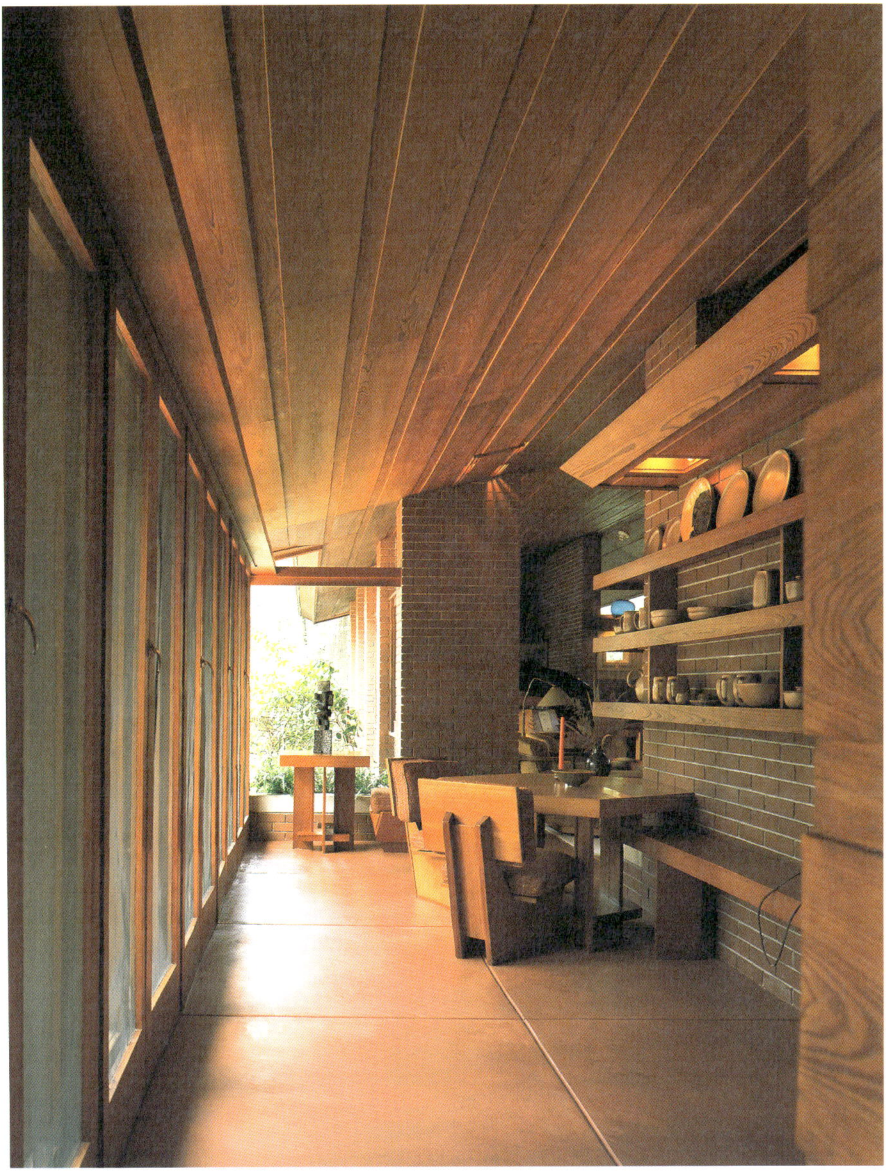

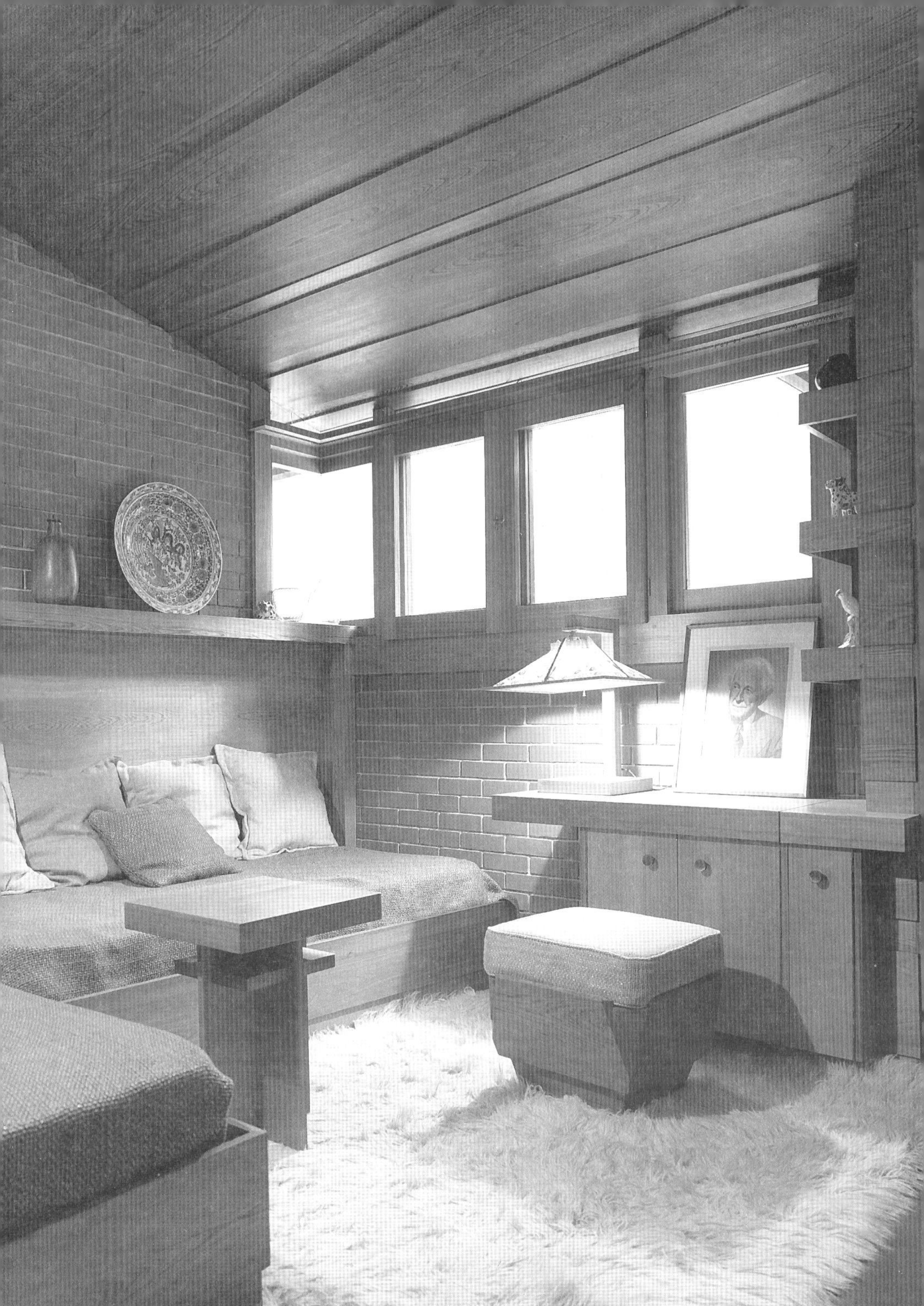

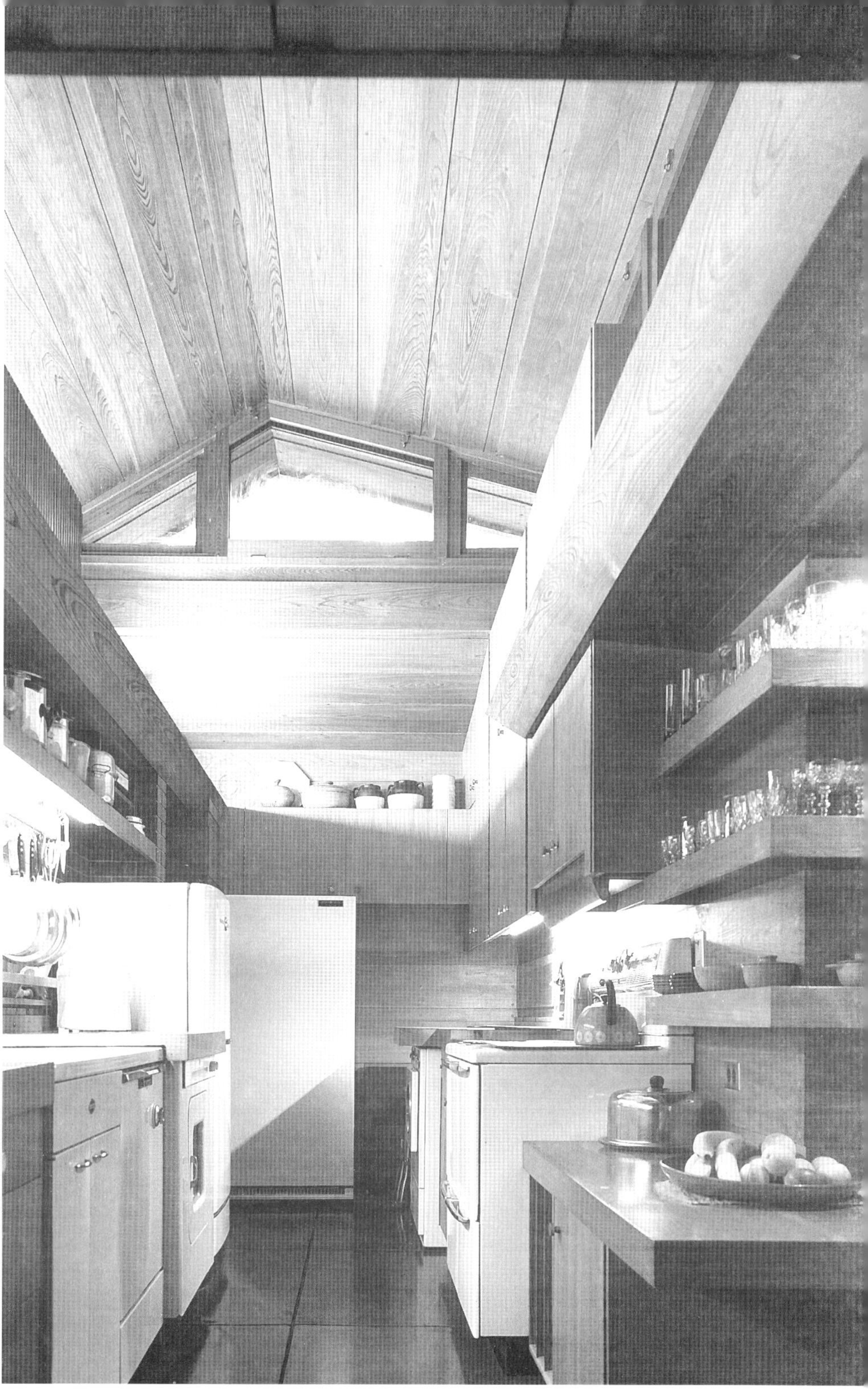

Harold Price House, "Grandma House"
Paradise Valley, Arizona, 1954

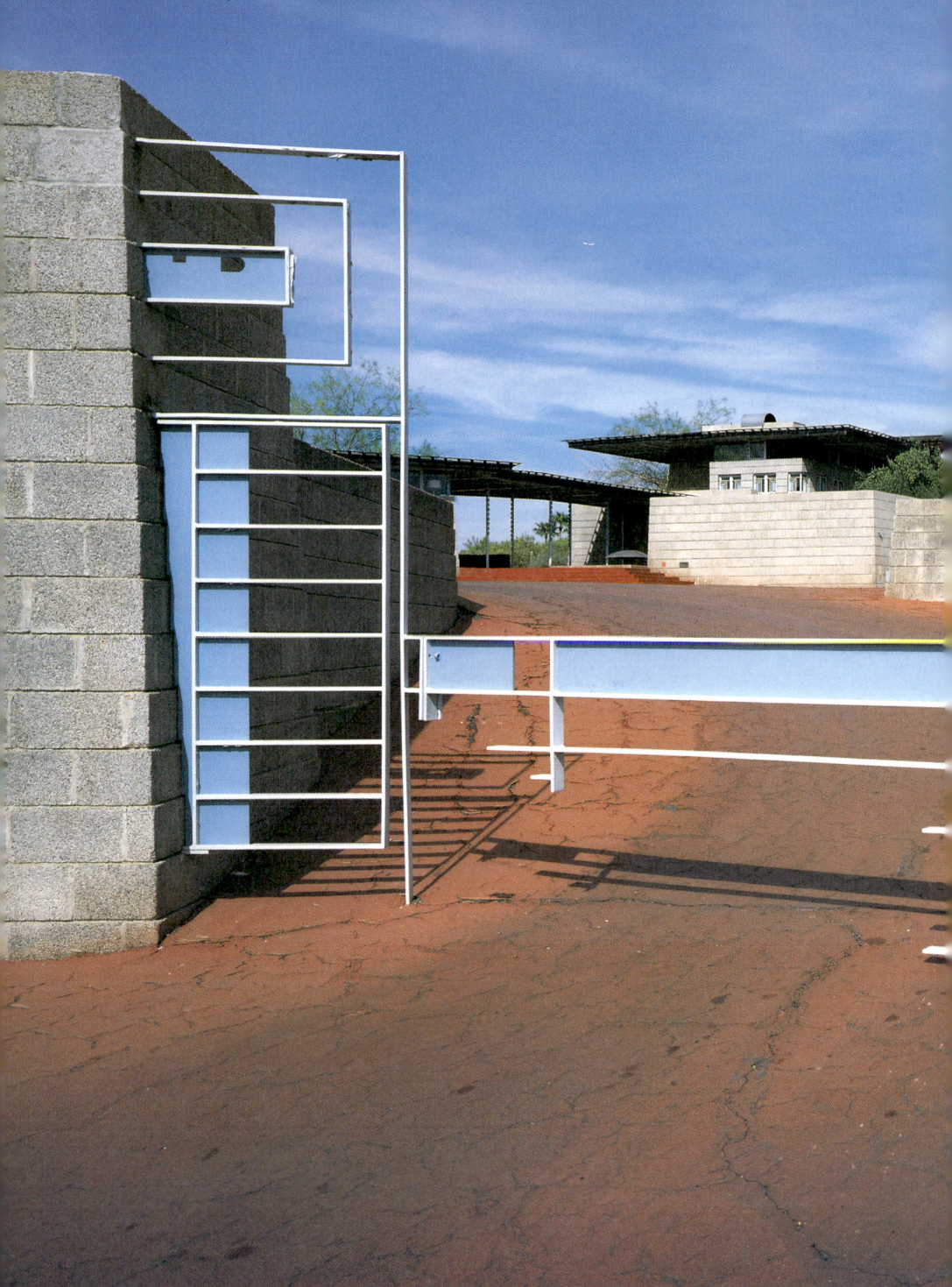

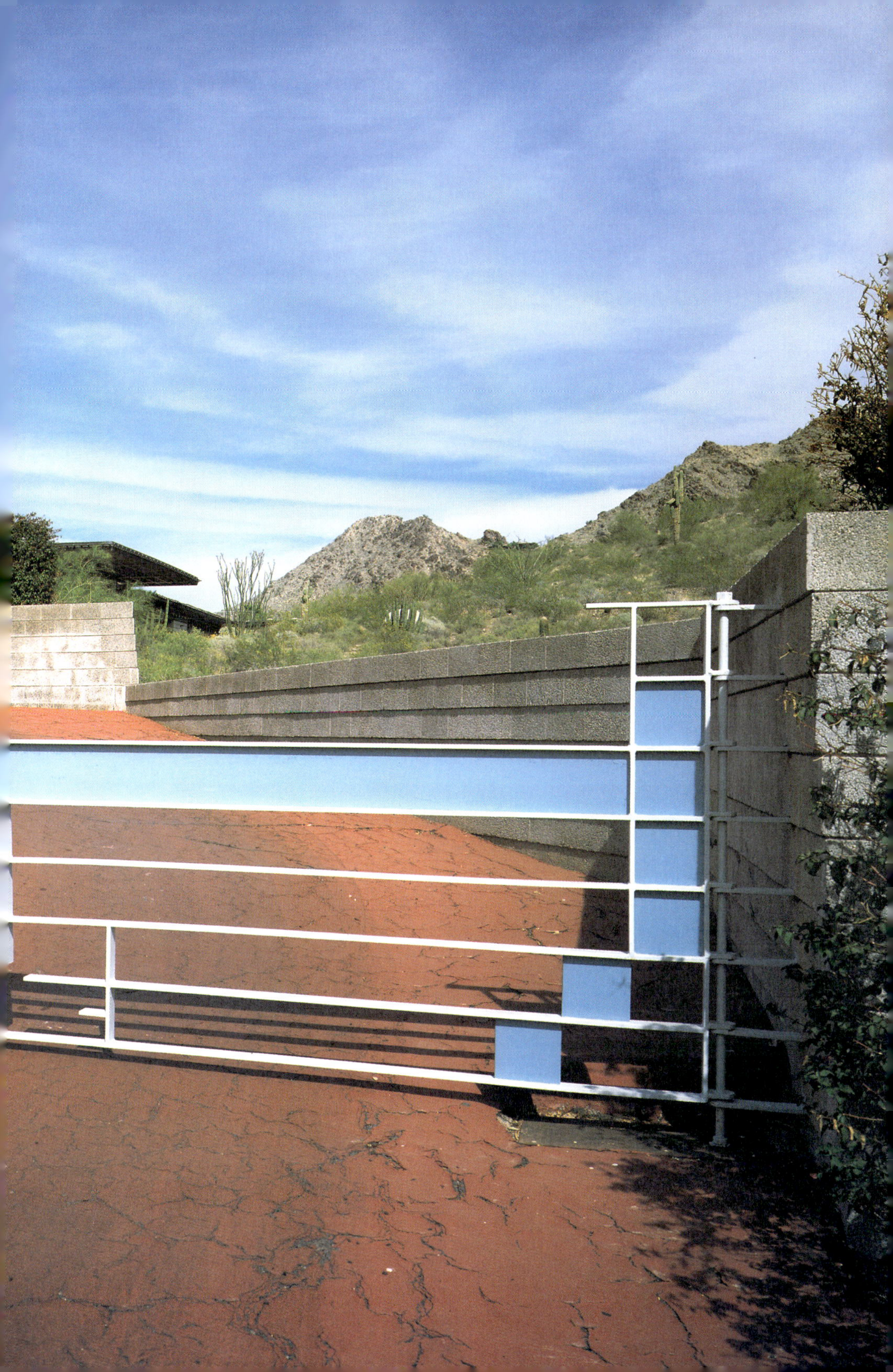

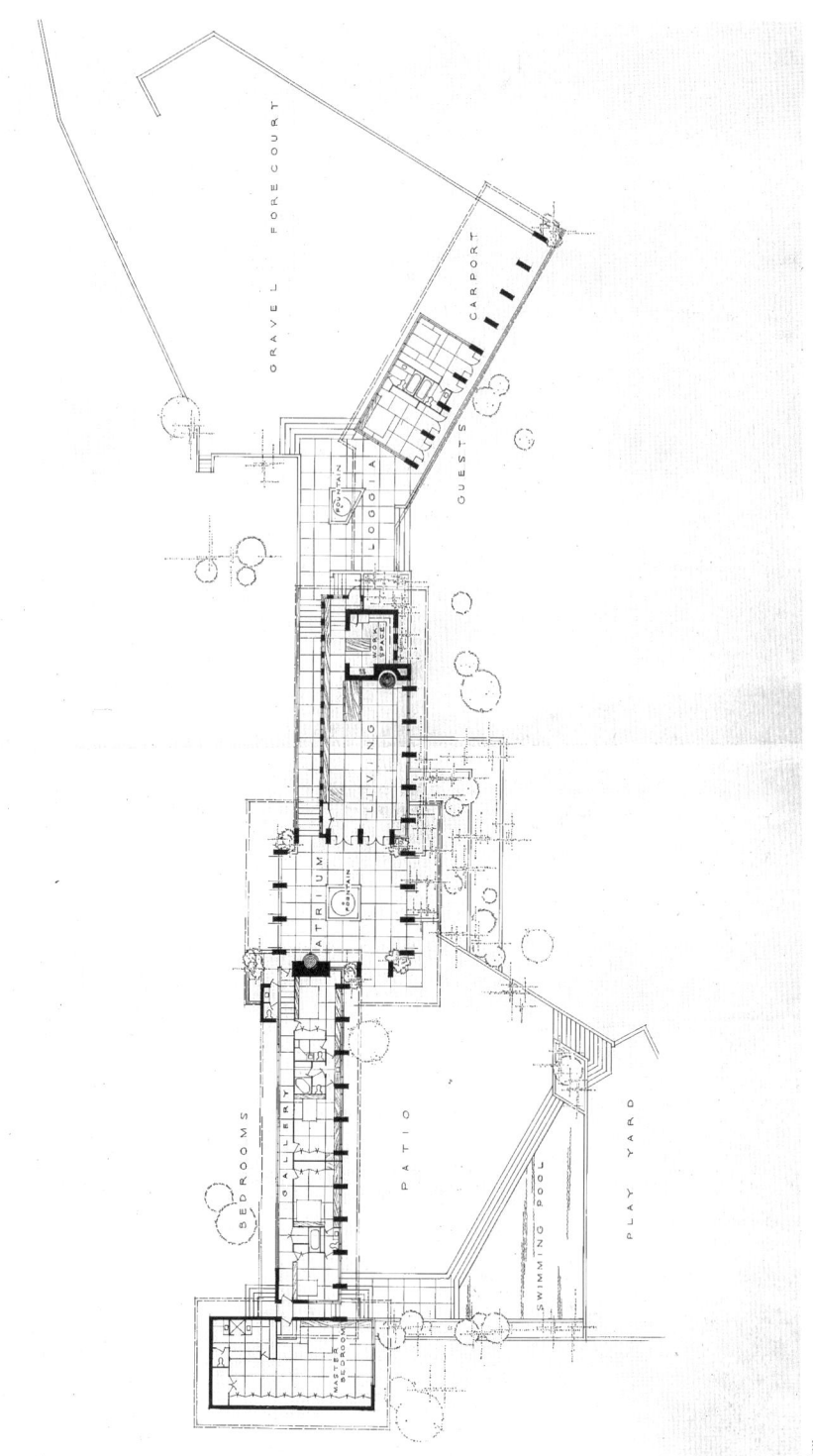

Plan

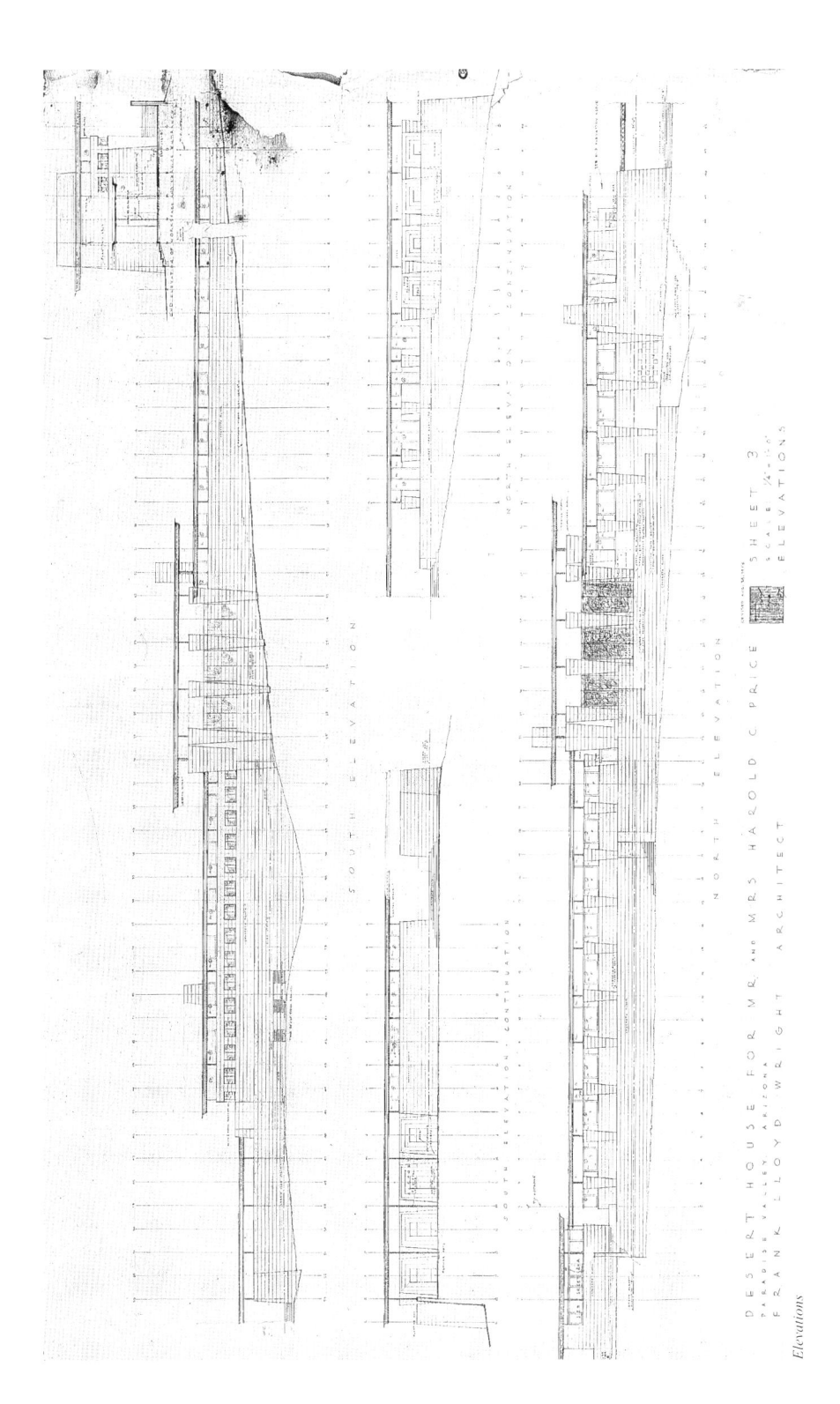

Elevations

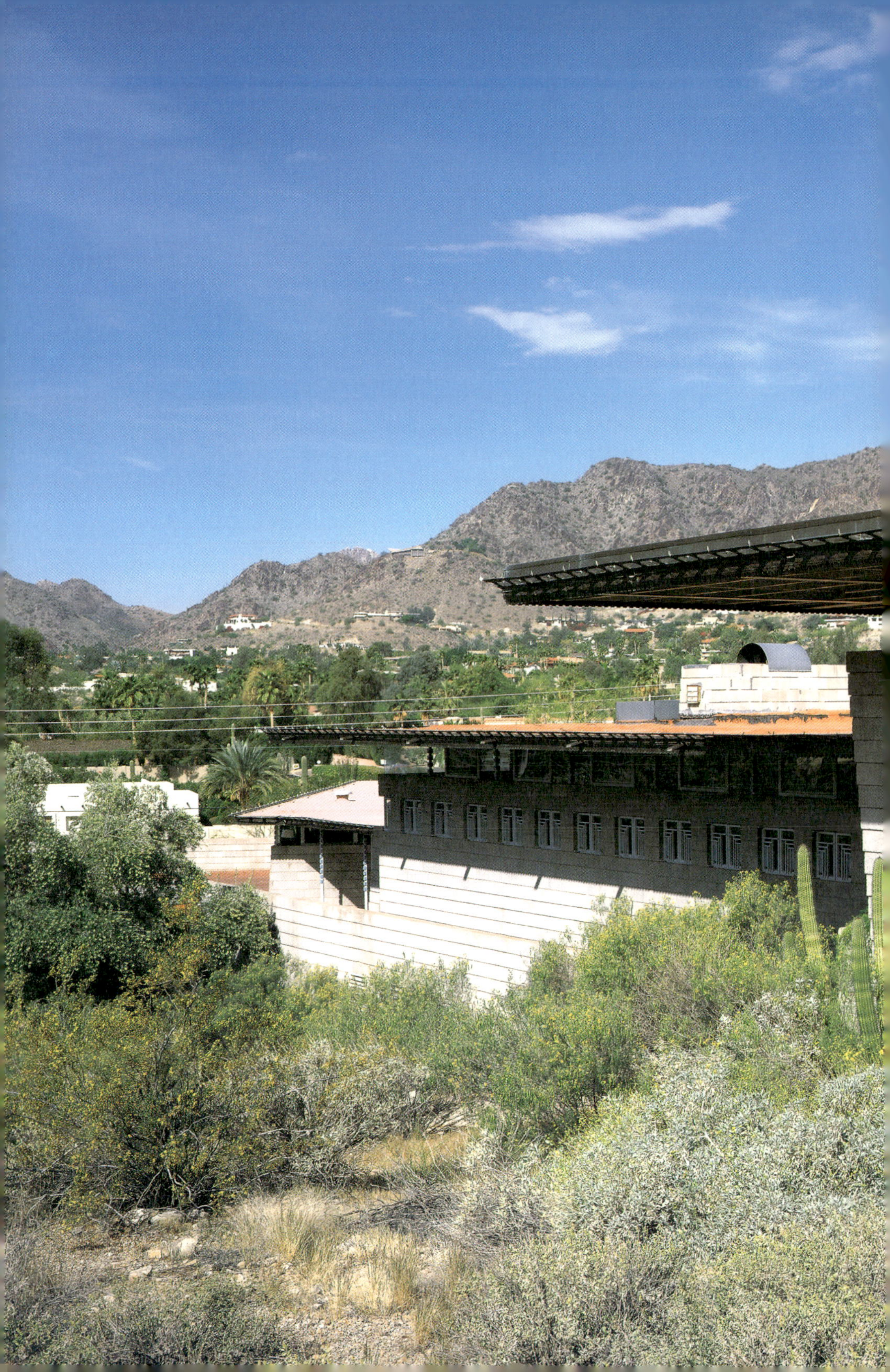

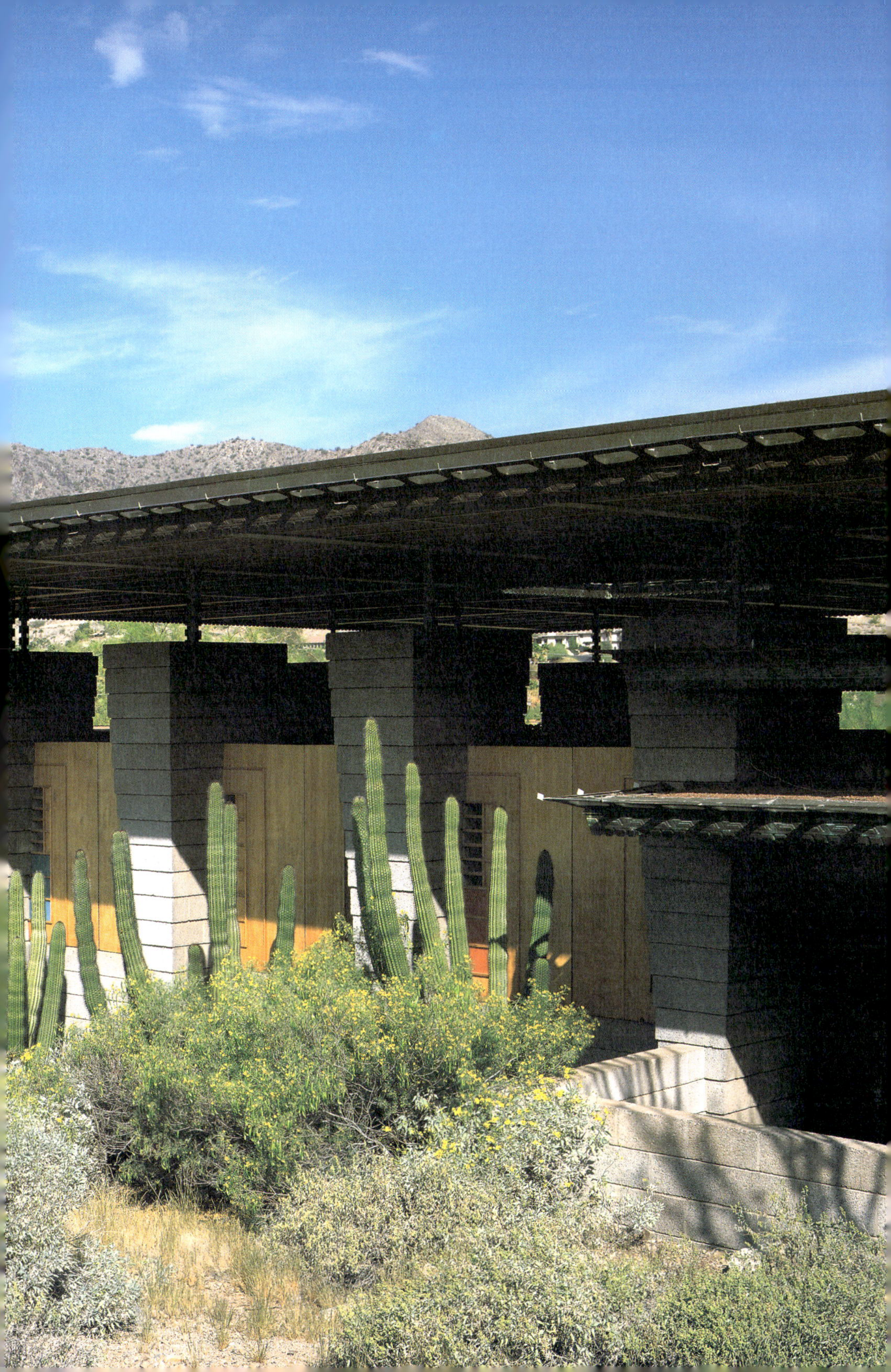

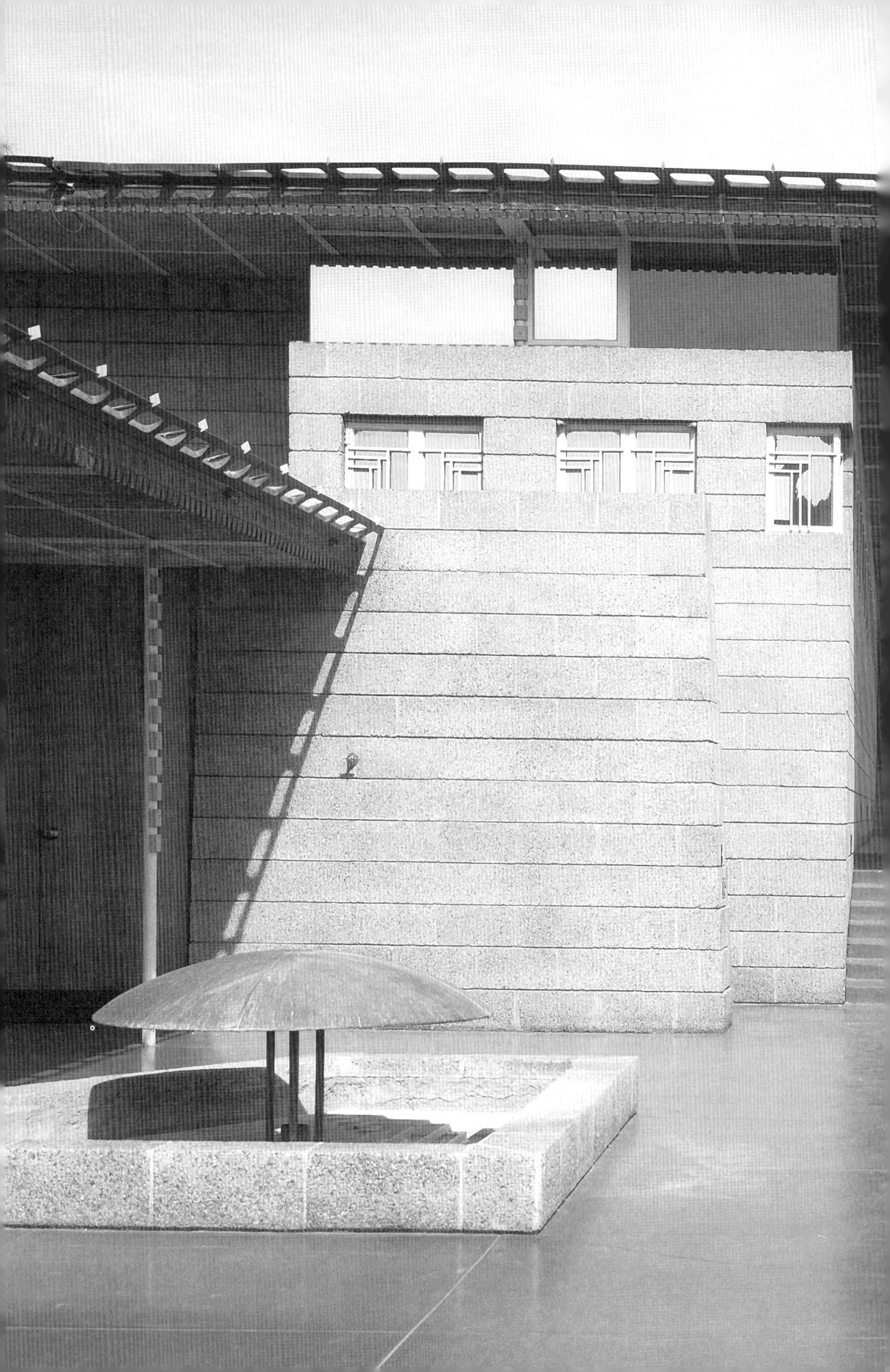

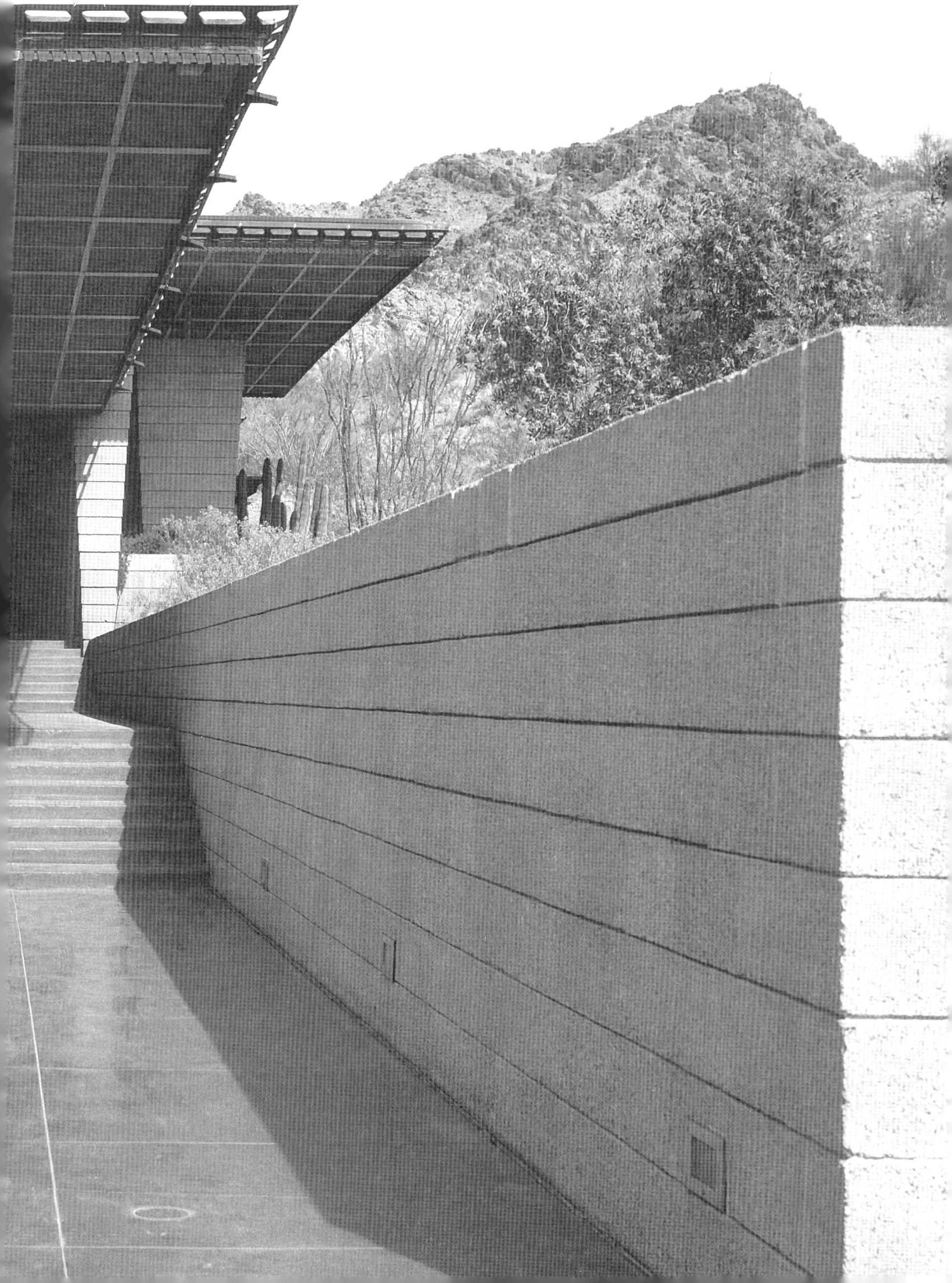

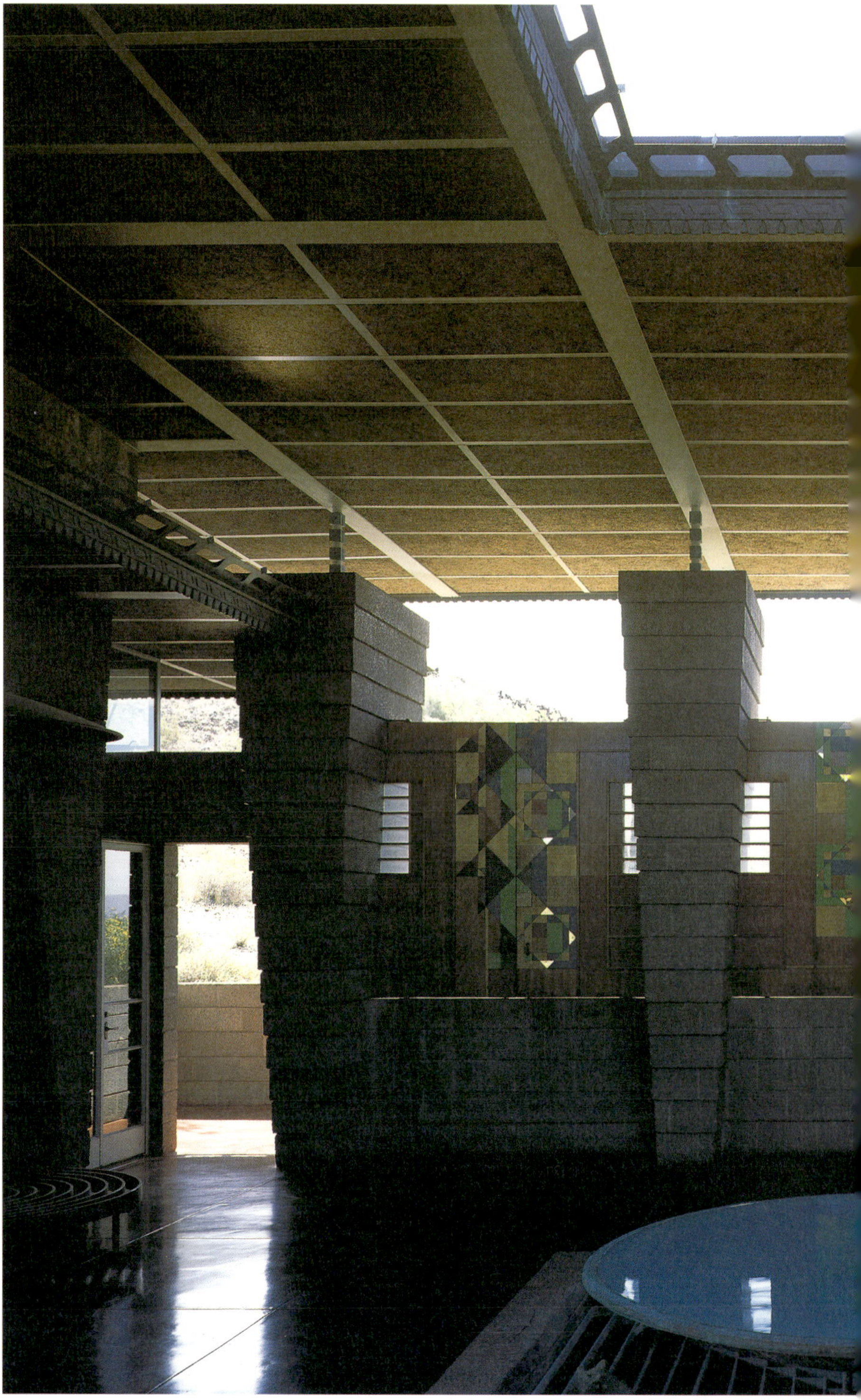

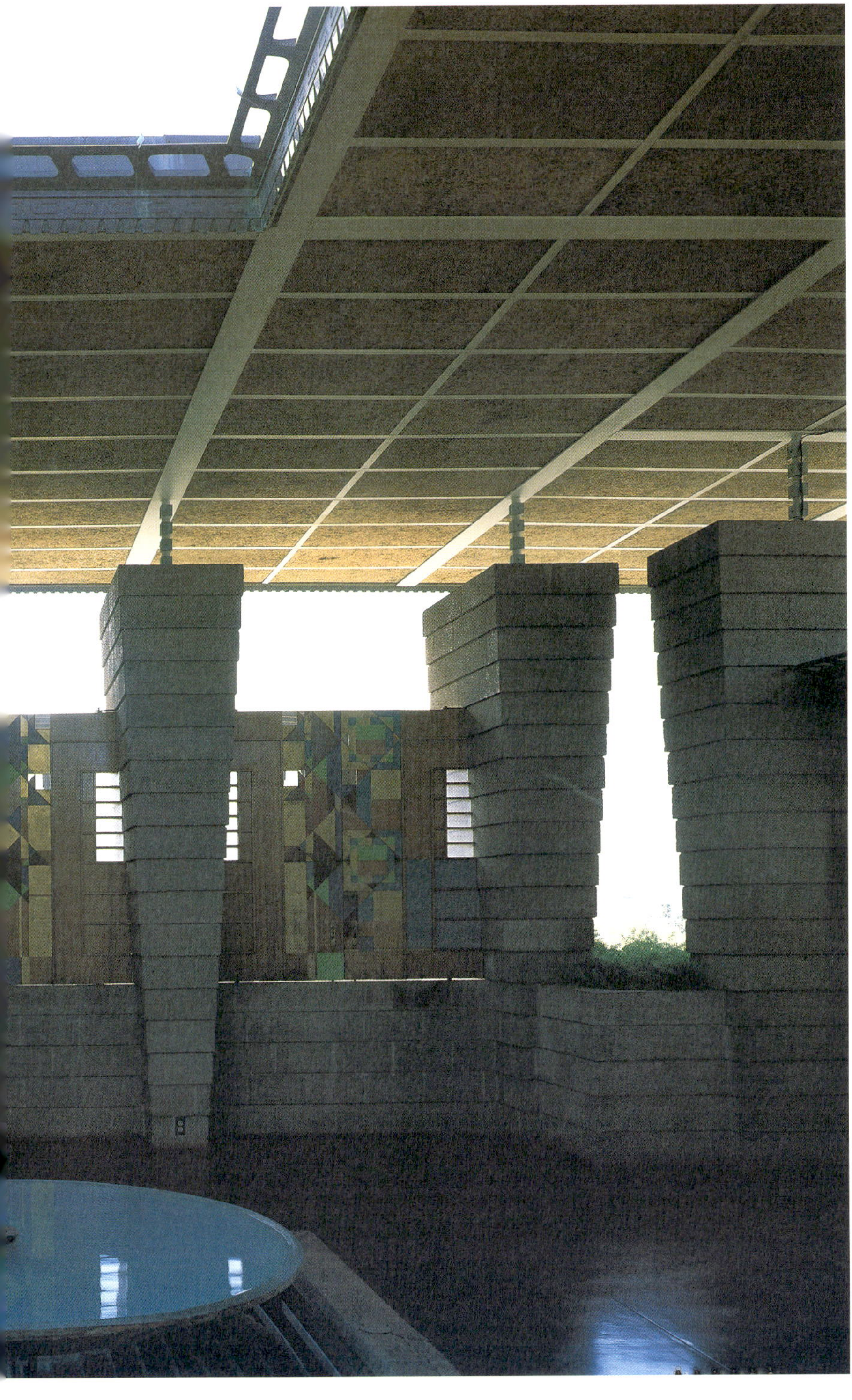

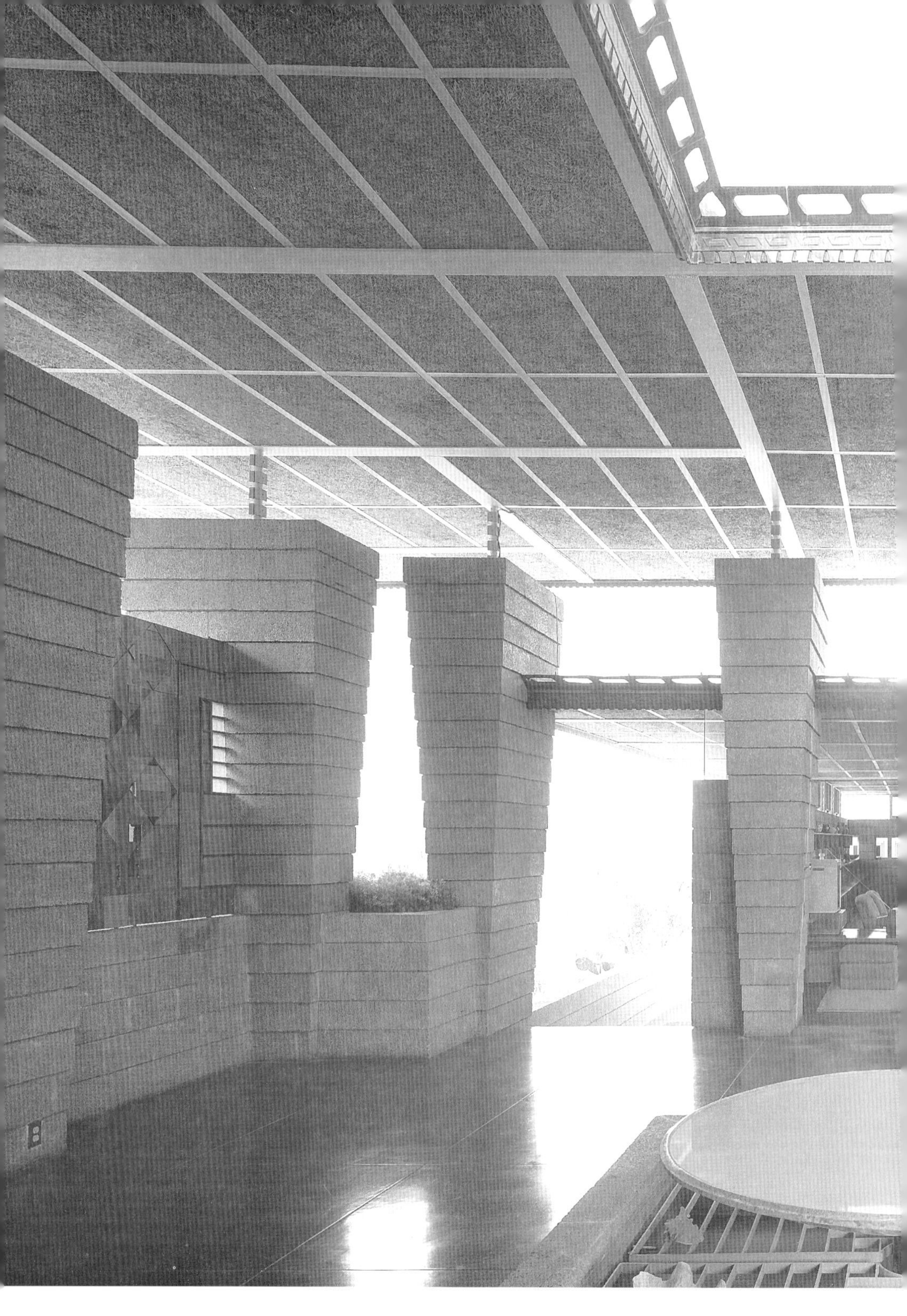

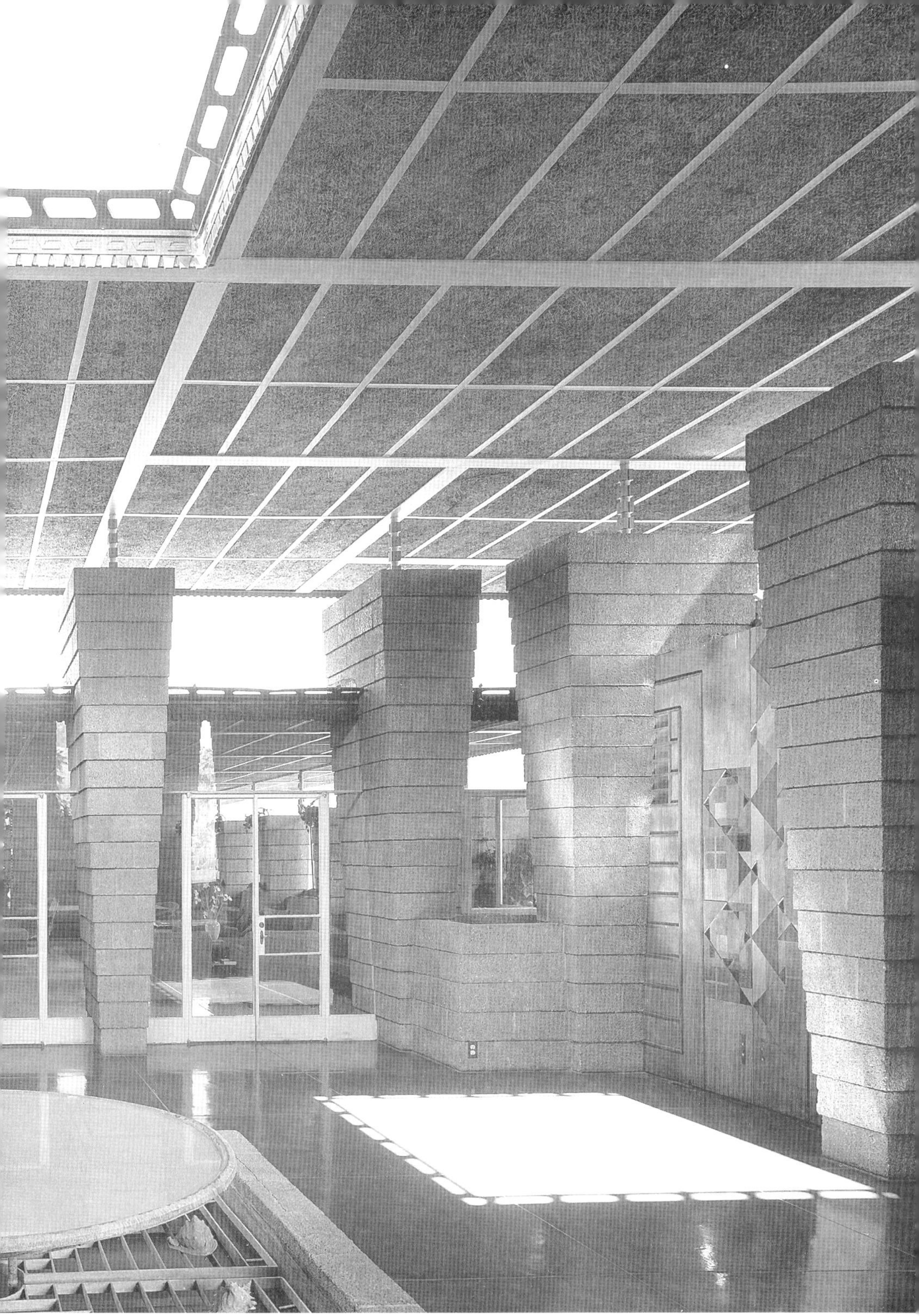

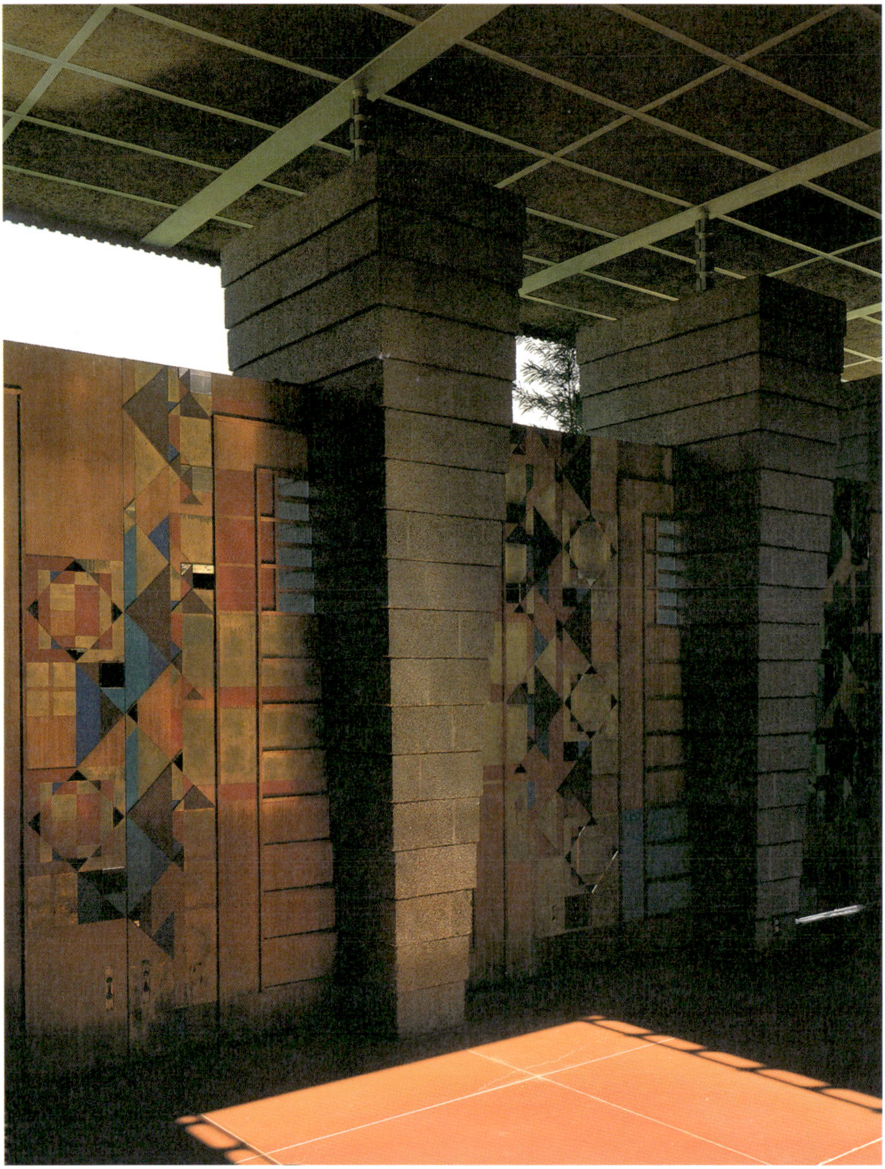

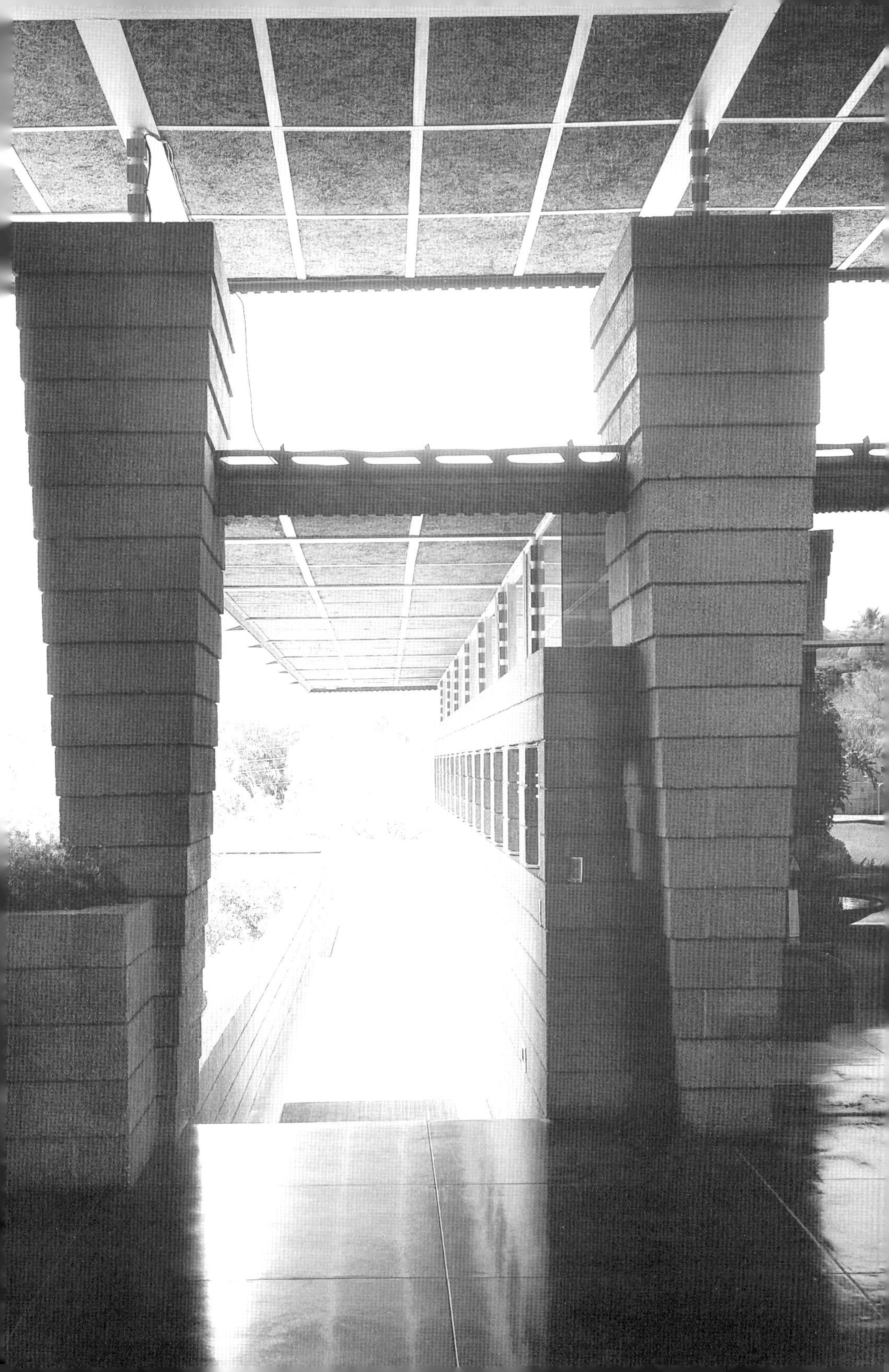

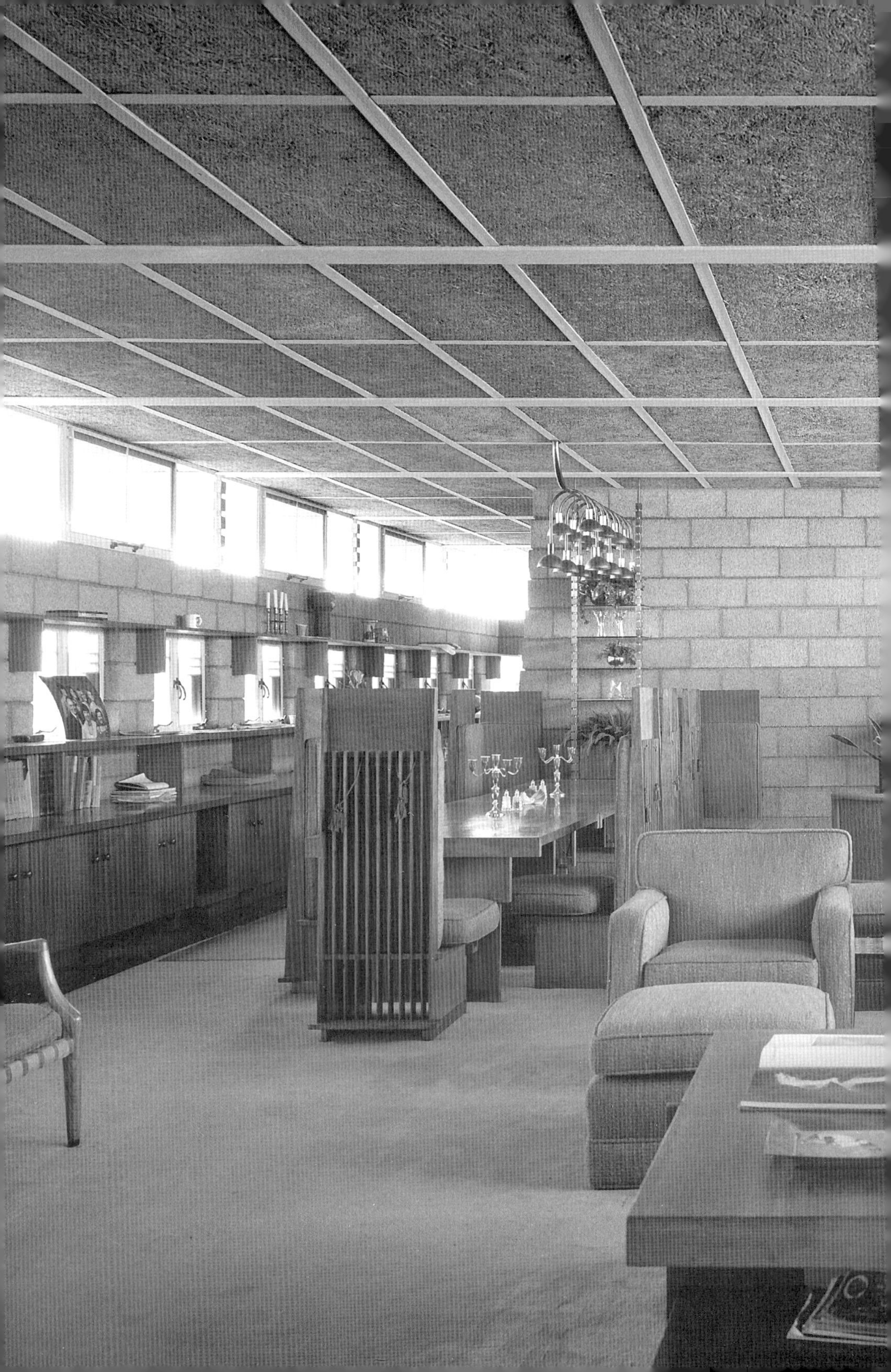

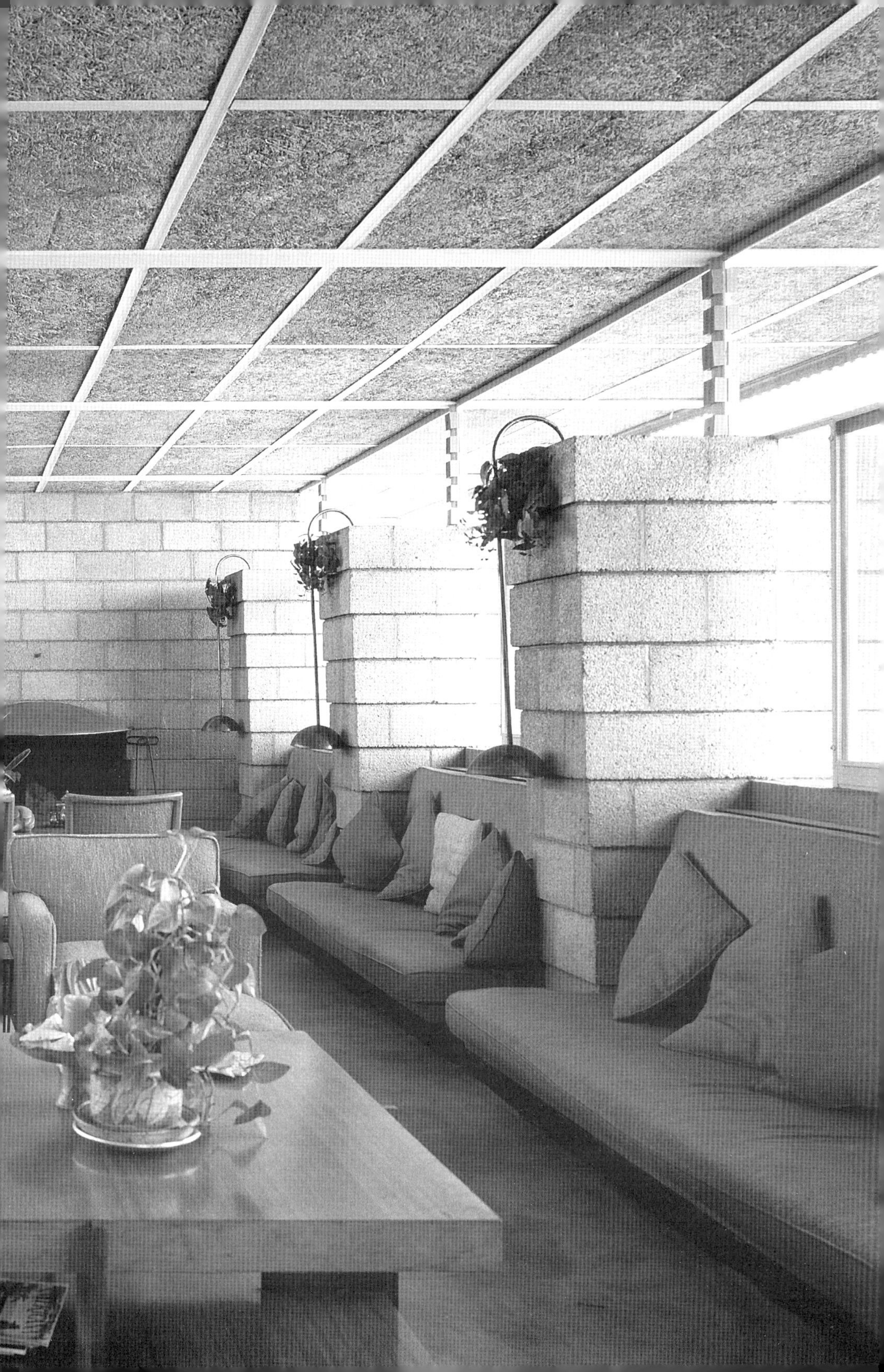

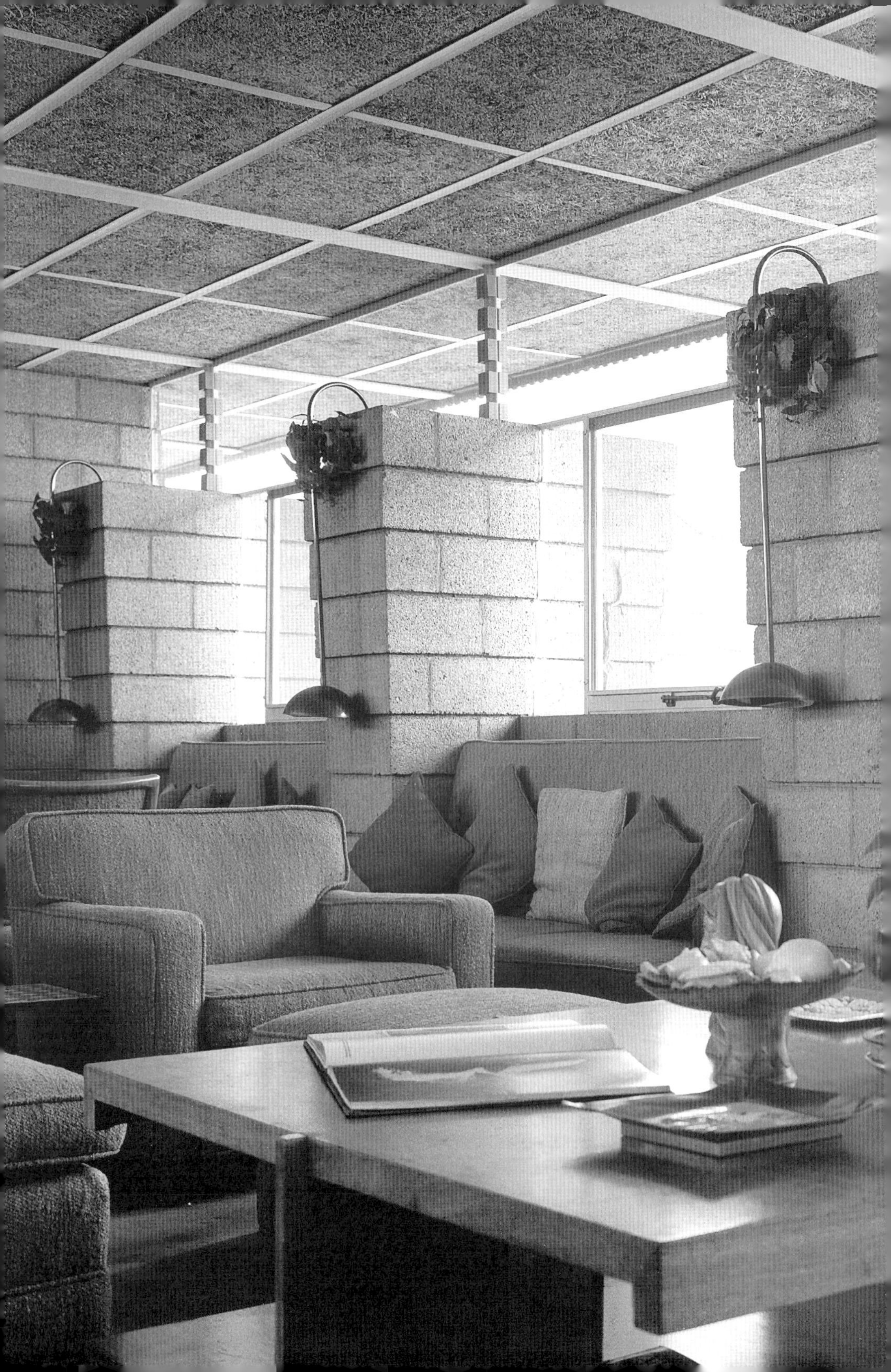

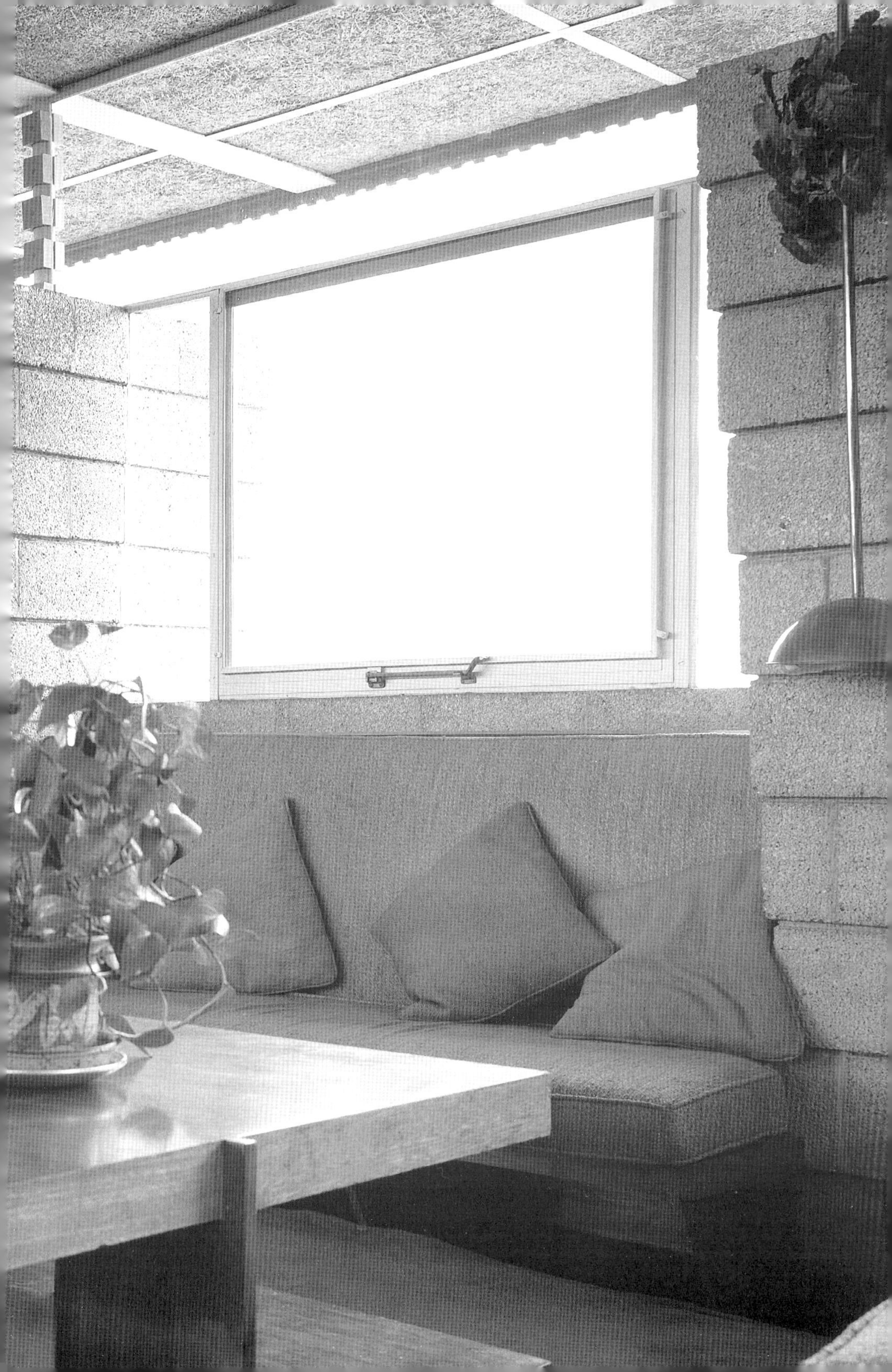

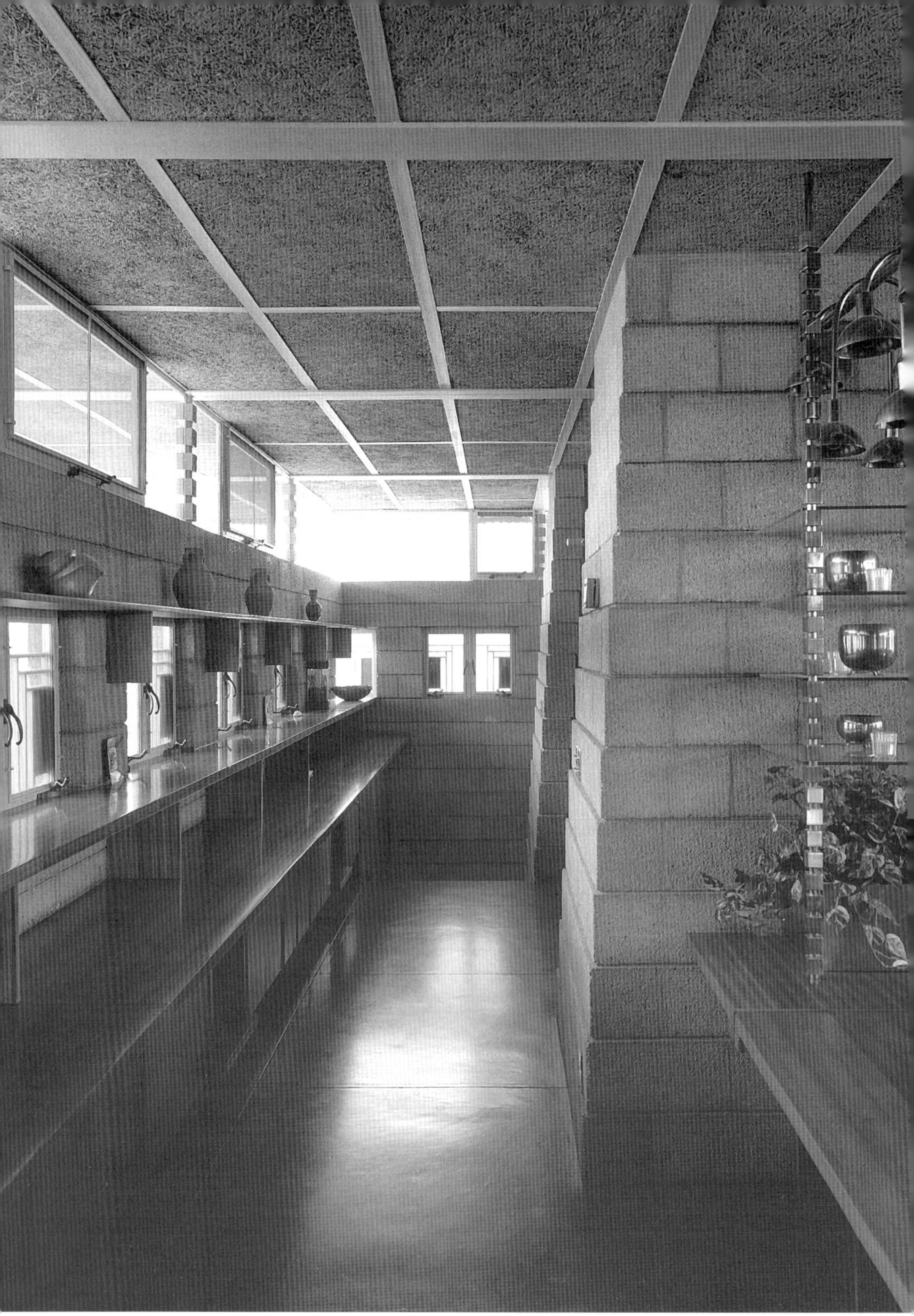

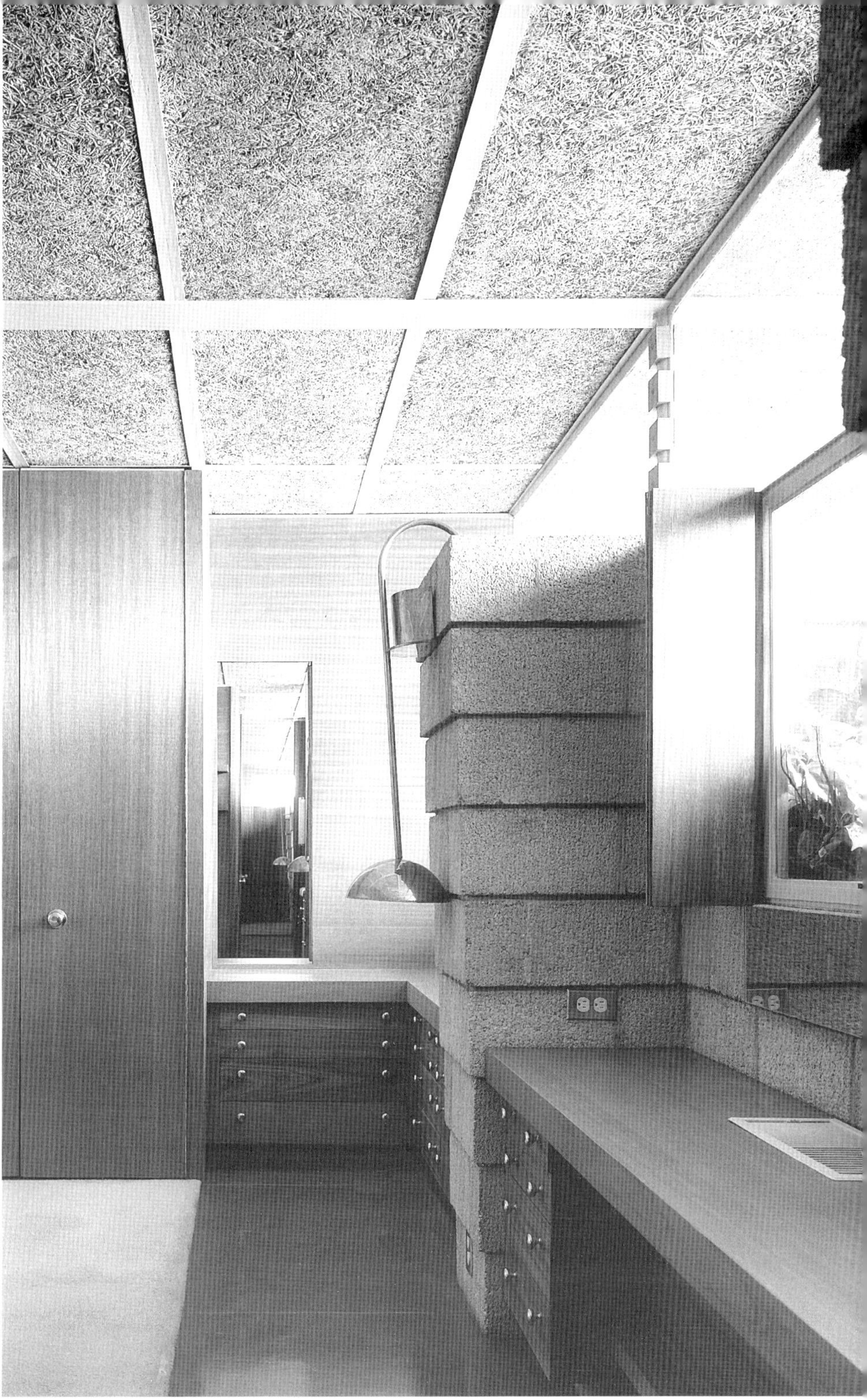

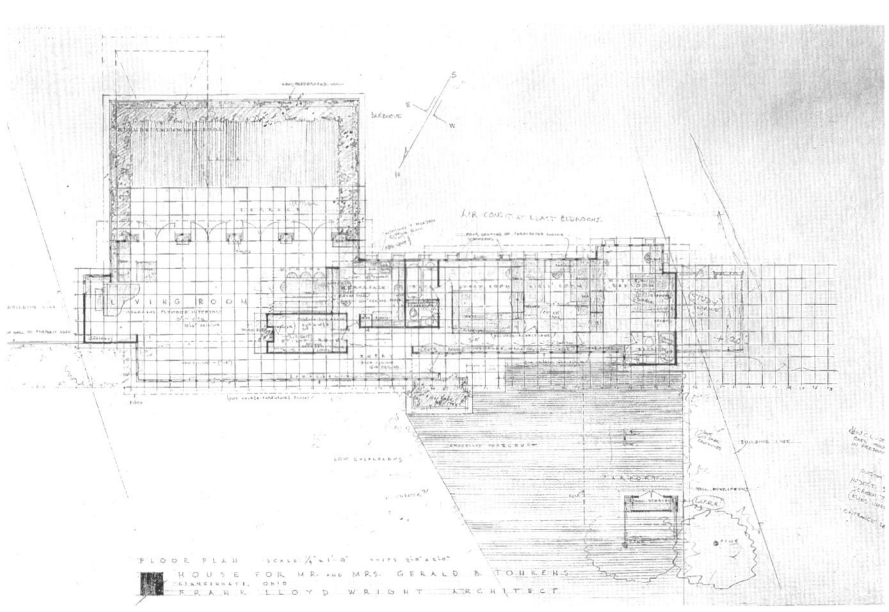

Gerald Tonkens House
Cincinnati, Ohio, 1955

Plan

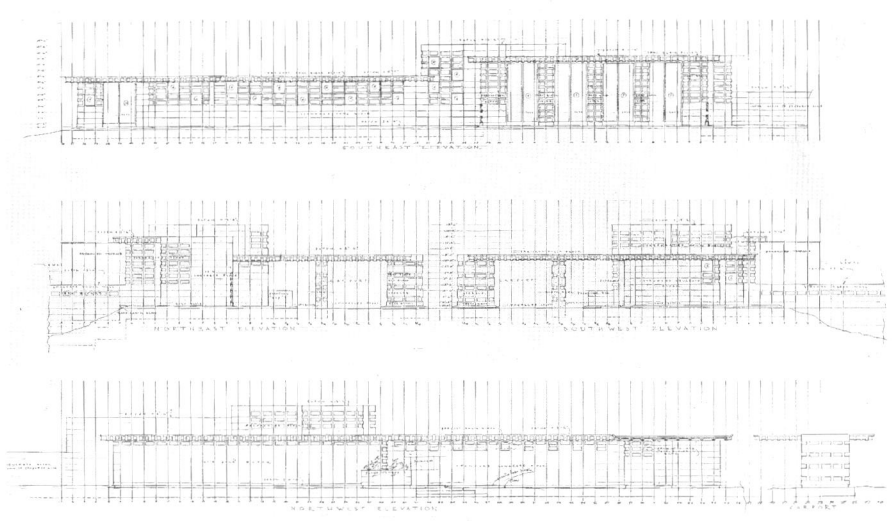

Elevations

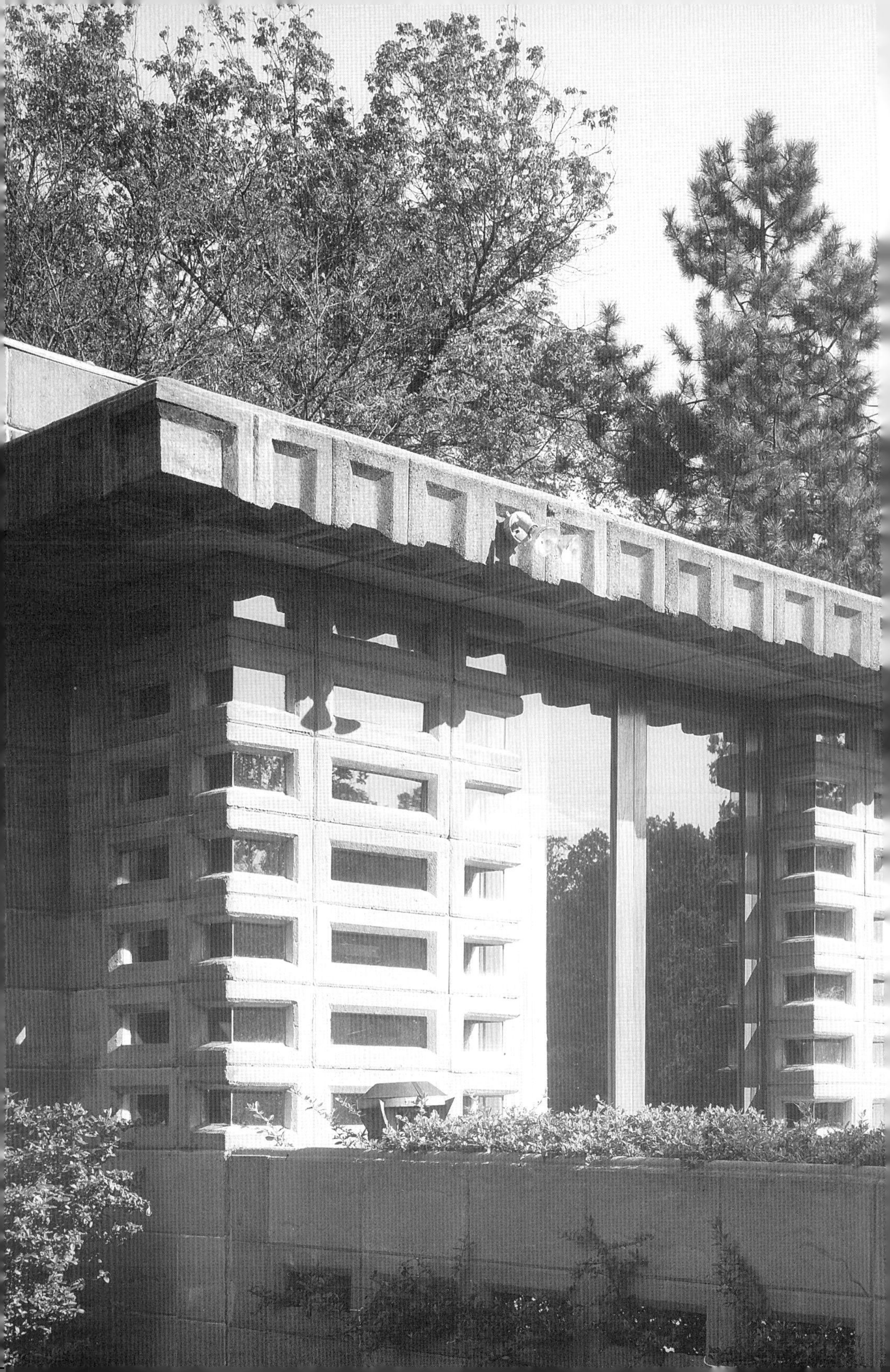

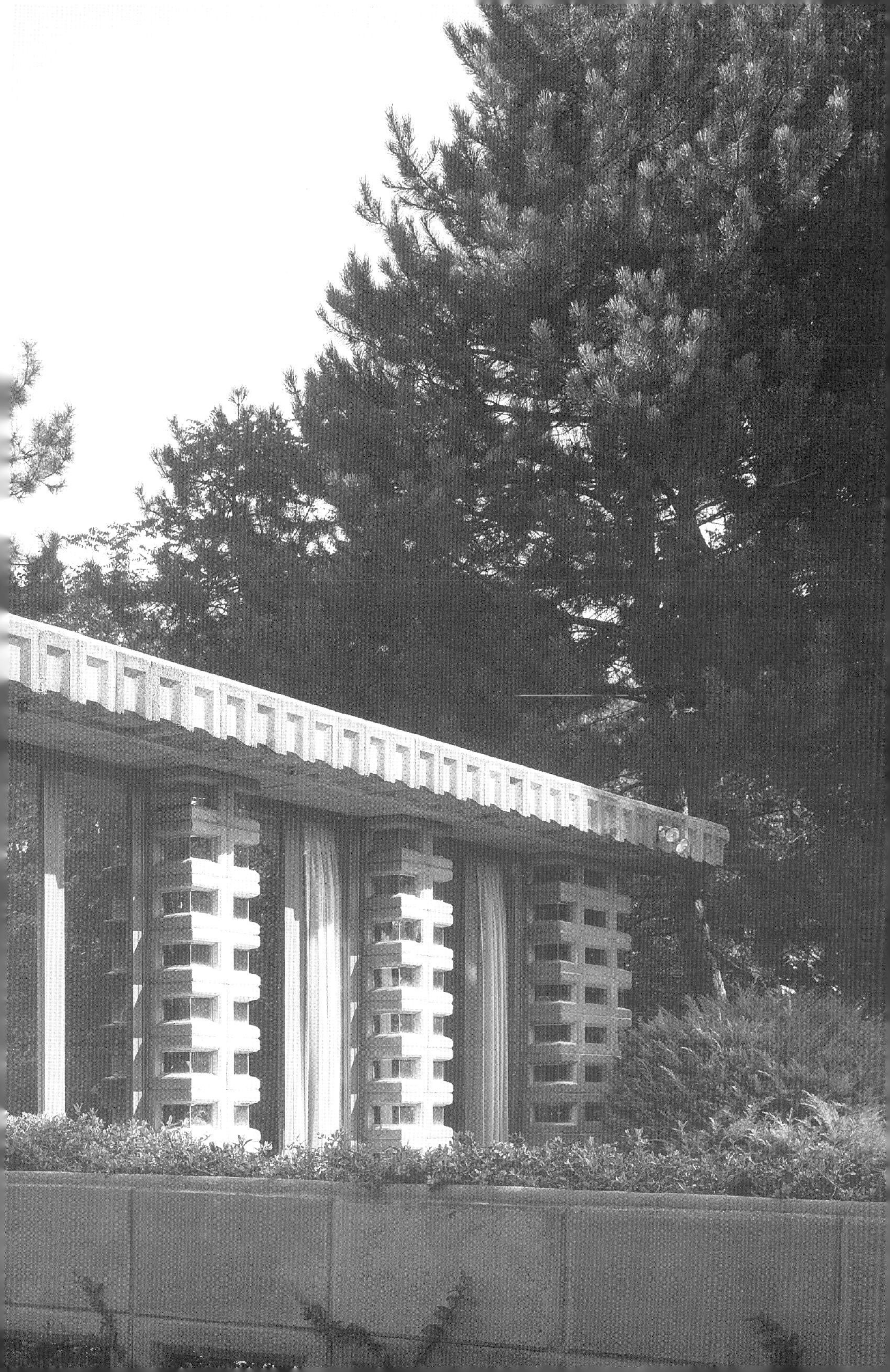

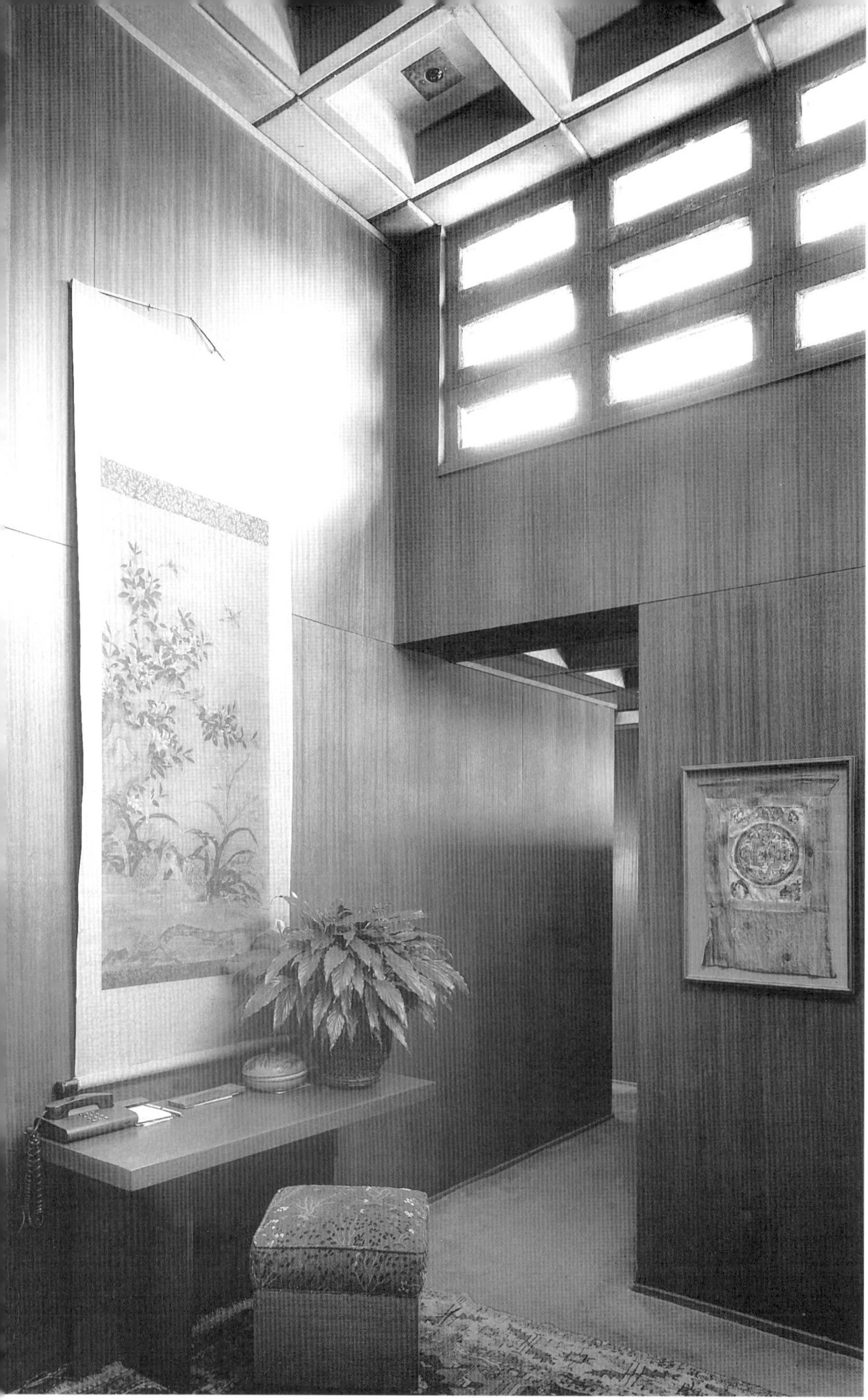

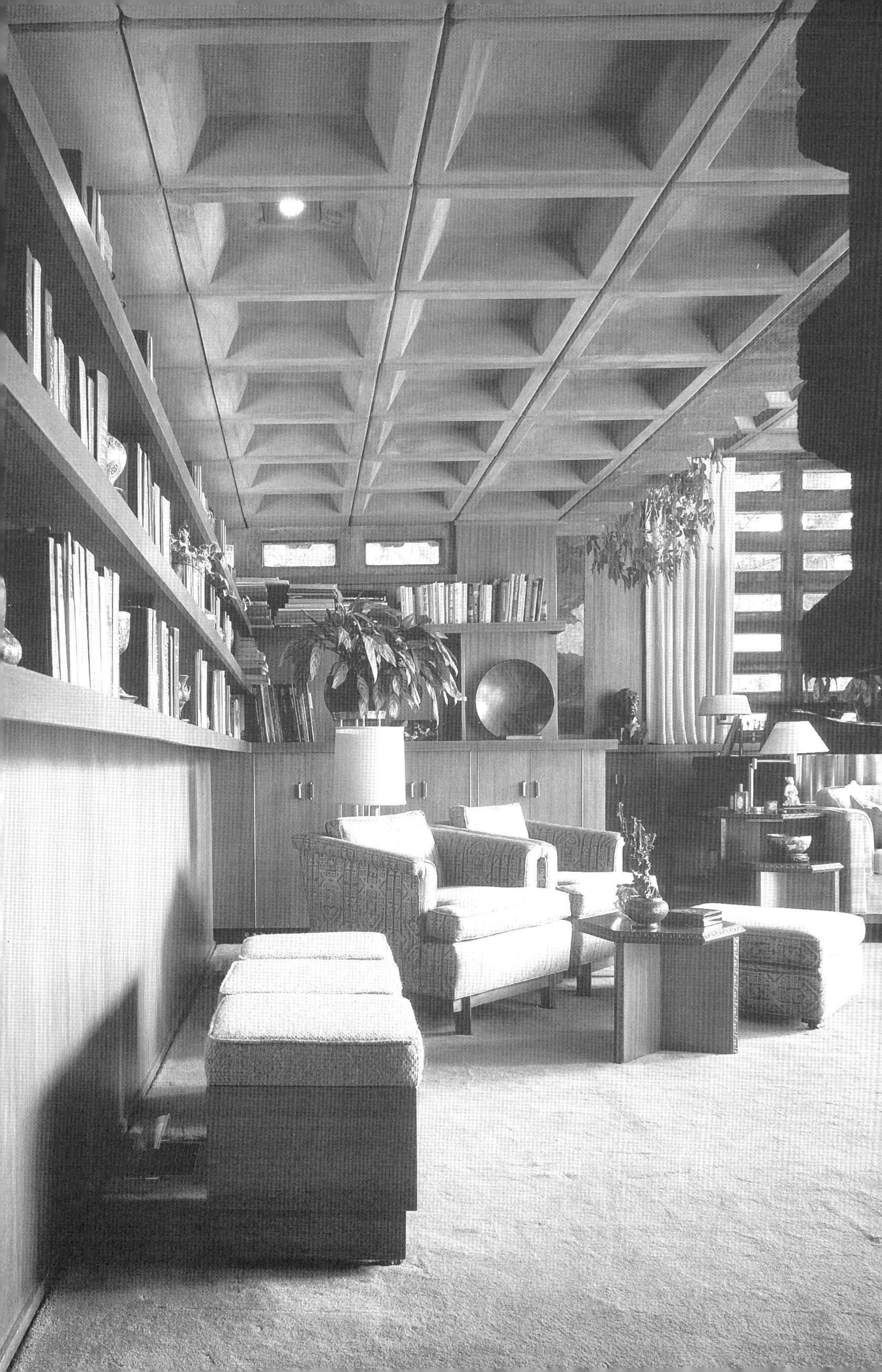

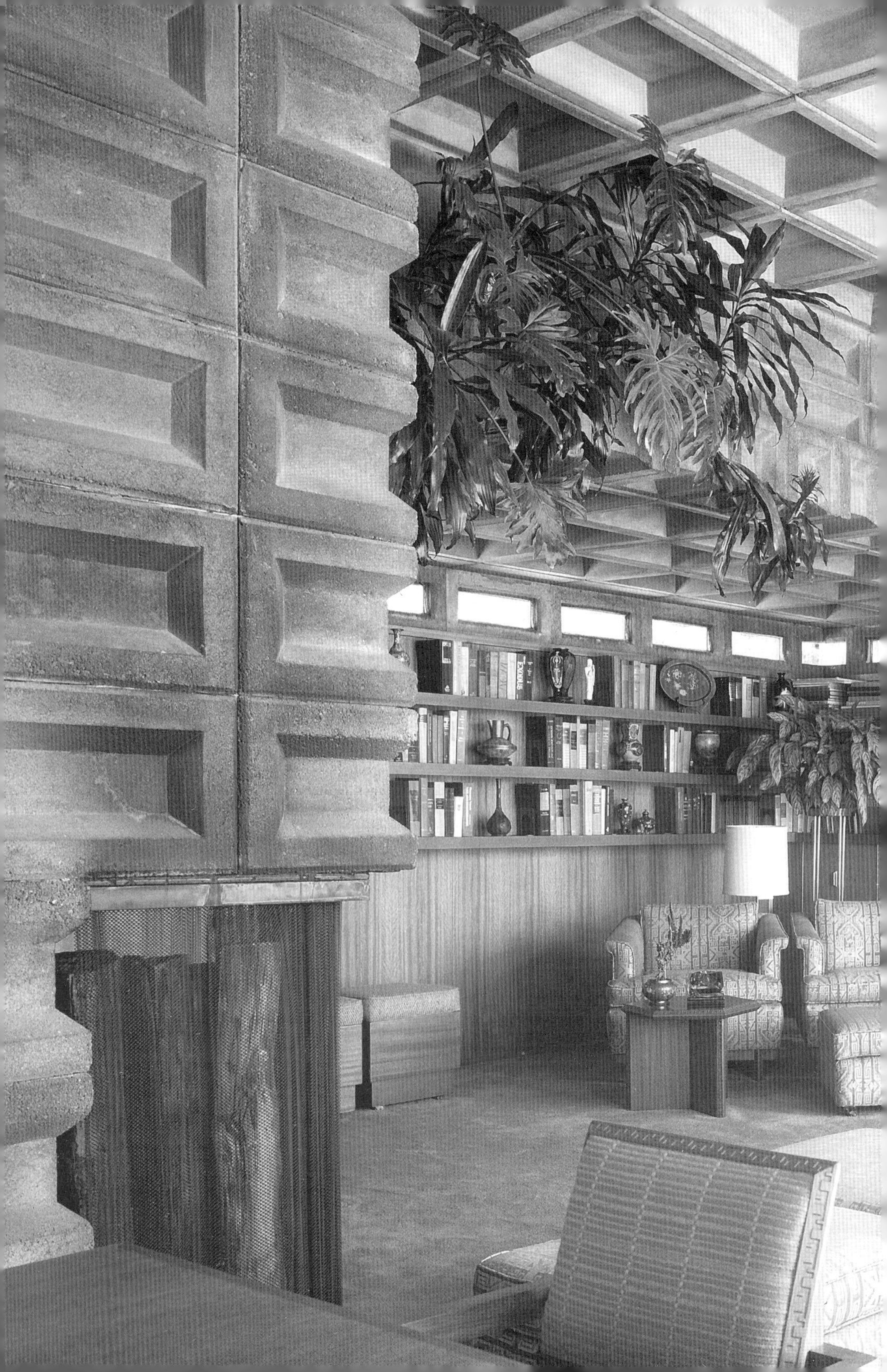
EXODUS

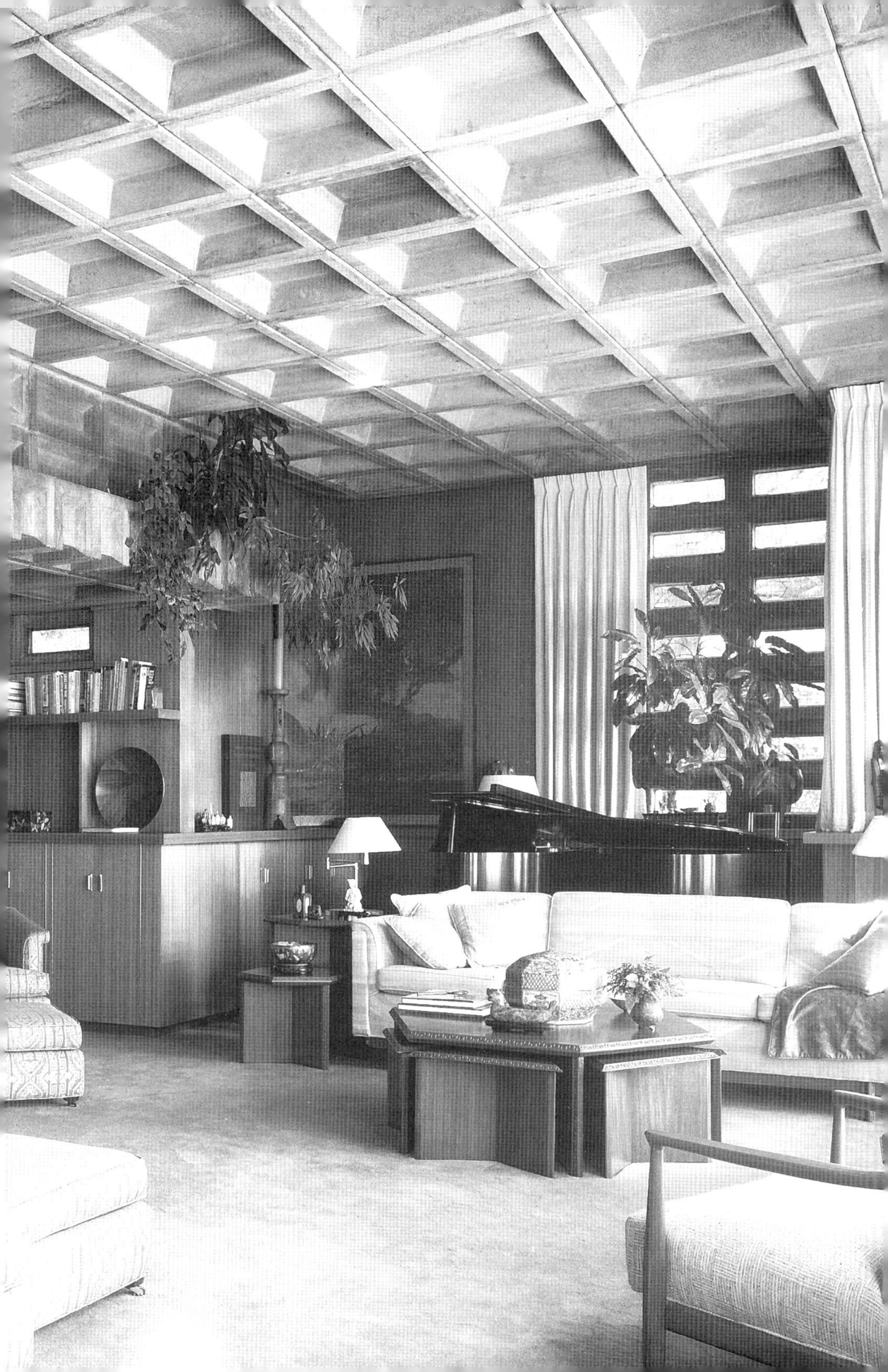

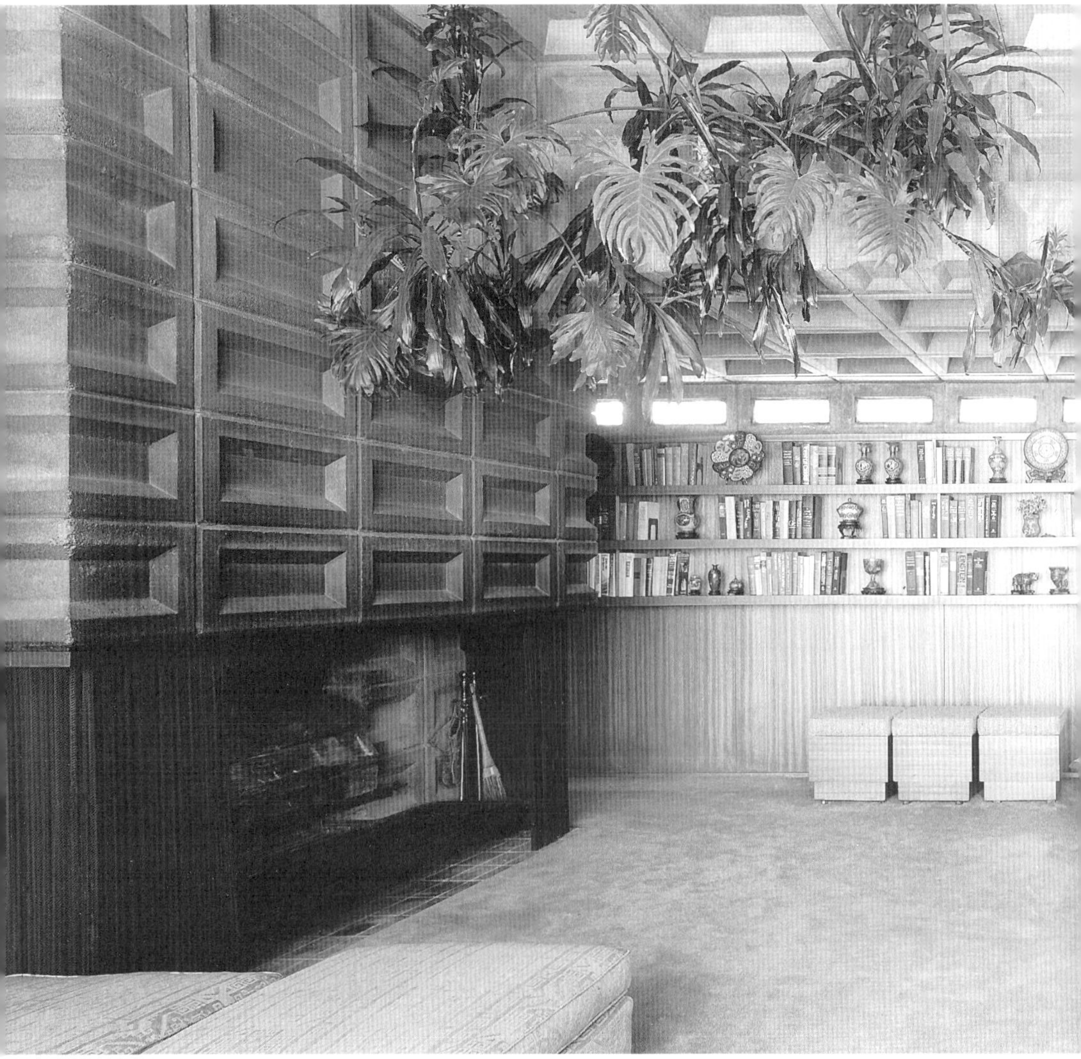

BEETHOVEN
FRANK LLOYD WRIGHT
SELECTED DRAWINGS
PORTFOLIO
FRANK
LLOYD
WRIGHT

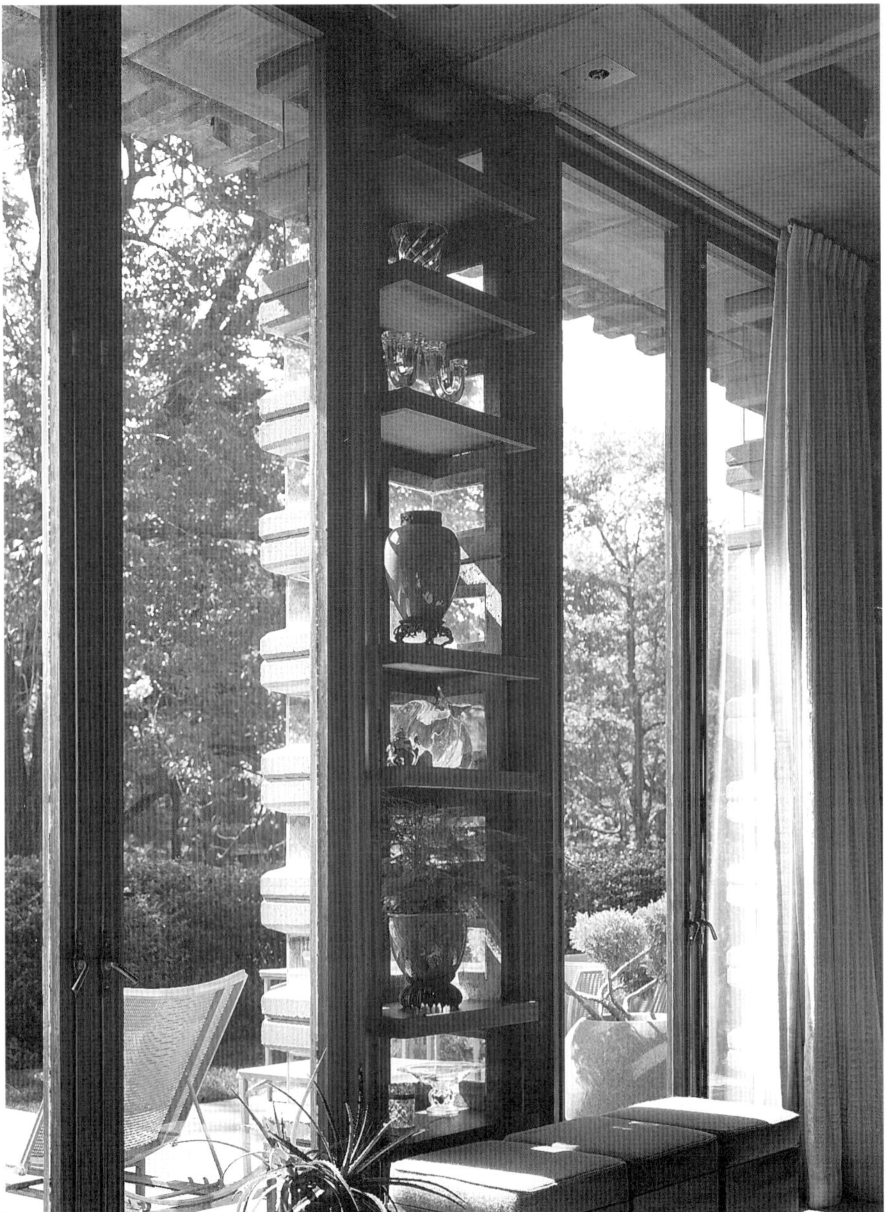

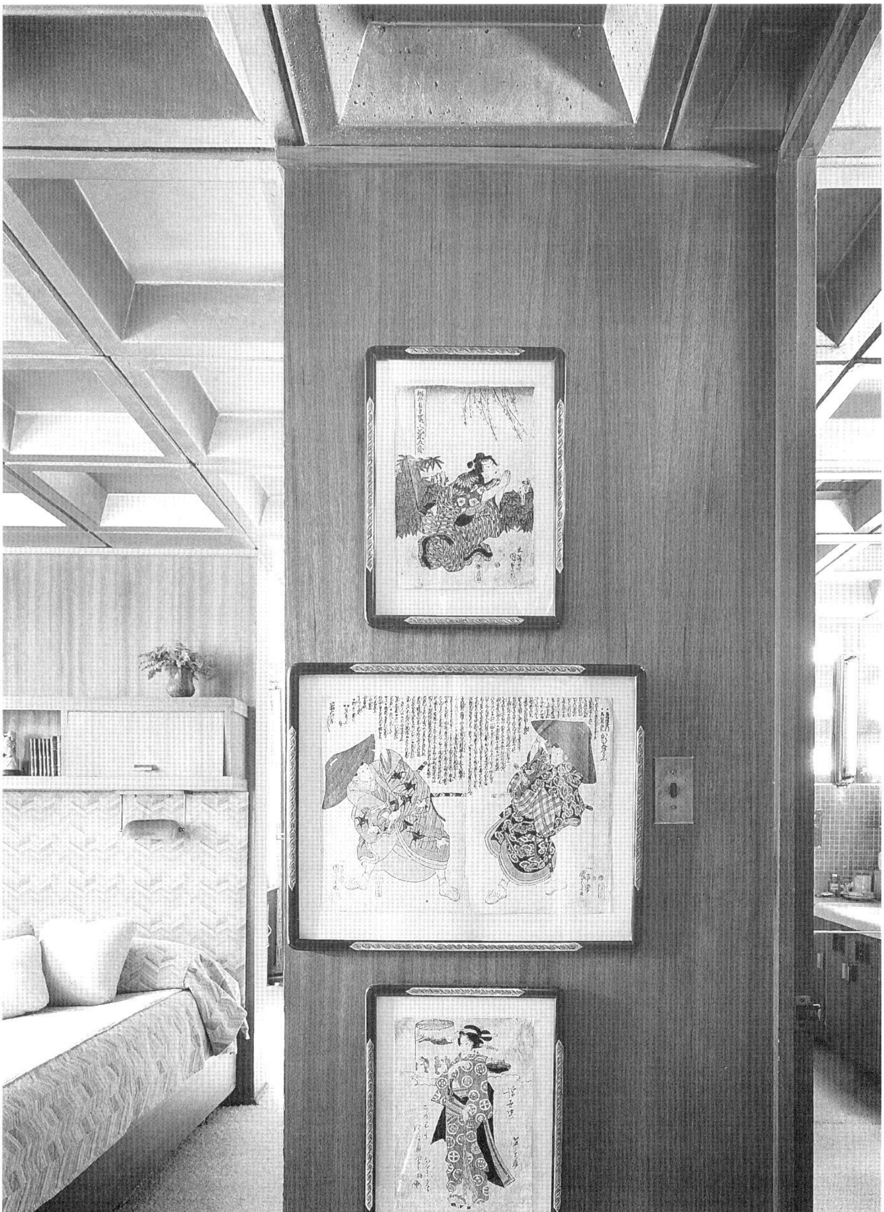

"Wingspread", Herbert F. Johnson House: view from approach — p.32-34

View from east — p.35-38

Cantilevered terrace — p.39-41

View from northwest — p.42-43

Guest and carport wing — p.46-47

Children's wing and swimming pool — p.50-51

Pergola of guest room — p.52-53

p.54-55 
Terrace

p.56-57 
Library

p.58-59 
Great hall

p.60-61 
Great hall

p.62-63 
Great hall: mezzanine level

p.66-67 
Library

p.68
p.69 
Mezzanine level  | View toward master bedroom

p.70-71 
Leigh Stevens House, "Auldbrass Plantation": stable and kennel

Overall view from lake — p.75-78

Main house — p.79-81

Terrace — p.82-83

Porch — p.88-89

Main house: bedroom on center and living room on left — p.84-85

Living room — p.90-91

Swimming pool and terrace — p.86-87

Living room — p.92-93

p.94-95 *p.104-105*

Living room: entrance on center

Lowell Walter House, "Cedar Rock": overall view from southeast

p.96-97 *p.106-107*

View toward entrance

View from south

p.98-99 *p.110*
p.111

Dining room

View toward entrance *Southeast corner*

p.100 *p.112-113*
p.101

View toward living room from entrance *Master bedroom*

Detail of concrete roof

p.102-103 *p.114-115*

View toward lake from dining room

Northwest corner

p.116-117

p.126
p.127

View toward garden room from entrance

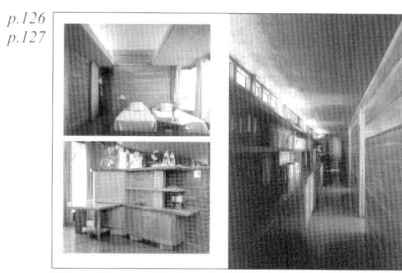

Above: master bedroom
Below: wooden furniture of garden room

Gallery

p.118-119

p.128-129

Garden room

Boathouse and pavilion on the edge of the Wapsipinicon river

p.120-121

p.130
p.131

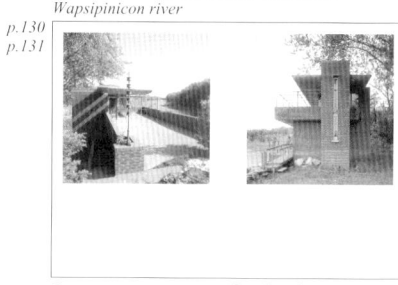

Garden room

Terrace

East facade

p.122-123

p.134-135

Garden room

Herman T. Mossberg House: view from street

p.124-125

p.136-137

Garden room

Entrance

264

Overall view from garden — p.138-139

Terrace — p.140-141

Exterior view of living room — p.142-143

Entrance *Loggia* — p.144, p.145

Living room — p.146-147

Living room: entrance on right — p.148-149

View of living room from second level — p.150-151

Staircase *Thin concrete slabs hung on steel rods* — p.152, p.153

Dining room — p.154-155

Gallery *Gallery: view toward staircase* — p.156, p.157

p.158
p.159

Staircase from second level

Above: daughter's bedroom
Below: master bedroom

p.160
p.161

Daughter's bedroom

Corner of master bedroom

p.162-163

Kenneth Laurent House: view toward terrace

p.166-167

Terrace

p.168-169

Curved terrace and roof

p.170-171

Living room

p.172
p.173

View from entrance

Above: alcove
Below: workspace

p.174-175

Living room

p.176-177

David Wright House: view from approach

p.178-179

Court: view of living room from ramp

p.180-181

Exterior view of master bedroom

p.192
p.193

Steps to entrance   *Entrance*

p.182-183

Living room

p.194-195

Exterior view of living room

p.184-185

Dining alcove

p.196-197

Exterior view of living room

p.186
p.187

Living room   *Gallery*

p.198
p.199

View toward living room from entrance    *View from workspace*

p.190-191

William Palmer House: view toward entrance from carport

p.200-201

Living room

267

Living room

p.202-203 p.212-213

Terrace

p.204
p.205

p.214-215

Dining area   Workspace

Exterior view of living room

p.206-207 p.216-217

Master bedroom   Study

Living room

p.208-209 p.218
p.219

Isadore J. Zimmerman House:
overall view from garden

View toward living room   Window of living room
from entrance hall

p.210-211 p.220-221

Overall view from street

Living room

p.222-223　　p.234-235

Living room : quartet stand designed by Architect　　Loggia: steps to entrance

p.224-225　　p.236-237

Corner of living room　Dining area　　Atrium

p.226-227　　p.238-239

Guest room　Workspace　　View toward living room from atrium

p.228-229　　p.240
　　　　　　　p.241

Harold Price House, "Grandma House": gate and entrance court　　Murals on wooden doors in atrium　　Entrance

p.232-233　　p.242-243

South elevation　　Living room

269

Living room — p.244-245

Living room: corridor to workspace — p.246, p.247
Bedroom

Gerald Tonkens House: overall view from south — p.248-249

Exterior view of living room — p.250-251

Entrance *Living room* — p.252-253

Living room — p.254-255

Living room — p.256-257

Detail of corner block with glass *Master bedroom* — p.258-259

GA トラベラー 006
フランク・ロイド・ライト
〈エレガント・ハウス〉
2002年11月22日発行

企画・編集・撮影	二川幸夫
文	ブルース・ブルックス・ファイファー
翻訳	菊池泰子
ロゴタイプ・デザイン	細谷巖
発行者	二川幸夫
印刷・製本	図書印刷株式会社
発行	エーディーエー・エディタ・トーキョー
	東京都渋谷区千駄ヶ谷3-12-14
	TEL. (03) 3403-1581 (代)

禁無断転載
ISBN4-87140-616-4 C1352